Disability and Culture

Disability and Culture

EDITED BY

Benedicte Ingstad
Susan Reynolds Whyte

UNIVERSITY OF CALIFORNIA PRESS
Berkeley   Los Angeles   London

University of California Press
Berkeley and Los Angeles, California

University of California Press
London, England

Library of Congress Cataloging-in-Publication Data
Disability and culture / edited by Benedicte Ingstad, Susan Reynolds
  Whyte.
      p.   cm.
  Includes bibliographical references (p.   ) and index.
  ISBN 0-520-08360-1 (cloth). — ISBN 0-520-08362-8 (paper).
  1. Handicapped—Cross-cultural studies.   I. Ingstad, Benedicte.
II. Whyte, Susan Reynolds.
  HV1568.D55   1995
  305.9'0816—dc20   93-38479
                                                                              CIP

Printed in the United States of America

1   2   3   4   5   6   7   8   9

The paper used in this publication meets the minimum requirements of American
National Standard for Information Sciences—Permanence of Paper for Printed Library
Materials, ANSI Z39.48-1984 ⊗

for Edwin
and
for Michael

CONTENTS

PREFACE

Impairments of the mind, the senses, and the motor functioning of the body are universal. Everywhere there are people who must live with biological defects that cannot be cured and that inhibit, to some extent, their ability to perform certain functions. But the significance of a deficit always depends on more than its biological nature; it is shaped by the human circumstances in which it exists. This book is about disability in its cultural context. We examine the ways in which people in very different settings understand and react to impairment. We ask how it affects the unfolding of their lives and the pursuit of the values that are most important to them—whether they find meaning in accumulating cattle, having children, or self-development. And we discuss historical changes in conceptions and practices related to disability.

The contributors to the volume have done intensive field research in the communities about which they write. Some have experience of impairment in their own lives; some have worked with rehabilitation programs and have undertaken research agendas primarily focused on disability. Others came to the issue through an interest in health, identity, personhood, and processes of cultural construction. In general we bring to our common project a mix of practical, empirical, and theoretical concern.

The history of this cooperation dates back to 1983. One of the editors, Susan, had just finished a consultancy in Tanzania for the World Health Organization and the Danish International Development Agency, which involved a study of attitudes and practices relating to mental impairment. Benedicte stopped in Copenhagen to discuss this work on her way to Botswana, where she was to undertake a two-year study of cultural aspects of disability in general and the WHO program for community-based rehabilitation in particular. At this first meeting we lamented the lack of literature on disabled people in developing countries. Most of the scholarly work dealt with Europe and North America.

While in Botswana, and on several later occasions, Benedicte met with Dr. Einar Helander, then head of the WHO Rehabilitation Department in Geneva, and "father" of the WHO Community-Based Rehabilitation (CBR) Programme. She pointed out the lack of cultural analysis and awareness in the implementation and evaluation of CBR programs. Generously, Dr. Helander took up this challenge and offered some economic support from WHO to set up a network of studies on beliefs and attitudes toward disabled people in various cultural settings.

This was done by encouraging graduate students of anthropology at the University of Oslo to choose "disability and culture" as the topic of their theses, by affiliating one student who had already undertaken such a study on his own initiative, and by persuading colleagues who were about to start fieldwork to include the topic in their research. The network came to include projects from nine countries. In 1990 we conducted a workshop at the University of Oslo, sponsored by the Norwegian Department of Foreign Affairs, in which these projects were presented, together with papers by invited scholars from Zimbabwe, Mali, Kenya, Sweden, and WHO in Geneva. The proceedings from this workshop were published as a working paper, and four of the contributions have been further developed for inclusion in the present volume (chaps. 3, 4, 8, and 10).

Other chapters were solicited from people who had relevant material or were already working in this area. We wrote to Robert Murphy, who expressed interest in our effort and a hope that he might be able to contribute something when he had finished work underway. After he died, his wife, Yolanda Murphy, kindly agreed to allow us to include a chapter from his book *The Body Silent;* we wanted him to be a part of this project.

Our colleagues in Oslo and Copenhagen encouraged and supported us in the work that led to this volume. Susan would also like to thank Bente Jensen at the Institute of Anthropology in Copenhagen for help in preparing parts of the manuscript, and the Department of Social Medicine at Harvard University for the hospitality of a visiting associate professorship while she completed revisions.

We are grateful to Gelya Frank for her advocacy and helpful suggestions when we needed them. At the University of California Press, Stan Holwitz welcomed our plan, and Michelle Bonnice and Linda Benefield treated our manuscript with kindness, thoughtfulness, and care.

We envision this volume as serving three types of readers: our social science colleagues and students; people working with health or rehabilitation programs, particularly in developing countries; and people with disabilities, who may find in these pages new perspectives on their situations. We hope that this book will provoke discussion and further research, and enhance understanding of the cultural dimensions of disability.

Introduction

ONE

Disability and Culture: An Overview

Susan Reynolds Whyte and Benedicte Ingstad

A preliminary common-sense definition of disability might be that it is a lack or limitation of competence. We usually think of disability in contrast to an ideal of normal capacity to perform particular activities and to play one's role in social life. Sickness also inhibits ability, but we distinguish between sickness, which is temporary (whether ended by healing or death), and disability, which is chronic. In principle, disabled people cannot be cured; they may be rehabilitated. Disability is used to refer to limitations resulting from dysfunction in individual bodies and minds. By metaphoric extension, we may speak of social disabilities such as poverty or race. But the core meaning of disability for most of us is a biopsychological one. Blindness, lameness, mental deficiency, chronic incapacitating illness—these are prototypical disabilities.

The International Year of Disabled Persons in 1981, followed by the United Nations Decade for Disabled Persons declared by the United Nations in 1983, put disability into a global context and posed the question of how it may be understood in a multicultural world. How are deficits of the body and mind understood and dealt with in different societies? How is an individual's culturally defined identity as a person affected by disability? What processes of cultural change shape local perceptions of disability? Through a series of case studies, this book provides some preliminary answers to these questions.

A great deal of work has been carried out by psychologists and sociologists on disability and rehabilitation in Northern (European and North American) societies. A rich literature and several journals attest to the empirical and theoretical development of the field. Rather belatedly, anthropologists are now beginning to write about disability as well. In the introduction to a recent special issue of *Social Science and Medicine* devoted to cross-cultural perspectives on disability, Nora Groce and Jessica Scheer (1990) point to the slow emergence of anthropological research in this field and the need for holistic conceptualizations of persons in their cultural contexts. Yet the articles in that issue are based on research in North America, as are most of the earlier anthropological contributions (Ablon 1984; Edgerton 1967; Estroff 1981; Groce 1985; Murphy 1987). Work on disability in Southern countries (we use "Southern" to mean non-European and non-North American countries) has been mostly in the area of mental health; chronic mental illness, epilepsy, and mental retardation have attracted more attention than sensory or motor disabilities. Robert Edgerton was a pioneer here, not only through his East African research but in his attempts to formulate general cross-cultural questions about disability and deviance (Edgerton 1970, 1985). He showed that attitudes toward people with impairments of their mental facilities varied greatly in non-Western cultures, from negative discrimination, to acceptance, and even to the positive attribution of supernatural powers.

Much research in medical anthropology has a "therapeutic theme." It has concentrated on conceptions of illness and disease, on modes of healing, and on the interaction between patient and practitioner. Studies of disability require us to move away from the clinic toward the community, where individuals and families live with deficits. Cultural assumptions about the body and personhood must be seen in the context of ordinary social interaction. We are less concerned with disease than with its long-term consequences and more concerned with adjustment than with therapy. Impairment raises moral and metaphysical problems about personhood, responsibility, and the meaning of differences. Questions about autonomy and dependence, capacity and identity, and the meaning of loss are central.

There is a growing consciousness in Europe and North America of disablement as a human and social issue that touches us all, the disabled and the "temporarily abled" as well. Powerful popular accounts by and about persons with disabilities articulate the experience of impairment (e.g., Sacks 1985, 1989). Political activism by interest groups has created awareness of how society handicaps people with disabilities. Moreover, the transition from acute to chronic morbidity and the perceived failure of biomedicine to cure other conditions as effectively as it does infectious diseases means that disablement poses an ideological challenge, indeed a crisis, for health care in industrialized society (Williams 1991). It is timely and instructive to examine some of these issues in a cross-cultural perspective.

The method of cultural juxtaposition (Marcus and Fischer 1986:157ff.) is well established in anthropology as a way of providing perspective on our own situation. In assembling articles about disability in very different cultural contexts, we follow the tradition of juxtaposition, and we hope that these accounts will be useful for those primarily interested in disability in

Northern countries. But we want to be wary of a pitfall of cultural juxtaposition: our tendency to look at other cultures in terms of our own problems and thus to fail to grasp the premises upon which other people are operating. We have tried to be sensitive to this danger, in part through awareness of the assumptions about disability we bring to the study of other cultures. This is particularly necessary as rehabilitation programs are established in Southern countries; we hope that people working with health development in those settings will find the juxtapositions illuminating as well.

A UNIVERSAL DEFINITION?

Attempts to universalize the category "disabled" ran into conceptual problems of the most fundamental sort. Differing definitions made it difficult to document the extent of the problem. The first estimates by the World Health Organization were that 10 percent of any population was disabled. Later these figures were modified to 6 or 7 percent, giving a global figure of 245 million disabled people (E. Helander 1993). Estimates depend on what counts as disability (the first figures included malnutrition), on how severe an impairment must be before it is considered disabling, and on how categories are implemented in actually gathering data. Although a number of surveys have been carried out in developing countries, we can still make only a qualified guess about statistics (Renker 1982). Any epidemiological study involves cultural factors (Johansson 1991), and cultural factors are especially involved in attempts to count cases of disability.

The World Health Organization definition of disability is logically stringent and designed for universal application. The *International Classification of Impairments, Disabilities, and Handicaps* (WHO 1980) is based on the model of the International Classification of Diseases, but because it attempts to categorize the consequences of disease, it includes a consideration of social contexts.

An impairment is defined as "any loss or abnormality of psychological, physiological, or anatomical structure or function" (WHO 1980:27). The concept bears close resemblance to Arthur Kleinman's definition of disease as "a malfunctioning of biological and/or psychological processes" (Kleinman 1980:72). Like disease, impairment is defined "primarily by those qualified to judge physical and mental functioning according to generally accepted standards" (WHO 1980:27).

While impairment relates to constituents of the body (the "organ" level), disability has to do with "compound or integrated activities expected of the person or of the body as a whole, such as are represented by tasks, skills and behaviour." It is defined as "any restriction or lack (resulting from an impairment) of ability to perform an activity in the manner or within the range considered normal for a human being" (WHO 1980:28). Handicap relates to the social consequences of deficiencies in organs and activity performance. It is defined as "a disadvantage for a given individual, resulting from an impairment or a disability, that limits or prevents the fulfilment of a role that is normal (depending on age, sex, and social and cultural factors) for that individual" (29). Handicap depends on valuations and expectations that put the disabled person at a disadvantage. The WHO manual states explicitly that valuation depends on cultural norms.

The formulation of these concepts represents a valuable attempt to move beyond the restrictions of straight biomedical classifications. Nevertheless, the taxonomy is based on a biomedical concept, that of impairment; disability and handicap are consequences of impairment (itself a consequence of disease or trauma). It is on the basis of the biomedical definition of impairment that the classification is proposed as a universal tool. The primacy of the biomedical concern is reflected in the fact that the list of impairments is far more extensive and detailed than that of disabilities, which is again more elaborated than that of handicaps.[1] Most anthropologists would prefer a cultural relativist position rather than the universalizing approach proposed by the WHO (and this is reflected in the fact that few of them have chosen to use the WHO definitions systematically).

An example may illustrate the problem. A Malian and a Norwegian researcher set out to describe those qualities of an individual which might inhibit the ability to play normal roles among the Kel Tamasheq (Tuareg). They explain the Tamasheq notion of fault, or "default," and exemplify it by citing old age and immaturity (making one physically dependent), illegitimate birth (making one socially anomalous), and ugliness (rendering it difficult to marry). They list Tamasheq terms for a variety of faults, including deafness, excessive freckles, protruding naval, absentmindedness, and flabby or small buttocks (Halatine and Berge 1990:58–59). Most of these impairments are not on the WHO list and several, like illegitimate birth, are social and not "organic" problems. Others are organic but would never be seen as impairments by biomedical authorities. But the point they want to make does not have to do with identification and classification, but with the very notion of "fault" itself and the Tamasheq view of personhood.

Cultural relativism, the idea that phenomena must be understood within their relevant cultural contexts, takes two forms. Within discussions of disability, a "weak relativist" position is common. The point here is that the disadvantage posed by a disability depends on the capacities most prized or needed in a particular context. One of us remembers visiting the Alhambra many years ago—the lovely view over the town with the Sierra Nevada rising magnificently above, and the plea chalked on a wall of the fortress: "Give alms, woman, for there is nothing worse in all the world than to be blind in Grenada." The idea that it is worse to be blind in the midst of beauty, or mentally retarded in a setting that values educational achievement, or crippled where all earn their living by hard physical labor, is commonly accepted. However, few anthropologists would be satisfied with this form of relativism, because it remains at the level of specific functions and tasks and ignores the way in which culture structures whole life worlds, imbuing individual variations of the human condition with significance more far-reaching than the simple ability to perform a given activity.

"Radical relativism" seeks to reveal basic assumptions about what it is to be a person, and what kinds of identities and values exist in given social contexts. How important is individual ability as a source of social identity? What is it people are trying to achieve? The strong version of relativism questions the terms of analysis and attempts to uncover the categories implicit in other worldviews. The concept of disability itself must not be taken for granted. In many cultures, one cannot be "disabled" for the simple reason that "disability" as a recognized category does not exist. There are blind people and lame people and "slow" people, but "the disabled" as a general term does not translate easily into many languages. In this volume, Aud Talle (chap. 3) explains that the Maasai term used to translate the English word *disabled* actually refers to a lizard that walks in an awkward way. The emphasis is on physical movement, so conditions like mental retardation or chronic mental illness are not included. The concepts of disability, handicap, and rehabilitation emerged in particular historical circumstances in Europe.[2] As a social identity, "disabled" is only now being created in most Southern countries—through surveys, research projects, rehabilitation programs, and government policy.[3]

EURO-AMERICAN DISABILITY

Cross-cultural studies of disability must involve consideration of its cultural construction in Western society. We need this clarification not only in order to understand case studies from Europe and North America but also because Western (or Northern) concepts, organizations, and practices are carried over to other contexts and because culturally specific assumptions are often implicit in our analyses.

A fundamental theme in the contemporary Western discourse on disability is the assumption of the desirability of equality—understood as sameness or similarity. The terms *handicap, disability,* and *rehabilitation* themselves provide clues to this supposition. Etymologically, *handicap* was originally a game, a kind of lottery, in which the winner paid a forfeit; the umpire held the money in his hand in a cap. Later, the term came to be used in relation to competitions in which unequal competitors were weighted so as to make the match more equal. Thus the word has connotations of competition and efforts to create equality. *Disability* implies a deprivation or loss of a needed competency or qualification, in contrast to *inability,* which suggests an inherent lack of power to perform a thing. This notion of loss is underlined by the response to disability, *rehabilitation,* which implies restoration to a previous condition. There is an underlying ideal of equality lost and restored, and of the *right* to be able to participate equally.

Western concepts of equality and individual rights are central to a notion of person that Louis Dumont has called "Homo aequalis." Dumont traces a distinction between a notion of equality as a political ideal that recognizes innate differences (the kind of equality of which Rousseau wrote), and the nineteenth-century American concept of equality, which tended toward an ideal of innate similarity. In discussing Tocqueville, Dumont writes:

> If equality is conceived as rooted in man's very nature and denied only by an evil society, then, as there are no longer any rightful differences in condition or estate, or different sorts of men, they are all alike and even identical, as well as equal. This is what Tocqueville says: where inequality reigns, there are as many distinct humanities as there are social categories, the reverse being true in egalitarian society. (Dumont 1980:16)

It is this theme of similarity and difference which Henri-Jacques Stiker (1982) follows in tracing the history of impairment in Western society. While neither he nor Dumont is interested in a cynical deconstruction of the idea of equality, both draw attention to possible consequences of the pursuit of equality: intolerance of innate diversity and individualism which denies the social nature of persons. This concern is so fundamental for Stiker that he begins his history by declaring his own position—that the love of difference leads to humane social life, while the passion for similarity brings repression and rejection.

Western conceptions of disability are formed in the context of a centralist state that imposes a universal code through legislation. Stiker argues that legislation gives to infirmity an existence and a consistency it never had before—definition, criteria, and degrees of severity. People with infirmities become a marked group; they are given a social identity, as citizens who have the same rights as others and should be integrated like ordinary people. They have a double self-image: as injured beings and as citizens/workers like everyone else. "Paradoxically, they are designated so as to disappear, they are named so as to go unmentioned" (Stiker 1982:149; our translation).

Stiker draws attention to the contradictions of this situation; the culture of "as if" would negate handicap, but in pretending that everyone is identical, it does not make them equal. In fact, this may be seen as a kind of confinement—of the different in the common and familiar. It is this contradictory situation that Robert Murphy and his coauthors call "liminal." The word may be misleading, in that it suggests the possibility of transition to another state. But the point they make fits well with Stiker's assessment of the paradoxical position of people with impairments. In American middle-class culture, disability is treated as unspeakable and invisible. Children are taught not to point, stare, or mention the impairments of people they meet. "And so we are treated to the paradox of nobody 'seeing' the one person in the room of whom they are most acutely, and uncomfortably aware" (Murphy et al. 1988:239). Such differences are painfully embarrassing in a society where differences are supposed to be compensated so that the ideal of equality cum similarity may be maintained.

Euro-American assumptions about disability are not only based in a particular political philosophy but are elaborated through a set of laws, administrative procedures, medical diagnoses, welfare institutions, professional specializations, and business interests. In Europe and North America, disability is a political privilege entitling one to financial support and a series of services. The state assigns to physicians the task of determining who is entitled to these rights. In this way, the political issue of redistribution, which involves separating the deserving from the undeserving, becomes a clinical problem (Sundby 1990). In the Scandinavian countries, doctors must decide at what point alcoholism is severe enough to entitle one to an "invalid pension." In the United States, Social Security benefits can be awarded only to sufferers of persistent pain, "when medical signs and findings show a medical condition that could be expected to produce the pain" (Osterweis et al. 1987:51). In her analysis of the history of disability as an administrative classification, Deborah Stone (1984) examines the tendencies toward expansion of the category. Various interests are served by maintaining flexibility in definitions and by continually incorporating new conditions (chronic fatigue syndrome, fibromyalgia) as disabling. Although cast in biomedical terms, the determination of disability involves political decisions about the distribution of social goods. "Instead of seeing disability as a set of objective characteristics that render people needy, we can define it in terms of ideas and values about redistribution" (ibid.:172). Nevertheless, the ongoing discussion *is* about objective criteria and measurements of incapacity, precisely because the state must be seen to be distributing (increasingly) scarce goods in a (seemingly) fair and systematic way.

The development of disability as a concern of the state was accompanied by the emergence of rehabilitation as a medical and paramedical specialization, beginning in the struggle for professional control over the damaged bodies of the First World War (Gritzer and Arluke 1985). In the United States, as the population aged and suffered more chronic diseases, as federal legislation on disability expanded, and as the health insurance industry developed, disability became big business. In a political-economic approach to rehabilitation in America, Gary Albrecht (1992) argues that disability has been institutionalized and reified, and that rehabilitation goods and services have become commodities with an ever-increasing market. A consequence of this trend is that people with disabilities become consumers; they develop an identity and form groups as users of the services available to them. The disability rights movement is still young and involves only the most active consumers. But it demands a part in shaping the rehabilitation marketplace to reflect the needs and values of the consumers themselves (ibid.:285ff.).

Thus disability in Europe and North America exists within—and is created by—a framework of state, legal, economic, and biomedical institutions. Concepts of personhood, identity, and value, while not reducible to institutions, are nevertheless shaped by them. Notions of citizenship, compensation, and value lost through impairment and added through rehabilitation are institutionally reinforced constituents of disability as a cultural construct. So is the idea that disability is a medical condition for which technical expertise (educational, psychological, social) is the answer. In countries of the South, where this kind of institutional infrastructure exists only to a very limited degree, disability as a concept and an identity is not an explicit cultural construct. The meaning of impairment must be understood in terms of cosmology and values and purposes of social life.

DIFFERENCE AND PERSONHOOD

One of the basic questions for cross-cultural research on disability is that of how biological impairments relate to personhood and to culturally defined differences among persons. Are people with impairments impaired people? Are they valued differently than other members of society? Irving Zola speaks of the invalidation and infantilization of disabled people; one's validity as a full person is denied. Being different means being less (Zola 1982:235–237). Murphy uses concepts of liminality and impurity to characterize this state of ambiguous personhood. The Norwegian author Finn Carling captured his sense of being not only devalued but dehumanized, in the title of his book *And Yet We Are Human* (1962).

In order to begin to deal with such issues, it may be useful to distinguish between humanity and personhood. Accounts from some societies suggest that individuals with certain kinds of impairments or biological characteristics may not be considered human. Or rather, there may be a point at which such an individual's humanity is in doubt. In many Northern countries, the abortion of a defective fetus is considered more acceptable than that of a "normal" one, suggesting that the "human" status of an impaired individual is more negotiable. The debate about whether severely impaired infants or even adults should be kept alive also involves the attribution of humanity, as the revealing term "human vegetable" implies. In many societies, birth defects are more likely to be seen as inhuman than defects acquired later in life, when humanity and personhood are already established. The ethnographic literature contains many reports of infants who are not anthropomorphized and are expected to die. Nancy Scheper-Hughes describes how impoverished women in northeast Brazil neglect these "poor little critters" and compares them to Nuer "crocodile infants" and Irish "changelings," all excluded from the realm of humanity. "The sickly, wasted, or congenitally deformed infant challenges the tentative and fragile symbolic boundaries between human and nonhuman, natural and supernatural, normal and abominable" (Scheper-Hughes 1992:375). What is significant for our purposes at the moment is that the cultural conceptualization of humanity is variable; the anomalies that may be seen as inhuman differ greatly from one society to another, and they do not correspond directly to biomedical definitions of impairment. Twins are not considered human by the Punan Bah (chap. 2) nor are children born with teeth by the Bariba (Sargent 1982).

Such examples may easily become stereotype generalizations about the cultural construction of disability; in fact they are only a simple beginning to an investigation of disability and personhood. If personhood is seen as being not simply human but human in a way that is valued and meaningful, then individuals can be persons to a greater or lesser extent. There may be kinds and degrees of personhood, and the qualities of a person are evolved and confirmed throughout life. (Personhood refers to the evaluation of others in contrast to the reflexive sense of self.) So what are the significant characteristics of a person? Individual ability? Community membership? Family? There is no single answer for any culture, nor is there a universal set of priorities. For several of the societies described in this book, being a member of a family and having children are far more important to being a person than work capacity or appearance. The contrast between egocentric and sociocentric concepts of personhood (Geertz 1973; Schweder and Bourne 1982) provides one kind of comparative framework here. Where a person's worth is conceived in terms of individual abilities and achievements, we would expect impairment to diminish personhood. But where persons are primarily considered in terms of relations to others, this would not necessarily be the case. Such a dichotomy must be used with care, however, for both kinds of qualities are recognized everywhere. The real challenge lies in understanding the way particular characteristics, be they impairments or gifts, inhibit or facilitate individual achievements and relational integration in a given cultural world.[4]

One of the recurring themes in the American (and European) conceptualization of disability is that of autonomy and dependence. In fact, Murphy asserts that they are universal aspects of all social relationships and that dependency is a problem that all disabled people must confront (Murphy 1987:156). But he also shows how reliance upon another person may be encompassed by love and a feeling of mutuality. That is to say, dependency may have different values and implications. We have already suggested that in some cultures, sociality (family and community membership) may outweigh individual ability as a value. Ann Goerdt's study of physical disability in Barbados makes an interesting comparison because it falls somewhere between the egocentric concern with independence and the sociocentric one with community. The Barbadian conception of personhood emphasizes a balance between autonomy and connectedness. "At the same time that one should demonstrate autonomy, one must not be too independent of others. . . . for the unity of the group depends not only on the contribution of each member, but also on each member's willingness to accept help from others" (Goerdt 1984:88). Thus Barbadians conceptualize disability not just in terms of helplessness, dependence, and infantilization (failure of autonomy) but also in terms of limitations on social interaction (failure of connectedness), which they sometimes describe as "hiding."

SOCIAL ORGANIZATION AND DISABILITY

Cultural conceptualizations of difference must be seen in relation to social contexts. Cross-cultural literature on disability employs two general ways of doing this: examining overall features of social organization, and focusing on the implications of specific social characteristics (gender, age, class) within a society. The first concern has been the most common, because of the interest in juxtaposition and comparison of whole societies, indeed of whole kinds of societies.

A broad social structural hypothesis has been proposed by Scheer and Groce to explain the differing situations of disabled people in small-scale and complex societies. They suggest that where face-to-face contact between individuals is frequent, and people have multistranded and diffuse relations with one another, social identity is based on a variety of family and other characteristics.

> In such situations, a single personal characteristic, such as a physical impairment, does not generalize to define one's total social identity. In complex societies, however, social relationships and contexts are more impersonal and task specific, and individuals are not related to each other in varied contexts. Accordingly, visible physical characteristics are commonly used to classify and socially notate the individual's identity. (Scheer and Groce 1988:31–32)

The distinction made here between traditional, small-scale societies and complex societies involves a contrast not only in types of social identity but also in social participation and support of disabled individuals. From several studies, a picture emerges of a kind of "natural integration" of disabled people as members of families and communities in simpler societies.[5] Perhaps the best-known example is Groce's own ethnohistorical study of deafness on Martha's Vineyard, in which she describes a society where everyone, hearing and deaf, spoke sign language, and where deaf people farmed and fished, married and had children, participated in town meetings and ordinary social interaction. They were remembered as unique individuals, never as "the deaf" (Groce 1985:4).

Of the contributions to this volume, both Ida Nicolaisen's article on Punan Bah of Sarawak (chap. 2) and Aud Talle's on the Maasai of Kenya (chap. 3) describe situations where disabled individuals are integrated and accepted. Kinship identity, residence in a longhouse or large compound, and rank or membership of an age-set are more important factors in social identity than impairment. One is truly handicapped when unable to marry or participate in the community, and it is up to the family to insure that this does not happen.

However, we will argue that as an analytical tool, the dichotomy between traditional/small-scale and complex societies has significant limitations. Not all relationships in complex societies are impersonal and task specific; in many situations, identity is based on criteria other than physical characteristics. And even in small-scale societies, there are kinds of impairments that may dominate social identity; inability to have children limits the strands in relationships. Not all relationships are multistranded, unless one never leaves one's own village; while people may not attribute a primary identity as impaired to their own neighbors, they are likely to do so in relation to people they know less well (see Goerdt 1984:26–27 on madness, and Whyte, chap. 12, on epilepsy). Furthermore, very few societies in the world today are small-scale in the sense of being untouched by national institutions and the global economy. Nicolaisen suggests that wage labor and the timber industry impinge upon the possibilities for disabled Punan Bah individuals to be economically integrated. Talle shows how Maasai families may use national institutions such as schools and the home for disabled children.

The point that identity does not generally derive from impairment in small-scale societies should not distract us from recognizing that there may well be roles and activities where impairment is the central criterion for recruitment. All deaf children from Martha's Vineyard were sent to the American Asylum for the Deaf and Dumb in Hartford from the time of its founding in 1817 and at state expense; in the nineteenth century, they were better educated than other islanders (Groce 1985:77–78). In this respect, the island was not small-scale, and the identification of individuals by their impairment supported their participation in island life.

The other example that Scheer and Groce use as an illustration of a simple society with diffuse social roles is the community of San Pedro Yolox in southern Mexico, studied by John Gwaltney. Many adults, especially older ones, had been blinded by onchocerciasis, and Gwaltney shows how deeply embedded they were in village life through ties of real and fictive kinship. He also writes about the importance of begging expeditions, from which blind people "derive a great sense of approved, purposeful participation in the life of their pueblo" (Gwaltney 1970:112). People were supposed to beg in other villages, but some also did so in their own. Clearly, begging requires identifying oneself as disabled,[6] and begging in other villages is a task-specific social relationship requiring a particular physical characteristic. In ordinary social interaction as well, blindness is an important part of identity, to judge from Gwaltney's account of how individuals expound upon their misfortune and receive commiseration (114). While Scheer and Groce point to an important dimension in relating role structures to social identity, the problem is that the polarity of two ideal type societies is too simple for the analysis of real cases.

In examining the characteristics of social organization relevant to disability, there are three important questions. First, what is the ability of the family to care for an infirm member? Demographic factors such as family size as well as the organization of the economy and social activities are important here. It has been claimed that the "phenomenon of the handicapped" emerges in European society in part as a function of the difficulties of the nuclear family in bearing the burden of care. Sociality (work, leisure, education) is disaggregated in space and time; the technical constraints of special care and training may require removing the person from the home, at least part of the time. This, together with the normative demands for conformity and achievement, places an enormous practical and psychological burden on a family, often on a mother (Stiker 1982:175).

Research in Africa has examined the way that households cope with caregiving in contemporary circumstances there. In Tanzania, Susan Whyte (1991) found that people with mental illness, retardation, and epilepsy were almost always cared for by their families and care was regarded as a family, not a community, responsibility. Because families were large, the burden of care could be shared. However, labor migration and poverty transform family situations. Sidsel Saugestad (1990) describes how in Zimbabwean villages it is often grandmothers who care for disabled children because parents (or unmarried mothers) are working in town. From Botswana, Benedicte Ingstad and coauthors (1992) describe a similar pattern. Labor migration takes away the healthy and able household members, leaving the old, the very young, and the infirm to survive on subsistence farming and often irregular remittances. Loyal and affectionate care may well mark the relations among these "weaker" members of a family. But that does not eliminate the need for cash and other assistance from the most "able" relatives. Coping with care is a matter of the disposition of family resources (Walman 1984) and also of the willingness to give such care priority over other needs and goals. Increasing pressures on families in developing countries may be instrumental in creating a demand for programs for the disabled, and thus a social category of "the disabled."

The second question in examining social organization and disability is, How does the occupational structure of the society incorporate people with impairments? The organization of production, the degree of specialization, and the nature of the work affect the degree to which people with impairments are able to participate. Where the family is the basic unit of production, it seems easier for people with disabilities to make a contribution. Working conditions are flexible, tasks are varied so there is almost always something they can do, and there is support from other family members and neighbors. Impairment does not usually disqualify people for work in subsistence production, domestic tasks, or even home-based handicraft production for the market. When labor is a commodity sold on a competitive market in fixed time and skill units, the participation of people with disabilities is more problematic.

We can take this question a step farther by asking whether impairments actually qualify people for certain occupations or whether some jobs are thought specially suitable. (For the moment we leave aside national vocational training programs for the handicapped.) The information on this point in historical and ethnographic literature is limited. In some places, blind people were more likely to become singers, storytellers, or learned religious men. M. C. Narasimhan and A. K. Mukherjee (1986:2) mention the Surdasi, blind singers of India, called after a famous blind vocalist. In many countries, impairment is a valuable qualification for the occupation of begging. Studies from India describe the techniques of beggars displaying their defects: "arousing . . . compassion by skilfully exhibiting their physical disabilities and diseased condition" (Chaudhuri 1987:33); "Some sat silently . . . exposing their diseased part or physical handicap and thereby they tried to bang on the emotion of the passersby" (Misra and Mohanty 1963:40). In premodern Taiwan, beggars who lacked a suitably "pitiful image" might fake disability or exploit an impaired person as "a begging implement" (Schak 1988:47). Yet even though mendicancy is the most widely mentioned special occupation for people with impairments, probably no more than a fraction actually engage in it in societies where it is an option.

A final question concerns the existence of special programs, institutions, and organizations for disabled people. These may comprise laws and welfare benefits for the disabled as a generic category, as well as institutions and interest groups for people with specific kinds of impairment. Some excellent fieldwork accounts are based on participant observation in such institutions (Zola 1982) and with people defined in relation to an institution (Edgerton 1967; Estroff 1981) or organization (Ablon 1981; May and Hill 1984). By contrast, many disabled people in developing countries are not (yet) touched by any kind of special program; where deafness and blindness are not as common as they were on Martha's Vineyard and in San Pedro

Yolox, a deaf or blind person might not know anyone else with the same impairment.[7] And special privileges are not usually granted *because* one is disabled (with the possible exception of the right to beg). However, as programs are introduced, and as organizations of disabled people are formed in developing countries (often with support from sister organizations in Europe and North America), new options are made available. Nayinda Sentumbwe (chap. 8) shows how "in-marriage" emerges from programs for the blind in Uganda. Goerdt (1990) examines relations of patronage in vocational programs for disabled people on Barbados. Even though nearly every country has at least some disability institutions, there is great variation in their accessibility and in the ways they touch people's lives.

SOCIAL POSITION AND DISABILITY

So far we have discussed ways in which general qualities of social organization are related to disability. The emphasis has been on characterizing societies or identifying social features that affect impaired people in general. We turn now to the issue of variation within societies. How does impairment interact with factors like sex, age, and economic standing to create different situations within a social universe?

Recent work in North America is beginning to examine gender differences in disability. Adrienne Asch and Michelle Fine (1988) point out that disabled women are less likely to marry than disabled men, and if they do marry after the onset of their impairment, they are more likely to have a disabled spouse. The high value placed on women's appearance and fitness in American culture is only part of the explanation for this pattern. Asch and Fine emphasize the emotional components of American marriage, in which women are expected to be nurturant and to satisfy men's unacknowledged needs and dependencies (ibid.:17). It is assumed that disabled women, burdened by their own needs, are less able to meet those of husbands. Murphy summarizes the different consequences of having an impaired spouse for men and for women: "Husbands become part-time nurses, which goes against social conventions, and wives find themselves with an additional child, which doesn't" (Murphy 1987:159).

Sentumbwe (chap. 8) found that in Uganda, even though blind women seemed to be at a disadvantage compared to blind men in terms of marriage, they also had an important option—to have children, even when unmarried. Through children a woman is fulfilled and respected; she develops new relationships through her children, and, paradoxically, she becomes more independent because she has someone to rely upon. Disabled men are not able to achieve parenthood so easily; future research may pursue the implications of this gender difference in relation to disability.

The way in which parenthood interacts with disability has been examined by Shlomo Deshen and Hilda Deshen (1989) in their research on the relation between blind parents and seeing children in Israel. The authority of parents over their children is undermined by the general stigmatizing of blindness in Israel, of which children soon become aware. In order to strengthen their position, parents may emphasize blindness-linked assets, such as their ability to move officials to compassion or the fact that they are often better educated than their sighted relatives. A study of hearing children of deaf parents in the United States also shows the relationship between parent-child dynamics and the wider society. Paul Preston (1991) speaks of deaf people as constituting a highly endogamous, clearly demarcated cultural community. Hearing children born of deaf parents identify with this community and experience it as normal. But ultimately their membership is ambiguous because they can hear. They have a polarized understanding of deafness as viable and normal, and as stigma and deficit. Preston concludes by emphasizing that the meanings of disability are ultimately dependent on social context. It is necessary to examine significance from particular social positions.

The point in the life cycle at which disablement occurs may well be crucial for the meaning and implications of disability. An impairment incurred later in life, after one's social and economic position is well established, and when the debilities of age are more or less expected, has a different significance than a loss experienced as a young adult. A study from the United States suggested that while lifelong disability may be a "master status" dominating one's identity, disability in old age is a subordinate one. Marriage and children were far more important than "validity" for the status of old women (Simon 1988:218–219). This may hold in many other societies as well, though in Botswana (Ingstad et al. 1992) it is not just a matter of having children, but of being respected and supported by them. In China, government policy has been to encourage, if not require, family care of disabled elderly people. A study in Canton (Ikels 1991) found that restrictions on labor mobility, residential stability (in part due to a housing shortage), early retirement, and pension and medical benefits facilitate family caregiving. And the lack of alternative care necessitates it. But the power of morality and the meaning of generational relations are mobilized as well. People are encouraged to care for elderly disabled persons because of respect for their age and indebtedness to them as members of the revolutionary generation.

A final point regarding the social positioning of disability is that differences in a family's social and economic status may be decisive. Bernhard Helander (1990:42–44) compares the perceptions and situations of two Somali boys with apparently comparable degrees of mental disability. One belonged to a prestigious patrilineage and was well treated in the village. His "problem" was explained as due to the fact that his mother was not of sufficiently high status, but he was not regarded as mad nor was he humiliated in any way. The other boy was a homeless orphan, said to be possessed by a spirit. He was teased and despised, and children sometimes threw stones at him "trying to hit the spirit." Helander's message is that the explanatory models of disability in Somalia are partly shaped by the social positions of the actors. Among the Tuareg, Susan Rasmussen (1989) shows similar patterns of variation in explanations of impairment according to socioeconomic status.

Disabled people and their families construct the meaning and value of disabilities in the choices they make concerning production and reproduction. Didier Fassin's (1991) study of people with physical handicaps in Dakar demonstrates the economic constraints and potentials involved in marital and income-earning strategies. To marry off a disabled daughter means accepting a lower bridewealth than would be paid for a "normal" woman. But to obtain a wife for a disabled son requires the payment of a larger than normal bridewealth, a project that may take many years to realize. Sending disabled family members onto the streets to beg gives an immediate return; apprenticing them requires an investment of money that the family may not have and may well increase the profits of the employer. Beggars use their impairment as a tool to work for their families; apprentices provide a labor force for their masters, and only in the long run do they have a chance of obtaining worthwhile work that may benefit their families. Whether or not impairment handicaps one on the marriage market or becomes a tool for work as a beggar depends not on Senegalese conceptions of disability alone; it is also determined by the economic and social situation of the family.

Research in rural Botswana showed that most families cared well for their disabled members. In the few cases that seemed to show abuse and neglect, the family was in extremely difficult circumstances. Care was less a function of "attitudes" toward disabled family members than of household resources. In situations of extreme poverty, people with disabilities are particularly vulnerable.

ANALYZING PROCESSES

Medical sociology has long been concerned with the processes of interpreting, negotiating, and labeling impairments. Since the 1960s, within the general approach of symbolic interactionism, analytical issues have emerged which continue to shape disability studies. One is the notion of stigma and the ways in which it is negotiated in social interaction (Goffman 1963). Related ideas of "spread" and "deviance disavowal" (Davis 1961) are tools for analyzing the interpersonal management of difference. Another is the concept of "career," used to describe the ascription of a social role and identity to a "deviant" individual. One of the points of labeling theory is that the identification of a singularity by social agencies has consequences for the subsequent career of the impaired person; primary deviance, once labeled, is encompassed by secondary deviance that is socially determined (Scheff 1966; Scott 1970). Whether describing face-to-face interaction and the problems of identity management, or the interaction of individuals and families with therapeutic institutions, the emphasis in symbolic interactionist studies is on the social production of reality and on the way in which individuals are both subjects and objects in interaction with others. Interpretations are social processes.

This kind of approach to the dynamics of disability has been influential in anthropological studies as well, although certain differences in emphasis are evident. In this book, Lisbeth Sachs (chap. 11) follows the process of labeling an infirmity, demonstrating how complex this process can be in a changing, multicultural situation, where different conceptions coexist. There is no simple acceptance of the doctors' identification of the problem. Sue Estroff finds it characteristic of anthropology to show how people identified as deviant "adopted, elaborated, and/or rejected their deviant identities while interacting with the culturally defined values and actions of others" (1981:211). She examines the cultural values and practices of American society toward "crazy" people and the way those so defined manipulate and use the dominant values. Like Sachs and others (Murphy et al. 1988), she tries to characterize broader cultural patterns of meaning and value, rather than social situations or social careers. In contrast, some of the sociological studies tend to take culture for granted.

In an overview of sociological research on chronic illness, Uta Gerhardt (1990) points to a convergence between medical sociology and ethnography in their common "self-consciousness" about fieldwork and methodology. There is a recognition that reality is constructed in a double sense: researchers make (second-order) constructions of actors' (first-order) interpretations. Applied to the study of disablement, this entails a careful examination of the processes by which disabled people and their families define their conditions and situations as well as critical attention to the way in which data on disability are represented in analysis.

The concern with processes of construction and representation is reflected in the intense interest in discourse analysis, which alerts us to the necessity of looking critically at how and by whom a picture is drawn. A discourse is a way of talking about or dealing with a phenomenon. By words, institutions, and practices, discourses realize certain assumptions or views and thus construct their object in a particular way. Rehabilitation specialists present images of the pathetic situation of disabled people in developing countries, ethnographers make elegant analyses of the cosmology of anomaly, while families themselves may cast their situations in terms that are neither pathetic nor congruent with one systematic cosmology.

Life histories and narratives by disabled people have assumed a central place in the literature on disability. In part this reflects the desire to insert the individual into social and cultural analyses (Whittemore et al. 1986). In part it mirrors the experiential and interpretive concern of contemporary sociology and anthropology. The interest in texts and narrative analysis also fits in with the popularity of individuals' stories. But for our purposes, what is significant about life histories is that they invite a diachronic and processual view of disability.

We may distinguish various kinds of accounts as well as different analytical definitions of process. Life histories or case histories may be defined as accounts compiled by a researcher in cooperation and interaction with an informant. They may incorporate descriptions of context and observations made by the researcher (Good et al. 1992; Kleinman 1988; Langness and Levine 1986; Wilson 1947), and they may include considerations about how the account was produced and what it means (Crapanzano 1980). Many accounts of lives with disabilities are elicited through interviews in which individuals tell the history of their impairment and search for treatment, and of the way their problem is interlinked with other aspects of their lives (Good et al. 1992). Autobiographical narratives of the kind analyzed in chapter 6 are written on the subject's own initiative and are not directly a product of dialogue, but they are products of communication in an extended sense. They are influenced by the writer's motivations, and they are created in and for a social context.[8]

The production of a personal narrative about disability is itself a process and has an effect on producers and listeners. The narrative reconstruction of lives may be a mode of normalizing problematic experiences by asserting the legitimacy of suffering and the moral competence of the narrator (Gerhardt 1990:1154). By telling the story in a meaningful way, the narrator is transformed. Moreover, the story may also serve as a "model for" other sufferers who are seeking a meaning in their experience (see Geertz 1966). Judith Monks and Ronald Frankenberg (chap. 6) call this the exemplar function—the narratives show "the way it is" and "the way it should be."

Both the form of these narratives as autobiographical accounts of disability and the content with its emphasis on self and body through time appear to be characteristic of European and North American culture. We have virtually no autobiographical material on the experience of disability in non-Western contexts and very few life histories. Even the case examples sprinkled through the literature as illustrations do not thematize the dynamics of self and body, or the existential problems of the individual. To the extent that processes of narrative reconstruction can be traced, they seem to be concerned with asserting moral competence through interpreting the causes of disability rather than the process of living with it. There is an emphasis on events preceding the onset of impairment, and on moral relations to other people and spiritual beings. Through these kinds of accounts, the impaired individual is construed in relation to other people and the cosmological environment, rather than as a self in relation to a body. The temporality involved is not that of individual development; it is the link from an event like a parental curse or the breaking of a taboo to the resulting infirmity in a family member.

HISTORICAL TRANSFORMATIONS

The kinds of processual analysis mentioned so far have to do with the movements and efforts of people within the possibilities of a given place and historical period. But any overview of disability and culture should also consider the historical processes through which the range of possibilities and the nature of practices change. One way of analyzing such processes is Foucault's "genealogical method" (Armstrong 1990), which traces the social history of discursive practices. Aside from Foucault's own study of madness (1973), the best example of that method applied to disability is the work of the French scholar, Henri-Jacques Stiker (1982), which appears to be virtually unknown by anglophone researchers. Susan Reynolds Whyte (chap. 14) summarizes some of Stiker's analyses of European discourses on infirmity, in which Stiker examines the emergence of rehabilitation as technical and social adjustment of the individual. While Stiker's sweeping characterizations may be objectionable, his method of "historical juxtaposition" is stimulating and provoking. He succeeds in revealing the conditionality of the categories, assumptions, and institutional practices by which disability is constructed. Aside from the Foucaultian work, there are a number of historical studies of disability and rehabilitation in Northern countries (Albrecht 1992; Gritzer and Arluke 1985; Stone 1984; Straus 1965). However, there is little analysis of the historical processes under way in the countries of the South (but see Narasimhan and Mukherjee 1986 for an informative description of this process in India, and Farquhar 1987 for a biography of a remarkable figure in the history of rehabilitation in Zimbabwe).

The programs introduced in developing countries can be seen in terms of different models for work with disabled people, each model with its own historical and ideological background (Satapati 1989). We can distinguish specialized services, outreach programs, community-based services, and interest organizations. It is through the efforts of these programs, often with government or donor support, that legal, biomedical, and social identities for disabled people are being formulated.

Specialized, institution-based services are often the first type of organized assistance instituted in developing countries. They are impairment specific, with schools for the blind among the first to be established. Usually they are started by organizations in the colonizing country, often on a religious or philanthropic basis. They are financed by a combination of sister organizations in the North and local contributions, sometimes with a little state support. This means a chronic situation of underfunding; in the case of schools, fees have to be charged, and that makes it impossible for many children to attend. Selectivity is further determined by the location of such institutions and their very limited capacity.

Previously, such specialized institutions sometimes became places for minimal care and confinement. (This was especially true of mental institutions, which in the early days were hardly more than depositories for people considered dangerous or whose families could not keep them.) Today there is an increased emphasis on special education and vocational training, a tendency that has also characterized institutional development in Northern countries.

A consequence of such institutional care and training is that "clients" are isolated from normal social life and may find it difficult to adjust to life in their communities when they leave the institution. Partly to counter such effects, many developing countries now offer special education to pupils living at home in the form of nursery schools, day centers, special schools, or special classes in normal schools.

Outreach programs sometimes grow out of specialized institutions in an effort to extend services beyond the fraction of disabled people who can get a place in the institution. In comparison to the need, however, these programs still cover only a few people. Even where decentralized special services are not an extension of an institution but an independent program, capacity is a problem. Costs are high and when resources are limited, appropriate services can only be offered to a few, selected according to criteria such as location, type of disability, or age-group.

Community-based rehabilitation (CBR) is the alternative, and it is the dominant discourse (in the sense of both rhetoric and programmatic practice) in developing countries today. In line with the promotion of primary health care, WHO developed a plan for integrating rehabilitation services into local-level health care in order to make them generally available (E. Helander 1993). The key principles are low cost, simple technology, use of local resources, and community participation. The concept of CBR has now been taken up by many organizations and implemented in different versions.

A simple instruction manual for health workers, disabled people, and their families has been worked out by WHO and made available in various languages (E. Helander et al. 1989). Rehabilitation aids should be made of local materials, and family members should train the disabled in activities of daily living. Schools, workplaces, and neighborhoods are encouraged to include them on an equal footing. Ideally CBR should be implemented through existing structures and based in the community in a cultural sense.

The CBR model developed by the International Labor Organization focuses more specifically on vocational training and the establishment of small production units based on local resources. The ILO program calls for the adoption of a legal requirement that 2 percent of all jobs in plants and public institutions be reserved for disabled people.

David Werner proposes yet another version of CBR in his book *Disabled Village Children* (1987), written on the model of his pioneering handbook *Where There Is No Doctor* (1979). On the basis of his experience in a Mexican village, he sets forth a program with emphasis on mobilizing the disabled people themselves as the major force in rehabilitation work, which he describes mainly as medical and physical treatment.

To what extent have these visions actually been realized in developing countries? Besides the usual donor reports, there are few independent studies of CBR programs. In Zimbabwe, Deliane Burck (1989) did research connected to an ILO project in which she problematized the principle of community basis. If it is to be taken seriously, greater attention must be paid to local conceptions of disability, folk and professional therapeutic practice, and the social position of disabled people, all of which she describes in her study. Patrick Devlieger (chap. 5) also emphasizes the necessity of taking local ideas and practices into account in implementing CBR programs. Benedicte Ingstad (chap. 13, and 1991) followed up a WHO project in Botswana over a two-year period, partly to evaluate the CBR model and partly to gather basic information on the conditions for disabled people in a rural African setting in light of the commonly expressed view that they were hidden and neglected by their families. She found that although the program was intended to be community based, it was in reality implemented from the top down and never really managed to activate the community in the rehabilitation process. It became more of an outreach than a CBR program.

The establishment of programs for the disabled proceeds at different paces and through different historical circumstances in each country. War and the subsequent efforts of governments to offer services and compensations to the injured veterans may precipitate development. Just as World War I, with its terrible production of mutilated men, led to a consciousness of disability and a whole set of rehabilitation institutions in Europe and North America, so have wars in countries of the South led to efforts to care for and recompense those who have suffered disablement. In the case of Nicaragua, government programs for disabled veterans were instituted as other organizations for disabled people were also becoming active. Frank Jarle Bruun (chap. 10) shows the interplay of these forces in the development of a social identity for the handicapped in Nicaragua. In Zimbabwe, which also suffered a devastating civil war, the first major effort toward rehabilitation was the construction of a large institution for disabled veterans. Later, this institution was reorganized as a resource center for several disability groups, and the government has implemented a policy of decentralized community-based rehabilitation for not only war veterans but all disabled people.

While organizations *for* disabled people, charity organizations, have a long history in North America and Europe and are fairly well established in countries of the South, organizations controlled *by* disabled people themselves are relatively new in developing countries. They are based on the model of Northern groups and often cooperate with them. In Northern countries, such organizations are mainly concerned with the rights of disabled people; through publicity and lobbying, they attempt to change laws and policies in order to promote integration in all sectors of society. In Southern countries, the groups themselves often feel that the most immediate needs are for practical programs of rehabilitation. Many donors prefer to channel aid through such groups, and the future will no doubt see a considerable expansion in their numbers and activities. The question is to what extent such groups can represent and reach out to the broad majority of disabled persons and their families living in rural areas.

We began our introduction by mentioning the difficulty of trying to survey the global extent of disability. It may be fitting to conclude these remarks on historical changes by noting that the attempt to count was problematic in another way as well. In order to plan projects when the International Year of Disabled Persons was launched, surveys were carried out in several developing countries. In some cases, the surveys were so costly that they devoured the few resources available to institute programs. The very act of interviewing people about their infirmities raised their hopes that something was going to be done for them. A consciousness about disability was created without any follow-through. In a nutshell, this suggests a danger in the present situation—that people will come to be identified as disabled without any of the benefits to which that label might entitle them and which they may have been led to expect.

In this book we wish to relate disability to fundamental assumptions about humanity and personhood in different cultures. We ask if and how impairment affects one's value as a human being and one's position as a social person. Are persons with impairments impaired persons? To answer this question, our contributors relate concepts of disability to notions about power and bodies, normality and order, individual capacity and social existence. But concepts of personhood and disability are not just "found in" cultural analysis. They are asserted by the media, the clergy, health personnel, and development agencies; they are negotiated by parents, represented in ritual, contested or ignored by people with impairments. As anthropologists, we know that they are grasped or glimpsed through the interaction and dialogues of fieldwork, systematized more or less rigorously, and written with varying degrees of authority and sensitivity. So the one question about disability and personhood leads to other questions. How is disability constructed in everyday interaction, in the telling of narratives, in the representations of scholars and the discourses of experts? How do these constructions change over time?

The chapters are grouped in two sections, each with a short introduction to give the reader a preview of what is in store and how the chapters relate to one another. In the first section, the theme is disability and the concept of personhood, examined in five cultural settings. In the second section, seven contributors explore the social contexts and processes in which impairments are interpreted and experienced. The final chapter is an epilogue that further considers the analytical issues involved in dealing with disability and culture. It suggests directions for further research and shows how the essays in this book point the way.

NOTES

1. WHO experience with the *International Classification of Impairments, Disabilities, and Handicaps* (ICIDH) indicates the difficulties of universal taxonomies for phenomena subject to cultural variation. The foreword to the 1993 reprint of ICIDH, looking ahead to the planned revision of the document, remarks upon the problem: "An important task in the revision of the ICIDH will be to improve the presentation and illustration of the way in which external factors affect the ICIDH components. . . .These factors . . . are strongly culture-bound. It is unlikely that a universally acceptable classification of these determinant factors is achievable at present, for the same reasons that preclude a universally accepted classification of the determinants of health" (WHO 1980:5).

2. Two French sociologists have argued that in European history, the category of "the sick" has assumed meaning in relation to capacity to work and is the product of a double movement toward the individualization and the socialization of illness (Herzlich and Pierret 1987:50, 53). The same point can be made, perhaps even more strongly, about the status of "disabled," which connotes the incapacity of an individual to perform or achieve and at the same time suggests a group identity in relation to society.

3. The identification of individuals who were chronically unable to work began in early censuses in British African colonies. In Tanzania, in 1983, village offices were

supposed to keep records of the number of adults in the village unable to work. These examples represent steps toward establishing a general category of "disabled people" based on working ability.

4. How impairment is thought to affect individual ability is culturally variable. The notion of "spread"—deficit in some functions also spreads to others—has been identified in American culture. Murphy provides the example of how the waiter gives everyone a menu except the man in the wheelchair, assuming that he cannot read. This contrasts with the idea of "compensatory forces" held by the Kel Tamasheq of Mali: they say that "God does not close an eye without opening another," that is, people who are disabled in one way are gifted in another. Blind people are good listeners, the lame are good advisers, and ugly women have a spellbinding smell (Halatine and Berge 1990).

5. It has been claimed that some societies have not yet reached the developmental stage in which they discriminate against disabled children (Grünewald and Jönson 1981). Although this way of putting it seems to be based on a combination of evolutionism and admiration for the noble savage, it points to the same contrast between simple and complex societies.

6. Begging has been described as a form of interaction which negates the usual rules of exchange in social life in that the beggar makes demands not on the basis of what he can give in return, but on the basis of what he lacks (Gomm 1975). Although a bodily or mental deficit does indeed function as a lack for which one is entitled to receive something, the giver may also be recompensed in achieving virtue. In this sense there is a kind of general exchange operating. Christianity, Hinduism, and Islam enjoin charity and mercy toward those in need. Thus disability is reported to have value as a source of income in Hindu India (see Bjune 1992). With the exception of Gwaltney's account (1970), most indications are that mendicancy is associated with cities and towns, marketplaces, and other centers, where it is possible to beg from people with whom one does not have other relationships.

7. Leper colonies form an important exception; the ones in Cuttack, India, were largely endogamous and had their own political organization, recreation, and ritual life. They were associated with an institution, however; most of the inhabitants had been discharged from a nearby leper asylum (Misra and Mohanty 1963).

8. Many autobiographical and life history accounts of disability are parents' narratives and document the family experience of having a disabled child. Particularly in the case of mental retardation, the point of view is almost always that of the parents (Whittemore et al. 1986:2–3).

REFERENCES

Ablon, Joan
    1981   Dwarfism and social identity: Self-help group participation. *Social Science and Medicine* 15B:25–30.
    1984   *Little People in America: The Social Dimension of Dwarfism.* New York: Praeger Publishers.
Albrecht, Gary L.
    1992   *The Disability Business: Rehabilitation in America.* Newbury Park, Calif.: Sage.

Armstrong, David
 1990   Use of the genealogical method in the exploration of chronic illness:
          A research note. *Social Science and Medicine* 30(11):1225–1227.
Asch, Adrienne, and Michelle Fine
 1988   Introduction: Beyond pedestals. In *Women with Disabilities: Essays in
          Psychology, Culture, and Politics,* ed. M. Fine and A. Asch. Philadelphia:
          Temple University Press.
Bjune, Gunnar
 1992   Tuberkulose og lepra som folkehelseproblem [Tuberculosis and lep-
          rosy as public health problems]. In *Samfunnsmedisin: Perspektiver fra
          utviklingslandene* [Social medicine: Perspectives from developing
          countries], ed. B. Ingstad and S. Møgedal. Oslo: Gyldendal.
Burck, Deliane Jannette
 1989   *Kuoma Rupandi (The Parts Are Dry): Ideas and Practices Concerning Dis-
          ability and Rehabilitation in a Shona Ward.* Research report no. 36. Lei-
          den: African Studies Centre.
Carling, Finn
 1962   *And Yet We Are Human.* London: Chatto and Windus.
Chaudhuri, Sumita
 1987   *Beggars of Kalighat Calcutta.* Memoir no. 75. Calcutta: Anthropologi-
          cal Survey of India.
Crapanzano, Vincent
 1980   *Tuhami: Portrait of a Moroccan.* Chicago: University of Chicago Press.
Davis, Fred
 1961   Deviance disavowal: The management of strained interaction by the
          visibly handicapped. *Social Problems* 9:121–132.
Deshen, Shlomo, and Hilda Deshen
 1989   Managing at home: Relationships between blind parents and sighted
          children. *Human Organization* 48(3):262–267.
Dumont, Louis
 1980   *Homo Hierarchicus: The Caste System and Its Implications.* Chicago: Uni-
          versity of Chicago Press.
Edgerton, Robert B.
 1967   *The Cloak of Competence: Stigma in the Lives of the Mentally Retarded.*
          Berkeley and Los Angeles: University of California Press.
 1970   Mental retardation in non-western societies: Toward a cross-cul-
          tural perspective on incompetence. In *Social-cultural Aspects of Men-
          tal Retardation,* ed. H. C. Haywood. New York: Appelton-Century-
          Crofts.
 1985   *Rules, Exceptions, and Social Order.* Berkeley, Los Angeles, London:
          University of California Press.
Estroff, Sue E.
 1981   *Making It Crazy: An Ethnography of Psychiatric Clients in an American
          Community.* Berkeley, Los Angeles, London: University of California
          Press.
Farquhar, June
 1987   *Jairos Jiri: The Man and His Work.* Gweru, Zimbabwe: Mambo Press.

Fassin, Didier
1991   Handicaps physiques, pratiques économiques et strategies matri-
            monales au Senegal. *Social Science and Medicine* 32(3):267–272.
Foucault, Michel
1973   *Madness and Civilization: A History of Insanity in the Age of Reason.* New
            York: Vintage Books.
Geertz, Clifford
1966   Religion as a cultural system. In *Anthropological Approaches to the Study
            of Religion,* ed. M. Banton. London: Tavistock.
1973   "From the native's point of view": On the nature of anthropological
            understanding. In his *The Interpretation of Cultures.* New York: Basic
            Books.
Gerhardt, Uta
1990   Qualitative research on chronic illness: The issue and the story. *So-
            cial Science and Medicine* 30(11):1149–1159.
Goerdt, Ann
1984   *Physical Disability in Barbados: A Cultural Perspective.* Ann Arbor: Uni-
            versity Microfilms.
1990   Patron-client relationships for the employment of people with dis-
            abilities. In *Disability in a Cross-Cultural Perspective,* ed. F. J. Bruun and
            B. Ingstad. Working paper no. 4. Oslo: Department of Social An-
            thropology, University of Oslo.
Goffman, Erving
1963   *Stigma: Notes on the Management of Spoiled Identity.* Englewood Cliffs,
            N.J.: Prentice-Hall.
Gomm, Roger
1975   Bargaining from weakness: Spirit possession on the south Kenya
            coast. *Man* 10:530–543.
Good, Mary-Jo DelVecchio, Paul E. Brodwin, Byron J. Good, and Arthur Kleinman,
eds.
1992   *Pain as Human Experience: An Anthropological Perspective.* Berkeley, Los
            Angeles, London: University of California Press.
Gritzer, Glenn, and Arnold Arluke
1985   *The Making of Rehabilitation: A Political Economy of Medical Specializa-
            tion, 1890–1980.* Berkeley, Los Angeles, London: University of Cali-
            fornia Press.
Groce, Nora E.
1985   *Everyone Here Spoke Sign Language: Hereditary Deafness on Martha's Vine-
            yard.* Cambridge, Mass.: Harvard University Press.
Groce, Nora, and Jessica Scheer
1990   Introduction. *Social Science and Medicine* 30(8):v–vi.
Grünewald, K., and T. Jönson.
1981   *Handikappade Barn I U-länder* [Handicapped children in developing
            countries]. Lund: Natur och Kultur.
Gwaltney, John L.
1970   *The Thrice Shy: Cultural Accommodation to Blindness and Other Disasters
            in a Mexican Community.* New York: Columbia University Press.

Halantine, Fatima, and Gunvor Berge
  1990   Perceptions of disabilities among Kel Tamasheq of Northern Mali.
              In *Disability in a Cross-Cultural Perspective,* ed. F. J. Bruun and B. Ing-
              stad. Working paper no. 4. Oslo: Department of Social Anthropol-
              ogy, University of Oslo.

Helander, Bernhard
  1990   Mercy or rehabilitation? Culture and the prospects for disabled in
              Southern Somalia. In *Disability in a Cross-Cultural Perspective,* ed. F. J.
              Bruun and B. Ingstad. Working paper no. 4. Oslo: Department of
              Social Anthropology, University of Oslo.

Helander, Einar
  1993   *Prejudice and Dignity: An Introduction to Community-based Rehabilitation.*
              United Nations Development Program Report No. E93-III-B.3. New
              York: UNDP.

Helander, Einar, Padmani Mendis, Gunnel Nelson, and Ann Goerdt
  1989   *Training the Disabled in the Community: A Manual on Community-based
              Rehabilitation for Developing Countries.* Geneva: WHO/UNICEF/ILO/
              UNESCO.

Herzlich, Claudine, and Janine Pierret
  1987   *Illness and Self in Society.* Translated by Elborg Forster. Baltimore:
              Johns Hopkins University Press.

Ikels, Charlotte
  1991   Aging and disability in China: Cultural issues in measurement and
              interpretation. *Social Science and Medicine* 32(6):649–665.

Ingstad, Benedicte
  1991   The myth of the hidden disabled: A study of community-based reha-
              bilitation in Botswana. Working paper. Oslo: Section for Medical An-
              thropology, University of Oslo.

Ingstad, Benedicte, Frank Bruun, Edwin Sandberg, and Sheila Tlou
  1992   Care for the elderly, care by the elderly: The role of elderly women
              in a changing Tswana society. *Journal of Cross-Cultural Gerontology*
              7:379–398.

Johansson, S. R.
  1991   The health transition: The cultural inflation of morbidity during the
              decline of mortality. *Health Transition Review* 1(1):39–68.

Kleinman, Arthur
  1980   *Patients and Healers in the Context of Culture: An Exploration of the Bor-
              derland between Anthropology, Medicine, and Psychiatry.* Berkeley, Los
              Angeles, London: University of California Press.
  1988   *The Illness Narratives: Suffering, Healing, and the Human Condition.* New
              York: Basic Books.

Langness, L. L., and Harold G. Levine
  1986   *Culture and Retardation: Life Histories of Mildly Mentally Retarded Persons
              in American Society.* Dordrecht: D. Reidel.

Marcus, George E., and Michael M. J. Fischer
  1986   *Anthropology as Cultural Critique: An Experimental Moment in the Human
              Sciences.* Chicago: University of Chicago Press.

May, T. J., and R. F. Hill
    1984   How shall we see them? Perspectives for research with disabled organizations. *Social Science and Medicine* 19(6):603–608.

Misra, Bidyadhar, and Amiya Kumar Mohanty
    1963   *A Study of the Beggar Problem at Cuttack.* Bhubaneswar: Dept. of Rural Economics and Sociology, Utkal University.

Murphy, Robert F.
    1987   *The Body Silent.* New York: Henry Holt.

Murphy, Robert, F., Jessica Scheer, Yolanda Murphy, and Richard Mack
    1988   Physical disability and social liminality: A study in the rituals of adversity. *Social Science and Medicine* 26(2):235–242.

Narasimhan, M. C., and A. K. Mukherjee
    1986   *Disability: A Continuing Challenge.* New Delhi: Wiley Eastern.

Osterweis, M., A. Kleinman, and D. Mechanic, eds.
    1987   *Pain and Disability: Clinical, Behavioral, and Public Policy Perspectives.* Washington, D.C.: National Academy Press.

Preston, Paul
    1991   Mother father deaf: The heritage of difference. Paper presented at the American Anthropological Association Annual Meeting, Chicago.

Rasmussen, Susan
    1989   Accounting for belief: Causation, misfortune, and evil in Tuareg systems of thought. *Man* 24:124–144.

Renker, K.
    1982   World statistics on disabled persons. *International Journal of Rehabilitation Research* 5(2):167–177.

Sacks, Oliver
    1985   *The Man Who Mistook His Wife for a Hat and Other Clinical Tales.* New York: Summit Books.
    1989   *Seeing Voices: A Journey into the World of the Deaf.* Berkeley, Los Angeles, Oxford: University of California Press.

Sargent, Carolyn Fishel
    1982   *The Cultural Context of Therapeutic Choice: Obstetrical Care Decisions Among the Bariba of Benin.* Dordrecht: D. Reidel.

Satapati, Purushottam Rao
    1989   *Rehabilitation of the Disabled in Developing Countries.* Frankfurt: AFRA.

Saugestad, Sidsel
    1990   Cases of disability in a social context. In *Disability in a Cross-Cultural Perspective,* ed. F. J. Bruun and B. Ingstad. Working paper no. 4. Oslo: Department of Social Anthropology, University of Oslo.

Schak, David C.
    1988   *A Chinese Beggars' Den: Poverty and Mobility in an Underclass Community.* Pittsburgh: University of Pittsburgh Press.

Scheer, Jessica, and Nora E. Groce
    1988   Impairment as a human constant: Cross-cultural and historical perspectives on variation. *Journal of Social Issues* 44(1):23–37.

Scheff, Thomas J.
1966   *Being Mentally Ill: A Sociological Theory.* Chicago: Aldine Publishing.
Scheper-Hughes, Nancy
1992   *Death without Weeping: The Violence of Everyday Life in Brazil.* Berkeley,
            Los Angeles, London: University of California Press.
Scott, Robert A.
1970   *The Making of Blind Men.* New York: Russell Sage.
Shweder, Richard A., and Edmund J. Bourne
1982   Does the concept of the person vary cross-culturally? In *Cultural Con-
            ceptions of Mental Health and Therapy,* ed. Anthony J. Marsella and
            Geoffrey M. White. Dordrecht: Kluwer.
Simon, B. L.
1988   Never-married old women and disability: A majority experience. In
            Women with Disabilities: Essays in Psychology, Culture, and Politics, ed.
            M. Fine and A. Asch. Philadelphia: Temple University Press.
Stiker, Henri-Jacques
1982   *Corps infirmes et sociétés.* Paris: Aubier Montaigne.
Stone, Deborah
1984   *The Disabled State.* Philadelphia: Temple University Press.
Straus, Robert
1965   Social change and the rehabilitation concept. In *Sociology and Reha-
            bilitation,* ed. M. Sussman. Washington, D.C.: American Sociological
            Association.
Sundby, Per
1990   Norwegian welfare politics as promotor of cultural change. In *Dis-
            ability in a Cross-Cultural Perspective,* ed. F. Bruun and B. Ingstad.
            Working paper no. 4. Oslo: Department of Social Anthropology,
            University of Oslo.
Walman, Sandra
1984   *Eight London Households.* London: Tavistock Publications.
Werner, David
1979   *Where There Is No Doctor.* London: Macmillan.
1987   *Disabled Village Children: A Guide for Community Health Workers, Rehabil-
            itation Workers, and Families.* Palo Alto, Calif.: Hesperian Foundation.
Whittemore, R. D., L. L. Langness, and P. Koegel
1986   The life history approach to mental retardation. In *Culture and
            Retardation,* ed. L. L. Langness and H. C. Levine. Dordrecht: D.
            Reidel.
Whyte, Susan Reynolds
1991   Family experiences with mental health problems in Tanzania. In *The
            National Mental Health Programme in the United Republic of Tanzania,* ed.
            Fini Schulsinger and Assen Jablensky. *Acta Psychiatrica Scandinavica,*
            supplement no. 364, vol. 83:77–111.
Williams, G. H.
1991   Disablement and the ideological crisis in health care. *Social Science
            and Medicine* 32(4):517–524.

Wilson, Peter J.
    1947   *Oscar: An Inquiry into the Nature of Sanity.* Reprint. New York: Vintage
                Books, 1975.
World Health Organization
    1980–   *International Classification of Impairments, Disabilities, and Handicaps.*
                Geneva: World Health Organization. Reprinted annually.
Zola, Irving
    1982   *Missing Pieces: A Chronicle of Living with Disability.* Philadelphia: Tem-
                ple University Press.

PART ONE

Disability, Cosmology, and Personhood

Introduction

The significance of an impairment depends on the values and assumptions that people have about the nature, functioning, and goals of persons. What are the ideals and expectations against which people measure themselves? How are persons understood in relation to cosmological patterns and forces? What is human and what is inhuman? The chapters in this section examine disability in terms of the culturally constructed worlds in which people move.

Patrick Devlieger (chap. 5) illustrates the value of a holistic approach to cultural categories of humanness. Among the Songye of Zaire, physical abnormality of children may fall into three types. There are "ceremonial children," whose birth is in some way exceptional (e.g., twinning or unusual presentation); they are particularly valued and often have special powers, including the ability to heal. "Faulty children" have bodily deficits (motor impairment, spasticity) that indicate distorted relationships, and they are liminal in relation to ordinary people. "Bad children" (including albinos, dwarfs, and hydrocephalics) are inhuman, and though they are cared for, their families know that they came to the world not to live but to die. Thus biological abnormalities may be interpreted as superhuman, ambiguously human, or inhuman. But what is central for the Songye understanding of physical disability is not so much the classification of bodily singularities as the embeddedness of embodied persons in networks of relations. Answers to the question "Why disabled?" are sought in problematic relationships.

The relational concept of personhood is elaborated in different ways in several of the cultures described here. Among the Punan Bah of Sarawak, according to Ida Nicolaisen (chap. 2), being a person depends on having a socially recognized father and thus a rank and a kinship identity. Illegitimate children cannot achieve this any more than nonhumans like twins, witches, or spirit children. More than that, personhood is realized through marriage and children. Some kinds of impairment may render this difficult, but it is the responsibility of the family to make it possible, if necessary by giving a child to the impaired individual. Thus personhood is not dependent on individual ability so much as on social identity and family obligation.

Similarly, for the Maasai, Aud Talle (chap. 3) proposes that the defining characteristic of personhood is sociability—living communally with other people. "Disability," which for the Maasai primarily refers to practical incompetence in performing daily tasks, does not detract from personhood. Physical differences are accepted as a normal part of life; they are remarked upon, but they do not inhibit sociability. Everyone should have the chance to marry or at least have children, for a person exists with and through others. The person who is truly disabled is the one who is excluded from the community, as in the case of the boy Parmeleu, who was cursed by his father.

Bernhard Helander's approach to personhood among the Somali (chap. 4) is to analyze basic cultural assumptions embedded in cosmology and health practices. While kinship identity is important, individual differences and abilities are recognized and appreciated. Personhood involves flexibility, growth, and change; thus infirmity, which inhibits this, is a diminishment of personhood. As Helander shows, accepting that a condition is incurable means acquiescing in stagnation. The idea of adjustment and development through rehabilitation does not fit with this view; incurable conditions deserve mercy but they cannot be changed. Helander's article reminds us that concern with individual dynamics is not limited to Western cultures as the simple dichotomy between individualistic and sociocentric concepts of personhood suggests.

Judith Monks and Ronald Frankenberg (chap. 6) work with processes of individual change in relation to disability as well, but they deal with subjects reflecting on their own situation, rather than as perceived by others. In examining autobiographies written by people with multiple sclerosis, their concern is less with context and more with the content and dynamics of the stories themselves. They analyze conceptions of time, body, and self and the way in which these are interlinked in the chain of the narrative. In doing so, they reveal fundamental assumptions in European culture and they identify patterns in the process of construing the meaning of personhood in the face of impairment. The person of these accounts is the autonomous, reflexive self—the individual located in consciousness but incarnate in a body that has physical and medical as well as experiential aspects. The unfolding of the narrative is effected through different conceptions of time, and at different phases, attention and time seem to be devoted more or less to the self and the body. As the narratives close, self-time comes to predominate but in

conjunction with an acceptance of disease, with its limitations on the experiential and physical body.

The concern with the cause of impairment is predominant in all the contributions from Southern contexts. Personalistic causal agents in the form
of spirits or human beings reflect the relational nature of personhood in
these settings. Individuals are so fundamentally involved with other beings
that their bodies and minds are readily affected by agents outside themselves. Just as causes are relational, so are the life expectations against which
people with disabilities are measured.

The Europeans with multiple sclerosis who wrote accounts of themselves
are less concerned with relations to other people and far more attentive to
their own states of mind and their bodies. Perhaps we might expect this in
view of the body-mind dualism that is one aspect of personhood in this culture. The importance of biomedicine in constructing the body, or at least
one kind of body, is explicit in this analysis. Biomedicine has a much greater
cultural salience in Euro-American concepts of disability and personhood
than in those of the other examples here.

The authors of these five chapters suggest an approach to disability which
we hope will be followed up with studies from other parts of the world. Instead of seeing impairment in terms of ability to perform specific tasks, they
ask about personhood in relation to cosmology. They illuminate indigenous
classifications and evaluations and provide a rich variety of case stories and
examples that give life to the ideas they describe.

TWO

Persons and Nonpersons: Disability and Personhood among the Punan Bah of Central Borneo

Ida Nicolaisen

"What is the point in feeding him, he is a spirit." Those were the very words of his father. That was his opinion, when he saw this one. That was the opinion of Ake I. [the child's father's mother] as well, you see. Inan T. [the child's mother] did not want to take him in her arms. Just take a look at him yourself. Look at his hands, look at his feet, look at his face. So what do you say? He is a spirit, this one. Inan T. did not feel like nursing him. She did nothing. She just stayed put. Day after day he got nothing. No one fed him. Only then did his father take pity on him. He could not bear to see him and bought some milk powder. That is what happened. His father bought milk powder. That is why he is still alive, this one. His father took pity, you see.

The old woman turned her full attention to the betel she had been preparing, as we sat together on a mat in her room in the longhouse. She placed a piece wrapped in a betel leaf smeared with chalk in her mouth and lapsed into silence. I did not mind. I valued the confidence the old woman had shown in me by speaking about her grandchild, the intimacy that colored our relationship and allowed us to sit peacefully without talking to each other. Her dim room was pleasantly cool in contrast to the burning tropical sunshine outside, which seemed to silence even the insects and birds of the surrounding rain forest. The other inhabitants of the room were absent, working in the rice fields, I presumed, or gone visiting in the longhouse. The children were playing on the longhouse veranda and at the river bank, except for the handicapped boy, who for once was not along but was sitting quietly between us eating a durian fruit.

I looked at "the spirit." He was about five years old, a skinny boy, small for his age, and severely impaired by deformed limbs. He lacked fingers and toes. His face was scarred by a harelip, and mentally he was somewhat retarded. He had the appearance of a child impaired by thalidomide, a drug that by no means could be ruled out as the cause of his calamities, considering the totally uncontrolled way that medical drugs find their way to and are used by ethnic groups in Central Borneo. More likely, however, his handicaps were brought about by an unsuccessful abortion. That was the opinion held by the grandmother and other women in the longhouse. Abortion is frequent among Punan Bah women, often provoked with a pointed bamboo knife smeared with pounded black pepper. The boy's deformities could well be the result of damage done that way to the embryo.

I contemplated his situation and his grandmother's remarks. What did she mean by saying that the boy was a spirit, *otu*? Was it a mere figure of speech, or did the Punan Bah actually perceive him as being of another kind, being a nonhuman spirit? I was aware that he had no proper personal name, the only Punan Bah I came across who did not. He was called Otun, an abbreviation of *motun*, which means cut off or truncated, a name that clearly alluded to his deformed limbs. Why had it been the child's father who had decided his fate? Why did the mother not want even to touch her child at first? I pursued these and other questions related to the conception of disability during ensuing stays among the Punan Bah and observed their behavior toward the physically and mentally impaired whenever the situation lent itself.

This conversation with an old woman back in 1975[1] puts us on the track of the line of analysis and the questions to be pursued in this chapter to generate new insight into the cultural construction of disability and to bolster our ability to cope more adequately with the social and psychological problems created by loss of competency. Disability has been defined as a biological or physical impairment that limits major life activities like walking, seeing, hearing, speaking, breathing, learning, and performing manual tasks. Rooted in a Western medical view, this definition is by no means objective or value-free, as pointed out by Susan Whyte (1990:197–198). The perception of disability varies between societies and even within multiethnic ones, and we can deal scientifically and practically with disability only if we are sensitive to the cultural, social, and psychological structures in which it is embedded. Every culture poses a challenge to preconceived notions and forces us to ask anew how disability is understood, conceptualized, and dealt with. Thus we must choose frameworks that facilitate the generation of a scientific body of knowledge from which cross-cultural generalization can be extracted. A promising line of investigation, it seems to me, is to look into the ways in which societies define and conceptualize personhood. Lately this field has captured the interests of anthropologists and generated a substantial body of literature (see Carrithers, Collins, and Lukes 1985; Frank 1990; Harris 1989). I shall argue that we need to go beyond the classical approach to this field, in which personhood is defined and described in terms of social properties, and analyze the cultural perception of the biological constitution of the human being itself, in order fully to grasp the meaning of disability in a given culture and its social significance.

Every culture must come to terms with the anomalies that defy its basic assumptions, and the way in which societies do so tells much about their structure. Mary Douglas (1966) has demonstrated that matter that cannot be neatly categorized is conceived as threatening to the social order and hence as dangerous and polluting. Danger lies in transitional states, she writes, simply because transition is neither one state nor the next (ibid.:96); it is indefinable, a line of thought further elaborated by Victor Turner, as we shall see. We may expect therefore to find notions of pollution and taboo as symbolic demarcations of boundaries between those conceived as normal or full social persons and the disabled, such as in Western society, where the disabled are set apart, are conceived as a category.

A considerable number of the studies of disability in the Western world have approached the field from the angle of deviance, as pointed out by Robert Murphy and coauthors (1988). Disability has been described primarily in terms of handicap, as in Erving Goffman's work on stigma, and the disabled seen as persons socially marginalized, at times branded by their impairment. Goffman distinguishes between the following types of stigma, all sociological, in his exploration of the structural factors by means of which social labeling and discrimination take place: physical impairment, character deficiencies, and tribal or kin-based stigma, by which he means race, nation, and religion (Goffman 1963:17). These are criteria that in themselves or in combination, loaded with positive or negative value, are applied in shaping, affirming, or discrediting social identities and cultural conceptions of normality, he argues. Goffman's concept of stigma is so inclusive, however, that it is of limited applicability to our endeavor to probe into the cultural criteria and social structures that define and shape notions of personhood and disability.

A recent article advocates the view that the social situation of the disabled should be analyzed as a state of "liminality" (Murphy et al. 1988). The concept was used as early as 1908, by Arnold van Gennep in his book *Les Rites de passage.* Van Gennep argued that life-crisis rituals are symbolic expressions of the transfer of individuals from one social position to another, and that they, if examined in terms of their order and content, are composed of three stages: one of detachment of the individual from his or her former identity, one of transition, and one of incorporation as a new person into society. Van Gennep denoted the transitional, the in-between situation, the liminal stage of the ritual. Sixty years later Victor Turner took up where van Gennep had left off. He argued that social life in itself must be conceived as a dialectical process, in which individuals are constantly on the move from one status to another, in the process passing through a limbo of statuslessness or liminality (Turner 1969:97ff.). Liminal people are in an interstructural position; they have been declassified but are not yet reclassified. For this reason they are dangerous people, and interaction with them takes place within the protective armor of ritual formalism (Turner 1967:93ff.).

Murphy and his coauthors claim that in American culture the disabled find themselves in a similar indefinite state of neither/nor, and that a parallel can be drawn between the situation of those who go through a puberty rite of passage and the disabled. Like the initiate in the liminal condition, the disabled are set apart. They are neither sick nor well. They are without clear status, and like the initiates in a bush school, they are spatially secluded from society. They are avoided and treated as if they are invisible. Murphy gives the powerful example of how any user of a wheelchair, although noticed by everyone in a room, still experiences that he is acknowledged by nobody (Murphy et al. 1988:238).

Let us return to the Punan Bah, whose ideas, values, and social life constitute the ethnographic field for the ensuing analysis, to explore the dynamic interrelationship between their ideas of disability and the cultural premises and social structure of their society. We shall probe into Punan Bah conceptions of the human being and personhood, which form the framework for their understanding of disability. On this background we shall look closer at the relations between the cultural construction of disability and Punan Bah values and attitudes toward the impaired. We shall apply Douglas's ideas as a methodological device to isolate conceptual boundaries between categories of persons, insofar as they exist, and discuss the applicability of Murphy's concept of the disabled as liminal people within the social reality of the Punan Bah.

THE PUNAN BAH, THEIR SOCIETY AND CULTURE

The Punan Bah are a minor ethnic group of about fifteen hundred people who live in seven longhouse settlements in Central Borneo, more precisely in the Fourth and Seventh Divisions of Sarawak, Malaysia. Here they subsist on swidden agriculture, fishing, hunting, and gathering. Cash income is procured by selling game, fish, ironwood, and jungle produce such as rattan, by tapping rubber, and by working as wage laborers for timber companies. Punan Bah society is stratified. It consists of a small but highly influential aristocracy and many commoners. Until well after World War II it included slaves, who formed part of aristocratic households.

Over the past 150 years, the period during which we can follow Punan Bah history fairly closely, their society has undergone a series of transformations in dynamic response to social, economic, and political incentives imposed by the state and other external agencies. For example, when the Brooke Raj put a final stop to head-hunting in Sarawak in the 1920s, the Punan Bah made changes in the *Save* ritual, the high point of their religious ceremonies, as they no longer could procure fresh human heads for the obligatory sacrifices to benevolent ancestral guardian spirits. In the 1950s, when logging first began to influence their way of life, the adherence to omens was abandoned as being incompatible with wage-labor, and the Punan Bah chose to adopt the syncretistic *Bungan* religion. This enabled them to maintain, as far as can be assessed, basic ideas that structure their understanding of the world and the human condition. Their perception of the human body and the person appear to have undergone but little change over the years, and these are, as we shall see, at the core of the system of conceptions with which the Punan Bah perceive disability and on the basis of which they react to it.

BODY IMAGES AND DISABILITY

To the Punan Bah human reproduction is in part a physiological, in part a spiritual process. A fetus is created, that is, given body or shape, out of the man's "liquid," *ileang*. This flows as blood in his veins and is ejaculated as semen in intercourse. The woman's womb provides a nest, in which the fetus feeds and grows on menstrual blood. While a man must take care not to waste his "liquid" indiscriminately, be it as blood or semen, as his body holds but a limited quantity of this precious fluid, a woman has liquid or blood in abundance. Each month it runs over from her heart and out through her vagina. Upon conception the fetus grabs her blood in its tiny hands, shuts them tightly, and lives on this nourishing fluid until it lets itself be born.

This understanding of the man as the creator and the woman as the nourisher finds symbolic expression in a series of taboos that the Punan Bah claim they adhered to as long as they followed the *Save* religion. Though no longer considered mandatory, young men and women assured me that they recently had and intended to continue to observe various of these taboos. While the taboos adhered to by the man during his wife's pregnancy serve to ensure that nothing unfortunate happens to the child or hinders its smooth delivery, those observed by the woman while expecting the baby have a bearing on the delivery only. Unlike her husband, a woman should observe taboos also after she has given birth to protect the child against illness and insure that it thrives.

Physical forms of impairment are explained in terms that are congruent with this understanding of human conception and the roles of the two sexes in this. As the creator of the child, it is largely the father who can be held responsible for congenital physical impairment, while the mother's behavior may influence the delivery and the fate of the child once born. An exception is blindness, which may be blamed on the mother. If she allows her husband or any other man to have intercourse with her during pregnancy, the eyes of the child may be damaged, "pierced by the man's sword," as the Punan Bah say. Neither the man nor the woman is necessarily blamed for the congenital disability of the child, however. Whether they are blamed depends on a complex set of social factors that shape public opinion. These are intimately related to the social competition between families, to fights for status or "news," as this is often called. For example, a young man was held responsible by his in-laws for the fact that his firstborn suffered from spasticity. The impairment, which manifested itself at first by the inability of the child to hold his head upright, was blamed on the child's father because he had killed a tortoise by cutting off its head during his wife's pregnancy. His parents-in-law and their siblings alluded to this unfortunate happening again and again, well aware that they made the life of the young couple and of the man in particular virtually unbearable. The issue at stake was not the impairment of the child. Casting the blame was part of an overall effort on their behalf to make their daughter, the wife, divorce him, because they were dissatisfied with his social background, economic performance, and general behavior.

Conception relies also on spiritual forces—more specifically, on the will of ancestors to let themselves be reborn by a couple. The body of a newborn child is considered little more than a physical shell, a mere carrying basket, *alat*, the Punan Bah say. It is only when an ancestor spirit takes permanent residence in the child that it becomes a proper human being, *linou*. Until then it is but blood, *da*, and it comes as no surprise that abortion entails no moral problems under these circumstances. That a newborn baby has become a proper human being is indicated by its ability to turn its body or by the breaking through of the first tooth, which happens at the age of about six months. Only then is it given a name and considered a person in its own right, a new member of the society, of a given family and class. Only from then on will it be properly buried in case of death with rituals that guide its soul to the realm of the dead, and with reburial rites to ensure that it can return to this world to be reborn once again and secure the continuation of the family. Up to the age of half a year, children are basically neither truly human nor socially defined as persons. They are not labeled with a personal name or addressed with a kin term but are known only as babies. They are liminal people in an interstructural position, to cite Turner (1967:93ff.), and, in accordance with Douglas's observations, they are considered to be polluting—in this case to all men, except the father, out of whose sperm they were given body.

Newborn twins constitute a particular case of this category of liminal people. The birth of twins is a social disgrace and believed to pose physical danger to both mother and children. The birth of twins is generally explained as an indication of insatiable sexual urge, a sign that the couple did not refrain from intercourse during the woman's pregnancy, as they ought to have, and hence they produced doublets. These are given life, however, by the ancestor spirits, which "have decided to let themselves be reborn." At birth these spirits do not enter the bodies of the babies—that happens only later—but they take up residence at the bosom of the mother. To shelter two such powerful spirits, the Punan Bah explain, is dangerous for the woman. Today a family will arrange, if possible, for one twin to be given away in adoption to non-kin in another longhouse. If they fail to do so, one of the twins withers away. There are no adult twins among the Punan Bah to the best of my knowledge.

Severe congenital deformity likewise places individuals in a liminal position. Individuals who suffer such impairment are classified as nonhuman, as spirits, as in the case of the old woman's grandson. In order to understand why this is so, we must look a little closer at the Punan Bah understanding of the human being. They believe that men have seven souls, women only six. Which soul women lack is of little concern to them today and shall not occupy us here. The most important soul to both sexes is the one known as the soul of the body, *bluou omar*, or the soul of life, *bluou urib*. This soul is associated with breath, *ingad*, and ultimately located in the liver, the stem or center of life, *po'o urib*. In a wider sense *ingad* denotes the human mind and spirit. It embraces intelligence and memory, as well as feelings, conscience, character, and disposition. The soul of the body is thus considered the spiritual ego, the personality, and it is in essence the ancestor reincarnated. It is believed to look exactly like the body and to resemble the ancestor reincarnated. Traditionally the Punan Bah used divination to determine which ancestor had let him- or herself be reborn in order to find the correct name for the child.

Throughout life the soul of the body may leave its physical shell and wander about for short intervals. This happens normally without the knowledge of the individual and is revealed for example by the fact that an individual appears in someone else's dreams. Souls may be scared away from the body by the thoughtless or malicious behavior of fellow human beings or chased away by spirits. In any event, the soul must be brought back, or sickness and death will prevail. The distinction between body and soul, and the belief in the volatility and vulnerability of the latter, form the explanatory principles of Punan Bah understanding of major congenital handicaps like those of the boy, as well as of mental disturbances and a variety of other illnesses. The boy's appearance was interpreted as being caused by a nonhuman spirit, which had taken possession of the boy's body instead of a proper ancestor spirit. The boy looked monstrous, as do such spirits; hence he was one.

Down's syndrome and other forms of severe mental retardation have not come my way among the Punan Bah. I suspect that children born with such impairments "wither away" as do one out of two twins, or die at an early age. Milder cases of mental deficiency do occur. Such individuals are talked about as being half-human, *stenga linou*, and their impairment is said to be caused by the soul of the body being no good. It is fully accepted that they are unable to carry out tasks like normal people or fulfill social roles. "J. [is like] chaff, [there is] no grain. She wanders aimlessly hither and thither, and knows nothing," a man said of a young, mentally retarded person. She was well taken care of, however, as were others in a similar condition. Each of the five mentally retarded persons that I have known well lived comfortably with and were treated as part of their families. The families made no effort to arrange marriages for them, however. "It would not be a proper thing for people who are only half to marry," I was told. "Such people ought to remain unmarried because they are unable to look properly after a spouse and possible offspring," the argument went. I have nevertheless come across two couples who on their own arranged to live together, in both cases to the worry of their families, who judged the couples unable to take proper care of possible children. In this they proved right.

Epilepsy (*lanon*) and madness (*bangen*), be it psychosis or neurosis, have still other causes in Punan Bah interpretation. They are brought about by nonhuman spirits who invade and partly take over the body, relegating the soul of the body to a secondary position. Such illnesses are hence perceived as partly dehumanizing the individual, perhaps only temporarily. Mad people are considered dangerous to their families or fellow longhouse inhabitants only when behaving violently. Depending on the concern and wealth of the family, more or less effort will be put into the curing of mad persons. The Punan Bah distinguish between a variety of mental illnesses yet do not always specify their identity or cause. For all, treatment relies on spirit mediums. Health can only be restored if the "disturbing" spirit is split into two parts. This is done symbolically with a sword by a spirit medium during an extended nightly seance. One half of the disturbing spirit is chased away by the helping spirits of the medium, the other transformed into a benevolent guardian spirit, said to protect the individual against future attacks, and enabling him or her to carry out corresponding rites of curing for other mentally disturbed individuals. When the spirit of madness has been exorcised, the mediums retrieve the soul of the body, carry out a symbolic rite of purification, and restore the soul in the individual. With such an understanding of mental disturbance it is little wonder that the Punan Bah have but limited faith in treatments offered by Western physicians, although they do seek such treatment in difficult cases. They believe, however, that only their traditional rites with the invocation of and assistance rendered by helping spirits, rites which for days on end put the patient at the center of public attention, prove effective in the long run. It would come as no surprise if they were right in some cases. By perceiving the mentally ill as temporarily dehumanized, and singling them out for particular treatment, which for the rest of their lives, if they so wish, enables them to treat other mentally ill, and by finally subjecting them to food taboos, they define the mentally ill as a special category of people in the society. While their illness prevents them from taking full part in social life in practice, the community will generally try to cope with their situation so as not to deprive them of the social relationships that define adult personhood, as we shall see.

It is a different story for those accused of being witches, *nyamanin*. Witchcraft occurs if a guardian spirit that a person had acquired by being successfully cured of mental illness suddenly gets a craving for human blood. What causes it to change its nature is not explained. That it is happening is proven, in the view of the Punan Bah, by the withering away of persons in the longhouse, by the occurrence of inexplicable deaths, and through dreams that are related to the doings of the person suspected of witchcraft. Witches are inevitably old people, mostly socially marginal ones, although there are exceptions. Witches are not aware of the deeds of their guardian spirit until rumors reach them, or they become aware that they are being feared and avoided by others. There is nothing they can do about the accusation, which well into this century might end with a public execution. Witches constitute still another category of dehumanized people. Their identity as human beings has been overruled, they are shunned, their bodies associated not with benevolent but with evil powers, a situation of serious consequence for the accused.

It is clear from the preceding that the Punan Bah do not hold the physically and mentally impaired responsible for their condition. Lack of competence in various fields that we lump together and label disability is given different explanations and holds disparate implications for the person thus impaired. This can be further illuminated by looking at Punan Bah understanding of physical impairments such as blindness, deafness, deafmuteness, and motor disability (e.g., limping). None of these calamities cause those who suffer from them to be perceived as less human. The calamities are not associated with the soul of the body and do not therefore counter an appreciation of the person as fully human. They are due, it is claimed, to the imperfection or absence of one or more of the other souls with which a person is normally imbued. These other souls are linked with the senses, that is, with sight and hearing, and with motor capabilities. Congenital blindness may be explained as caused either by the absence of the soul of the eye or by the sexual activity of the mother during pregnancy, while a gradual loss of sight due to cataract or glaucoma is said to be caused by the soul of the eye gradually absenting itself. The stomach soul is in control of the digestive system; another soul controls sexual urge. These souls arrive gradually and independently of one another in the body in accordance with sensory, motor, and sexual development. It is in congruence with this view that those who suffer from sensory or motor impairment do not acquire compensatory forces. The extent to which they are capable of making up for their disability depends on the nature of the impairment, the personality and intelligence of the disabled individual, and the compassion of his or her family.

SPATIALITY AND VISIBILITY

The conditions and qualities of life offered the disabled by the comparatively affluent and highly differentiated, specialized, and secular Western society with its pronounced separation of work and home life and stress on individual performance are in radical contrast to those found in the materially poor, fairly homogeneous, and nonspecialized Punan Bah society, where daily work, rituals, and family life are closely integrated and value is ascribed to sociability. In Western society personhood is tied in with individual capability and accomplishment; among the Punan Bah it is associated primarily with social relations, as is the case in many other societies based on kinship. One who fits in, who "knows how to be with others," is socially esteemed. Yet individuality is not played down. The Punan Bah distinguish between socially generated personhood and individualism, and there is leeway for those who "follow their own way."

The very layout of a Punan Bah longhouse with its public space in the common verandah, from which a door leads to the room occupied by each family, contributes to the Punan Bah form of personhood. This common verandah is the place where parents, grandparents, often aunts and uncles, and siblings and cousins with their spouses and children eat, entertain, work, rest, and perform rituals. It creates an environment in which the individual, disabled or not, experiences him- or herself as embedded in society. Spatial seclusion is not possible in the longhouse, nor are the disabled otherwise segregated there. Only mad persons may be driven by their illness to take up residence apart from the longhouse and live temporarily on a nearby farm. Such separation is not caused by social pressure, but by the incapacity of the mad person to stand the bustling life in the longhouse. The mad are set off from normal life only symbolically by a series of food taboos that vary according to the diagnosis of their illness, taboos they will maintain even after recovering. The physically and mentally impaired live as members of their extended families. They stay in their family room and eat and sleep with their relatives. Leisure is spent in the company of fellow longhouse inhabitants, and they partake to the extent of their ability in social events and rituals. Depending on their handicap, they do their share of the daily household work in accordance with their age and sex, demonstrating more or less diligence, as any other member of the family. The disabled women I have known, be they crippled, mentally retarded, or incapacitated by old age, look after small children, do part of the cooking, chase chickens away from rice laid out on mats for drying, mend clothes, make sun hats, cut tobacco, and weave baskets and mats for household use or to generate cash income. Disabled men are likewise engaged in productive work, and, like the women, they may be almost indispensable in families short of adults. Disabled men craft tools, make chicken cages and fishtraps, and mend and make fishing nets, tasks that are necessary to the subsistence of the household. I was taken aback more than once by the capabilities of some of the disabled, in particular those congenitally so. A blind man, well into his forties, was the prime climber of coconut palms. He went fishing with a child and managed to partake in the clearing of young secondary forest for swiddens with his jungle knife. I have seen a blind man stand in the prow of a longboat punting it through rapids with but a few words of guidance from a boy sitting in the rear. As far as I could observe, the Punan Bah treat their physically and mentally impaired children as they do their other children, but there may be subtleties I did not discern. The disabled were not singled out by nicknames connoting their impairment, nor were they often referred to in terms of their disability. This is so, as far as I can discern, because they are recognized fundamentally both as humans and as persons. They have a soul of the body, the ancestor reincarnated, which must be respected, or illness or bad luck may strike the inconsiderate. During the almost three years I lived among the Punan Bah, I came across no individuals so mentally or physically impaired that they were unable to look after their own basic needs. Only children and very old or sick persons are found in such helpless condition that they need extensive care.

The physically and mentally impaired are thus neither invisible nor spatially segregated as is typically the case in Western society, according to Murphy and his coauthors (1988). The spatial layout of the longhouse, limited specialization, and a division of labor only according to age and sex enable physically impaired and mentally retarded individuals to carry out their share of the daily tasks and to take part in social and ritual events. Persons ill with diseases believed to be contagious like leprosy and tuberculosis are not spatially secluded either, though measures are taken to keep their plates and glasses apart. Disability is not unspeakable. The Punan Bah talk openly about physical or mental impairments, and it is not considered poor manners to do so in the presence of the impaired person. Nor will the disabled abstain from discussing their handicap quite freely. In contrast is their handling of ugliness, a matter it is most tactless to bring up in the presence of the person considered plain. We shall take this lack of symbolic segregation and stigmatization as a stepping-stone for our further endeavors to delineate Punan Bah concepts of social competence and the criteria that in their eyes are critical to the achievement of full personhood.

PERSONHOOD AND DISABILITY

Any society has a plurality of symbolic structures in terms of which individuals are perceived not as mere unadorned members of the human race but as persons, that is, as representatives of certain distinct categories founded on social relationships, as Clifford Geertz (1973:363) has pointed out. It was the classic Marcel Mauss (1938) study on personhood which inspired anthropologists to explore concepts of the person in various cultures and to make a clear distinction between the social concept of the person and any human being's self-awareness. In any society concepts of the person explain a wide range of behavior, emotions, and events. It is by looking closer at the symbolic forms through which personhood is both perceived and expressed that we may dig deeper into the conceptualizations that structure Punan Bah understanding of and reactions toward disability. In what follows I shall continue to use the term *individual* to refer to the mortal human being, the object of observation, so to speak, and *person* to refer to concepts that lend the object social significance and identity, following Jean La Fontaine (1985:126). Concepts of the person and of the negative qualities that inhibit full participation in social life are shaped in dynamic response to the specifics of the social context. They are contingent on the organizational structure as well as on ideas of society itself, the nature of authority, beliefs, and morality. We can deal with only certain aspects of this complex whole and shall turn directly to those which have a central bearing on Punan Bah conception of disability.

The social relations that primarily shape Punan Bah notions of the person are defined by kinship, rank, marital status, and age. Persons are labeled accordingly by personal names, kinship terms, teknonyms, necronyms, and birth-order names. We have already heard how the notion of the person is intimately associated with a conceptualization of kin ties revitalized. Fundamentally, any living Punan Bah is a personification of an ancestor. However, every child must be recognized as the legitimate offspring of a man through a symbolic exchange of valuables in order to be placed as a member of and with the same rank as the paternal kin group. Individuals whose paternal kin have not been established for one reason or another are known as "children of dogs," *enea au*. They are in a liminal position, with ties to their maternal kin only. Their social position is severely weakened. They have no paternal family to draw on. The men have no father's sister, real or classificatory, who can, for example, amass the valuables necessary for the payment of bridewealth, and they are hence unable to marry well. Few individuals end up in this unfortunate situation, but those who do are unable to achieve full personhood.

A person is defined moreover by criteria of sex, age, and marital status combined as: *kolovi*, "child(ren)"; *kolovi oro/kolovi elei*, literally "child-woman/child-man," a category that embraces unmarried young persons, be they physically mature teenagers, adult spinsters and bachelors, or divorced persons still young enough to reconsider marriage; *oro/elei*, literally "woman(en)/man(men)," a labeling that implies married status (specified in the case of doubt by an addition of the word *pauvo*, married); and finally *balu/bluai*, which means "widow/widower." What is noticeable is that adult, fertile, but unmarried persons are classified as child-woman/child-man, re-spectively. We are here approaching a key issue for the understanding of Punan Bah conception of disability: the fact that another prerequisite to the achievement of full personhood is marriage and the begetting of offspring. To be unmarried and in particular to be childless is to be in a liminal state, neither child nor fully adult but an in-between person, a child-woman or child-man. This liminal state is symbolically expressed in a number of ways, in particular through the ascription of specific roles during the reburial rit-uals, which serve to secure the rebirth of the dead person, and thus ulti-mately can be considered a fertility rite.

Any unmarried person is a member of and lives with his or her family. As time goes by and marriage becomes ever more unlikely, both spinsters and bachelors will feel marginalized and be perceived increasingly as ap-pendages to the household, which will be run by a sister or an even more distant female relative. By not being one of a couple, the individual is barred from asserting him- or herself socially, be it by entertaining guests or by performing certain rituals. Most important, the unmarried person is barred from establishing a semi-independent economic unit within the household and an entirely independent one in due time. I shall not elabo-rate on these aspects of personhood but proceed to the key factor for the achievement of full personhood, the cultural and social importance at-tached to having offspring.

Children not only satisfy emotional needs, secure a continuous labor force for the household, support and care for aging parents, and bolster the status of the family by adding to its size but ultimately are wanted and cul-turally ascribed significance because they secure the continuation of the family. Offspring provide the precondition for the possible rebirth of those currently alive; they ensure the continued existence of the family room. Punan Bah conceive of society as established once and for all by divine an-cestors. It is based on the idea of tradition and is perceived as a projection of a previous form. This is symbolically expressed in the practice of a div-ination to name children correctly after the ancestors of whom they are basically reincarnations. In this society personhood is essentially the fulfill-ment of a socially significant career, of which parenthood is the alpha and omega. All individuals do not achieve full personhood here, as is the case in culturally similar societies (see La Fontaine 1985:136–139). "You have lost out," *lugi kuou*, the Punan Bah will say, when they hear that you have no chil-dren, and it is to this deeply serious aspect of childlessness that the remark ultimately refers. To be adult yet not married, to be a child-woman or child-man, is a natural state as a teenager. Yet even teenagers are constantly asked if they have sweethearts, if they are soon going to get married. For the ulti-mate aim is to produce children, legitimate ones that is.

The symbolic identification of parenthood as a key step toward the achievement of full personhood is reflected in the widespread use of teknonyms and necronyms. When a child gets its personal name at the age of about six months, sometimes a little later, it is turned into a person and must be respected as such. The child is a relative, defined, if legitimate, by links to both its father's and mother's family. The forging of these ties is symbolically confirmed by the use of kinship terms for address and reference to the child. If it is a firstborn, its parents will concurrently assume teknonyms as father of A., *Oman A.*, and mother of A., *Inan A.*, the grandparents as *Ake A.*, and the great-grandparents as *Ake Alop A.* These teknonyms may be seen as forming a scale associated with increasing authority. They are labels that connote the achievement of full personhood. The personal names of the parents are never applied again, and it is poor manners ever to use them, except if the child dies. In this case the parents will adopt the appropriate necronym, grand- and great-grandparents likewise. They will not do so, however, if the child is still but a few years old, an age at which its position as a proper person is still fragile. When the reburial of the body has been carried out and the period of mourning completed, their personal names will come into use again, or they may be called by mixed teknonym and necronym, the latter being the one carried by the next child in line, the bereaved sister or brother of the dead one. This will be in use until they can adopt a teknonym of a grandchild. Teknonyms are just one of several symbolic expressions that the achievement of personhood depends on having children.

Granted the limitations inherent in using a concept like disability to describe Punan Bah reality, in which no equivalent exists, I shall argue that we may distinguish between two categories of people who under these conditions may be seen as the disabled. One category embraces those who are set apart as nonhuman and hence unable to become social persons, as well as persons temporarily or permanently dehumanized. The latter is the case for witches. Considered a danger to society at large, witches are treated as marginal persons. People are afraid of them, avoid them, and at the same time dare refuse them nothing. They are stigmatized, and their position makes rehabilitation impossible. No spirit medium is brave enough to intervene and challenge the blood-craving guardian spirit of a witch. The other category embraces illegitimate children, the "children of dogs," who are without paternal kin and rank. These too cannot be "rehabilitated," in contrast to those who lack offspring. These too are disabled, as it is only when one has offspring that one is able to be reborn as a member of the same family, that one has a safe place in the kinship system. Without offspring one is not in the descent line but wavering in the social system, which embraces the living as well as the dead.

The notions of the Punan Bah can be seen as having similar consequences for the perception of full personhood as those of the Tallensi.
Meyer Fortes tells us that among the Tallensi, where ancestor worship plays
a significant role, only the completion of a proper life qualifies an individual for full personhood. If a person leaves no children, then this has not
been attained (Fortes 1973). Factors that hamper marriage and the begetting of children are thus potentially disabling. They range from severe physical and mental impairment to infertility and bodily deformities such as
limping, harelip, blindness, and deaf-muteness. Other factors, such as ugliness, be it due to a dark complexion, poor teeth, being overweight or skinny,
or personality characteristics like a hot temper, laziness, or selfishness may
curb marriage possibilities as well. Does this not indicate then, that we after
all are dealing with disability as a category, one that relates to individuals
impaired in the above-mentioned ways? The answer in my opinion is no.
First, because these factors do not necessarily prevent marriage. Second,
and as significantly, because the Punan Bah deal with this issue of achieving
full personhood as a social and moral problem, not of the individual but of
the family, and they cope with it accordingly through adoption.

It is the moral duty of sisters and brothers, a category which in Punan Bah
conception includes first cousins, to give a childless sibling one of their own
children. To do so is not only an expression of compassion but of responsibility, and it lends the person and his or her spouse the utmost esteem. The
Punan Bah perceive of such an exchange between siblings or first cousins
as a gift, not an adoption. In their conception the latter occurs between un-
related or more distantly related couples only. Due to this custom few Punan
Bah are left without a child of their own. A parent-child relationship may
also be created through dreams. We have also heard how mentally retarded
persons engaged in marriage on their own and had children. The net result
is that to my knowledge no one ends up being denied full personhood in
this society; no one is structurally disabled.

CONCLUSION

Physical or mental inability that hampers or outright prevents individuals
from carrying out normal day-to-day tasks is recognized as a problem in all
societies and in most is considered a handicap for the individual. To what
extent such impairments block the achievement of a full social life, of full
personhood, varies from society to society, however. Jean La Fontaine has
argued, drawing on Weber and Fortes, that

> in modern states with their bureaucratic hierarchies, society is conceived of as
> an organization of competing individuals, citizens of the state. In such soci-
> eties person and individual are virtually indistinguishable. By contrast, where
> society is seen as the descendants of founding ancestors, personhood is the ful-

fillment of a socially significant career, of which a crucial element is parent-hood. (1985:138–139)

Punan Bah reality confirms this thesis. Among the Punan Bah, individual ability is not crucial for the formation of social identity. This is fixed by po-sition in kin groups and wider social entities, such as the longhouse com-munity and the ethnic group, and personhood is not prevented by physical and mental impairment. Those disabled this way are neither perceived as a category, bounded by concepts of pollution and danger (see Douglas 1966), nor spatially segregated, set apart as "invisible," and considered liminal peo-ple, as is the case in the West (Murphy et al. 1988). The significant cultural and social distinctions between individuals are of another kind. A distinc-tion is drawn between nonhuman and human individuals, and between nonpersons and persons. At birth every individual is defined as nonhuman. Only those become humans who reach the age of at least six months—and some do not, as we have seen—only they will be defined as persons, as kins-men, and social persons of the rank of their fathers. As such they are to be respected, impaired or not, or the wrath of the ancestors will be incurred. Even those who become seriously mentally ill and hence temporarily de-humanized because their bodies are partly taken over by evil spirits are not disqualified as persons. Another distinction is drawn between social per-sonhood and antisocial (non)personhood, as exemplified by witches. These are stigmatized, and in the past were killed.

The Punan Bah definition of personhood is intimately associated with Punan Bah conception of society and of themselves as mortal beings. They envisage themselves as existing in a world of visible and invisible, good and evil beings. They are themselves the living exponents of an ethnic group that at a basic level of understanding embraces the invisible souls of those already dead and those yet unborn. It is a social entity constantly threatened with extinction by outside forces, be they evil spirits or hostile fellow men. A prime concern is hence the securing of ethnic and family continuation. This is obtained by behaving considerately in order not to endanger the life of oneself and others, by taking part in subsistence activities to satisfy phys-ical needs, by the begetting of children, and by the carrying out of elaborate funerary and secondary funerary rites to safeguard the rebirth of the de-ceased. The mentally and physically impaired are part of this social entity. They too are living incarnations of ancestors, and it is a moral obligation of their next of kin to take proper care of them, whether they be of limited in-telligence or suffering from mental illness or bodily impairment. They must be paid due respect in this world or there will be ancestral punishment, and they must be cared for at death so that their souls do not get lost. Only those defined as nonhumans are set apart. As nonpersons they are not embraced by the web of social rights and obligations. They are not cared for or about, traditionally with fatal consequences for the individual so defined.

This cultural conception of society and hence the situation of the physically and mentally impaired is being threatened by the current socioeconomic transformations in Sarawak in general and of Punan Bah society in particular. The extensive logging of the rain forest alters the economy and hence the entire way of life of the Punan Bah and the many other ethnic groups of Central Borneo. The large extended households break up into nuclear units or small extended family units, and sharing and cooperation between family members is on the decrease. Since the beginning of the 1980s, the Punan Bah have relied increasingly on cash income earned by the wage labor of young men for the timber companies and generated by trade and services in the wake thereof. Money has also been acquired in the rapidly expanding public sphere. Lesser weight is accorded subsistence activities such as swidden agriculture, hunting, and the collection of jungle produce, a shift that by implication puts the disabled in a less favorable position. It diminishes the number as well as the significance of a wide variety of tasks that they were able to carry out, tasks that moreover lent them social value. I am thinking here of the preparation of roofing material for huts on the farms or of fishing nets by men, and the making of hats and baskets and the weaving of mats by women. The latter is a typical example. Rattan, which for decades has been collected for consumption and trade, is becoming increasingly scarce due to damage caused by pulling out timber with Caterpillar tractors. It is more time-consuming to collect, and hence more difficult for the disabled and elderly women to get for the making of mats, an activity that once earned them both social respect and money. Hand in hand with these socioeconomic changes goes a cultural transformation, a decreasing knowledge of and faith in a range of traditional beliefs, a tendency enforced by less effort put into ritual activity. A redefinition of personhood seems on its way, one more in tune with the capitalist Western values that imperceptibly permeate Punan Bah view of themselves and the world. This may save the life of children impaired like the "spirit" boy, but it may well make the lives of many others considerably less fulfilling and more difficult.

NOTE

1. Extensive field research among the Punan Bah of Sarawak, Malaysia, was carried out in 1973, 1974–1975, 1980–1981, 1983–1984, and 1986.

REFERENCES

Carrithers, M., S. Collins, and S. Lukes, eds.
  1985   *The Category of the Person: Anthropology, Philosophy, History.* Cambridge: Cambridge University Press.

Douglas, Mary
1966   *Purity and Danger: An Analysis of Concepts of Pollution and Taboo.* London: Routledge and Kegan Paul.
Fortes, Meyer
1973   On the concept of the person among the Tallensi. In *Religion, Morality, and the Person,* ed. Jack Goody. Reprint. Cambridge: Cambridge University Press, 1987.
Frank, A. W.
1990   Bringing bodies back in: A decade review. *Theory, Culture and Society* 7(1):131–162.
Geertz, Clifford
1973   Person, time, and conduct. In his *The Interpretation of Cultures.* New York: Basic Books.
Goffman, Erving
1963   *Stigma.* Reprint. København: Munksgaard, 1975.
Harris, Grace
1989   Concepts of individual, self, and person in description and analysis. *American Anthropologist* 91:599–612.
La Fontaine, Jean S.
1985   Person and individual: Some anthropological reflections. In *The Category of the Person: Anthropology, Philosophy, History,* ed. M. Carrithers, S. Collins, and S. Lukes. Cambridge: Cambridge University Press.
Mauss, Marcel
1938   A category of the human mind: The notion of person; the notion of self. Trans. W. D. Halls. In *The Category of the Person: Anthropology, Philosophy, History,* ed. M. Carrithers, S. Collins, and S. Lukes. Cambridge: Cambridge University Press, 1985.
Murphy, R., J. Scheer, Y. Murphy, and R. Mack
1988   Physical disability and social liminality: A study in the rituals of adversity. *Social Science and Medicine* 26(2):235–242.
Turner, Victor
1967   *The Forest of Symbols: Aspects of Ndembu Ritual.* Ithaca, N.Y.: Cornell University Press.
1969   *The Ritual Process: Structure and Anti-Structure.* London: Routledge and Kegan Paul.
van Gennep, Arnold
1960   *The Rites of Passage.* Trans. Monika B. Vizedon and Gabrielle L. Caffee. Chicago: University of Chicago Press. Originally published in French as *Les Rites de passage,* 1908.
Whyte, Susan R.
1990   Problems in cross-cultural research on disability. In *Disability in a Cross-Cultural Perspective,* ed. F. J. Bruun and B. Ingstad. Working paper no. 4. Oslo: Department of Social Anthropology, University of Oslo.

THREE

A Child Is a Child: Disability and Equality among the Kenya Maasai

Aud Talle

Even if you are clever, God does not give you everything at the same time.

These words of wisdom from a Maasai elder provide the background for the concept of disability and the way physically impaired people are perceived and treated among the pastoral Maasai in Kenya.[1] The moral of the statement is that you cannot take anything for granted in life because its course is shaped by forces beyond human control. Fortune and misfortune, two sides of the same coin, are distributed at random, and you never know when and where one or the other will strike next. Being nomads by tradition, the Maasai pastoralists are accustomed to moving household and herd at the vagaries of nature. Their adaptation to a rather hazardous and unpredictable environment has given them experience in coping with the unexpected.

The Maasai do not regard people with a disabling condition as a single, unified category toward whom they relate by a standardized set of behaviors. In other words, "disability" is not a criterion for classifying people or of interaction. The Maasai recognize many forms and degrees of physical impairment; the perception and attitudes toward people in this situation and the relations in which they engage vary and are not primarily related to their impairment. In line with this argument, I would claim that the "disabled person," with whom we are so familiar in a Western context, is a phenomenon not encountered among the Maasai. The different conceptualization of physically impaired people in Western versus Maasai society must be understood with reference not only to Maasai ontology but also to the extent to which these people act in roles and are involved in relations that construct social persons (see Fortes 1987).

Being "human"—being a person (*oltungani*)—among the Maasai is to live communally with other people (i.e., be "social") in extended residence groups where sharing, generosity, and cooperation are virtues of highest degree. Maasai hold that in this setting of communality, men and women will multiply and prosper. In order to live a full life as a Maasai it is imperative to marry and beget children. Maasai elders who have been blessed ("lucky") by old age and high fertility in children and animals embody the image of the good life (*enkishon*).

THE PASTORAL MAASAI

The Maasai are seminomadic pastoralists and inhabit large tracts of savanna on both sides of the Kenya-Tanzania border. Their total population amounts to some three hundred thousand people. Patrilineal kinship and the male age-set organization are crucial structural principles defining the social identity of the individual.

The Maasai pastoralists live in large scattered settlements comprising several independent polygynous joint families. Each married woman has her own separate house within the settlement where she resides with her children. A Maasai settlement may consist of ten to twelve houses or more. Territorial mobility and shifting of people and animals between seasonal settlements used to be an integrated part of Maasai adaptation to a rather arid environment. During recent decades the pastoral Maasai have become increasingly sedentarized. The tendency in residence pattern has been away from large groups toward smaller units founded on the individual family only (see Talle 1988). Maasai identity and self-definition are closely associated with pastoral praxis.

Livestock is the mainstay of their economy. Families live on the milk, meat, and blood that the herds and flocks of cattle, sheep, and goats provide, and they also sell animals to obtain cash to buy nonpastoral foodstuff and other necessities. Maasai have a marked cultural preference for pastoral food; they believe it keeps them strong, fit, and healthy. Livestock products are also highly valued and extensively used in the care and treatment of sick people. Goats, for instance, are often slaughtered at times of illness. Goat soup made of bones, fat, and blood is considered to be very nutritious and palatable, and when cooked with various herbs from trees, bark, or roots, it serves as medicine for sick people. Freshly drawn blood from cattle is always given to newly circumcised girls and boys and to women in confinement to substitute for the blood lost and to restore strength. These people are not considered sick, but they are weak, a condition that, if not remedied, may cause illness. In fact, blood and fat are standard diet for people under physical strain. Other animal products used as curatives for various ailments are milk, fat, urine, and cow dung.

The modern health care system among the Maasai has hitherto been addressed to curative rather than preventive health. The government operates dispensaries in all major localities, and at the district headquarters there is a hospital to which the dispensaries refer difficult cases. There is at least one rehabilitation home for disabled children in the study area run by the African Inland Church. The rehabilitation center regularly has about seventy in-patients for whom it provides treatment and education. It also cares for and feeds more than a hundred malnourished children who attend daily as out-patients.

In a survey from one Maasai locality not far from the study area it was found that while roughly 25 percent of the Maasai seek treatment at government institutions when they become ill, about the same percentage consult private "doctors" or traditional healers. A majority do not seek any professional assistance at all, preferring to try to treat themselves in various ways (Nestel 1985). Self-medication with traditional medicines as well as purchased drugs (which are available in most local stores) is very widespread among the Maasai. Traditional medicines are produced chiefly from the bark, roots, or leaves of various trees and plants; actually the word for medicine and tree (*olcani*) is the same in the Maasai vernacular. Knowledge about the medicinal properties of trees and plants is not confined to healing experts; it is common to most Maasai adults. There are some males and females from certain lineages, though, who are considered to be medical experts to some extent, and consequently they are renowned for the "strength" of their medicines and ability to cure certain diseases. The degree of medical specialization among the Maasai is, however, limited. Products such as soda ash, soot, battery acid, red pepper, honey, and purchased fat are widespread ingredients applied alone or mixed with animal products in curing and healing procedures.

The treatment alternatives that a Maasai will choose for a certain disease, whether dispensary, private "doctor," traditional healer, or self-medication, will depend on a number of circumstances, such as the definition and explanation of the cause of the disease, the distance to the various health care options, and the confidence that the patient and his or her family have in the different curative methods.

WHO IS DISABLED?

When trying to define the notion of disability among the Maasai, we are confronted with some severe problems of cultural translation and language use. The English word *disabled* usually denotes somebody who is unable to use his or her body properly. The word, however, has connotations far beyond the simple recognition of a physical impairment. As a historical and cultural construct, the notion of disabled, in the Western context, is heavily charged with implications of social inferiority or stigma. Because of this culture-specific meaning of *disabled*, I find it hard to apply the term directly to the Maasai case. For the sake of convenience of language, however, I retain the word, but put it in quotation marks to underscore that I use it only in its denotative meaning.

"Disabled" people everywhere are different in one way or another: physically, mentally, or socially. So also among the Maasai. Who is identified as disabled, however, and by what signs, when, and for what reason, is culturally variable. What is crucial for the present analysis is to know to what extent the physical or mental differences observed in the individual are socially and culturally constructed as a "difference" implying notions of hierarchy and requiring extraordinary actions and practices.

To the Maasai the concept of disability has a very strong dimension of practical incompetence. A person who is recognized as being disabled is basically one who is unable to help him- or herself practically (lame, crippled, amputated) or is constrained in his or her activities by one or another disabling condition (blindness, deformity, epilepsy, or others). Mentally retarded or mad persons are not regarded as disabled in this physical sense but are more likely to be referred to as "abnormal" (*olmodai*, "fool"). People whose appearance deviates from the normal standard (harelip, excessive burns, etc.) are considered to be disabled only if their injury/damage also restricts them physically.

There is no single term in Maasai that embraces all categories of disabling conditions, which should indicate that they do not conceive disability as a meaningful concept in itself. The Maasai employ specific terms for a number of disabling conditions: *emodooni* (blindness), *emingani* (deafness), *enkiterria* (epilepsy, lit. "those who faint"), *oloirirua* (devil, mad in the sense of shouting and behaving wildly), *eng'oki* (dwarf, unlucky child), and others. The one single term that comes closest to the English *disabled* and that is used by literate Maasai when translating the English word is *olmaima* (crippled). Literally, *olmaima* means a big, brown lizard that has short legs and sways from one side to the other while walking; that is, it walks awkwardly, slowly, and with difficulty. The term emphasizes the physical impairment, the fact that the person cannot move and walk like others. In a nomadic society where mobility and flexibility in residence are called upon daily, the ability to walk and cover long distances quickly is a prerequisite for survival.

That Maasai apply an animal metaphor to describe disabling conditions in a human being should not be interpreted as meaning that the Maasai see similarities between a person whose movement is impaired and an animal, a lizard. The matter is rather, following Claude Lévi-Strauss, one of classification; certain "disabled" are distinguished from people who walk easily as lizards are distinguished from other animals capable of running fast. The word *olmaima* strongly signals the bodily focus in Maasai conceptualization of "disability."

It is noteworthy that a person who is temporarily limping because of a broken leg or any other leg damage may also be referred to as an *olmaima* in certain situations. Among the Maasai, a person who has a physical impairment, say being blind or deaf, is often identified and named by that particular quality. This practice of naming by referring to a marked physical trait that the person possesses is applied not only to those whom we would call disabled but also to people with any kind of prominent biological characteristic. For instance, Maasai frequently distinguish people by the color of their skin, the "brown/black one"; by their height, "the short/long one"; or by any other outstanding physical feature: the "thin/fat one," the "one with white/brown teeth," and so on. Naming by way of bodily characteristics should not be interpreted as having derogatory undertones; rather, such a practice reveals a cultural acceptance of differences.

However, a person who ridicules another person's impairment, by imitation, for instance, tempts fate. The Maasai recognize that the one who is "disabled" cannot be blamed for the condition because it is not the person's wish to be like that. Any physical impairment is considered to be an unfortunate or "bad" thing. Maasai hold that there is "strength" (*engolan*, "divine power") in the "sick thing," and if you incite it, it may reappear. To counteract adverse effects, Maasai frequently use euphemisms to avoid direct mention of a subject, either good or bad.

Provisionally, we may state that a person who is considered to be disabled in the Maasai sense of the word is primarily not one who deviates physically or mentally from what is defined as standard but rather one who is physically dependent on others for help in daily tasks. In this meaning even old people (*intasati*) may be regarded as disabled if they need a lot of practical help.

Among the Maasai, "disabled" people are a heterogeneous group; thus it is difficult to arrive at a common denominator for them because they are conceived of as having nothing in common. Like any other member of their society, they differ in personal characteristics, abilities, and resources. The fact that their physical competence is impaired, however, is for all to see and contemplate.

Our aim should not be to try to construct the "disabled" as a concept among the Maasai. Rather, for our project of cross-cultural comparison and translation we should deconstruct the concept and allow for specifications of the disabling conditions. This will enable us to clarify the kind of social and cultural phenomenon we refer to when discussing disability. A physical or mental impairment in itself carries little weight for our analysis.

BELIEFS ABOUT DISEASES AND DISABILITY

In every society there exist beliefs about sickness and health care. Such beliefs are common and shared cultural knowledge and are embedded in the cognitive structure of the society. In the individual case of sickness, however, these general beliefs may be more or less relevant as guidelines to explain and interpret a particular disease case. People usually have their own specific understanding of the cause and development of a disease case that draws partly on the repertoire of general beliefs but also on situational factors of social, economic, and political nature. The lack of agreement between such shared general belief systems and the diagnosis of the individual case done by the patient and his/her close relatives and the health practitioners has inspired Arthur Kleinman (1980) to make the analytical distinction between "beliefs" and "explanatory models" in disease explanation and cure. These two levels are necessarily interrelated, and there is a continuous process of feedback between them. I find Kleinman's distinction both valid and important. By keeping our analysis on the general, overall level of belief systems as well as on the individual, interactional level simultaneously, we are able to describe and depict how belief systems are generated and reproduced. This perspective opens the way for a dynamic analysis of disease explanation and interpretation. In trying to understand Maasai conceptualization of disability, for instance, it would be misleading to describe it with reference only to cultural beliefs. A contextual analysis of the disability case is instructive if we want to grasp and understand this phenomenon in its full social and cultural setting. I will refer to some general beliefs about disease and disability prevalent among the Maasai, but at the same time I will give a few case accounts in order to point at the complexity and situational character of this cultural realm of human life.

The Maasai perceive disease as a sign of social or cosmic disorder projected on the human body. Therefore the most effective prevention against diseases and other misfortunes is to care for and manage social and divine relations properly. Hence moral misconduct and transgression of normative rules may easily lead to disasters like incurable diseases.

Normally, the Maasai distinguish between two categories of diseases: rare and serious ones (*enkeeya*, same term as death; often used with reference to fatal livestock diseases) and common ones (*emueyian*), such as fever, flu, malaria, and so on (Galaty 1977; Århem 1989). These two categories of diseases require to some extent different curative and healing methods. The latter may be cured by anyone who cares to slaughter animals and prepare the medicine; the cure of the other, however, needs more refined healing methods and is a matter of ritual expertise. Disability is a borderline case in this discussion because it is not a straightforward disease, although it may begin as a common disease (e.g., trachoma, *baasha*) and gradually develop into a disabling condition (blindness). In view of this dichotomization of rare and common diseases, disability cases of the kind that are not congenital are likely to fall within the first category.

To give birth to a physically deformed child is generally categorized as misfortune (*entorroni*, "bad thing," "offense"). Spontaneous abortions, infertility in women, prolonged droughts, cattle losses, and other inexplicable occurrences are also defined as *entorroni* and are "bad" because they threaten life-giving forces and prosperity. Misfortune is something that is basically caused by "nature" or God (*Enkai*) and is regarded as an unavoidable and integrated part of the harsh living conditions to which the Maasai are subjected. In other words, a disabled child is a fact of life which Maasai in general accept. Statements like "we just met him like that" (referring to a child who was born disabled) convey the message that the child's impairment is an act of *Enkai* and cannot be explained otherwise. It is beyond human comprehension and ability to cure; it strikes randomly and without warning. Maasai try to prevent such accidents by way of supernatural and practical measures, above all by the performance of prescribed blessing rituals at certain events in the life span of a person, as well as by practicing everyday rites in the homestead and, most important, by wise management and care of social relations. An overriding principle of interaction and social order is the notion of *enkanyit*, which may be translated as "respect" or "obedience" to structural superiors. The concept of *enkanyit* is, in fact, a guiding principle for interaction between men of various age-groups and between men and women in the Maasai society.

A term sometimes used with reference to a deformed child is *engoki* (sin), meaning a child with "bad luck." The term implies that there is some kind of inherited sin within the family. An ancestor may have left a bad reputation behind when he died. One cardinal misdeed, as the Maasai see it, is neglect of old parents. *Engoki* is held to be a kind of curse, not inflicted by people on people, but by divine powers on human beings. God wants this to happen, and the supernatural "punishment" for the ancestors' sin comes in the form of the disabled child. The child, however, cannot be blamed for it.

Various kinds of disability and disease, however, may also be caused by cursing and sorcery, or by misbehavior of women during pregnancy or when nursing the child. Clairvoyant people (*ilkonjek*, "people with eyes") may also, consciously or unconsciously, harm fellow human beings in various ways, not necessarily by making them permanently impaired but by bringing about accidents or injuries that may result in states of disability. Clairvoyant people are individuals who "admire" (in the meaning of envy) certain parts of your body or another ability you may possess, such as having an extraordinary talent for dancing or singing. Except for those people, like the diviners, who are known and feared for their strong eyes, people with "eyes" are not easily detected or identified but are likely to appear in certain encounters. Some categories of people are more susceptible to "eyes" than others. Babies, in particular, are vulnerable, and Maasai mothers take great care in covering their newborn when they move in public. Likewise Maasai warriors when they come from their meat camps in the bush to the homesteads smear coal around their eyes to protect themselves from the gaze of married women. After two or three weeks in the meat camp, where they have slaughtered livestock, the warriors appear healthy, strong, and attractive. Radiating growth and fertility, they are an object of great admiration to the women. Furthermore, a person who is wealthy in livestock and children is always in a dangerous position of attracting eyes. The Maasai deem it a bad omen to openly express admiration for anything good, such as a person's large cattle herd or healthy and numerous offspring. For such reasons they themselves will not count their animals or children. If inauspicious words are uttered by accident, however, the person speaking them should immediately spit to neutralize the negative effect.

Disabilities that are caused by humans may not differ in kind from those inflicted by the deity, but the former may be identified and can potentially be healed. Polio (*oltung okigile*, being "broken" or *tarrush*, "lame"), for instance, may be inflicted either by God or by human intervention. When the disease first appears in a person, those around him will try to treat and cure it by the traditional and modern healing methods at their disposal. If the disease is not stopped in time, however, it may result in severe physical impairment. A disease that develops into a disabling condition is of course an experience very different from that of giving birth to a child with a congenital deformity. The latter is more readily explained as a direct or indirect act of *Enkai*, while the former is more ambiguous and may have various causes: curse infliction, sorcery, normative misconduct, or violation of rules of "respect." There is, however, no clear distinction between these two models of explanation; rather, they intersect. The interlinkages between different causation theories and their relative explanatory value vary from case to case and can best be described and analyzed through case material.

A curse (*oldeket*) is a ritual sanction that is spelled out publicly. It is pronounced by a person toward another in front of "witnesses." In contrast to *engokai* (divine curse), its effect is more or less immediate. Maasai believe strongly in the power of the curse; actually, a large portion of misfortunes befalling people is said to be linked to curse infliction. Cursing is an aspect of several close social relations in the Maasai society; *inter alia* fathers may curse sons/daughters; wives may curse husbands (and vice versa), and mothers may curse children. Other relatives may also curse each other, and senior age-sets may curse junior ones. The most potent curse is the one inflicted by "seniors" on "juniors" as these categories are defined within the age-set system. One general rule, however, is that a curse has to be morally justified to be effective. The infliction of a curse, or more often the threat of it, brings things back into order.

Sorcery (*esakutore, esakut*), although different from cursing, is also an intentional way of harming people by using spiritual power, but the wished result from the ill-willing person's side is not stated overtly. The person who wants to harm another prepares some "medicine" (*ulogi*; often referred to by the Kiswahili word *dawa*) from various poisonous herbs or trees and mixes it with other ingredients. Except for the sorcerer, nobody actually knows the various components of the medicine or the procedures of preparing it. The medicine may also be bought from experts of other tribes. The Kamba, a Bantu-speaking people living to the east of the Maasai area, are particularly famous for their skills in preparing medicine used in sorcery. The sorcerer mixes the medicine with some substance from the targeted person, such as saliva, hair, or a piece of cloth, and puts it in a place where the one to be harmed is bound to come in contact with it, say at the entrance of the homestead or in the middle of the cattle corral. Women who have several miscarriages one after the other are often suspected of being bewitched. So are people who turn mad. The word itself, *oloirirua* (madness), alludes to the fact that the person has been possessed by the devil. Bewitchment or sorcery is usually executed by a malicious person who is envious of or bears a grudge against the bewitched. The sorcerer might be a full brother or a distant neighbor. You can never be sure of who wants to bewitch you; in fact you cannot even always be sure of whether you have been bewitched or not. If you suspect that somebody is trying to bewitch you or intends to do so by interpreting certain signs in your surroundings, the best way to counteract the effects of the bewitchment is to consult a diviner (*oloiboni*). The *oloiboni* will "read" his divinatory stones and give the victimized person his blessing.[2] This particular blessing is accompanied by "sacrifices" of a specially prepared medicine of bush herbs which has been processed beforehand. While uttering words of blessing, the *oloiboni* sprinkles the medicine by spitting it onto the patient (*inkamulak*, blessing that combines words and saliva). The consultation and blessing of the *oloiboni* is taken to be a cure against the bewitchment or curse. His blessings in this instance are also taken to be a general prevention against wicked forces that threaten growth and prosperity among people and livestock.

By their behavior during and after pregnancy women may cause children to become sick and weak, even deformed in exceptional cases. Maasai women have to observe several precepts while they are pregnant. One of them is that they should abstain from sexual intercourse from the third month of pregnancy onward. Those who are careless about these precautions may risk miscarriages or give birth to stillborn or deformed children. It is believed that the fetus gets bruised by the force of the penis or is harmed by the semen, which enters the womb during intercourse and either chokes the child or defiles its body with white spots (*eryatata*, "a child coming out with spots"). While nursing the child, the mother still should not have sexual relations, because sexual activity during lactation is reputed to spoil the milk and cause diarrhea in the child.

A young, newly married woman who had a suckling child suffering from repeated outbreaks of diarrhea was accused of transgressing the rules of sexual abstinence during lactation. After three months of almost continuous diarrhea, the child, then in a very poor condition, was removed from the mother and given to the father's mother living in the same homestead. In fact, the two women were next-door neighbors. From that day on the grandmother took full responsibility for the care and upbringing of the child. She fed him on milk, tea, and gruel. Luckily, the child improved, but he was still very weak and malnourished when I saw him several months later, and he showed signs of apathy and physical impairment. The family had not sought any professional help for the boy, but had relied on their own interpretation and knowledge of the cause and cure of the disease. The ill health of this boy was explained by the moral misconduct of the mother.

In the introduction to this section, I stated that Maasai have certain beliefs about diseases and their management and cure, but at the same time I noted that the explanatory value of these beliefs in the individual disease case fluctuates. The case of the mother described above and that of Parmeleu, which follows, reveal that beliefs can be very forceful in certain situations, and particularly when they concern the morals of women. The case of Parmeleu is particularly instructive because it touches the very basis of Maasai society and moral order, namely that of sexual relations between men and women as these are governed by the age-group system.

PARMELEU: A CURSE CASE

Parmeleu was cursed by his father (that is, his social father, his mother's husband) when he was born because his mother had conceived him with another man. The age-group organization, as a fundamental principle of Maasai society, regulates and defines relations between men of various age-categories as well as relations between men and women. Within this system, although a woman may have sexual relations with men of the husband's age-group, it is strictly forbidden for married women to have intercourse with men not of the husband's age-group. Parmeleu's mother had taken a lover from a younger age-group than that of her husband; the physiognomy of the boy clearly revealed his biological father. The birth of Parmeleu was a scandal, and everybody in the locality where they lived knew about the incident. The father is a practicing diviner. He is now rather old, but he was formerly an influential man in the community. He cursed Parmeleu in front of his mother, saying, "I will not bring him to die, but he will become nothing." "To become nothing" meant that Parmeleu would remain a poor man without cattle, children, and influence.

While growing up, Parmeleu was always a bit different from other children mentally. He could not see well and his perception seemed to be slower. At the same time he was strong and helpful. He herded the animals with his brother and half brothers (his father had several wives). At the age of sixteen or seventeen Parmeleu was circumcised along with a slightly younger half brother. They belonged to the same age-group and spent the time together as young warriors. Up to this point in his life Parmeleu had passed the mandatory rituals of growing up. Even Parmeleu's elder brother, I was told, was somewhat different. He had poor sight and stammered. He was, however, the favorite son of his father. The brother died while he was still young and newly married. The mother also suffered from impaired sight like her sons.

The father always referred to Parmeleu as a "fool" (*olmodai*). He would tell the mother to "take away her fool." As Parmeleu grew up, the mother also began to dislike him because he constantly misbehaved in various small ways. Among other things, he had the habit of stealing food from her house. Parmeleu also frequently ran away from home. He obviously reacted to the treatment he was subjected to, first from his father and later from his mother. The other people in the settlement felt sorry for him, but their sympathy could not alter the fact that his father had cursed him.

When I first saw Parmeleu, he was almost blind and he sat idle all day murmuring to himself. He hardly moved, but reacted when somebody spoke to him, although they had to shout to get his attention. Nobody took much notice of his presence. He was given his food and he slept in the homestead. After all, he counted as a member of the family. For long periods he stayed away from home. None of his relatives appeared to worry too much about his whereabouts. One day in 1981 he left and had, by 1986, not been back to his home. Some years after he disappeared, the family received news that he had been seen locally outside the Maasai area, but they never tried to trace him. To his family Parmeleu is considered to be a "dead person." He exists as a human being, but as he has neither married nor begotten children and thus not established the relations that make him a person in the Maasai sense of the word, Parmeleu is a "lost" member of his community.

People relate Parmeleu's fate to the curse that his father inflicted on him, although his mother is to be blamed for it. It was not the weak sight or slow perception that made Parmeleu ill, people said, but the fact that he was cursed by his own father. The father refused to release the curse under the pretext that he wanted to punish the mother. Simultaneously, we may speculate, he wanted to confirm his reputation as a strong diviner. Parmeleu's deplorable situation made it evident to everybody that his father was powerful. Just as Maasai diviners are regarded as potent blessers, they are known to have an effective curse and to be potentially dangerous sorcerers.

Through his bad eyesight, Parmeleu is definitely physically impaired, but his true disability within the Maasai society derives from his unfortunate fate of being the product of a sinful relation that has marginalized him as a person.

TREATMENT OF AND ATTITUDES TOWARD DISABLED PEOPLE

To my knowledge, Maasai do not have any special cure or care for disabled people. In some cases a disabled person may be looked upon as a sick person whose recovery requires the normal procedures of disease diagnosis and treatment. This, for instance, is the case with people who are stricken by po-lio. Such individuals undergo various treatments, at least during the first stages of the disease. Any cure depends on the cause of disability and whether the person was born disabled or contracted the condition later. Maasai seem to accept that the disease that has been caused by Enkai has no actual cure.

Children who are born with some kind of deformity or bodily impairment or "weakness" (with a low birth weight)[3] are treated in much the same way as other children; that is to say, they are neither mistreated nor neglected nor particularly favored. They are given the same diet as other children and are subjected to the same prescribed ritual blessings and ceremonial procedures while growing up. The social and psychological advantages of being inte-grated in a social group has its disadvantages as far as survival of the child is concerned. The fact that disabled and weak children are not offered any spe-cial cure or treatment often results in early death. That may partly explain why travelers who were struck by the absence of disabled people among the Maasai drew the erroneous conclusion that Maasai practice infanticide on children with congenital deformities (Merker 1910:51).

According to Maasai informants it is wrong to kill or mistreat deformed or impaired children, because they are of the "same blood," meaning that they are human beings. The child who has been conceived by a man and woman in a legal union is by definition a member of a social world consist-ing of relations preceding its birth. Although the child has to go through a number of humanizing and socializing rituals to be a full member of its so-ciety, it is no doubt a social being at the time of its birth. To mistreat such a child would be a sin (*engoki*) against God and interpreted as mismanage-ment of divine as well as human relations.

Since Maasai keep livestock and live in an intimate relationship with them, they also experience animals being born with deformities. It may be pertinent to mention that Maasai would not kill a deformed calf, kid, or lamb either. This would be a loathsome act, the consequences of which would be difficult to predict. In serious cases, however, they may let nature take its course and allow the animal to die. There is a story of a three-legged goat that gave birth to twenty-seven kids and became the pet animal in the homestead. I was also told of other examples of deformed animals that had become very useful to their owners. "Disabled" children, in spite of their in-capability, may also multiply and become useful. Maasai emphasize that no matter what the child looks like, the parents will always care for and take re-sponsibility for it and value it as any other child. I have heard Maasai tell many stories about parents who devote a tremendous amount of care to their impaired children.

One such case involved a girl who fell out of bed into the fire on the floor while she was a baby. The mother was drunk and fast asleep and did not notice what had happened.[4] The girl's hands and arms were damaged in this accident. The right hand had to be amputated; the left hand was deformed, with only two fingers intact. The mother cared extremely well for this girl and they were always in each other's company. Some of the neighbors said that the girl was spoiled. The mother constantly worried about the future of her daughter. She foresaw the difficulties she would have in finding a husband due to the fact that the girl was unable to carry things and thus would need somebody to assist her with collecting firewood and fetching water, among other things. Even the most commonplace female task of tying a baby to the back would surpass her competence. The mother claimed that she would educate the girl, visualizing an easier future for her that way. As far as their physically disabled children are concerned, Maasai parents often perceive formal education as a real option to the rough and demanding nomadic lifestyle they pursue.

Another case of parental protection was that of a young girl with a deformed leg, whom people said had been bewitched. When she approached marriageable age and was circumcised, she was not pushed to marry a man and move to his home and live among foreign people as is the common practice, but was allowed to remain in the homestead of her parents and reproduce herself there. Her children would become members of her own lineage and legal heirs of her parents' property. This practice of keeping daughters in the own home after circumcision (*entito enkang*, "girl of the homestead") is in fact an alternative to marriage that quite a number of parents, for various reasons, choose for their daughters. It is not a special arrangement for the physically impaired. Maasai claim that this alternative is particularly favored by fathers who have only girls and want a male heir, or those who are exceptionally fond of their daughters and would hate to see them being mistreated by other men. A "girl of the homestead" has a privileged position among women; she lives amid her own people and, more important, she does not have to succumb to the will of a husband. Even though such a girl is single, she still gives birth to legitimate children and these become her entrance to full participation in all community events.

A caring attitude of Maasai parents toward their disabled children was confirmed by missionary workers at the children's rehabilitation home. They narrated stories of fathers who had carried their lame or deformed children vast distances to bring them to the rehabilitation home for treatment.

Sometimes one hears opposite views, though. An educated Maasai woman who works with a primary health care program in the Maasai area told me how a mother who had brought all her children for vaccination, among them a mentally retarded child, had referred to the "disabled" one as *enguguu*. This term designates an animal-like creature (monster)—a being that transgresses the boundaries of the human world. The woman cited this incident in support of her view that Maasai are not very considerate with their "disabled" children. We should note, however, that, after all, the mother brought the retarded child to be vaccinated. In light of that fact, the mother's direct naming of the child's mental and physical impairment (i.e., the difference observed) should not be interpreted as mistreatment. On the contrary, her behavior reflects openness and acceptance.

Taking into consideration that the Maasai shift residence frequently and often hastily, the care of "disabled" family members, particularly those unable to walk alone, implies considerable additional work for the rest of the family. When they are presented with alternatives for the care of those who are severely physically impaired, they may take the opportunity to rid themselves of the toil. The rehabilitation home has proven to be one such opportunity.

It is firmly laid down in the Maasai moral code that impaired children should be treated exactly the same way as other children. "A child is a child whatever it looks like" is a statement commonly heard. The norm that there should be no discrimination between the children applies not only to their upbringing and feeding while young but also to marriage and the inheritance of parents' livestock. All children, unless they are disqualified through grave misconduct or neglect of rules of "respect" or are severely mentally retarded, are given chances of marrying or having children; this testifies to the strong conviction of the Maasai that any member of their society should enjoy the most basic of all human rights, namely reproduction. It is first and foremost through parenthood that an individual becomes a person; that is what makes him or her into "someone." A Maasai who dies childless is leaving "nothing" behind; his or her name will be erased from memory.

NORMALITY IN DIFFERENCES

"Disabled" people are as far as possible integrated in the daily routine of the homestead and the community. This is not only because the Maasai feel there is no practical alternative; as I have noted above, Maasai do not stigmatize people who have a "disability," however serious the condition may be, by excluding them from the community. Physically impaired persons marry, become parents, and participate in all communal activities to the best of their abilities. A physically disabled man, if he is intelligent and speaks well, may even become the elected political leader of his age-group (olaiguenani), which is the highest political office in the Maasai society. I know of at least one such case, which involved a rather short hunch-backed man, a gifted speaker with high intelligence.[5] Even Parmeleu, until his health deteriorated drastically, underwent the socially prescribed rituals and observances preparing him for adult life. In other words, "disabled" people are neither hidden away nor taken to be impure or polluting. They live their lives alongside relatives and friends, thus allowing them to fully participate in the rewarding sociability of homestead and neighborhood.

The following two examples bring home the point that differences in people's physical or mental capabilities are not culturally constructed as differences having implications for a person's fulfillment in life. The first case concerns a man who was born without proper legs. He is married to two women, has a steady job as a clerk, a fair number of animals, and several children. For these qualities he enjoys much respect among his fellow Maasai and is defined as a successful man. People consider him to be "blessed" because he was taken to a rehabilitation center, where he was given education and later employment in the office. He moves around in a wheelchair that he was given by his employer. As far as I could ascertain, this man plays the usual role of the father and elder in his household. He makes the necessary decisions concerning the husbandry of the herd, performs obligatory rites at birth and circumcision of children, and so on. As he is not able to walk by himself, he is of course dependent on his wives for most practical things. The second wife of this man was married to him by capture, which occurs sporadically among the Maasai. He could not possibly participate in this ritual himself, but age-mates assisted him and brought the wife to his homestead. Members of the same age-group are considered to be so close that in most instances one can be replaced by another.

The other case is a woman who had had her foot amputated because she had been bitten by a snake when she was young. She was the only wife of her husband, had five children, and managed the household on her own. She walked with a very simple foot made of wood fastened with some leather straps to the leg. When she journeyed long distances on foot, she carried a stick. The fact that she had quite a severe impairment in the Maasai context did not prevent her from leaving her husband and returning to her own family who lived some twenty to thirty kilometers away when her husband began to drink heavily and misuse their livestock property. While away from her husband (and her children) she traveled widely among her own relatives to collect animals promised to her when she was circumcised as a young girl.

The sexual division of labor among the pastoral Maasai requires more physical prestations from women than from men, which has some consequences for how severe a disabling condition is considered to be for men and women respectively. Recalling that Maasai families live together in large settlements, help and assistance in practical matters are potentially close at hand. As cooperation in daily work and leisure is quite extensive within the homestead, the woman with the artificial foot could always rely on a female relative or neighbor to give her a helping hand when things got difficult. The man in the wheelchair could fall back on Maasai cultural institutions like polygyny and the age-set system for support and assistance. There are indications that the disintegration of the residence pattern into one-family homesteads in general increases the workload for many women, as well as isolating women from one another (see Talle 1988). Even male cooperation and sociability suffer from the changes in size and composition of homesteads. For a woman or man with some kind of disabling condition, this, of course, is an unfortunate pattern that will make it a greater handicap to have a disability.

I began this chapter by pointing out that among the pastoral Maasai in Kenya disability is not a basis for defining persons. The fact that an individual is impaired in one way or the other is just an aspect of his/her person, but does not make any difference in social and cultural terms. Certainly Maasai notice disabilities and look upon them as bad or unfortunate things. They both name the difference and mark it, but I argue that this indicates acceptance and lack of fear of the different or abnormal. To give birth to a disabled child is not culturally defined as a crisis, requiring specific actions and precautions. It is part of life's experience. The Maasai seem to have institutional and cognitive instruments for coping with such a situation, and thus, while marking the difference, they normalize it.

NOTES

1. The data on which the chapter is based were collected during field research among the Loodokilani section of the Kenya Maasai between 1979 and 1981 and on shorter follow-up visits later. My sincere acknowledgment to Moses ole Sharrar, who participated in the field research and contributed constructive views on an earlier version of the chapter. I am also greatly indebted to Melkiori ole Matwi for reading and commenting on the text.

2. The Maasai ritual experts and diviners (*oloiboni*, pl. *iloibonok*) are recruited from a subclan called *enkidongi*. They are endowed with supernatural powers to procure the well-being and fertility of people and livestock, call forth rain, and predict the future. The ritual power is inherited patrilineally, but only a few members of the lineage practice ritual skills of high degree. (Frequently, however, one hears the Maasai refer to any person capable of curing as being *oloiboni*.) The divinatory stones are kept in a special calabash or cowhorn, called *enkidongi*. The name of the subclan stems from this term. When performing divination, the *oloiboni* shakes the calabash and throws the stones on the ground, whereupon he interprets the pattern and constellation of stones for his client.

3. Weakness (*ameena*), weak in the sense of being thin, is not generally regarded as disability or as a disease, but it may very well develop into disability or disease if not treated. I mention it here because the Maasai look upon weakness as a sign of ill health.

4. Abuse of alcohol is not common among Maasai women, but it is widespread among men. There are women, however, who become alcoholics, and Maasai claim that their number is increasing.

5. The role of ritual leader (*oltuno*) of the age-group, however, can only be held by a person who is "perfect" (*sinyati*, "sacred") in all senses: physically, mentally, morally, and in terms of heredity. The role of *oltuno* is close to a "sacred" position,

and that is why great care is taken in selecting the candidate. The *oltuno* is considered to be the ceremonial "father" of his age-mates. Any physical, mental, or social handicap in the person chosen would be a bad omen for the whole age-set. The procedure of selecting the *oltuno* can be likened to the selection of slaughter animals at important rituals and ceremonies. The body of the animal must be without blemish; it must have no disfiguring marks, possess the right color (usually black, which is an auspicious color in Maasai symbolism), and have a good pedigree (*olkiteng osinyati*, "sacred oxen").

REFERENCES

Fortes, M.
1987   *Religion, Morality, and the Person: Essays on Tallensi Religion.* Ed. J. Goody. Cambridge: Cambridge University Press.

Galaty, J. G.
1977   In the pastoral image: The dialectic of Maasai identity. Ph.D. dissertation, University of Chicago.

Kleinman, A.
1980   *Patients and Healers in the Context of Culture.* Berkeley, Los Angeles, London: University of California Press.

Merker, M.
1910   *Die Masai: Ethnographische Monographie eines ostafrikanischen Semitenvolkes.* Reprint. Berlin: Dietrich Reimer, 1968.

Nestel, P. S.
1985   Nutrition of Maasai women and children in relation to subsistence production. Ph.D. thesis, University of London.

Talle, A.
1988   *Women at a Loss: Changes in Maasai Pastoralism and Their Effects on Gender Relations.* Stockholm Studies in Social Anthropology, no. 19. Stockholm: University of Stockholm.

Århem, K.
1989   Why trees are medicine: Aspects of Maasai cosmology. In *Culture, Experience, and Pluralism: Essays on African Ideas of Illness and Healing,* ed. A. Jacobson-Widding and D. Westerlund. Uppsala Studies in Cultural Anthropology 13. Stockholm: Almqvist and Wiksell International.

FOUR

Disability as Incurable Illness: Health, Process, and Personhood in Southern Somalia

Bernhard Helander

In much of contemporary anthropological work on the disabled there is a difficulty in defining and separating disability from disease. Partly to blame for that is a biomedical view according to which one sees "disability as a disease state . . . a temporary anomaly in an otherwise nondisabled population" (Groce and Scheer 1990:v). A common anthropological response is to focus investigations on a single or a limited number of types of disabilities (e.g., Ablon 1984; Estroff 1981; Frank 1984; Goldin 1990; Groce 1985; Gwaltney 1970), thus avoiding grappling with the definitional difficulties that emerge when the disabled are treated more generally. Yet among studies that approach the disabled broadly in relation to other social categories, there has been, as Robert Murphy and his coauthors (1988) suggest, a marked trend toward looking at stigma and other extreme sets of attitudes. Since stigma is not something that disabled people are uniquely subjected to, the disabled may therefore not be a relevant population of enquiry. As Benedicte Ingstad (1991) argues, the focus on stigma and severe maltreatment of disabled people may well be a product of our lack of understanding of other fundamental social processes that shape the lives of the disabled.

However, problems related to the definition of disability are not simply an analytical phenomenon. Studies of the disabled in non-Western societies (e.g., Halantine and Berge 1990; Talle 1990) indicate vast discrepancies between Western notions and those of other cultures. When I was first asked to collect material for a paper about the disabled in Somalia, I had some difficulties in clarifying the topic both to myself and to the Somali people I discussed it with. The difficulty stemmed from the fact that in the parts of Somalia where I worked there was no clear border between what we call disease and disability. Certainly words exist that are more accurately rendered as one than the other, and certainly some people are said to be disabled rather than ill. But the difficulty is not just a terminological one. Through-out the whole process of identifying a disability, acting on the discovery, learning to cope with it, trying to cure it, or any of the other routes that people may choose to follow, there is no distinct set of attitudes or actions reserved for the disabled. On the contrary, both in classification and treat-ment, Somalis appear to regard the disabled as ill and impairment as dis-ease. If any profound difference is seen, it is only that what we term disability is regarded as more difficult to cure than ordinary disease.

My aim for this chapter is to sort out the various implications that the lack of clear distinction between disease and disability have on the way that dis-abled are regarded and treated in Somalia. My approach is to look on the process that shapes disabilities from three different angles: I shall first try to put the Somali notions of disabled in the context of their theories of per-sonhood, and then situate their ways of approaching disabilities within the general pattern of health seeking. I will also consider the way that labels for illness are constructed throughout the health-seeking process. I shall argue that while the theory about how a human being is constituted is extremely adjustable to shifting circumstances, it cannot accommodate immobility. A person is a totality that is thought to be constantly changing. Imperfect people may be subjected to amendments, but when repeated attempts to restore health are unsuccessful, a disabled person appears permanently incapacitated and cut off from the stream of life. As long as a disorder can be regarded as illness, it may be acted on. However, when such attempts fail or are judged as hopeless, only despair ensues.

The data are primarily drawn from my field studies in a community in the Bay region in southern Somalia.[1] The group I worked among is a clan called Hubeer with some fifteen thousand members. The Hubeer are agro-pastoralists. They cultivate sorghum and maize around their villages in the clan homeland and graze their camels, cows, and small stock in pastures that they share with neighboring clans. The Hubeer, like the vast majority of other Somali, adhere to the Shafi'ite code of Sunni Islam. Like other Somali clans, they are organized in a system of patrilineally segmented descent groups to which they attribute a major role in social and political affairs (see B. Helander 1988a). The sedentary portions of the population also have vil-lages and other nonagnatic forms of community to serve as important foci for social affairs. Villages in the area often contain members of different clans. Even the clan itself is to a large extent a confederation of allied peo-ple and groups of rather mixed provenance. Externally, however, Hubeer represent themselves as descendants of a single ancestor, and they mostly act in accordance with that ideal.

Additional data for this paper were collected during brief periods of fieldwork in other areas of southern Somalia, including an outpatient rehabilitation center in the capital, Mogadishu, and a rural area in which a community -based rehabilitation scheme had been introduced. Some supplemental information was obtained from southern Somali refugees living in Sweden.

DISABLED PERSONS

The Somali word that comes closest to the WHO notion[2] of disability is *naafo*. This is the term that rehabilitation workers in Mogadishu use for rehabilitation projects and for labeling centers for training of disabled people. To ordinary urban people the term at least partially covers people with moving deficiencies but focuses primarily on persons with amputated or seriously injured limbs, the epitome of whom are probably crippled soldiers. For many years Somalia has been the scene of war, which has left the country with a substantial number of invalids. Someone with an injured arm will first be thought to be a soldier. However, visual and hearing deficiencies are clearly not regarded as *naafo*, since nothing but terms like *blind* and *deaf* are ever used for them. It is unclear to what extent, if at all, learning difficulties are recognized as a particular category of disability. However, it is clear that neither fits, strange behavior, nor chronic tuberculosis (all of which are covered by the WHO definition) is covered by the term *naafo*. I lack information on whether leprosy is seen as *naafo*, but it is likely that some disabling effects of that disease would correspond to the image of a crippling condition that the concept conveys.

It follows that a significant feature of the Hubeer/Somali notion of disabled is that only in very specific circumstances are "disabled people" (*dadka naafada*) seen as or talked about as a unified category. If one lumps together people with different types of what we call disabilities, they would be described as "sick people." More commonly, disabled people tend to be addressed and discussed in terms of the specific disability they suffer from. A person missing an arm is often talked of and addressed as *gacanley* or *gacamey*, "armless." Someone with a limp may be nicknamed *jees*, "limpy." Similarly, deaf people are labeled *dhegoole*, "without ears," and the blind *indhoole*, "without eyes."

This way of talking about people with disabilities implies a stress on the disability itself. The habit would seem to establish an identification with the disabling symptom, at least in the eyes of other people. It is difficult to say whether such an identification is actually resented by disabled persons themselves; I have never myself seen any sign that a disabled person appeared particularly bothered by it, but I have heard it said that women sometimes may dislike such tags. It should be observed that disabled people are not alone in becoming identified with some personal peculiarity. I have elsewhere discussed how individual deviance is given cosmological sanction and religious legitimation by the astrological system (B. Helander 1988a: chap. 5; 1988b).

That way of defining individuality focuses above all on the mental strength of persons as displayed in daily discourse, and it is also something that is given a prominent place in religious healing. Apart from the interpretation of individual capacity that sheikhs may provide,[3] ordinary people give a great deal of attention to individual peculiarities and leanings. Nicknames (*naanaays*), which are very common in Somalia, are often both to the point and amusing, and they may also—at least in the case of men—feature an element of mockery. Traits singled out for recognition by a nickname may be some bodily attribute (e.g., *dhego madoow,* "black ears") or behavioral quality (e.g., *mashquul,* "busy"). The way of addressing disabled people by deriving a name from their disability is thus not an attitude uniquely applied to disabled persons but rather forms part of a system of attitudes in which great importance is attached to individual inclination, character, and deviation. Yet it is necessary here to give some further attention to the cultural definition of the person in relation to disabled individuals.

It is possible to say that the Hubeer ideas of how a person is constituted draw on two different strands of thought. On the one hand, there are aspects of a person that are known to all and that are fairly obvious. These include the genealogical standing and status of the person and his or her family; meritorious achievements by a person in areas like oratory, leadership, economics; and to some extent proven physical ability in one's work or in combat. On the other hand, the Hubeer recognize a number of less apparent influences on an individual's character. In the local variety of a Sufistic astrological tradition, a person is thought to be connected to the influences of astral bodies, seasons, elements, and Muslim saints. The combination of these influences is summarized by the term *burji,* which in Arabic means a sign of the Zodiac but for the Hubeer has a wider implication as a fundamental aspect of a human being, related also to emotional and mental abilities. If the concept were not so linked to a Western tradition, *burji* could perhaps be described as the inner essence of human beings.

While all of these major aspects combine in the totality of the person, they do represent distinct realms of thought and action. To the Somali in general, mundane arenas like clanship, politics, and economy should remain separate from religious phenomena. Even in the ideal division of roles, a "man of religion" (*wadaad,* or sheikh) could not also be a "spear bearer" (*waranleh*), that is, a person engaged in the political affairs of his descent group (see Lewis 1963).

What is so interesting about this particular way of defining a person is the enormous flexibility it implies. The person is never a given, never completed, but rather represents an array of continuously shifting influences. Even presumably stable aspects, such as the prestige that comes from belonging to a particular lineage, is in the Hubeer context adjustable. Also, the more indistinct traits of a personality, those which are thought to derive from various forms of obscure celestial influence, can be altered or manipulated. In brief, a fundamental trait of the Hubeer/Somali idea of "person" is that it is something positioned at the junction of continuously changing influences.

This shifting nature of their concept of the person bears some striking similarities with social forms in the Hubeer society. Hubeer men and women like to think of themselves as sturdy workers, with good reason. They praise industrious people and continuously stress the need to go about one's business in a meticulous manner. Indeed, to create the comparative affluence in which many of them live requires a tremendous input of heavy manual labor, and while most people appreciate some company over a cup of *shaah,* they return quickly to their duties when the break is over. A full day's work for the Hubeer can often amount to twelve hours of agricultural labor.[4]

The Hubeer regard productivity as affecting both self-esteem and social standing; similarly, they hold innate qualities like talent and mental strength, provided by their *burji,* to be to some extent dependent on the life events and experiences of a person. "To be eaten up by one's worries" is one of many ways in which they sometimes phrase their concern over loss of spirit. When there is a felt disturbance in the relations to some other person, it may often develop into somatic consequences. Conversely, some people may point to a particular event or person as being somehow auspicious to them.

The Hubeer notion of personhood appears to have some very marked implications for their attitudes toward deviance in general and for some types of disabilities in particular. That idiosyncrasies are not despised but rather seen as reflecting personality means that the Hubeer, and other Somalis too, often are extremely condoning when it comes to individual peculiarities. The threshold beyond which a type of behavior is ruled out is high, and while curious acts may be viewed with amusement, respect for individual leanings is also observed.

Although personal deviance is to some extent supported by the system rather than condemned by it, that does not place all disability on par. While, for instance, blind and deaf people have little to wish for in terms of community acceptance, people with some other kinds of disability do find Hubeer attitudes toward them much less tolerant. In particular, people who are seen as mentally aberrant run a risk of conflicting with Hubeer notions of *iska caadi,* "be normal," and *ha is waalin,* "don't be crazy for/by yourself." In contrast to the majority of other disabilities, mental disability is not generally regarded as disease. Although the treatment afforded mentally disabled people varies a lot from case to case and ultimately depends on factors such as the social standing of the concerned family (see B. Helander 1990a), the general attitude toward mentally disabled people is one of strong disfavor. In a sense, that attitude can be said to relate to a feeling of intellectual immobility of these people. A proverb says that words of wisdom told to a *doqon* (fool) are like semen provided for an infertile woman or rain that falls in the sea rather than on arable land. Infertility, death, inertia, and wasted wisdom are all close synonyms in this cultural logic.

The Hubeer way of regarding persons as entities that are somehow in a continuous state of flux has a distinct bearing on the way in which they see ordinary illness in relation to disability. Inactivity is probably the worst possible condition for a person to be in, and as they see it, inactivity is what will come out of severe illness. As I have said, there is no sharp line separating disease (*cudur*) from disability (*naafo*)—the very concept of *naafo* is too vague for that. Yet I have several times heard severely sick people explaining that although they were very ill they were not "invalids" (*boos*). Thus, although the terminology for disability is not very highly developed, such statements seem to reflect an opinion that disability is what lies at the end of the line when all attempts to restore health have failed. As the Hubeer see it, invalids and disabled people are permanently bedridden and cut off from the flow of social life.[5] While ordinary persons are influenced by a constant dynamic, the disabled are fixed and stagnant. Most people with disabilities in Somalia end up having to accept rather circumscribed roles for themselves. Often they support themselves from begging and come to be mixed up with a category of people referred to as *masaakinta*, "the poor." That would seem to distance them even further from normal people, since the poor and needy—often talked about as "God's protégés," *magan Allah*—are often attributed magical powers in compensation for their lack of political power. Among the disabled in Mogadishu and their families it was striking how close at hand the begging alternative seemed to be, even if it took the form of negative statements like "we did not want him to sit in the street, that's why we keep bringing him to the rehabilitation center." The association between the poor and powerless and the disabled is not of a straightforward kind. Rather, the reasoning seems based on the attribution of all kinds of misery and misfortune to the poor, and therefore it is only natural to find disabled people among them, too.[6]

THE HEALTH-SEEKING PROCESS

To understand the way health management practices affect the situation of disabled people, it is necessary to stress the social character of this process. All aspects of it are located in a network of social relations and dependent on social resources of various kinds. The actions initiated by the detection of bad health in the family may be described as a pendulum movement between the family members' discussions and labeling of the symptoms and their seeking of external assistance. This movement comes to cover a widening sphere of people. And over time, a similarly widening geographical area may be covered.

At the onset of abnormal symptoms in a child, mothers frequently regard the condition as something they should cope with more or less on their own. For the most common children's diseases there are a multitude of dietary and herbal treatments, collectively known as *baano*,[7] that usually become the first choice of therapy. Especially in the case of children, these types of treatments may be attempted for an extended period. If *baano* treatments are unsuccessful, the mother may turn to women in the hamlet or neighborhood for advice, and visiting relatives will undoubtedly also become engaged in the case. Men's involvement at the initial stage of illness detection varies a lot among families, but even where their engagement amounts to a minimum (which is rare), men will have a say if consulting some kind of expert is being considered. The increased availability and use of pharmaceutical drugs have probably served to make mothers' health decisions more independent, at least in the initial stages of illness. For adults who get sick, a visit to a local pharmacy is an increasingly common first choice, and frequently women (and men) turn to pharmacies to obtain medicines for their children, too.[8]

If, after an initial period of attempts to restore the child's health, no signs of improvement are visible, the issue will be regarded as more serious and receive more attention among other family members. Typically, matters of health are discussed in the evenings after supper, often as the people sit outside the houses. Since this is the time of day when people pay visits to others' homes, family discussions concerning the health of one of the members often involve other people, too. There is a common format for such discussions. The assembled people usually agree rather quickly on what is wrong and define a particular label for the symptoms. To distinguish such labels from biomedically established diseases, I shall refer to them as "illness-labels," which I discuss separately below. Once an illness-label has been found, there is often less agreement concerning how the illness best could be combated, and whom, if any, of the local experts one should consult. Should the family decide to consult an expert, they commonly present their case by using the illness-label and not by giving a detailed account of the detected symptoms. While illness-labels may be reformulated and reconsidered in the process of health seeking, they retain a primary role both in determining generally the course of action and also in relation to more specific decisions that have to be made, such as the selection of healer.

An essentially pluralistic medical tradition such as the Somali one offers many alternative health resources outside of the family. An ordinary Hubeer village hosts several religious healers with varying skill and recognition. There are also specialists in herbal treatments and experts in some other traditional healing techniques, for example, scarification, bone setting, and surgical techniques. In addition one can find drug peddlers in the markets, and some larger villages even have well-stocked pharmacies. The latter are often synonymous with primary health care. The local terminology divides these health resources into three major categories: *dawo Soomaali,* "Somali medicine"; *dawo casriga,* "modern medicine"; and *diin,* "religion" (see B. Helander 1989). An ordinary-sized village will usually have around ten recognized healers, each with slightly differing specializations. The treatments offered by the different practitioners are not regarded as exclusive alternatives, but rather as complementary paths that can be explored simultaneously or successively. In the case of prolonged illness, several alternative treatments almost always will be attempted.[9]

Seeking health for a sick family member is a process that may last for years. It is also something that must be done along with regular chores. For most Hubeer households even a quick visit to a doctor's private clinic in the regional capital, Baydhabo, eighty kilometers away, requires careful planning. Ill people rarely travel alone, so a companion has to be appointed. Since city food is not appreciated and is too expensive, sorghum for a few days consumption is prepared. That normally means taking it out of the underground granary and grinding it. Although lorries leave for Baydhabo several times a week, the fares are high, and to pay the fares additional sorghum has to be prepared and sold.

A household's ability to meet the various expenses of cash and labor involved in health seeking naturally depends on factors such as its size and economic standing. However, there is another constraining factor of great consequence for how decisions are made in the health-seeking process; the personal ties a family has with a healer influences the readiness to make use of his or her services. As the search for expertise outside the sphere of the household commences, people who are known from previous contacts are always turned to first. When the resources in the social vicinity have all been explored, most people will then approach even unknown specialists. It is common, particularly at later stages of a health-seeking process, for hopes to be ignited by rumors about some miraculous treatment that someone else has received. But before reaching that point, unmediated contacts with unknown healers are generally avoided. To some extent this conforms to the pattern in which all social contacts are managed among the Hubeer: interaction without previous acquaintance or mediation by a third person is rare, and simply belonging to the same clan is not sufficient basis for most social purposes. Establishing new social ties in the process of health seeking is also a matter of costs, because accepting advice or free services implies a new future reciprocal obligation to be met.

COMMUNICATING AND EVALUATING

Throughout the health-seeking process the effects of the various remedies are subjected to evaluation. If the sick person is an adult, his or her subjective experience will have a great influence on whether further treatment is pursued. The way in which evaluations of health are communicated primarily focuses on the amount of present pain and the degree of mobility. To illustrate this I shall quote from a conversation between a woman who was believed sick with *dabeyl* ("polio," see the next section, "Illness-Labels") for several years and a female visitor. The visiting woman had called on the sick woman some weeks ago and at that time recommended that the family consult a sheikh in a neighboring village. The husband of the sick woman had at first disapproved of that since he himself was a sheikh. However, persuaded by a brother of his wife, he had eventually called the other sheikh, who had performed a *marre* for the woman.[10] When the woman came again I was interviewing the sick woman in the house. I heard the visitor meet the husband outside the house and ask him about his wife's condition. The husband must have been slightly embarrassed because of his resistance to her suggestion. Although there had been no improvement in his wife's health after the *marre*, he responded politely and said that she was "a little bit better (*kistoo roonta*)."

In enquiring about somebody else's health in Somali some precautions have to be observed. Since most illness may be caused by the evil eye, questions usually must not be too direct. The more imprecise and general the question the better, for in that way there can be no suspicion of hidden malice. For instance, it is not good to ask straight out, "Is your leg aching? (*Lugta ma ku xanuuneysaa*)," but better to say, "How is it with your leg? (*Lugta iska warran*)."[11] Another factor in a conversation between a sick person and a visitor is that the format for a well-mannered conversation, one with mutual assurance of good health, cannot be abandoned. In the case of the woman who called on her sick friend, a further issue was involved. The visitor had not been told during her first visit what illness-label the sick woman's family believed in. Perhaps this was because that particular illness-label borders on the other illness-labels in which a suspicion of human agency of some kind exists; such illness-labels cannot be told to someone who theoretically could have caused the affliction.

When the visiting woman entered the house, the sick woman, who was lying in bed, made her voice very feeble. They started to exchange the conventional greetings asserting that they both were *faylan*, "fine," "good," and "healthy." After that the visiting woman asked once more, "How is it with your health? (*Caafimaadka ii warran*)." In responding to that and the following questions the sick woman made use of some of the expressions that routinely are used to describe a poor state of health. She explained that she was still lying down (*jiifo*), that she felt "completely flat" or "exhausted" (*tacabaan*). She mentioned that she even felt too weak to drink tea. She also described the pain she felt by imitating a sound like that made by scratching ("cararash, cararash, gorong, gorong") while pointing to the various places of her body where she felt the pain. She added that the visit to the sheikh recommended by the other woman had relieved her from the fever she had before and that she had also taken a few Dawonool tablets.[12]

Although this conversation involved a severely ill woman, the terminology she and others used to describe her condition is typical for how the Hubeer communicate health matters, both among themselves and when they contact experts. The degree of mobility is described, often by referring to some common act that the person no longer is able to carry out. The terms *tacabaan* and *boos* represent the extreme end of immobility,[13] and in the case just described the sick woman had apparently begun to identify with this condition. Typical, too, is the vivid description of particular symptoms, mostly the amount of pain. In cases of impaired limbs the term *naafo* will be applied at a stage when the injury appears irreversible from changes that have emerged in function, color, or shape of the limb. Terms like *naafo, boos,* and *tacabaan,* when used in a rural context, suggest a finality—nothing more can be done. It is ironic therefore to find that crippled soldiers are probably among those who receive the best rehabilitation of all—even though they are often labeled *naafo.*

The decision on whether to go on in health seeking or not is formed not only with regard to the state of health. When many treatments have been tried, the issue of the costs involved becomes more and more distressing. Particularly in the case of disability for which several therapeutic alternatives have been unsuccessfully attempted during an extended period, it is common to find tensions in the social vicinity relating to different opinions about how to proceed. An often-quoted proverb is quite explicit about that: "Much is [or has to be] spent on a sick person." Actually, the same proverb can, with only a minor alteration in pronunciation, also express the sense of duty among the relatives of a sick person: "A sick person governs [orders about] one hundred [people]."[14] The latter, with the change of one vowel, can mean that many people give advice to a sick person.

One aspect of the sick woman's case is that it had been going on for a few years and that active attempts made by her family to cure her had become increasingly less frequent. As I mentioned, the husband had even tried to stop the last visit paid to an expert. The family, even the three children of the woman, had in a sense grown used to having the woman in a state of more or less permanent, or at least incurable, illness.

The *dabeyl* sick woman is not alone. Since most disabled people are treated as sick people, very few are able to report any success of their health seeking. When families find their disabled member impossible to cure, one can often sense how the hopes previously attached to different medicines or healing have given way to despair and resignation. Such emerging feelings often appear to be parallel to—or find nourishment in—the cumulative costs of health care.

ILLNESS-LABELS

What I call an illness-label is strictly speaking a combination of several different things. In some cases it is nothing more than a local name for a medical condition, such as the local name for common cold (*hergab*). Frequently, however, even such terms involve a local theory of what has brought about the illness and therefore, although the locally recognized symptoms may correspond to those recognized by medical science, the meaning of the illness is totally different. A good example of that would be *walkoraad*, which phenomenologically corresponds more or less to hydrocephalus but is locally believed to be caused by the shadow of a bird. Most illness-labels, however, appear to group symptoms differently than in biomedical science. For instance, the local term *helmeeso* includes measles but also some other cases where children suddenly get high fever.

It should be underlined that there is probably not *one* consistent nosology in Somalia. Rather, the different therapeutic traditions tend to see the same set of symptoms in the light of different theories and sometimes apply different labels accordingly. Adding to that pluralism is the social heterogeneity of the Hubeer and the neighboring clans, which has brought people with slightly different notions on how to handle health matters to inhabit the same villages.

Two aspects give a particular character to Somali illness-labels. First, they are produced primarily by the household and not by healers or experts. Thus, although the labels are influenced by both herbalism and Islam, and also have picked up concepts like "vitamins," "germs," and "blood pressure," they belong to an independent folk tradition of divination and are a property of the laity rather than experts. Second, despite the range of variability, there are a limited number of internal bodily functions that are both important for a large number of different illness-labels and that also cross the boundaries between the different therapeutic traditions. In a sense these reflect the same general preoccupation with fluidity and mobility that is present in communicative patterns concerning different degrees of illness.

One such bodily function is digestion. Constipation, *qaras*, is regarded as having far-reaching, and in some cases even lethal, consequences. A sizeable number of traditional herbal remedies are designated as treatments for *qaras*, and people's own illness stories often mention that their stomach was "standing still," "did not move," and so on. Another bodily function attributed great importance is the condition of the blood. Old blood or black blood, supposed to have been held up below the skin, is blamed for a variety of disorders. It is also common to blame illness on blood that is "little" or "much." Some internal organs like the liver are also the focus for both religious healers and Somali traditional doctors.

The range of illness-labels and subsequent therapeutic endeavors in which these bodily functions are invoked is enormous. Bad blood, it is held, could get stuck in the liver and damage it. I have seen cases of heartburn or ulcer that were treated on that premise. However, probably because the liver is often both figuratively and literally pointed to as a seat for deeply felt emotions, some healers make frequent reference to the liver in treatments designed for disorders of a more psychological nature as well.

Some illness-labels directly suggest a type of therapy to be applied. When, for instance, spiritual attacks are suspected, the range of applicable therapies is limited to different religious types of treatments or the spirit possession cults. However, even for some ordinary physical disorders like infants' diarrhea, the most common illness-labels directly indicate how the disorder ought to be dealt with.

Illness-labels are often synonymous with an agent that is believed able to cause a wide variety of afflictions. Among such general illness-labels "the evil eye" (*isha, il-dad, dejis,* etc.) is most frequently cited. The evil eye is seen as an extremely powerful force that many result in almost any kind of sickness for the victim. It is said that if a person eats in front of someone desiring that food, the food will turn poisonous and hurt or kill the one eating it. Similarly, exaggerated praise of the possessions of somebody else may be harmful to that person or the item itself. A man who is told of his daughter's beauty by another man will often be suspicious because he fears the intentions of that man. Numerous stories tell of people and livestock that have been struck dead or crippled for life, due to the desire, praise, or envy of others.

No specific set of symptoms is associated with the evil eye, but it is one of the primary possible causes of any unforeseen misfortune which people will consider in their search for an explanation. The evil eye is not believed to strike randomly or to be caused by just any person. I have noted that it is often believed to come from people who occupy a somewhat peripheral position in their network and to have been triggered by some neglected duty or obligation of the victim. In cases that I came across it was often distant relatives and temporary acquaintances who were (secretly) blamed for having brought on the affliction in question. Often this was said to be due to some minor shortcoming of the victim, such as a failure to respond to a greeting, insufficiently shown hospitality, arrogance, and so on.

In seeking a remedy for inflictions believed to be caused by the evil eye, the suspected person often is brought to the sickbed of the victim. The suspect is usually not told the real reason for the visit; instead, the visitor is told that the victim requested his or her presence and display of affection and concern as a favor and in keeping with the Somali tradition that sick people must be visited.

Another illness-label that is synonymous with the agent causing it is the curse. Curses are believed to be the cause of many afflictions, diseases, and disabling conditions. Curses (*inkaar, habaar*) have, like the evil eye, a distinct social component. However, in contrast to the evil eye, curses do not work on the periphery of one's social relations. Rather, it is within the sphere of closely bound relatives that curses may be effective. Curses are intimately bound up with the authority of parental generation(s) (*waalid*). All members of these generations possess the capacity to curse members of the descending generation(s) (*ilmo, carruur*). They are believed to have this capacity to a greater or lesser degree. The strongest curse—and the one people fear most—is that of the maternal uncle.

When a person is struck by a curse, it is held to have been incurred by the transgression of rules or a failure to fulfill obligations toward the elders. There is no specific type of disability or sickness that is caused by curses. If asked, people state that it leads to "unhappiness" (*bacaaw*) and sometimes illustrate it by mentioning that your livestock will die or stop producing milk, that your fields will cease yielding, and that you may die without offspring. Some informants mentioned that curses can "wither your limbs," and it is common for people who are not acquainted with the circumstances of a disabled person to spontaneously attribute his or her disability to a curse. I have, for instance, heard it said about people who walked uneasily that this was due to a curse from their parents. The very expression "to stagger along" (*heedheeda dareere*) refers to an unsteady way of moving and to a lack of success.

Once an illness-label is arrived at, it need not be stable; often it is dependent on factors such as the circumstances during which the illness was acquired, the probable causes, the gender of the sick person, and, in some cases, the gender of the illness itself. A good example is the various categories of polio. The name *dabeyl,* which literally means wind, is derived from the agent that is believed to cause it, and this is how many illness-labels are chosen. Certain types of winds, for instance, the small tornados that may develop on large areas of cultivated land, are believed to be harmful, bringing both disabilities and sickness. The wind has been blamed for bringing various epidemics such as cholera, but more commonly and in a more general sense it is seen as a cause of polio.

Beliefs about *dabeyl* represent a mixture of suspected causes behind a symptom and descriptions of the symptoms as such. This issue was particularly well illustrated in a series of interviews I conducted with two polio victims and people in their social vicinity. One of them was a forty-year-old man who had suffered from polio in his youth. The other was a mother of three children who was sick at the time of the interviews and whose way of presenting her illness was described in the previous section. The interviews suggested that the standard translation of the term *dabeyl* as "polio" may not always be accurate. For both these informants the concept *dabeyl* covered a wide range of symptoms, disorders, and causes of misfortune in general.

Among the Hubeer *dabeyl* is subdivided into four major types. They are *dabeyl insi* (the wind of the evil eye), *dabeyl jinni* (the wind of the spirits), *dabeyl lab* (the male wind), and *dabeyl dheddig* (the female wind). *Dabeyl insi* is said to be synonymous with *af-dad*, "people's vicious tongues," and *cayu-umanaas* (from Arabic), "evil eye." It is a type of *dabeyl* that is believed to be incurable by both modern and traditional methods. As will be noted, the term itself identifies the disease with its supposed origin but says little about the nature of its effects. The same observation applies to *dabeyl jinni*. This is a type of *dabeyl* that is believed to originate with invisible spiritual beings, which may, for instance, enter the stomach of pregnant women. Finally, the distinction between the "male" and "female" varieties of *dabeyl* relates to the severity of the symptoms, whatever these may be. The more severe *dabeyl* afflictions are regarded as "female," while lighter (*khafiif*) types are "male."

The various subtypes are not exclusive classes. The "wind of the spirits" and "the wind of the evil eye" distinguish between sources of the disease, and the other two types distinguish the severity of affliction.[15] Thus, even when the illness-label *dabeyl* has been agreed upon, the flexibility of subtypes appears to give room for radically new interpretations of the same basic symptoms.

As cases of illness stretch out in time and a variety of treatments has been tried, the labels are affected. It may happen that a specialist whose treatment involves divinatory practices discards the illness-label presented by the sick person or the family and provides an entirely new definition. More commonly, however, illness-labels are redesigned by drawing upon the associations that a particular label may have with other illness-labels. In the case of the *dabeyl*-struck woman this was precisely what had happened. The original illness-label that the family had arrived at some two to three years previously was "pain in the legs." As the symptoms became worse, the term *dabeyl* was used more and more frequently. At that point no suffix had been appended, but gradually, and in the course of trying out different treatments, an understanding had emerged that no *jinni* could be held responsible for her ailments. Her affliction originally had been very "light," so it was regarded at first as a "male" type of *dabeyl*.

The woman was generally held to have been exceptionally beautiful, and many people who were close to the woman explained that because of her beauty she had fallen prey to the evil eye of others. The family was actually never quite explicit about this. The woman herself, however, said that it was quite clear to her that even if her illness was *dabeyl*, it had been brought on by someone who wanted to do her harm, and her suffering must therefore be regarded as caused by the evil eye. In a way, the family's hesitance in admitting this to others was a confirmation of that suspicion, since the best treatment for afflictions caused by the evil eye is to have the person responsible come to the sickbed of the affected person without being aware of the suspicions.

At the time of my meeting with her, the family and the woman herself were still adhering to the definition of her problem as *dabeyl,* but they had appended to the illness-label the fact that she appeared incurable. It was now regarded as *dabeyl* of the "female," hard kind. It was apparent that the husband had exhausted the range of resources he had access to. Even the woman's brothers, who previously had been urging the husband to continue his efforts, now seemed more and more disengaged. To some extent it was the in-built dynamics of the illness-label itself that had allowed this situation to emerge. While it originally directed the family's search for treatments in a certain direction, it also provided a rationale for inactivity and a reason for the failure of the various treatments that had been tried.

MERCY OR REHABILITATION?

There is in Somalia no articulated idea that a handicap is the result of a combination of physiological constitution and social circumstances. Disabled people who lead "normal" lives are held to do so through their own personal ability, but the importance of the support extended to them is usually neglected. Such measures are seen as a religious duty of showing mercy and are not deemed to have any role in enhancing the opportunities of the disabled. In a similar way, people pay considerable attention to the problems of the disabled in their communities and families. However, they do this out of pity or mercy, and there is little awareness of the potentials for rehabilitating, finding roles, or developing adapted life-styles for the disabled. Although it is possible to find cases of successfully rehabilitated individuals,[16] they are not held up as examples for others. Their success is held to derive from their own personal abilities, whereas the role of the training they received is little appreciated. In other words, there seems to be no idea that the quality of the support system that a disabled person may rely upon can affect the degree to which the impairment will become disabling for that person. In this view, the disability cannot be altered by training or rehabilitation; all treatments are designated as treatments for the impairment only.

This is not to say that these Somalis hold that one should not care for disabled people. However, to my knowledge there is no notion that such care and support may in any way affect the disability as such. It is regarded as compulsory to show mercy to the disabled. This attitude finds some support from religious texts[17] and in a general feeling for how one should behave toward severely sick people. That feeling was once explained to me in a way that captured some of the attitudes toward immobility: there are two categories of people that one must always visit and even, when it is called for, bring food. They are the imprisoned and those who are sick for a long time. However, these special provisions for some categories of ill people are not seen as something that will enable the person to ease the constraints that the disability imposes. Nor can food brought to someone in prison set that person free. It should be done as a matter of mercy, guided by religious duty. Families are held to be able to perform this duty more or less satisfactorily, depending on their circumstances, but whatever the case might be, it is the impairment that affects the disabled, not their families.

CONCLUSION

A difficulty in approaching issues relating to disabled people in Somalia is the fact that the Somali definition of disability is much more limited than the Western one(s). If the disabled are singled out as a unified category at all, the concept covers only those with very visible physical impairments, and they are hardly representative of the majority of Somali disabled. Most disabled people are instead seen and treated as sick people, and that, I submit, is a key factor shaping the situation for the Somali disabled. On all levels, resource allocation in family health management proceeds from the small to the large; a first sign of illness—in the case of children at least—will be observed and acted upon only by mothers. Gradually, beginning within the household, other people are introduced to the problem. As expertise external to the household is consulted, personal relations and kinship guide the selection of the healer. Even with such a widening sphere of people and resources mobilized, there is a final point beyond which further health seeking is seen as pointless, or where costs in money, time, and relations would be too high.

Yet the process of disability is not determined only by cost-benefit calculations along the various routes of health seeking. Equally important is the way in which self-diagnosis and household labeling of illness relate to both selection of experts and communication with them. Illness-labels that summarize the causes of a health disorder and indicate the most salient symptoms serve within the household to attract attention to particular aspects of a member's health. In communicating with experts and healers, the illness-labels replace detailed presentation of etiologies, and many of the labels that most frequently apply to the disabled are of a nature that directly suggest the type of healer to consult. While illness-labels are chosen at a fairly early stage of a disability process, they are continuously changed or modified to represent the current state of health and the outcome of cures received. When household resources are exhausted, illness-labels appear to provide a mirror for the despair and reflect—in health terms—the incurability of the disease. That view is also reified by metaphoric imagery of the illness in terms of immobility.

I have attempted to take seriously the fact that the Hubeer do not discriminate firmly between disability and disease. The practices and ideas surrounding disabled people can be described within the framework of health seeking and health management through which all health problems are processed. There is good reason to do so; not only is the line between being disabled and being sick indistinct, but the same values and indicators of health are used for both categories. In fact, some of the constraints on disabled people's roles relate to them being subjected to the same criteria for evaluation as people with "ordinary" disease.

Such criteria are the subjective experience of being well or ill, often expressed in terms of the degree of pain, and the ability to move about and take part in the stream of social events. For the Hubeer a normal person is a mobile person. The values attached to mobility are not restricted to peoples' movement but are also reflected in the concerns they have for fluidity of the blood and expeditious digestion. Inactivity signals that something is wrong, and prolonged immobility is a sign of severe illness.

Although Hubeer culture draws no sharp line between normality and deviance but to the contrary encourages an amount of deviance as an aspect of personal identity, the immobility imposed by a physical handicap tends often to separate disabled and nondisabled people. Personhood to the Hubeer is a becoming; it is never fixed but continuously shifting and growing with the accumulation of experience and age. Frustrations, disappointments, and illness affect the totality of the person as much as triumph and success do. Both positive and negative influences are calculated ingredients of life, but there is a point beyond which one's ability to cope with disappointment begins to vanish and when no strength remains for seeking remedies for an undesired situation. At that point the Hubeer apply terms like *naafo* or *boos,* concepts that imply that nothing more can be done. For some disabled people, this may leave no alternative but begging. As a beggar, a disabled person will be confined to a role as "God's protégé," pitied, feared, and subjected to the mercy of others. Even if most disabled people do not end up as beggars, the very fact of their immobility seems to produce attitudes similar to those normally reserved for the destitute.

Just as the Hubeer appreciate mobile persons, they also value an agile mind. Stupidity and madness are likened to infertility and death, and the mentally disabled are often treated harshly outside of their families. A person is defined by being in the nexus of a series of continuously shifting influences, but that also puts high demands on receptivity. A physical impairment may reduce one's ability to respond to changes in life situation, but a mental defect does not even allow such changes to be perceived. That is probably a major reason why so few cases of mental disability enter the process of health seeking, compared to other types of disability.

The process through which a disability is created among the Hubeer is linked to, and to a large extent shaped by, their pattern of health seeking. In a system like the Somali one, it is impossible therefore to approach a single category of disabilities, or even the whole field of disability, without relating it to how health care is managed more generally. I suggest that this may have a more general validity for the anthropology of disability, for in any society the range of resources available for the disabled emanates from the same sources within the household as those for sick people in general. Disabilities everywhere are socially produced through processes that often are related to those that handle ordinary illness. It is therefore highly relevant to direct further attention to precisely how different local health traditions mold the lives of the disabled.

NOTES

1. Fieldwork in the Somali Democratic Republic was carried out during 1983 and 1984–1985 and was supported by generous grants from the Council for Research in the Humanities and Social Sciences (HSFR) and the Swedish Agency for Research Cooperation (SAREC), and the Helge Axelson Johnson Foundation. A brief field study in 1988 was funded by SAREC, WHO, and UNICEF. The work in a community-based research project area and a rehabilitation center was facilitated by the kind cooperation of the Norwegian Red Cross and the Somali Red Crescent Society. I would like to thank B. W. Andrzejewski, Ellen Gruenbaum, Einar Helander, Amina Warsaame, and Susan Reynolds Whyte for their constructive criticism of earlier drafts of this chapter.

2. In discussing various types of disabilities, I will occasionally make use of the WHO categorization as outlined by E. Helander et al. (1989), and now used globally as a basis for community-based rehabilitation (CBR). While the WHO definition is functional, it should not be forgotten that it is a desktop product, founded in a particular ethnomedical tradition—that of Western biomedicine (Hahn and Kleinman 1983). Whenever I speak of "the disabled" here, I do so in a general sense referring to a state of personal activity limitation established by the social recognition of an impairment or functional limitation.

3. The cosmological dimension of personal identity is a kind of knowledge that has sacred attributes and is regarded as a privileged domain of the clergy (B. Helander 1988b).

4. One afternoon I was sitting with an assistant outside my hut transcribing tapes from interviews. A woman who was passing by yelled at us asking what we were doing. My assistant answered, slightly annoyed, "Go away, we are working." The woman replied: "How can you be working when you are sitting down?"

5. The reduced mobility that comes with increasing age does not have that so-cially confining character. On the contrary, it is regarded as natural that old people should like to sit and do little but talk with one another.

6. This is reminiscent of the way in which medical labeling in the European tra-dition has assigned particular physiologies to different social statuses (Foucault 1963). See also Sontag 1977.

7. For many Somali the term *baano* designates primarily food supplied dur-ing convalescence and not so much the treatments applied during initial stages of illness.

8. I have elsewhere given a more detailed description of the medicinalization of rural health care (see B. Helander 1990b).

9. For a more complete inventory of traditional health resources and types of healers, see A. M. Ahmed 1988.

10. A *marre* is the reading of the entire Koran once. Sometimes more than one such reading may be performed.

11. However, when it comes to making positive remarks about others, one should, conversely, avoid phrasing them in a general way because that could be in-terpreted as envy. For instance, rather than saying "your shirt is nice," one should say "that shirt is nice for you."

12. A common painkiller of Kenyan origin. Its name in Somali means "good medicine."

13. It should be added that both terms, and particularly *tacabaan,* can be used in conversations with much less of the serious overtones that they have when applied specifically to describe one's state of health.

14. The proverb is *nin buka boqol u tali,* and it means literally "spend a hundred [shilling, sheep, etc.] on a sick person." If instead the final vowel of the word *buka* is long, *bukaa,* the subject and object of the verb *tali* change, and the meaning becomes instead that the sick person commands many people. I am grateful to Professor B. W. Andrzejewski for his valuable expertise on this issue.

15. From the cases I came across, it appeared that the spirit type of *dabeyl* was more capricious and could end as suddenly as it had begun, whereas the evil eye type gave more permanent injuries. Hence the latter type would more often develop into a "female" type of affliction.

16. For examples, see B. Helander 1990b.

17. The Fourth Surah of the Koran ('Women'), which deals with marriage and inheritance, bids believers to manage the property of the feeble-minded and to pro-vide for them from it.

REFERENCES

Ablon, J.
  1984   *Little People in America: The Social Dimensions of Dwarfism.* New York: Praeger Publishers.
Ahmed, A. M.
  1988   Somali traditional healers: Role and status. In *Proceedings of the Third International Congress of Somali Studies,* ed. A. Puglielli. Rome: Gangemi Editori.

Estroff, S.
 1981   *Making It Crazy: An Ethnography of Psychiatric Clients in an Ameri-
             can Community.* Berkeley, Los Angeles, London: University of Cali-
             fornia Press.
Foucault, M.
 1963   *The Birth of the Clinic.* Reprint. London: Routledge, 1976.
Frank, G.
 1984   *On Embodiment: A Case Study of Congenital Limb Deficiency in Ameri-
             can Culture.* New York: Wennergren Foundation Working Papers
             in Anthropology.
Goldin, C. S.
 1990   Stigma, biomedical efficacy, and institutional control. *Social Science
             and Medicine* 30:895–900.
Groce, N.
 1985   *Everyone Here Spoke Sign Language: Hereditary Deafness on Martha's Vine-
             yard.* Cambridge, Mass.: Harvard University Press.
Groce, N., and J. Scheer
 1990   Introduction. *Social Science and Medicine* 30:v–vi.
Gwaltney, J.
 1970   *The Thrice Shy: Cultural Accommodation to Blindness and Other Disasters
             in a Mexican Community.* New York: Columbia University Press.
Hahn, R. A., and A. Kleinman
 1983   Biomedical practice and anthropological theory. *Annual Review of
             Anthropology* 12:305–333.
Halantine, F. Q., and G. Berge
 1990   Perceptions of disabilities among the Kel Tamasheq of Northern
             Mali. In *Disability in a Cross-Cultural Context*, ed. F. J. Bruun and B.
             Ingstad, Working paper no. 4. Oslo: Department of Social Anthro-
             pology, University of Oslo.
Helander, B.
 1988a   The slaughtered camel: Coping with fictitious descent among the
             Hubeer of Southern Somalia. Ph.D. thesis, Uppsala University.
 1988b   Individuality as mysticism: On the Somali concept *burji.* In *Proceed-
             ings of the Third International Congress of Somali Studies,* ed. A. Puglielli.
             Rome: Gangemi Editori.
 1989   Incorporating the unknown: The power of Southern Somali medi-
             cine. In *Culture, Experience, and Pluralism: Essays on African Ideas of Ill-
             ness and Healing,* ed. A. Jacobson-Widding and D. Westerlund. Stock-
             holm: Almqvist and Wiksell International.
 1990a   Mercy or rehabilitation: Culture and the prospects for disabled in
             Southern Somalia. In *Disability in a Cross-Cultural Context,* ed. F. J.
             Bruun and B. Ingstad. Working paper no. 4. Oslo: Department of So-
             cial Anthropology, University of Oslo.
 1990b   Getting the most out of it: Nomadic health care seeking and the state
             in Southern Somalia. *Nomadic Peoples,* no. 25–27:122–132.

Helander, E., P. Mendis, G. Nelson, and A. Goerdt
    1989   *Training the Disabled in the Community: A Manual on Community-based Rehabilitation for Developing Countries.* Geneva: WHO/UNICEF/ ILO/UNESCO.
Ingstad, B.
    1991   The myth of the hidden disabled: A study of community-based rehabilitation in Botswana. Working paper. Oslo: Section for Medical Anthropology, University of Oslo.
Lewis, I. M.
    1963   Dualism in Somali notions of power. *Journal of the Royal Anthropological Institute of Great Britain and Ireland* 93:109–116.

Murphy, R., J. Scheer, Y. Murphy, and R. Mack
    1988   Physical disability and social liminality: A study in the rituals of adversity. *Social Science and Medicine* 26:235–242.
Sontag, S.
    1977   *Illness as Metaphor.* New York: Random House.
Talle, A.
    1990   Notes on the concept of disability among the pastoral Maasai in Kenya. In *Disability in a Cross-Cultural Context,* ed. F. J. Bruun and B. Ingstad. Working paper no. 4. Oslo: Department of Social Anthropology, University of Oslo.

FIVE

Why Disabled? The Cultural Understanding of Physical Disability in an African Society

Patrick Devlieger

A society reveals itself in the way it handles certain important phenomena.[1] Disability is one such phenomenon (Stiker 1982:25). Looking at disability from a cultural point of view starts with asking questions such as, What does disability mean in a certain society? How is the status of the person with a disability determined by the culture in which he/she lives? What are the most important issues when talking about disability in a certain society?

These questions are linked here to development of services for persons with disabilities in so-called developing countries. New developments in service provision have not eliminated previous cultural beliefs (Jackson and Mupedziswa 1988). We are now beginning to see that rehabilitation concepts and procedures must not be drawn only from developments in Western countries, neglecting contributions from beliefs, practices, and attitudes in local culture, such as that of the Songye of Zaire, the subject of this study. The notion that cultural beliefs are only barriers to development is changing.

Traditional beliefs "have to be understood before implementing any kind of community-based rehabilitation" (Momm and König 1989). Understanding is the basis for a dialogue between service providers and persons with disabilities in a local society. In such a dialogue, people should be given a chance to discuss elements of their culture and reinterpret them. This understanding of culture, supplemented with skills of counseling and guidance, will give the service provider the ability to work "with," not necessarily "against," culture. An understanding that is complemented by the necessary skills would greatly contribute to the emergence of genuine African concepts of rehabilitation.

I make a first attempt to develop such a concept in this chapter. Following Henri-Jacques Stiker (1982), my attempt is semiotic because I am interested in understanding a cultural universe. However, it is also pragmatic, since it concerns the development of rehabilitation services. There are inherent limitations in this attempt. First, the data on which I rely reflect the ideas of only one African people, so that generalizations for Africa as a whole should be excluded. Second, the collection of data was limited to persons and relatives of persons with physical disabilities of the upper and lower limbs. No generalization to other types of disabilities should be made.

The methodology used here involves examining the various categories of abnormality in a cosmology and contrasting them with the Western concept of disability. Further, I demonstrate the kinds of issues disability raises in a given culture, showing that whereas the concern of Western societies is to improve on the lives of people with disabilities, in some African societies, such as the Songye of Zaire,[2] the primary interest is in explaining why they are as they are. Traditional medical treatment of illnesses is very common in Songye society, and disability might at the onset be treated as if it were an illness. However, the idea of rehabilitation as a continuous effort of improving and accommodating the living conditions of persons with disabilities is basically a Western idea that is foreign to Songye thought. Instead, the Songye have developed in their culture alternative ways and means of coping with disability. Living with the limits of the disability rather than surpassing them seems to be the most important norm.

I will first put the social status of the child with a disability into a holistic picture of cultural categories and then show how the social status of the person with a disability is shaped by cultural beliefs.

PHYSICAL DISABILITY AND SOCIAL STATUS

Normality is a culturally construed notion that is strongly ethnocentric (Fougeyrollas 1987:54). This will be illustrated here by examining the Songye conceptualization of abnormal children.

For the Songye, deviations in the body can induce a higher, lower, or undetermined status in comparison with able-bodied people. Therefore, not all deviation is stigmatizing, and not all persons with disabilities are marginalized because of their disability. Within Songye society, three categories of children are distinguished as being abnormal: ceremonial (*mishinga*), bad (*malwa*), and faulty (*bilema*) children. The English word *disability* does not correspond to any of the categories that are distinguished in the Songye terminology. Although both "bad" and "faulty" children would be classified as having physical disabilities in most Western societies, these are different categories in Songye society. Bad children are associated with the dead; faulty children are not.

Ceremonial children receive special ceremonies, they are given specific names, and some of them are believed to have special power and healing ca-

pacities. All these characteristics confer a higher status. Examples of ceremonial children are: the child who holds off the rain,[3] twins, and children
born with the umbilical cord around the neck, with a hand on the cheek, or
with feet or hands first. In Western societies these characteristics are regarded at most as medical phenomena, which do not affect the social status
of such a child.

Bad children, in contrast, are considered inferior to other members of
the society, not even human beings. They are supernatural because they
were in contact with the anti-world of sorcerers. They come to this world to
stay for a short time and afterward return to their own world. In this category are albino, dwarf, and hydrocephalic children. They are given basic
care, but all parents expect them to die sooner or later, for the Songye believe these children did not come to earth to live but to die. Such children
are truly marginal, and hence their interaction with their surrounding
world is limited.

Faulty children (*mwana wa kilema*, lit. "a child with a fault") are those with
not only an imperfection of the body but also a distorted relationship. In
fact, attention is more geared toward the distorted relation than toward the
disability itself and the person who has it. These children have deformed upper or lower limbs as the result of diseases such as poliomyelitis, or birth
complications that result in spasticity or congenital deformities such as clubfoot. In contrast to ceremonial children, they are not given higher respect
because of their nature, nor do they, as in the case of bad children, receive
an inferior status. Their status is betwixt and between (Turner 1967), undetermined. This is probably because the fault is permanent, without any
change. Bad children, in contrast, are expected to die. The undetermined
status that characterizes faulty children has been called the liminal status
(Murphy et al. 1988).

The liminal status of faulty people, their ubiquitous presence in everyday
life, and the fact that services for people with disabilities are very much limited in Songye society mean that an attitude of indifference toward improvement of the person's situation prevails. Much more attention is given
to interpreting the fault. That issue is tackled by the family in a search for the
cause, a process in which the person with the fault may be left out completely.
In this view, the fault is only a symptom of something more important.
Hence, a solution needs to be found for the problem that underlies the fault.

The positive side of this situation is that the person with a disability is
seen not as an abnormal, a marginal, or a deviant figure but as a liminal
one. This does not give the person an a priori negative status that has to be
changed; the person, like any other, is seen as having "potential," with a
right to development.

Persons with disabilities are not necessarily viewed negatively by able-
bodied people. A popular proverb says, "Do not mock the faulty; God keeps

on creating you" (*Tosepanga lemene; Efile kiakupanga*). Some proverbs even induce an attitude of respect, such as "When the person with a fault enters, the door is completely shut" (*Ha mulemane utwela, kibi e kubuwa kingo*). This proverb means that the wisdom of a person with a fault can be used; one may discuss problems with a faulty person that should not be heard by the indiscreet.

Some other proverbs, however, indicate that people with faults should not try to surpass themselves and should engage only in activities that fit their capacities: "When the drums go fast, the dance should go fast too" (*Ngoma lubilo, masha lubilo*). This means that those who do not know how to dance fast should not dance. This idea is even better expressed in proverbs from other African people, such as the Wolof proverb "A blind man should not jump holes" (*Gumba du tëb pax*).[4] People with faults are at the same time part of normality and not part of it. These proverbs are clear messages for people on how to cope with a fault. The message is that disabled people deserve a certain respect, but that they also should accept their limitations.

COPING WITH DISABILITY IN SONGYE SOCIETY

There are many patterns of coping with a disability of the upper and lower limbs in Songye society. Children and adults who are not able to walk long distances are given specific tasks in the village. Children with walking problems are responsible for looking after younger brothers and sisters and taking care of the house in the absence of their parents. Simple devices are used to facilitate walking, such as a stick or wooden blocks. The simplicity makes these devices superior in many ways to more complex ones because their maintenance and replacement are very easy. In the course of a development project for children with physical disability, when these children were given calipers, although simply made by Western standards, these devices could not be maintained or replaced, and the children eventually returned to homemade devices.

For a Songye woman, however, major disability of the upper or lower limbs that inhibits daily activities such as fetching water, cutting wood, and washing clothes is a serious situation, since performing these tasks is imperative for an adult woman. The marriage chances for such a woman are virtually nonexistent, in contrast to marriage potential for men with a similar disability.[5] However, there is a pattern of coping for such a woman which leads ultimately to a more or less independent life. Such a woman may conceive a child and stay with her parents until the child is approximately ten years old. At her parents' home, the woman performs activities that can be done seated. Once her child is capable of performing simple daily tasks that the mother cannot perform, such as fetching water, cleaning, and bringing messages, a house is built for the woman and her child. With the help of her child and without ever being married, the woman leads a more or less independent life.

DISABILITY ISSUES SHAPED BY CULTURE

For the Songye, the most important issue concerning a fault is answering the question "Why?" They seek the cause of a fault through exploring the relation between human beings and their environment, in search of an ultimate answer to the question "Why disabled?" This question is afforded fewer answers in a Western context (Ingstad 1988) and receives, therefore, less attention. What Robert Murphy (1987:89) writes might be true for many persons with disabilities in the West: "In all those years since the onset of my illness, I have never consciously asked, 'Why me?' I feel that this is a foolish question that assumes some cosmic sense of purpose and direction in the universe that simply does not exist." In the African context, Murphy's view is unacceptable. "Coincidence" is an unsatisfactory answer to those personally involved, and their search for reasons lends itself to explanation in terms of the supernatural (Cheater 1986:166). Just as the question "Why?" is of less importance in a Western context, so the mechanics of improving the living conditions of persons with disabilities is not of paramount interest in the traditional Songye context. Since the question "Why?" is central, not much attention is given to the person with the disability as an individual. That person is integrated into normal life in an indifferent way, without ceremonial, without a lot of medical attention, but without being hidden.

The reason for disability will be sought through profound analysis of various hypothetical levels of relationship between human beings and their environment. Relationship with the *physical environment* will be examined, as will relationship with *family members* through sorcery and bridewealth, and finally relations with the *ancestors*. If none of these relations can be identified as distorted, then God is seen as the cause of the disability. God is a residual category that is used when no other cause can be found. God denotes the sphere beyond the control of human beings (Burck 1989). These various levels of relationship are distinguished here for the sake of clarity of explanation and may, therefore, give a somewhat static impression. However, the actual exploration of relations is a dynamic process that is the result of consultation with many significant others. In this process people might change their opinions about the cause of the disability as a result of these consultations or as a result of important events that occur. In the course of time some explanations of the cause, for example, in terms of sorcery, might become irrelevant and be replaced by more general or less harmful explanations, such as attributing the cause to God.

It is appropriate here to clarify the relation between the emic category of thinking about the causes in terms of *relationship,* and thinking in terms of *congenital* or *acquired,* which could be called an etic category. At first view one would imagine that a "congenital disability" (etic) would fit with "caused by God" (emic) and an "acquired disability" (etic) with "caused by human beings through sorcery" (emic). Although this would be true in many cases, it does not always hold; there are clear cases in which congenital disability is interpreted in terms of relationships.

PHYSICAL ENVIRONMENT

The relation with the *physical environment* finds expression in the food prescriptions and sex taboos that pregnant women must observe. The nonobservance of some of these taboos leads to disability. Important to the Songye are the taboo (*bishila*) on eating certain types of meat and the prescription to eat more of other types. It is believed that eating forbidden types of meat will cause the characteristics of the animal to be transmitted to the child, which will be apparent at its birth.

A child born with a certain characteristic, for example, too weak, without hair, or having small sores, might remind the parents that they did not respect the food or sex taboos. Such children are said to be "born with a habit" (*batandika na kipikua*), which is considered impossible to heal or to treat. In such cases, people merely watch how the habit develops. If the habit evolves negatively, it is considered "a fault" and the child is placed in the category of children with faults (*baana ba bilema*).

The Songye observe many food taboos in order to ensure the birth of a healthy child. Some foods forbidden to pregnant women are the meat of antelope (*mbudi*), which is to prevent the child being born with hemorrhoids (*lupusu lwa mbudi*); the meat of sheep (*mukooko*), which can cause a child to be born like a lamb (weak and unable to hold up its head); and the meat of snake (*nyoka*) because "the snake cannot stand up," which results in a child called *kisheta,* who crawls too long before walking. The consumption of other foods is recommended, such as monkey (*nsoko*), which will influence the child to be astute, or mongoose (*nkankalankala*), which makes a child have harmonious movements. If a child is identified at birth as having a habit, the mother, father, or both parents are reprimanded for their behavior by their relatives and reminded to behave well in future.

SORCERY

Sorcery is the most important explanation of evil among the Songye. It is the cultural instrument that explains disability as the result of infringed relations between members of the same family. Most important are the relations between the parents and their close relatives and between co-wives.

The Songye of Zaire identify different types of sorcery to explain different types of evil. For example, the strongest type of sorcery, *masende*, causes the immediate death of its victim. The world of sorcery is the opposite of the normal world, like night to day, like death to life. It is believed that some people live an ordinary life during the day while they live the life of a sorcerer at night. The sorcerer seeks an increase of power through evil. The easiest victims are found among people who are weak because they did not respect certain rules or have shown bad behavior. In this sense, sorcery comes to people as a punishment for their weak moral state. Therefore, sorcery happens in families where the family ties are not tight. Sorcerers "attack" in families where there are quarrels.

From there, it can be understood that sorcery functions as a strong social control system. The occurrence of disability in the family is the starting point for an inquiry into the relations of the family. If bad relations are discovered to have existed prior to the occurrence of the disability, sorcery will be blamed for the disability, as in the following example.

> The cause of spasticity in a child was sought in the quarrels between the mother and her brother-in-law when the mother was pregnant. In the course of those disputes, the brother-in-law had told the mother she would vomit her child instead of delivering it in the normal way. The mother had never forgotten the words of the brother-in-law and believed that she was the victim of sorcery. However, she did not accuse her brother-in-law because she could not prove that he practices sorcery.

The primary importance of an investigation of relationships is also clear in a situation where the cause of the disability is attributed to envy (*kifita*) as a motive for sorcery. A family that distinguishes itself from other families by its prosperity can be affected by envy, resulting in a child that is different from other children. The belief that children with disabilities occur more often in rich and polygamous families is quite widespread. The following account given by a Luba boy who was born with a clubfoot illustrates the belief in envy as a cause of disability.

> My birth is surrounded with a history. In the 1960s, we left Kananga to settle down in East-Kasai, namely in Katanda, my birth village. When my mother came from Kananga, she had eight children. The family was rich and we lived easily. All this made the villagers envious and that has caused my disability.

The relation between co-wives is another fertile ground for seeking the cause of disability, as in the following case.

The cause of the disability of a girl who had polio was sought in the relationship with her half-sister (the daughter of the first wife of her father). This half-sister had several times declared that the second wife was a sorcerer. In addition, she had declared, in the presence of her father, that she would bewitch the second wife and her children.

When a disability, a deformed leg, became apparent in the second wife's child, the second wife complained to her husband about earlier statements made by the first wife's sorcerer-daughter. The husband acted on that and took the sorcerer-daughter to a healer. The girl vomited. In the vomit, a piece of meat, fire, a chair, and a snail shell were discovered. The healer said the meat symbolizes the material through which the sorcerer-daughter was introduced into the world of sorcerers, the fire symbolizes their bad force, the chair stood for her presence during the meeting of sorcerers, and in the snail shell the power of sorcery was kept. A long time later the sorcerer-daughter was brought to a prophet of a religious community. There, she vomited the shell of a tortoise, also a symbol of bad forces. Then the sorcerer-daughter was healed from sorcery.

It is important to consider here that the belief in sorcery and the inquiry into relations within the family assume that the problem of disability is not a problem of the individual but rather a problem of the family. Disability is made a relational problem between human beings. The search for a cause of the disability in terms of relationships is different from an explanation in biomedical terms. In biomedicine the distinction between what happened before and after birth is decisive, and from there, the distinction between a congenital and an acquired disability is made. These biomedical categories do not make sense when searching for the cause of disability in terms of relationships.

ANCESTORS

When a disability is obvious at birth, it will be attributed to sorcery only when there is a clear remembrance of bad family relations. Generally, the Songye belief is that a sorcerer does not have access to the womb of a pregnant woman. Thus in most cases the relationship with the *ancestor* becomes the focus in the search for the cause. Respect for the ancestor and the ancestor's rules is the issue.

Respect for the ancestor finds its focal expression in the burial. The Songye believe that an ancestor who was not buried with due respect can be reborn with a fault, manifesting his or her anger. The belief in reincarnation is very strong. A child who is born with certain characteristics will sometimes be considered to be an ancestor who has come back into the family. It can be any member of the family, or even a friend. The important point is that there was a very strong friendship between the deceased and the father or the mother of the newborn. The event is announced to the pregnant woman, usually in a dream. If a child is born with a "fault" (*kilema*), this can be taken to mean that the child is born with "the spirit of the ancestor" (*busangu*). It can be said that the ancestor was not properly buried. For example, in the case of a child born with a clubfoot, the interpretation was that the ancestor was not well buried; his coffin was too small so that his legs were pressed too much.

When the ancestral rules are not well respected, as in the case of adultery or theft, the ancestors may manifest their anger toward members of the family through the birth of a child with a disability or through abortion. Disability is then considered as a punishment for bad behavior. It is clear that these beliefs function as a strong social control mechanism.

BRIDEWEALTH

Another cultural system that is of great importance and sometimes related to the occurrence of disability in Songye belief is the *bridewealth*, the goods given by the family of the man to the family of the wife as part of the marriage arrangements. It is a compensation for the loss of a woman and is considered to be a proof of the seriousness and stability of the marriage.

When disability occurs in a family, the father of the child with the disability might ask his wife's family whether the goods that were donated for the bridewealth were well received and distributed in the family. The father might discover from his inquiries that his mother-in-law or some of the brothers did not receive enough and therefore they hold a grievance toward him. This would then be considered the cause of the disability. The father might solve the problem by asking the father-in-law to redistribute some goods or by donating other gifts. In contrast to reactions to disability in a Western context, the function of these Songye solutions is the restoration of relationships in the community.

GOD

In most cases Songye explain disability as caused by God (*Efile Mukulu*). When the cause of the disability cannot be deciphered in social-familial terms, God as absolute and unknown force remains as the only possibility and the final cause. God is considered to be the source of everything, good as well as evil. God is one entity which is at the same time favorable and unfavorable; this is a bifacial, ambivalent God. As God is the source of everything, he gives the liberty to cause evil. Sorcerers can cause evil with the authorization of God, in which case evil is like a test, or they can cause evil without authorization, when the evil is a "maleficio" (*kifita*). It is believed that the sorcerer who attacks with *kifita* seeks out easy victims, who are vulnerable because of poor relations with family members, ancestors, and even God.

For the Songye, an explanation of the cause of a disability can never be limited to the biomedical level. The explanation is part of a broader inclusive view. Although a biomedical explanation may be accepted, that does not mean it is sufficient. In biomedical thinking, of course, most of these relations are considered irrelevant.

CONCLUSION

In view of the tremendous emphasis on analyzing relationships when a disability is considered, we must conclude that a good understanding of the person with a disability goes far beyond the individual characteristics of the person and places him in the framework of a wider social-cultural system. The relational nature of explanations of disability has been emphasized as characteristic of African cosmologies in general (Cheater 1986) and has important implications for rehabilitation programs. The development of programs for persons with disabilities in Africa should take this information into account. However, in existing community-based rehabilitation programs and even family support services, an individual approach to the disabled child, based on an appreciation of the child's skills and the nature of the disability, is dominant. For community-based programs, whose aim is to support families with children with disabilities, a methodology should be developed in which knowledge of traditional beliefs is incorporated.

When developing such a methodology, the following guidelines should be observed:

1. An examination of focal points in relationships should be the core of such a methodology. Focal points in relationships are those moments that are recalled when people search for the cause of the disability. An examiner can usually obtain such background information rather easily, provided a relation of trust can be built up. Community fieldworkers can ask parents what they believe to be the reason for the disability of their child. They can also examine the cultural system of the family they are working with, provided they have a good understanding of these systems.

2. The background information on relationships should be used in a problem-solving action aiming at the formation of strong relationships and the restoration of any weak relationships.

3. Strong relationships will form a good basis for the integration of persons with disabilities. In the course of the problem-solving work,

important persons in the context should be identified who can support the person with the disability and the family.
4. The identified important persons should become the first target
   group to be persuaded that those with disabilities are capable and
   have rights to education and employment equal to those of able-
   bodied persons. The same people may become very important resource persons in fulfilling conditions that can lead to integration.

The development and implementation of such a methodology could lead
to community mobilization on a small but effective scale. The condition for
this is a revision of the prevalent attitude that African thinking cannot be incorporated in service delivery because it is unscientific, primitive. It is now
recognized that there is a cultural dimension in development, and even
more, that culture should be the basis of all development (Verhelst 1987).
Further, it should be understood that there is a need for a methodology
in which "relationship" is the core concept, for it is clear that in African
thinking, the person with a disability is not the direct and primary focus
of solutions. Points in the broader environment, such as the disabled person's family, ancestors, and God, are the focus. Giving consideration to
these relationships will strengthen the family and benefit the person with the
disability.

An examination of relations should also be of interest in a Western context. One of the strengths of an African understanding of disability is the
recognition that it is not simply an abnormality of the individual body but
also a disruption in the family. More attention should be paid to the relational context in which the person with a disability exists, and greater efforts
should be made to involve and support important others.

An African approach to disability is concerned with the meaning that
biological deviations have for society, for the family, and for the individual.
In Stiker's terminology, it is metaphysical, in contrast to the modern Western approach, which is technical, focusing on the improvement of functions
and activities of daily living. Many Westerners feel dissatisfied with this nar-
row technical perspective, and they may ask whether the African model provides a more satisfying alternative. The answers that African cultures provide
to the question "Why disabled?" are based in their particular cosmologies
and social worlds. Indeed, it may be that the question itself is less pressing
in the West; we are less concerned with identifying causes in the African
sense. But causal explanations are not the only kind of meaning which may
be attributed to disability. Everywhere people try to work out a sense of purpose for their lives, and they are concerned with the existential implications
of bodily deviations. Murphy himself, who declared his lack of interest in the
question "Why me?" was abundantly concerned with other metaphysical
questions. African culture can teach us to be more attentive to the "why" of

disability in this general sense of existential issues with which individuals and families must grapple.

NOTES

1. I am grateful to Jeffrey Tines, Susan Reynolds Whyte, and Benedicte Ingstad for their valuable comments on earlier drafts of this chapter.
2. The Songye are a people living in the East-Kasai province of Zaire. The data used in this article were collected from 1983 to 1985 while the author worked as a volunteer of Withuis voluntariaat (Belgium) in a medical project for children with physical disabilities.
3. When the rains fail, it is believed that a child who has yet to be born is stopping the rains. The child is known through a dream. It will be given a specific name (*Ntumba*) and surrounded with ceremonies when it is born.
4. I am grateful to Papa Fall for providing me with this proverb.
5. A woman with a minor disability might be married. However, her father would not request the bridewealth or would ask for only part of it, mostly dependent on the goodwill of the son-in-law.

REFERENCES

Burck, D. J.
1989   *Kuoma Rupandi (The Parts Are Dry): Ideas and Practices about Disability in a Shona Ward*. Research report no. 36. Leiden: African Studies Centre.
Cheater, A. P.
1986   *Social Anthropology: An Alternative Introduction*. Gweru, Zimbabwe: Mambo.
Fougeyrollas, P.
1987   Normalité et corps différents: Regard sur l'integration sociale des handicapés physiques. *Anthropologie et Sciences* 2:51–71.
Ingstad, B.
1988   A model for analyzing the coping behaviour of disabled persons and their families: Cross-cultural perspectives from Norway and Botswana. *International Journal of Rehabilitation Research* 11(4):351–359.
Jackson, H., and R. Mupedziswa
1988   Disability and rehabilitation: Beliefs and attitudes among rural disabled people in a community-based rehabilitation scheme in Zimbabwe. *Journal of Social Development in Africa* 1:21–30.
Momm, W., and A. König
1989   *From community-based to community-integrated programmes: Experiences and reflections on a new concept of service provision for disabled people*. Geneva: ILO.
Murphy, R. F.
1987   *The Body Silent*. New York: Henry Holt.

Murphy, R. F., J. Scheer, Y. Murphy, and R. Mack
   1988   Physical disability and social liminality: A study in the rituals of adversity. *Social Science and Medicine* 26(2):235–242.

Stiker, H.-J.
   1982   *Corps infirmes et sociétés*. Paris: Aubier Montaigne.

Turner, Victor
   1967   *The Forest of Symbols: Aspects of Ndembu Ritual*. Ithaca, N.Y.: Cornell University Press.

Verhelst, T.
   1987   *Des racines pour vivre. Sud-Nord: Identités culturelles et développement*. Paris/Gembloux: Ducolot.

SIX

Being Ill and Being Me: Self, Body, and Time in Multiple Sclerosis Narratives

Judith Monks and Ronald Frankenberg

Life stories and illness narratives of sick and disabled people are increasingly valued tools in the investigation of personal experience and its shaping within larger social and cultural frameworks.[1] Their particular value has been said to lie in their breadth of contextualization (identified at various levels and across different domains) and in the insight they provide into how illness functions as an idiom for discussing and defining more general societal and cultural concerns (Early 1988:66–67; Farmer 1988:80; Kleinman 1988:50–51; Lang 1989:308, 319–320). They may also be set critically against clinical and other accounts (Frank 1984:640; 1986:192; Kaufman 1988:226), and in addition their temporal aspect has provided a medium for understanding the processual character of the phenomenology of illness and disability (Corbin and Strauss 1987:261–264; Frank 1986: 214; Kaufman 1988:218). To date, narrative data have been drawn almost exclusively from interview or other spoken or unpublished forms,[2] or occasionally from autobiographically inspired but fictional literature (see, e.g., Brody 1987). They are also available in published form as autobiographies and personal illness accounts.

The major defining characteristic of the life story genre is that it deals with aspects of an *individual* life. The structure, content, and sense of personhood and individuality that a life story conveys will be rooted in cultural conceptions of persons and individuals, and of what "makes" a life and a story in more formal terms. Both the notion of individuality and the typical structure of life stories as these appear in materials from Western industrialized societies have been seen as particular. Specifically, the location of individuality in consciousness has been associated with an emphasis on rationality, responsibility, and the continuity of a self that exists independently of both the sociocultural environment and bodily changes (Frank 1979:79; Gordon

1988:34–37; Scheper-Hughes and Lock 1987:14). The development of autobiographical writing has been seen as integrally associated with the history of this conceptualization, and particularly with the notion of the detached self or "reflexive self," able to stand back from, describe, and evaluate its own life (Frank 1979:82–83; Freccero 1986:16–17). While some recent theoretical developments have given less primacy to an autonomous self (see, e.g., Heller et al. 1986; Turner 1984), as Thomas Heller and his coauthors point out (1986:12), these seem so far to have had little effect on Western popular culture.

With reference to North American society, Juliet Corbin and Anselm Strauss (1987) have identified three major dimensions to the biographies of people with chronic illness, namely: self, body, and time. They regard self as a matter of personal identity: "who I am over the course of my biography" (ibid.:252). The body they see as providing a medium for action, which feeds into self-identity. Biographical time flows from the past, through the present, to the future, and, within this stream, at a day-to-day level, "clock time" must be juggled to accommodate different demands. The achieved sense of balance might emphasize illness as a major life focus, or illness might be integrated into the "fabric of being," becoming part of the "texture of biography." Severity of bodily impairment is assumed to be implicated in the extent to which illness may become contextual in this way (ibid.:250–251).

In this chapter we take up the themes of self, body, and time in relation to eight published narratives by people with multiple sclerosis (MS). Drawing on these data we were able to develop the conceptualizations provided by Corbin and Strauss. Specifically, we looked at the question of balance in people's lives in relation to time devoted to the self (particularly to personal projects) and time devoted to the body and disease. We could thus note the various biographical strategies whereby self-time ultimately came to predominate in all of the stories. We were able to compare the often subtle modes of representation of the body by distinguishing its "incarnate," "corporeal," and "somatic" aspects (Frankenberg 1990). The incarnate body encompasses a notion of a historical and actively experienced and experiencing body, in the phenomenological sense of being in the world. The corporeal (or more loosely, physical) body refers to a bounded biological entity, while the somatic body is one defined by medical technologies and is usually fragmented. These distinctions draw on the differentiation in German between *Lieb* (the lived body) and *Körper* (the physical structure) (Ots 1990).

Similarly, we found biographical time to be represented in a number of forms other than a linear flow from past to future, and we found that time within different life periods might have one of several different qualities. In considering the sequencing of events and periods that people wove into their stories, we found it helpful to refer to the concept of "liminality." Frankenberg (1986), following Turner, proposed this term to describe periods of novelty or antistructure wherein the routine constraints of daily life are relaxed. Such periods may be marked by expression rather than instrumentality, and they tend to allow personal idiosyncrasy a relatively easy outlet. In the current context (as indicated below) they provided opportunities for self-reflection and reorientation, and a link between periods of conventional structure which were different in kind. We should note here that Robert Murphy and his coauthors (1988) have used the notion of liminality in relation to the lives of people with disabilities in a different sense. They have suggested that the life histories of such people may be seen as arrested and "dramatized in a rite of passage frozen in its liminal stage" (ibid.:241). Thus their "state of being is clouded and indeterminate" (ibid.:238), falling ambiguously between sickness and wellness, living and dead, participation and exclusion. Ronald Frankenberg's usage, on the other hand, refers to liminal phases of *expressive* quality *within* the course of disablement or chronic sickness. It thus provides a framework for comparison which highlights the processual nature of sickness and incorporates personal endeavor as well as social constraint.

In the following section we describe the background to the study and give a brief overview of the material to be discussed. Then for each of the three major phases of the narratives (beginning, middle, and end), we compare authors' representations of self, body, and time in relation to events and more extended temporal periods. Here we note particularly the difference in narratives by authors who are also qualified health professionals and those of others. Finally we discuss the significance of the texts as more or less permanent exemplars.

BACKGROUND TO THE STUDY

For almost a decade, the Centre for the Study of Health, Sickness, and Disablement (CSHSD) at Brunel, the University of West London, U.K., has been carrying out sociological research related to multiple sclerosis (MS). Multiple sclerosis is a long-term incurable disease that affects the ability of the central nervous system to conduct electrical impulses, and it is associated with a variety of signs and symptoms that frequently relapse and remit. It is more common in women than men and is usually diagnosed in early adulthood (the third decade) when life plans are still uncertain or perhaps just beginning to be realized. The disease is not fatal in itself, but potentially very disabling. The uncertainty of prognosis and very marked variability (not only among people but for each person, even over short stretches of time) makes its accommodation difficult, not only for the person directly affected but also for her or his associates.

As an extension of its bibliographical brief, the CSHSD recently began to collect published accounts of people with MS, including those appearing in journals and edited volumes, as well as those published as separate works, or which appear as part of more general texts on management. Eight such texts have been obtained to date. While it is not claimed that the collection is exhaustive, there are sufficient points of interest even from this number to make reporting worthwhile.

The accounts varied widely in both form and length. Two were in book form (Davoud 1985; Rubenstein 1989), although that by Renate Rubenstein was much shorter, and less a formal autobiography than a series of reflections on life with disability, which drew on her own and her knowledge of others' experiences. Another relatively short account had been published privately as a booklet (Parkinson 1982). Three were written by health professionals: one nurse and two doctors. The nurse's account appeared as a paper in a professional journal (Kinley 1980), while that of one of the doctors formed part of a general collection of accounts by sick physicians (Chellingsworth 1987). The other doctor included her "Story" as the first section of a text on MS for a lay audience (Forsythe 1988).

The remaining two accounts formed contiguous sections of an edited collection concerned with the psychosocial aspects of MS: the first by a man (Brown 1984) and the second by a woman (Lowry 1984). John Brown's account was in fact the only one written by a man. Three of the texts reviewed were by British authors (Chellingsworth, Forsythe, Parkinson), one author was North American (Kinley), one German (Rubenstein), one Belgian (Davoud), and one was a New Zealander (Brown). The nationality of the remaining author, Florence Lowry, was unclear.

THE BEGINNING

The Announcement . . . She [psychiatrist] came. It was, she said, multiple sclerosis. . . . Lucky me, I thought. . . . Then she explained what the disease actually was, and my desire to think "lucky me" vanished. (Rubenstein 1989:19, 21)

That the accounts were essentially of the lives of people with MS was established early in all of the texts through detailed reference to the poignancy of the diagnosis. The diagnosis was an event that effectively separated the prior problematic period from the equally problematic, but qualitatively different, period that succeeded it. The "eventfulness" of the diagnosis, however, was also constructed in a different sense. What was significant was not a single episode at a specific time (the "telling" alone, for example), but a series of episodes that were encapsulated and represented as a unitary marker. Typically these would include a visit to the family doctor followed by one to a neurologist and an assortment of tests, often as a hospital in-patient. All these episodes were usually represented in a relatively short stretch of text, although the time could be considerable, in John Brown's case amounting to five years.

To be diagnosed as having an incurable, untreatable, and potentially progressive disease is a social event with devastatingly negative cultural connotations. Diagnosis disrupted the taken-for-granted meanings of daily experiences, and assumptions about what was or would be possible or feasible. The routine activities through which life was constructed and experienced could no longer take place in the way that they had. The body—its corporeal or physical aspect—was no longer an efficient and reliable instrument. It seemed to set its own agenda and have its own requirements, which competed with and inconvenienced preferred activities. In that the physical body provided means through which the self, as incarnate body, performed its social roles, these too had to be renegotiated. All this needed to be accomplished in the context of an "appropriate" response to the diagnosis. The authors "took" and were frequently "given" time to live through their shock.

The poignancy of the postdiagnostic period, and particularly the associated threats to selfhood, are seen in the terms in which authors refer to it:

> I had to leave that silent building [after hearing the diagnosis] on my own . . . I gazed in vain through a mist of disbelief for someone to share my awful truth with. I felt lost; utterly alone . . . I became a dreary soul at that time. (Brown 1984:23–24)

> The idea of a slow but inevitable deterioration . . . was certainly a devastating threat and was really too upsetting to think or talk about seriously. . . . The diagnosis was impossible for me to understand and I suspect for them [her children] it was equally meaningless. I was left with an unspeakable threat to my future and they were left with a mother who was concentrating on her own survival and pinning all her hopes on an incredibly restricted diet and a bottle of sunflower seed oil which she slurped down every morning rapidly followed by an orange. What a picture of family life!

> My husband came home very rarely during that miserable year. (Forsythe 1988:11–12)

It was the (often liminal) *quality* of these periods that was highlighted, not their length in terms of measured time or the chronology of episodes occurring within them. The major tasks of the period included informing relatives, friends, and work colleagues, and negotiating roles in terms of the help or concern desired or thought reasonable by both parties. In addition, there was seeking of information about the disease and possible treatments, and attention to the demands of the diseased body itself. Explicit concern with the now prominent physical (and sometimes somatic) body, accompanied by feelings of estrangement, was marked for Elizabeth Forsythe, Florence Lowry, and Liz Parkinson. Forsythe summed up her feelings:

> I was damaged; I hated my body being damaged in the sight of everybody and therefore everybody must hate my body as much as I did. I had become in some way an outcast and unlovable but at least deserving of pity. (Forsythe 1988:13)

For John Brown and Miriam Chellingsworth, however, work routine provided a structure that deflected attention from bodily timetables. They present a more fragmented picture of the difference of their relations with others, in terms of the persons they now were. The suffering seemed to be felt less publicly. Keeping up appearances was more important, although John Brown discovered later that his colleagues had been more aware and silently supportive than he had known.

Events not only mark the beginning but also the close of periods. The postdiagnostic period ended by both a spatial and temporal entry by the authors into a life with a more satisfactory balance between self and bodily demands. Liz Parkinson and Anne Kinley resumed their jobs; Nicole Davoud broke her "reverie" by taking trips outside the house and discovering the practical advantages of a wheelchair. Renate Rubenstein and Elizabeth Forsythe went (literally) in search of healing, and John Brown similarly sought and found a "shoulder to cry on." Miriam Chellingsworth's symptoms settled and she went away on holiday. Exclusive concentration on the disease and the physical body had ceased.

In Florence Lowry's case, however, this focus on disease and body remained. No event intervened to separate antistructure from structure. Instead, antistructure *became* the *modus vivendi*. This was achieved textually by a switch from the sequencing of episodes to the use of the conditional past with its connotations of habituality: "I would abuse my husband . . . I would damn the rain . . ." Lowry had learned of her diagnosis just prior to her marriage. She had no previously stable and practiced roles on which to draw. Indeed, "the disease had become [her] only role" and remained so until liminality intervened again in the form of a period of hospitalization for depression.

THE MIDDLE

> Whenever they [friends] came I couldn't stop talking about my plans and my projects and my healer, and all the things that were happening around me. . . . strange as it may seem, despite every possible appearance to the contrary, the real me was back to normal. (Davoud 1985:62)

The *modus vivendi* that emerged after the liminal period following diagnosis was not necessarily a once-and-for-all affair. Nor did it consist always of a stable routine. Living with MS was portrayed as a *process:* an interplay between self-time, that is, time devoted to matters related to personal projects, and time devoted to the physical body and the disease. For all but Florence Lowry and Liz Parkinson, self-time remained the focus of their narratives. Their lives were recounted in terms of what was accomplished via their instrumental (incarnate) body, the physical aspect of their body intruding on occasions in more or less significant ways. However, the quality of self-time that was achieved and the way in which it was maintained was not similar across all of the relevant texts.

Perhaps the most striking example of the achieved predominance of self-time (for this was usually presented *as* an achievement) is shown in the account by Nicole Davoud. One might have supposed, because of the extent of Davoud's disability and the severity of some of her relapses, that attention to her physical body and disruption of self-orientated activities would have figured far more prominently. It is therefore worth considering Davoud's account in some detail. How was it that for the most part she was able to portray her physical body as of subsidiary importance?

Nicole Davoud suffered her first prolonged phase of liminality almost a year after she had learned of her diagnosis, on finding that her usual pattern of life could no longer be sustained. As she emerged from this period, she tackled the Multiple Sclerosis Society[3] for its lack of services for younger people and on what she felt was its negative portrayal of MS. Describing her feelings at this time, she wrote: "I now felt excited, more elated and more alive than I had done for a very long time. I recognised the old Nicole Davoud in me" (1985:48).

The "old Nicole Davoud" was someone whose personal development progressed through intellectual and social activity. The "downs" of her life were periods of secluded, routine domesticity, and overwhelming physical or mental incapacity. The "ups" were periods of widening social horizons, writing, and campaigning. Episodes dominated by the physical body were significant insofar as they affected the possibility of meaningful activity. Often symptoms were recognized only on reflection. They were separated from the normal flow of life. This then was how Davoud described the period leading up to the launch of CRACK MS, a new section of the Multiple Sclerosis Society in the founding of which she played a major role:

> I was in a complete state of euphoria, tired, but far too excited and overstimulated to sleep. I lay awake at night thinking if there was anything that I had forgotten, what else I had to do. Countless ideas and suggestions kept flooding into my mind and I would pester my colleagues on the phone the next day. My condition was deteriorating, but I wasn't even aware of it. Only if I was sitting up and I fell down on the bed, then I would notice it. But I didn't think about it or dwell on it. Cramps came back at night in the legs, but as I was usu-

ally concentrating on something else, or developing an idea or a thought, I hardly felt the pain at all. (ibid.:82)

Similarly, Davoud portrayed improvements in her condition through her increased ability to accomplish what she felt was important:

> I carried on with life as normal, doing more and more walking. I was able to go into [her son] Alexander's room now with my frame—albeit bent and moving rather awkwardly—but he had stopped mocking me. He was just glad to see me being more able to do things with him. We discovered all sorts of games which we could play which did not require too much physical effort. I would sit on his bed and we would invent stories and do puzzles together, practise drawing. My hand was actually getting stronger. Once or twice I managed to return a ball he threw at me. (ibid.:95)

It is not until the closing phases of this middle section, which covered a period of approximately eight years, that Davoud began to address her physical condition more directly. Here she began to describe herself as "ill" and "tired" and to discuss in much more detail the practical difficulties of her work and attendance at meetings. She was also lamenting the fact that her more general campaigning work had distanced her from the CRACK MS membership and thus from people who understood and cared about *her*. Paradoxically, her active involvement in MS and disability issues did not reflect to others her personal suffering:

> My looks belied the way I felt, and it was only when colleagues escorted me out after a meeting and saw the minicab driver lifting me up and putting me into the car—because I was simply too tired to do it myself—that they realised that things were not as good as they might be. The subject, however, was never mentioned either by them or me. In a way I wished I could have opted out and let go, but I knew that I couldn't. After all, I'd set the ball in motion. There was no question of stopping midway. (ibid.:167–168)

For the most part, however, Davoud was living her old life although in new terms. Her body's requirements and limitations were relegated to subsidiary, contextualizing categories of experience which became focal only on conscious reflection or where unusually problematic. Her attention was principally directed to MS and disability per se. Thus personal illness provided the context in which self-time was lived in terms of more generalized sickness.

Renate Rubenstein, too, when referring to the physical body or disease, did so with reference to generalized bodies and textbook MS. Indeed (since "one out of every two thousand people have MS") "it occurred to [her] that these 1999 other people should be grateful to [her] that it wasn't them. Statistically [she] was their saviour after all—for 1999 people [she] assumed the role of MS patient" (Rubenstein 1989:25–26). Where her personal illness was concerned, Rubenstein learned to "leave it" through concentrating on the present, and on her current abilities: "Practise cunning to counter disappointment and loss: start from nothing and let everything surprise you. You will die anyway, and remain dead ever after. In the meantime, every little finger you move is a bonus" (ibid.:27). Over the next thirty-one chapters we learn of the state of Rubenstein's own physical body through her reflections on her activities and preoccupations (for example, over what she will never do again), her use of alternative therapies and disability aids, her fear of rejection and of her disease being reflected in her writing. The "handicaps" through which "a disease has a habit of reminding you of its presence" (ibid.:86) could be dealt with through avoidance (of walking), drugs (spasms), or relegation to "lost time," being "sen[t] away with the garbage" (fatigue and pain). "So the handicaps are not too bad and they can be managed" (ibid.:87).

Other authors described the quality of self-time in the middle section of their narrative as much closer to that which they had known in the past. The separation of disease and the physical body from the concerns of everyday life was accomplished rather differently. John Brown and Anne Kinley, both attempting to live their old lives in their *old* terms, provided contrasting accounts of attempts to ignore or accommodate their physical condition:

> The "spell" was broken and by the time I was promoted to a job on my country's second largest morning newspaper, I thought I could forget about that uncomfortable diagnosis. But I did not know MS and I reckoned without its deceitful habit of coming back and hitting you with full fury!
> ... During Christmas 1972, one of my flatmates returned from work to find me almost in tears. The sight in my right eye had gone and I was terrified. ... A week later, my eyesight returned to normal. Still no-one told me why this could happen. For an answer to that, I had to wait a further six months when I returned to hospital for a reassessment, this time at my own request. The doctor had told me to come back if I wanted further help. I sure did. MS was beginning to get in the way of my life. (Brown 1984:24)

> During the next two months, I worked hard at rehabilitation, with the goal of returning to work part-time at the Children's Health Center and Hospital in Minneapolis. I returned to my job but problems developed immediately. We were short-staffed and had a concentration of seriously ill children to care for. Even though I was only working six days in each two-week period with a day off between working days, I was exhausted, and it was extremely difficult for me to carry a full load while being so dependent upon a cane.
> I became more and more overwhelmed and fatigued, and before I had managed even two full months back on the job, I was ordered by my neurologist to take another leave of absence. (Kinley 1980:275)

John Brown's symptoms (if he had any in the earlier phase) were apparently more containable than those of Anne Kinley, but for both their attempted mode of living was unsustainable, and the physical body demanded more attention than either had been willing to give it. As we shall see, however, this did not ultimately mean that the body *remained* focal. On the one hand, John Brown's eyesight problem was an event that heralded a new period marked, as for Nicole Davoud, by generalized disease as a lived category. Anne Kinley, on the other hand, redefined the problematic aspects of her physical condition as a failing in her psychological self.

Miriam Chellingsworth's account of this "middle section" contrasts with those described so far in its treatment of disease in terms of unique and manageable episodes of somatic bodily disorder, rather than as a state to be contained or forgotten:

> April 1983. I was settled, liked the new hospital, and was buying a house. . . . I began to have more problems. It started with a right hemianaesthesia, followed by weakness of the legs and more retrobulbar neuritis. Each of these episodes recovered only to be followed by the next.
>
> . . . Because I had moved, I had a new neurologist. Fortunately I got on extremely well with him. I think he was as frustrated as I was by my frequent relapses and, like me, was not keen on steroids. I started on azothiaprine. I would like to have been part of a controlled trial, but my symptoms would not stay stable for long enough. I continued to have minor relapses but managed to get back to work and even surprised myself by learning to insert permanent pacemakers. Again, my consultants and colleagues were extremely kind, although my absence made a great deal of extra work for them. (Chellingsworth 1987:91–92)

Chellingsworth's next period was marked "November 1984" and incorporated more symptoms and another job move. Throughout, experience of the body was described in somatic terms, seen in references to both measured time and medical terminology: an account not dissimilar in fact from a medical case history. Bodily episodes were interruptions to the normal flow of life; sporadic breaches often involving (abnormal) time off (normal) work. The chronicity of the illness was portrayed through an accumulation of *discrete* happenings. It is almost as if each one came as a surprise.

Elizabeth Forsythe's narrative shows a variety of features already identified in these other texts. The middle section covers a period of eleven years and is replete with events and more qualitatively described periods. By this stage, with the aid of regular visits to a particularly helpful neurologist, Forsythe had overcome her distasteful feelings toward her body, and we hear relatively little of symptoms or other physical problems. By the latter part of this middle section, she had "remained in very good health and with good stamina for several years" (Forsythe 1988:18). Symptoms, such as there were, were disregarded as being not obvious to others and containable within her daily life. By the time mobility problems prompted Forsythe to leave her job, MS had faded so far into the background that she failed to connect her difficulties with the disease at all. The unwelcome necessity of having to take account of and spend time on her physical body prompted a distancing of the latter from her "self" (followed later by a reconceptualization of the relationship):

> In November 1985 I had difficulty getting up the stairs at work. . . . I have no idea what I thought the problem could be in my leg. This may seem strange but I know that the thought of MS did not enter my conscious mind.
> . . . I went privately to a physiotherapist to ask her to do something about the leg. She used various treatments but the leg got no better. I realise while writing that "the leg" was no longer "my leg" or part of my body and I believe this was how I saw the problem at that time. "The leg" was letting me down literally as well as metaphorically and was therefore no longer an acceptable part of me. (ibid.:19)

While the physical problems of her disease did not, for the most part, cause Forsythe daily concern, her MS diagnosis itself remained constantly significant in the form of "an ever-growing fence" between herself and her husband. The "fence" was eventually realized in the form of separation. Once psychologically, as well as practically on her own, Forsythe seemed able to dismiss MS altogether, describing her state as one of "buoyancy and optimism" (ibid.:18).

It was not only Elizabeth Forsythe who portrayed close relationships as instrumental in balancing disease and self-time, and in determining the quality of self-time which was achieved. Following the end of John Brown's marriage, the catalyst for which was a lack of adequate explanation for his symptoms combined with the provisional diagnosis of a "tumour," Brown, like Forsythe, was able to forget MS, if only for a brief period. He referred several times at this point to the support and warmth he felt from his colleagues at work. Here the diagnosis and its implications were not issues as they were for Elizabeth Forsythe and Nicole Davoud in their relationships with their families.

Davoud, looking back on her life toward the end of her "middle phase," writes:

> The only reality, the only continuity that I found in those years, was the fact that I was still Raymond's wife and Alexander's mother. That was something to which I could relate and which I could understand and, thank goodness, although going through patches of great difficulty, that relationship, that nucleus, my roots, had remained untarnished. (Davoud 1985:137)

Paradoxically, Davoud's husband seemed unable to accept the implications of her diagnosis and was "supremely uninterested in [her] work." However, since this meant he "never over-protected" her and was "totally unflappable in any difficult situation" (ibid.:136), in general this contributed positively to her way of life. Relegation of *personal* MS by both Davoud and her husband seemed to disallow the increasing dependency described by Anne Kinley (1980:275) and feared by Renate Rubenstein (1989:81–82). In addition, the MS diagnosis itself was not in dispute. It could not then, as for Elizabeth Forsythe, be rendered as an "obstruction": a negative "interactional object" in her relations with family and friends (Hunt, Jordan, and Irwin 1989:953). Rather, Davoud and her husband lived a particular life in which personal illness remained ironically implicit.

The way in which the fact of MS and the experience of its implications is construed within social relationships is significant, not only for those relationships themselves but for the patterning and quality of time devoted to the self, the physical body, and the disease in the course of everyday life. For the most part, the authors mentioned above were able to deflect their attention from their disease and disability as such. Breaking of relationships allowed John Brown and Elizabeth Forsythe to dismiss MS almost totally as part of their daily lives. Nicole Davoud's MS did not figure as such in descriptions of her daily relationships with her son and husband, and Davoud seemed able to withdraw (both negatively by avoiding holidays and positively by entering hospital) when it threatened to do so. Davoud's family relationships were thus able to support her active, working life, while for Anne Kinley they only encouraged her self-defined inadequacy. In all of these texts the way in which MS was constituted within family relationships closely resembled the account of its realization in everyday life. In the two cases where incompatibility was implied, this centered on a failure to share the meanings of the given diagnosis: the validity and tolerability of the implicated sickness.

The accounts of Florence Lowry and Liz Parkinson differ from those described above in that self-time was not reestablished as the dominant form in this middle period. Disease and the physical body or their implications were not contextualizing features of life but the reference points from which the whole of life was envisaged:

> Friends were the major problem. I hated the solicitous patronizing. I resented those who made light of it. "What now?" or "What next?" led the cacophony of growing concerns. I would abuse my husband when he was overly concerned about me. He became an object on which I could vent my frustrations—one moment with anger and the next with sexual demands. My life became over-dramatized as I became the actress caught up in a crazy overindulgence in the Stanislavsky method: I wanted to go back to being me but the disease had become my only role. (Lowry 1984:32)

> I became very, very frustrated with the fact that practically the whole day was spent coping with the demands and care of my decrepit body, when I could have used the time to do all the things I really wanted to—productive, creative things. Very often, the couple or so of hours left to me were spent prone

on the settee, in an exhausted daze, trying desperately to recoup the energy spent on all the other things, too tired even to concentrate on the television. Painting was out of the question. No way could I be bothered with all the messing about it entailed, and even had someone else done this for me, my back was too tired for me to sit in a position from which I could paint. (Parkinson 1982:74)

These perspectives on life with MS harmonized (again) with those construed in significant social relationships. Florence Lowry described the suffering of her husband together with whom (as she had said earlier) she learned about MS, wondering "who is being hurt the most" (1984:30). MS was a "problem" that at least the close family seemed willing to meet, and "hospitals had become a haven. Frequent exacerbations had meant months in the cocoon of others worrying for me. I was willing to resort to self-pity and let others do the positive things for me" (ibid.:33). However, contacts outside the family were little mentioned and even giving up her job seemed to cause Lowry no great concern as it did, for example, Elizabeth Forsythe.

For Liz Parkinson, too, who stated simply, "It was understood between the management and myself that I would now be medically retired" (1982:47), employment seemed no longer within her range of vision or to carry any particular significance. Her "priorities were changing" (ibid.:34–35), and she gave up paid work along with household jobs that had also become too difficult. However, support from work colleagues had been valued earlier. Like Parkinson herself, they had taken an active interest in her condition and its treatment, on one occasion offering money for a course of acupuncture. It was only later, when Parkinson was living with her sister, that there seemed any sign of friction, but we are told little, and nothing about if and how this was resolved.

While forgetting or ignoring MS were disregarded as options by both Florence Lowry and Liz Parkinson, they could be said to have accommodated aspects of their MS in that these became matters of routine rather than recurrent but discrete episodes. For Parkinson, for example, "taking pills was [by chapter 7] merely a way of life. I was quite nonchalant about the odd one or two extra" (1982:47), in spite of her earlier frequent references to medication as a constant concern. Indeed the interplay of concerns as they moved to and fro between what seemed *focal* at a particular time and what seemed routine gives insight into their relative saliency. "Injections" or the "DEFLATULENT medicine," for example, never seemed to reach a level of normality equivalent to that of "taking pills." The significance of management techniques of symptoms that rendered them episodic rather than contextual seemed to lie principally in the extent to which they were socially intrusive. Parkinson's incontinence, the hair growth on her upper lip, and her lack of balance are unsurprising examples. Her curling fingers are less immediately obvious problems:

One little foible of the right hand, which had caused me no inconvenience, and had in fact been quite a party trick, was that when I tried to hold it in a cupped position, the fingers would automatically curl themselves up towards the palm, unless I put every ounce of concentration into holding it flat. Now this began to happen with the left hand. This was the hand which I customarily held out for change in the shops, whilst I clung to the counter like grim death with the right, doing my best not to fall over. Imagine my embarrassment when, as soon as the change was placed in my palm, my fingers closed greedily over it, like a Venus's fly-trap! Either that, or the fingers would decide to wave about uncontrollably, causing the money to drop through the gaps so formed, resulting in a mad scrummage amongst nearby shoppers, whilst I laughed it off as "one of my clumsy days." One day, I had to hurry out before the tears started to fall, after it had happened just once too often. (ibid.:19)

The perceived visibility of these symptoms made them poignant in a way that Elizabeth Forsythe's own "clumsy left hand" and "tendency to lose . . . balance" were not. The symptoms also remained *personal* (albeit anatomically so in relation to "the hands"). Florence Lowry, too, was concerned to understand her "*personal* needs and condition," failing to find help "from the vague literature of the [MS] Society . . . and the skimpy mumbo-jumbo of the medical texts" (1984:32, our emphasis). This contrasts quite strikingly with the generalized and statistical MS of Nicole Davoud and Renate Rubenstein and the medically defined (somatic) body described by Miriam Chellingsworth. In fact when Parkinson's urologist demanded "every little detail of the functioning . . . of [her] bladder," she responded with the thought, "How should *I* know" (Parkinson 1982:50). She had not practiced the kind of bodily observation being assumed.

These then are stories of *personal* bodies (both corporeal and incarnate) with *personal* disease and are set in corresponding qualitative time frames. For Liz Parkinson the principal concerns were the physical body, its symptoms and its management: body-time was played out in terms of good and bad days enveloped in seasonal changes, also bodily significant. There were no holidays; no breaks. Visits to hospital were simply part of the overall picture. We learn less of the details of Florence Lowry's life. Her account is one of a *state of being* in which she explicitly played the role of the disease (Lowry 1984:32). Hospitals were a haven where the role could be played more easily (ibid.:30). The quality of those early years of disease-time was set up to contrast with that of a later period, more positively portrayed.

There were then a variety of ways in which authors characterized the middle section of their narrative, each giving insight into a particular mode of balancing disease, different aspects of the body, and personal concerns. We have drawn out what we believe are the major similarities and differences and shown how each account is made internally consistent in terms of the characterization of the body and disease in personal and social domains, and the time frame(s) in which life is portrayed. After similarly examining the final sections of the narratives we will look for more general contrasts in the structuring of the texts as complete pieces.

THE END

> I dread finishing this chapter, because then I have to read back through the rest, and fear that it may be a load of tripe. . . . If it isn't, then I hope and pray that it will perhaps help someone, somewhere, even if only to see the funny side of life when it could be interpreted as tragedy. I don't believe it is a tragedy, anyhow. (Parkinson 1982:79)

The final major phase of the narratives for most of the authors was entered, like the middle phase, through a series of episodes that hung together as a significant "event," and that often incorporated a "liminal" period of hospital admission or other seclusion from previous routines. Typically the event centered on a perceived change in the physical body which prompted general reflection on the current state of affairs and its meaning for the future. The result of these deliberations seemed to have the quality of a revelation, often quite a sudden one.

Nicole Davoud, for example, while in a state of exhaustion, remembered a doctor's recent opinion that her illness (rather than her work itself) was the source of her physical problems: "He meant that I had no control over my illness. It was progressing, no matter what I did. The realisation hit me like a thunderbolt" (1985:186). On the other hand, Anne Kinley's "problems became clear" once she began to "analyse [her] behavior" (1980:275) after leaving her job and reacting to her diagnosis with hysteria, while Florence Lowry was "brought to reality" by "a myriad of things" beginning with a stay in a psychiatric hospital during which she "started to listen" (1984:33). For three of the authors, Renate Rubenstein, Liz Parkinson, and Miriam Chellingsworth, the passage from "middle" to "end" was more closely woven into the textual form. Their concluding sections were more *obviously* conclusions: reflections on what had gone before and a statement of general sentiments.

In each narrative (as might be implied in the decision to set out their experiences) in one way or another self-time ultimately came to predominate. A sense of permanence was also evident. The novel stability of the situation invariably required quite a different time perspective with a different organization of self and body-related forms. The emergent organization was more in the nature of a resolution than a straightforward dominance of one form over the other. Two sets of contrasts seem particularly evident: that between the narratives of Nicole Davoud and John Brown, and the rest, and then within the rest, that between the health professionals' narratives and those of the others.

For Davoud and Brown, the disease ultimately became and remained their "work." We have described how this occurred relatively early in Davoud's narrative, but following the thunderbolt of recognition that she was not controlling her MS, the particular meaning of this work, the quality of time devoted to it, and its place vis-à-vis family and other personal concerns, underwent a number of changes. Although she could no longer identify with the "fight, fight, fight" (Davoud 1985:191) of hope and recovery with which she had launched CRACK, there came:

> the realisation that whether I liked it or not, that motto had to be mine if I was to survive. It didn't matter that I might not get better, never mind recover completely. What mattered was what I did with my life with whatever faculties I still had available. (ibid.:191)

However, Davoud was feeling too ill to proceed at her usual pace. She "needed a period of seclusion in which to give in to the depression" (ibid.:191). Nevertheless she rejected this as an appropriate course of action, reminding herself that:

> I had never found a way out simply by looking for it. A way out, adjustments, acceptance, coming to terms, eventually came to me while my mind was busily occupied with something else. When I was founding CRACK I was not aware that I was adjusting to my multiple sclerosis, yet after I had launched it I was ready to come out into the world. (ibid.:191–192)

The seclusion Davoud needed was achieved through writing the book we have been discussing. Paradoxically she saw this as an "activity" that complemented her previous work. Meanwhile her reinterpretation of earlier activities as "therapy" allowed continuity with the past and set the context for the novel outlook on life described in her final chapter.

The period of authorship ended the rather troublesome period of transition that had begun with the thunderbolt. The last pages of Davoud's story are once again replete with references to self-oriented episodes: adaptations to her house, a holiday in Devon, her silver wedding anniversary, and the tenth anniversary of CRACK. Her work "still goes on, but it has changed a lot" (ibid.:196). She summarized:

> I seem to be on a relatively even keel, by my standards. Much of the pressure of past years is gone, and for the first time I am not particularly concerned or worried about where I will go from here. . . . I have no illusions that I shall ever get completely well. All I want is to be well enough. (ibid.:197)

Although the physical body and disease remained subsidiary for Davoud, there was a sense in which body and self had come closer together. Self-focused interests and activities, enacted through the body incarnate, were now an integral part of *caring* for that body itself. Perhaps they also cared for the corporeal body through allowing Davoud to survive at all. Self-time was also explicitly now disease-time, and related to a *personal* disease as well as a generalized one. John Brown's story carried a similar kind of conclusion. In fact the whole of Brown's final section concerned his adoption of generalized MS as the focus of his personal concerns.

The remaining authors also presented themselves as having accepted or adjusted to MS, or as having learned to cope. For Liz Parkinson it was a case of her having "become used to it all," and Renate Rubenstein learned to "take it" and then "leave it." There are some remarkable consistencies in the mode of life these authors describe.

One consistently recurring theme was the restriction of personal horizons. Changes in temporal horizons were mentioned most frequently, but sometimes these were combined with an intensified focusing on narrowly bounded spaces:

> You experience nature in a different way, not a landscape but a square foot of lawn, a titmouse or a wren in the garden are individually perceived. Pleasure is being able to stand up, to move your fingers as you wish, or to read and talk. (Rubenstein 1989:87)

> I had hit bottom physically and emotionally, but I felt that I could make it. I became active in my therapy program by trying to live each day for itself. . . . Life slowed down and I began to see, feel, and enjoy things that I had been too rushed to notice before.
>
> At this point I can honestly say that having MS is not all that bad. I am gaining from it the ability to live my life in a lower gear and am seeing much beauty along the way. (Kinley 1980:275)

Anne Kinley's description brings out a number of other themes which seemed to characterize this final period. Surfacing of spiritual and aesthetic concerns is evident in her novel ability to "see, feel, and enjoy things" and to see "much beauty along the way." Renate Rubenstein associated such pleasure with her ability to pay attention to detail. Similarly, Florence Lowry was able to "live around [MS] by recognising all the good things that life had brought [her]" (1984:35), and Liz Parkinson found that "the mind, love and faith, can take precedence over whatever happens to the body" (1982:79). Indeed, achieving this perspective often involved a kind of self-control over the disease and the demands of the physical body. The success of adjustment thus ultimately depended on the efforts of the individual self, although help and support from others were appreciated.

> Over the next two years I had to learn gradually and painfully that "the MS" could not be separated from "me" and that any sort of recovery was impossible without the full involvement of me.
>
> . . . It was a long, demanding, painful and dangerous path, and it could have been simpler and superficially safer to have remained sick and progressively sicker and more disabled. I do not know that my path is applicable to

anybody else but [it is] possibly a guide to any people with MS who want to find their own path back to some sort of health. (Forsythe 1988:22)

These are sentiments shared to some extent by all of the six authors. The major difference between the narratives relates to their temporality, the distinction being particularly marked between the stories of health professionals (Miriam Chellingsworth, Elizabeth Forsythe, and Anne Kinley) and the others (Florence Lowry, Liz Parkinson, and Renate Rubenstein). Differences are evident principally in the kinds of connections the authors made between this final period and those of the past, and the kinds of general sense they then made of their lives and the implications of this for their portrayal of the future.

The health professionals seemed particularly concerned with order, both from a temporal point of view related to the chronological order of events and episodes, and from a concern to systematize their experience: to identify stages in their lives and to make logical connections between these. Anne Kinley was the most explicit. One of the markers of the final section of her narrative was her realization that she "had been going through the textbook stages of adjustment—shock and denial—and had branched off into regression. . . . I realised that in order to adjust and get the most out of my life, I would have to face my illness, accept my new body image, and reorganize myself" (1980:275).

By the end of her story Kinley was able to say "I now accept the fact that I have multiple sclerosis" (ibid.:275) and to look to accepting any future problems in a similar way. Acceptance dispensed with the linear time frame that dominated Kinley's account of her previous stages. Now days had different qualities and values and were lived one at a time, each for itself. Different kinds of days were expected; life held no surprises and the future, even though unknowable, was portrayed as similarly manageable.

Elizabeth Forsythe also identified stages leading to acceptance, although she spelled these out in a separate chapter of her book dedicated to this purpose. Throughout her story, however, she frequently reflected back on her account to show how she interpreted events in the light of her present understanding. We are not told of events in the final section, only that this covered a period of two years. Progression here was primarily of a spiritual kind measured along a path, not of recovery of health (though this was important), but of change in mental attitude.

Miriam Chellingsworth, on the other hand, at the conclusion of her story was still looking toward an "eventually" of marriage and children. She did not tell of a shift in her understanding of *her* MS, only of one relating to MS in her patients, which she had developed gradually over the course of her illness. Although relapses and her handling of them were now spoken of in the realm of "usually," she still looked forward to a chain of events associated with her career, although within the context of her fear of losing her independence. The future stretched out ahead as it had always done, only now as "one day at a time" (1987:93).

Acceptance, adjustment, and coping for these authors, then, were similar to the stages portrayed in medical texts (see, e.g., Gorman, Rudd, and Ebers 1984:218) and by Corbin and Strauss in their discussion of "biographical work" in chronic illness (1987:265). Adjustment comprised a mature psychological state achieved characteristically following periods of less successful adaptation. It incorporated a realistic view of physical limitations which did not reflect back negatively on the self-image. The future was encompassed by this view, but not too much at a time. Days mounted up one by one on a road to more complete adaptation.

In contrast, the narratives of the three other writers, Florence Lowry, Liz Parkinson, and Renate Rubenstein, lacked a sense of forward progression, or even an indication that the future was important, at least on the level of day-to-day experience. Instead, the present seemed interminable; the foreseeable future was simply more of the same. For Renate Rubenstein "the future [was] so uncertain that there [was] no point in thinking far ahead" (1989:120). The reality of change was appreciated, but a sense of future was represented by discrete scenarios, unconnected directly to the present:

> When I distanced myself from the idea of disablement and looked at what really was there, I saw a future that may strike tomorrow, in a month, in a year or in five years, and deprive me of my independence. "When I can no longer turn over in bed, I want you to put an end to my life," I told the doctor. . . . For the fearful it is a very comforting thought that death remains an option. . . . But the future, however impressive statistically, is still an idea and not an everyday handicap. (ibid.:85)

Similarly, after mentioning an unexpected improvement in her "waterworks," Liz Parkinson considers what else might occur:

> Who knows—this could lead to better mobility, because a great deal of energy will be saved, and my anxiety is cut down considerably. . . . Were I ever to be totally helpless, I would not want to place such a burden on my family, but would much prefer to go in hospital—or perhaps better still, a Leonard Cheshire home. (1982:80)

Analysis that paid attention to the logical and developmental aspects of their experience seemed of subsidiary importance to these authors, if it mattered at all. Instead, the different phases of their life stood as qualitatively different, linked, if at all, through comparison or simple merger. Renate Rubenstein's disconnected stories-within-a-story is perhaps the exemplar. Some of her stories told of gaining new understanding but in a piecemeal way, directly related to personal experience. Her reference to "the literature for the handicapped" showed how she had found changes in outlook simply to "occur" rather than always to result from conscious effort:

> There is something mysterious that happens despite yourself. After a period of grieving over what you can no longer do, you begin to emphasize what you can do. All the literature for the handicapped recommends this attitude and when you first read it, you think: what nonsense, how terribly sad this all is. But if you are lucky, the change comes about of its own accord and then it is of course not at all sad. (1989:121)

Florence Lowry's narrative, as we noted previously, was built around a comparison between a lengthy early phase (where the diagnostic period merged with a more stable middle section) and a later, current phase that incorporated another lengthy but completed period of "learning to cope with herself." MS itself was never "coped with"; the diagnosis was simply "accepted." Again, these phases were idiosyncratic. They were allowed to flow into one another in the course of a narrative that (like Renate Rubenstein's) wandered across the boundaries of chronological time.

In the latter respect Liz Parkinson's narrative differed from those of both Florence Lowry and Renate Rubenstein. It was a more temporally ordered account in that episodes were related according to their remembered sequence. The time points, however, were principally those of the corporeal or incarnate (but seldom somatic) body. In this sense the form of Parkinson's story could be said to straddle those of the health professionals on the one hand, and of Lowry and Rubenstein on the other. Order *was* important, but this was an order of very personal occurrences, which were in no obvious way progressive, nor divided into tightly bounded stages. There was no ongoing reflection or reinterpretation. Instead, the narrative was held together by reference to seasonal change. It began in "the long hot summer of 1976" (Parkinson 1982:1) and finished with a seasonal analogy that encompassed past, present, and future:

> You know, I remember, in the Springtime, a sudden, cruel, unexpected fall of snow blighting the daffodils outside my window. I thought they'd die—but they bloomed again, as beautiful as before. There was still plenty of life, plenty of hope. (ibid.:82)

In the concluding sections of these eight narratives we were thus able to identify at least three general modes in which self- and body-related time could be resolved. The first (related by Nicole Davoud and John Brown) involved a definition of self-orientated activities as therapy for both the incarnate and corporeal aspects of the body, within a context in which much activity related to sickness per se. The second mode of resolution incorporated a restriction of temporal and spatial horizons and a consequent appreciation of limited ability and the beauty of detail. This had to be achieved by individual effort involving a self-conscious learning about the relationship between self and body and how the physical body might be controlled. The authors who were health professionals (Miriam Chellingsworth, Elizabeth Forsythe, and Anne Kinley) also identified stages, or a more traditional chronology, which they used to link the various phases of their life. The remaining authors (Florence Lowry, Liz Parkinson, and Renate Rubenstein) were more concerned with the qualitative differences between phases and with flows across boundaries.

LIFE STORIES AND ILLNESS NARRATIVES AS EXEMPLARS FOR THE LIVES OF PEOPLE WITH DISABILITIES

> Having an illness like MS has helped me in my work. I now understand what it is like to be on the receiving end of advice like "take a month off." How often do we think before we give such advice to patients? I hope I now stop and think carefully before I give a patient advice that may dramatically alter his or her lifestyle. I still wonder what would have happened if I had taken up paediatrics. Who knows? (Chellingsworth 1987:92)

Miriam Chellingsworth wrote her story in order to sensitize her medical colleagues to the subjective experience of long-term illness. Anne Kinley, publishing as she did in a journal for professional nurses, could be presumed to have had similar reasons. Conversely, though herself also a doctor, Elizabeth Forsythe wrote for others with MS, wishing to share not just her medical knowledge, but her personal beliefs. Liz Parkinson apparently had similar motives.

Reasons for authorship are important for they indicate something about intended audiences. John Brown's and Florence Lowry's stories appeared in what was described as a book "on the psychological and social aspects of MS for all those who work in the field of MS care, who study in this area and for those people with MS who wish to go beyond some of the pamphlets handed out to them on diagnosis" (Simons 1984:vii). However, for Nicole Davoud, as we have seen, writing was more of a personal project, as it was also for Renate Rubenstein:

> I've had this rotten disease for seven years now and I've always kept quiet about it (I had talked about it of course, but never written). The longer this silence lasts, the more difficult it becomes to break it, I've become intimidated by my own silence, I've created my own taboo. Let Van Dis [television personality who invited Rubenstein to appear on his show and discuss her MS] help me over the threshold, then I will finally be forced to write this book, which I've been thinking of for so long. (Rubenstein 1989:14)

Whatever the full complement of reasons, and those given above will clearly be selective, much of the material was written with a view of influencing the attitudes of others. Authors felt they had something particular to relate which might help other people either to live with their own MS or, where readers did not have MS themselves, to sympathize with those directly affected. Insofar as authors wished and felt able to do this, as Renate Rubenstein indicates above, they had perhaps achieved a certain equilibrium or perspective on their circumstances, which would set them apart from those for whom (literary skills apart) their life story would be an unwelcome or even impossible task. John Freccero (1986) has pointed out the paradox in Western autobiography: that a belief in the continuity of the self coexists with an ability of that same self to act as its own observer. Thus the reflecting self must, in some sense, be the product of a conversion. It must be a higher form, conscious of its past errors and able to view these from within a new perspective. This view gives understanding to some of the features of the final sections of the narratives: the revelations that mark their beginning, the reflective content, and their sense of difference and permanence. Other writers have also noted how biographical work is required to reconstitute the self after the onset of chronic illness (Corbin and Strauss 1987:265; Kaufman 1988; Williams 1984).

The personal and moral victory of the self over the physical and somatic body is then inherent in the autobiographical genre and available to readers, whatever the intentions of individual authors. Although not referring to published autobiographies, Norman Denzin (1986) and Gareth Williams (1989) have pointed to how biographical material of different kinds may indeed have far-reaching effects. Whether self-stories told in meetings of Alcoholics Anonymous (Denzin 1986:331) or a report in the newsletter of a self-help group (Williams 1989:149), the narratives may come to function as exemplars of both the way it is and the way it should be. L. L. Langness and Gelya Frank (1981:93) have also suggested that for members of marginalized sections of society, autobiographies provide models for the sharing of experience. If the life stories of people with long-term illness or disability might also become exemplars (and this is worthy of investigation in itself), we need to know more about how (or whether) they are differentially used. Whether, for instance, the stories of health professionals are regarded as more authoritative and, if so, by whom. We have discussed some of the ways in which narratives of doctors and nurses might differ from those of others. We have seen (and learned from Elizabeth Forsythe [1988:137–138]) how orthodox medical training may provide a perspective that is brought to bear even on a doctor's own illness: specifically a particular evolution of the relationship between self and body which culminates in a special kind of "self" control (see also Frank 1986:190–192; Gordon 1988). The readership of autobiographies of sick people holds clues to the significance of this material in producing and reinforcing different views of their experience and more generally within the moral economy of chronic sickness.

CONCLUSION

> This book is about being ill and about being me.
> You can't separate the two.
> It is an egocentric book,
> full of good advice to myself.
>
> (Rubenstein 1989:frontispiece)

What then may we learn from our reading of these eight narratives? Does it bring us any closer to understanding the relationship of "being ill" and "being me" in the process of long-term sickness?

Drawing on the texts, we have throughout distinguished between notions of self and body, and between conceptualizations of the body which relate to its instrumental and experiential, its physical and medical aspects. We have looked at the balancing of claims of self and body (in all its various forms) with respect to attention and time, and found this to vary, not only according to the individual but also according to the particular phase of the narrative. With regard to the narratives' structure, we noted how authors frequently marked significant periods by reference to composite events, and how such events and periods were often similar both in kind and in their general sequencing. We also pointed out, however, that authors' own interpretation of this sequencing, and in particular the kind of temporal framework in which it was understood, was different for those with and without a medical training. We pointed out the potential significance of these observations for the kind of understanding of the lives of ill or disabled people which is conveyed through published texts such as those under discussion. In doing this we have learned of a range of conceptualizations of self, body, and time that may shape people's own assessment of their lives in the societies from which the texts were drawn.

What we cannot say relates to the extent to which our observations might also be relevant to narratives by people with conditions other than MS or who live in other societies or cultures. Particular features of MS—its unpredictability, its frequent relapsing and remitting form, and the invisibility of many of its associated symptoms, for example—give it potentially a marked social significance for those affected. This is apparent in both the accounts of those who have MS and in studies devoted to exploring the associated problems (see, e.g., Brooks and Matson 1987; Cunningham 1977; Duval 1984; Robinson 1988). Peter Conrad has identified seven "recurrent themes in illness experience research," all of which are echoed in these texts on MS (1987:7–17). While some concerns might be particularly acute or enduring for people with MS, their representation in narrative might highlight their potential significance for those with other conditions. Similarly, the accounts of those with "sociological types" of chronic illness other than the "lived-with" MS, may inform our own reading by indicating where the particular features of MS narratives lie and which aspects are shared by those whose authors have other conditions. Murphy (1987), for example, in his story of "mortal illness," describes how he remains "embedded irrevocably" in the "logic and meaning of his paralysis." Liberation of the self ("a sense of what and where we are") does remain a possibility, paradoxically because it is easier to transcend the soma than the "thraldom to culture" endured by the disabled and the able-bodied alike. However, the real triumph in his story lies in the continuance of the wish for life per se (ibid.:178–179). Autobiographical material of the kind we have reviewed may therefore usefully contribute to a unified perspective on chronic illness and sickness.

All the examples we have used represent material produced through negotiation between author and publisher within the framework of Western industrialized society. As Nancy Scheper-Hughes and Margaret Lock (1987) have made clear and as we indicated in our introduction, the outcome will necessarily be shaped not only by these negotiations themselves but by a particular conceptualization of the self and of the temporal process of sickness, interwoven with a particular organization of health care and knowledge. In contrast to the accounts presented here, Junichiro Tanizaki, in his fictionalized *Diary of a Mad Old Man* (1965), presents a detailed biomedical model of chronology which Lock (personal communication, 1990) has suggested might reflect the practice of diary keeping by patients of Japanese traditional healers. Tanizaki ends his account, not with a resolution of self and bodily demands, but with the somatic focus of the medical records of his nurse and doctor. Cultural variation in thematic content is indicated by Fedwa Malti-Douglas (1988) through his critical reading of the autobiography of a blind Egyptian intellectual. He shows here how the themes of traditional versus modern and East versus West, concerns of the emerging modern Egyptian society, intertwine with those of the author's "personal" and "social" blindness. We do not claim ubiquity for the themes we ourselves identified in the accounts we reviewed, nor for their treatment by the authors concerned. We do propose that they represent some of the complexities with which our future reading of life stories and illness narratives will need to engage.

NOTES

1. We are grateful to Ruth Pinder for her valuable comments on an earlier draft of this chapter and to Ian Robinson for the benefit we have gained from discussions concerning his earlier work on life histories of people with MS. We would also like

to thank Christine Allport for her help in preparing the manuscript. We gratefully acknowledge the financial support given by Action and Research for Multiple Sclerosis to the CSHSD.

2. Kleinman's "illness narratives" are unusual in that they are constructed from his own case records, and in one case represent a composite of the narratives of three individual patients (1988:60, 88). Life stories of the kind we have in mind, such as they appear at all, are not treated as wholes, but as part of these meta-constructs (236–237). Thus, although early in the text Kleinman stresses the personal importance to patients of "retrospective narratization" (50) and claims to "analyze actual cases of chronic illness and thereby generalize them from the issues outlined in these first chapters" (55), in fact he concentrates on the clinical interpretation of clinically constructed data. It is not then surprising that he treats departures from the expected narrative unproblematically as, for example, denial (35) or heroism (144), or that he takes for granted the centrality of illness in people's lives (31, 44, 47). Both Kleinman's notion of illness narrative and his concerns and interpretive framework were therefore very different from our own.

3. The Multiple Sclerosis Society is a national British charity devoted to the furtherance of medical research into MS and the welfare of those affected.

REFERENCES

Brody, Howard
    1987   *Stories of Sickness.* New Haven, Conn.: Yale University Press.
Brooks, Nancy A., and Ronald R. Matson
    1987   Managing multiple sclerosis. In *The Experience and Management of Chronic Illness,* ed. Julius A. Roth and Peter Conrad. Greenwich, Conn.: JAI Press.
Brown, John
    1984   One man's experience with multiple sclerosis. In *Multiple Sclerosis: Psychological and Social Aspects,* ed. Aart F. Simons. London: William Heinemann.
Chellingsworth, Miriam C.
    1987   Multiple sclerosis. In *When Doctors Get Sick,* ed. Harvey Mandell and Howard Spiro. New York: Plenum Press.
Conrad, Peter
    1987   The experience of illness: Recent and new directions. In *The Experience and Management of Chronic Illness,* ed. Julius A. Roth and Peter Conrad. Greenwich, Conn.: JAI Press.
Corbin Juliet, and Anselm L. Strauss
    1987   Accompaniments of chronic illness: Change in body, self, biography, and biographical time. In *The Experience and Management of Chronic Illness,* ed. Julius A. Roth and Peter Conrad. Greenwich, Conn.: JAI Press.
Cunningham, Diane J.
    1977   Stigma and social isolation: Self-perceived problems of a group of multiple sclerosis sufferers. HSRU report, no. 27. Health Services Research Unit, University of Kent.

Davoud, Nicole
1985   *Where Do I Go from Here?* London: Piatkus.
Denzin, Norman K.
1986   Interpretive interactionism and the use of life stories. *Revista internacional de sociologia* 44:321–337.
Duval, Louise M.
1984   Psychosocial metaphors of physical distress among MS patients. *Social Science and Medicine* 19(6):635–638.
Early, Evelyn A.
1988   The Baladi curative system of Cairo, Egypt. *Culture, Medicine and Psychiatry* 12(1):65–83.
Farmer, Paul
1988   Bad blood, spoiled milk: Bodily fluids as moral barometers in rural Haiti. *American Ethnologist* 15(1):62–83.
Forsythe, Elizabeth
1988   *Multiple Sclerosis: Exploring Sickness and Health.* London: Faber and Faber.
Frank, Gelya
1979   Finding the common denominator: A phenomenological critique of life history method. *Ethos* 7(1):68–94.
1984   Life history model of adaptation to disability: The case of a "congenital amputee." *Social Science and Medicine* 19(6):639–645.
1986   On embodiment: A case study of congenital limb deficiency in American culture. *Culture, Medicine and Psychiatry* 10(3):189–219.
Frankenberg, Ronald
1986   Sickness as cultural performance: Drama, trajectory, and pilgrimage. *International Journal of Health Services* 16(4):603–626.
1990   Disease, literature, and the body in the era of AIDS: A preliminary exploration [review article]. *Sociology of Health and Illness* 12(3):351–360.
Freccero, John
1986   Autobiography and narrative. In *Reconstructing Individualism: Autonomy, Individuality, and the Self in Western Thought,* ed. Thomas C. Heller, Morton Sosna, and David E. Wellerby. Stanford, Calif.: Stanford University Press.
Gordon, Deborah
1988   Tenacious assumptions in Western medicine. In *Biomedicine Examined,* ed. Margaret Lock and Deborah Gordon. Dordrecht: Kluwer.
Gorman, Eunice, Ann Rudd, and George C. Ebers
1984   Giving the diagnosis of multiple sclerosis. In *The Diagnosis of Multiple Sclerosis,* ed. Charles M. Poser, Donald W. Paty, Labe C. Scheinberg et al. New York: Thieme-Stratton.
Heller, Thomas C., Morton Sosna, and David E. Wellerby, eds.
1986   *Reconstructing Individualism: Autonomy, Individuality, and the Self in Western Thought.* Stanford, Calif.: Stanford University Press.
Hunt, Linda M., Brigitte Jordan, and Susan Irwin
1989   Views of what's wrong: Diagnosis and patients' concepts of illness. *Social Science and Medicine* 28(9):945–956.

Kaufman, Sharon R.
1988   Illness, biography, and the interpretation of self following a stroke. *Journal of Aging Studies* 2(3):217–227.

Kinley, Anne E.
1980   MS: From shock to acceptance. *American Journal of Nursing* 80:274–275.

Kleinman, Arthur
1988   *The Illness Narratives: Suffering, Healing, and the Human Condition.* New York: Basic Books.

Lang, Gretchen C.
1989   "Making sense" about diabetes: Dakota narratives of illness. *Medical Anthropology* 11(3):305–327.

Langness, L. L., and Gelya Frank
1981   *Lives: An Anthropological Approach to Biography.* Novato, Calif.: Chandler and Sharp.

Lowry, Florence
1984   One woman's experience with multiple sclerosis. In *Multiple Sclerosis: Psychological and Social Aspects,* ed. Aart F. Simons. London: William Heinemann.

Malti-Douglas, Fedwa
1988   *Blindness and Autobiography: "Al-Ayyam" of Taha Husayn.* Princeton, N.J.: Princeton University Press.

Murphy, Robert F.
1987   *The Body Silent.* New York: Henry Holt.

Murphy, Robert F., Jessica Scheer, Yolanda Murphy, and Richard Mack
1988   Physical disability and social liminality: A study in the rituals of adversity. *Social Science and Medicine* 26(2):235–242.

Ots, Thomas
1990   The silent Körper—The loud Lieb. Paper read at the joint meeting of the American Ethnological and Southern Anthropological Societies, Atlanta, Georgia, April 26–28.

Parkinson, Liz
1982   Snow on the daffodils: MS, a personal experience. Manuscript. Available from Mrs. L. Aldridge, Sequal, Ddol Hir, Clyn Ceiriog, Llangollen, Clwyd, Wales, LL20 7NP, U.K.

Robinson, Ian
1988   *Multiple Sclerosis.* London: Routledge.

Rubenstein, Renate
1989   *Take It and Leave It: Aspects of Being Ill.* London: Marion Boyars.

Scheper-Hughes, Nancy, and Margaret M. Lock
1987   The mindful body: A prolegomenon to future work in medical anthropology. *Medical Anthropology Quarterly,* n.s., 1:6–41.

Simons, Aart F., ed.
1984   *Multiple Sclerosis: Psychological and Social Aspects.* London: William Heinemann.

Tanizaki, Junichiro
1965   *Diary of a Mad Old Man.* Tokyo: Charles E. Tuttle.

Turner, Bryan S.
1984   *The Body and Society: Explorations in Social Theory.* Oxford: Basil Black-
           well Publisher.
Williams, Gareth H.
1984   The genesis of chronic illness: Narrative re-construction. *Sociology of
           Health and Illness* 6(2):175–200.
1989   Hope for the humblest? The role of self-help in chronic illness: The
           case of ankylosing spondylitis. *Sociology of Health and Illness* 11(2):
           135–159.

PART TWO

Social Contexts of Disability

Introduction

The cultural analysis of impairment and personhood must be fitted to-gether with an examination of the social and political relations in which the meanings of disability are played out. The authors of the chapters in this section show how concepts and values are invoked in particular situations, emphasizing the importance of social position (such as gender and profession). They also explore the historical processes that generate change and multiple perspectives.

Robert Murphy's analysis of disability in America (chap. 7) begins with ideals and moves to social encounters, providing a bridge between the classic cultural approach and the sociological tradition of symbolic interactionism. He shows that impairment is an affront to the American ideal of the body beautiful and describes the awkwardness and avoidance characteristic of encounters between people with deficient bodies and able-bodied people. It is assumed that deficit in some functions also spreads to others; the waiter does not give the man in the wheelchair a menu, presuming that he cannot read either. This liminal state is not to be lumped with other kinds of stigmatizing deviance. Radical bodily difference arouses fear, avoidance, and denial because it is an affront to specific ideals of beauty, activity, capability, and success which are central to American concepts of personhood. Murphy shows the relevance of these values and meanings in different types of social interactions. His impairment had different implications for his relations to women and to men, to colleagues and to students, and to people of higher and lower status.

During his fieldwork in Uganda, Nayinda Sentumbwe (chap. 8) focused specifically on gender aspects of one type of disability. He found that the sexual and marital experiences of blind educated women in Uganda differed from those of men. Women might have sighted lovers, but were likely to have blind husbands, whereas blind educated men were more apt to have sighted spouses. Sentumbwe argues that gender roles, especially expectations about the role of wife, mean that blindness is a greater handicap for women than for men. Husbands depend upon their wives socially and economically; wives keep the home, produce the food, and cultivate crucial relationships to neighbors and kin. Hard work, efficient management, and sociability are more important qualities than physical attractiveness (a pattern Ingstad also found in Botswana). Given prevailing views of blindness as persistent sickness and general rather than limited incapacity, men and their families are reluctant to accept blind wives.

How do concepts of personhood and disability change, and how do national and international political processes affect the options available for people with impairments? Benedicte Ingstad (chap. 9) exemplifies the historical phenomenon of discourse transfer in which concepts and programs are planted in a new context in the name of development. Botswana, like other developing countries, has a number of rehabilitation projects and programs: special schools established by Christian missions, rehabilitation centers run by small nongovernmental organizations, and community-based rehabilitation programs administered by larger nonprofit organizations and by the government as part of its health services. The initiative and the funding behind these rehabilitation efforts have come largely from Europe. Norway is one of the major donors, and Ingstad shows how the elements of a public discourse on rehabilitation took shape in Norway in the context of a welfare state obligated to ensure equal rights for all its citizens. She discusses the problems of transplanting these elements to Botswana, where there has been no comparable indigenous political process and where assumptions about state, family, and individual are very different.

The situation in Nicaragua, as described by Frank Jarle Bruun in chapter 10, makes an interesting contrast to Botswana. Here the emergence of contesting constructions of disability is more closely related to national political processes. Disabled people are presented as heroic, as pitiful, and as autonomous and capable by different interest groups in Nicaraguan society. The war, which mutilated so many men, and the political struggle gave significance to the disablement of soldiers and created greater awareness of the situation of disabled people in general. Newspapers and organizations by and for disabled people drew on a variety of values, both indigenous and imported: machismo, Christian charity, and equal rights. Government programs of compensation, political slogans, sports events, and media coverage suggested identities for people with impairments. But as Bruun shows in the case of Carlos, a young soldier who came home from the mountains without his legs, the negotiation of identity is a complex affair.

Lisbeth Sachs (chap. 11) investigates such a negotiation. Although the setting is very different, it also involves a variety of perspectives and assumptions about impairment. Here, however, the purpose is to analyze the experience of one family moving through a complex social situation, rather than to provide a broader historical analysis. Sachs tells the story of an immigrant Turkish woman and her family in Stockholm and the process of interpreting and acting upon an abnormality. She shows how the mother of an infirm baby moves from seeing the child as not normal, to understanding it as "yes, disabled." The analysis has elements of symbolic interactionism; the interpretation is a product of interaction with others and has consequences for the way the mother and child are treated. Yet Sachs also has other concerns that are not typical of that more sociological tradition. She shows the coexistence of conflicting interpretations of the situation and relates these to differences in cultural background and to the necessity of working out new interpretations in the situation of migration.

The concern with processes of interpretation and representation is also present in Susan Reynolds Whyte's chapter on epilepsy in East Africa (chap. 12). She draws attention to a double process of construction, showing how researchers have tended to emphasize images of epilepsy that distance and decontextualize persons, ideas, and practices. Instead, stigma, contagion, social isolation, and "traditional beliefs" must be seen in actual social contexts where actors are making interpretations and getting on with their lives. There are always possibilities and contingencies in the process of construction, beginning with the choice of whether to call the problem "epilepsy."

Pronouncements by donors of financial aid or authoritative health officials are cultural constructions, as well. Ingstad's contribution in chapter 13 shows that the "myth of the hidden disabled" is a representation of others (whether unenlightened people in the next village, backward country people, or "under-developed" citizens of under-developed countries) who hide their impaired individuals, out of shame, heartlessness, or ignorance. The point is that this myth is a stereotype of what Others make of disability. It ignores the variety of their experiences and positions, and it devalues the efforts of families to care for their infirm members, emphasizing only that the Others do not conform to the raconteur's image. The picture presented here, with its specific examples of families and rehabilitation staff, supplements the overview of Botswana rehabilitation discourses in chapter 9.

Together, the articles in this section provide analyses of social processes at a wide range of levels, from the individual interacting with family and neighbors to the conflicts of national political movements to the world of international development aid. They show how social distinctions and power relations affect the significance of disability in a given setting. More than that, they raise methodological and analytical issues concerning processes of interpretation, the role of professional discourses, and the generation of change and complexity.

SEVEN

Encounters: The Body Silent in America

Robert Murphy

> *Our own body is in the world as the heart is in the organism; it keeps the visible spectacle constantly alive, it breathes life into it and sustains it inwardly, and with it forms a system.*
>
> —MAURICE MERLEAU-PONTY,
> *THE PHENOMENOLOGY OF PERCEPTION*

The recently disabled paralytic faces the world with a changed body and an altered identity—which even by itself would make his reentry into society a delicate and chancy matter. But his future is made even more perilous by the way he is treated by the nondisabled, including some of his oldest friends and associates and even family members. Although this varies considerably from one situation to another, there is a clear pattern in the United States, and in many other countries, of prejudice toward the disabled and debasement of their social status. This is manifested in its most extreme forms by avoidance, fear, and outright hostility. As Erving Goffman noted in his landmark 1963 book *Stigma: Notes on the Management of Spoiled Identity,* the disabled occupy the same devalued status as ex-convicts, certain ethnic and racial minorities, and the mentally ill, among others. Whatever the physically impaired person may think of himself, he is given a negative identity by society, and much of his social life is a struggle against this imposed image. It is for this reason that we can say that stigmatization is less a by-product of disability than its substance. The greatest impediment to a person's taking full part in his society is not his physical flaws, but rather the tissue of myths, fears, and misunderstandings that society attaches to them.

To understand why this is so, it is necessary to consider some of the central themes of, for example, American culture, especially our attitudes toward the body. The body is so important in American symbolism that most

From *The Body Silent* by Robert Murphy. Copyright © 1987 by Robert E. Murphy. Reprinted with minor changes by permission of Henry Holt and Company, Inc.

At the height of his career as professor of anthropology at Columbia University, Robert Murphy began to suffer muscle spasms and deteriorating physical coordination. In 1976, at the age of fifty-two, he was diagnosed as having a tumor of the spinal cord. Despite progressive paralysis, he continued his teaching, research, and writing until his death in 1990.

of us, including anthropologists, do not even realize that its care and nurture have changed from practicality to fetishism. This is not simply a phenomenon of the past decade. In 1956, the anthropologist Horace Miner wrote a wonderful, tongue-in-cheek essay on a people he called the Nacirema (*American* spelled backward). With unerring accuracy, Miner described the bathroom as a religious center where the inhabitants make their ritual ablutions in a cult of the body beautiful. Since that time, the bathroom, surely one of the cornerstones of our culture, has evolved even further; the rich now have huge, sunken tubs with built-in Jacuzzis, and the profane toilet bowl is segregated from the sacred bathing area. Whatever else may be said about Americans, they are a fairly clean people.

But the body must be more than clean; it must have a certain shape. The anthropologist Marvin Harris notes that whereas corpulence used to be an indication of wealth and prestige—Diamond Jim Brady and J. P. Morgan come to mind—it now is a sign of lower-class status and an overly rich diet. The reigning beauties of the Gay Nineties would be buxom, even fat, by today's standards, for our twentieth-century ideals of beauty have evolved from Lillian Russell to Marilyn Monroe to Twiggy. Today's bodies must be lean and muscular, an injunction that is almost as binding for females as it is for males. The feminine ideal has shifted from soft curves to hard bodies.

And how does one attain the body beautiful of the 1980s? By exercise, diet, and other mortifications of the flesh. If you want the right kind of body—presumably the passport to romantic love and economic success—then you must get out there and jog several miles a day. The craze for jogging soon turned to running frenzy, for it has been deemed necessary to get the heart pumping hard. Another route to the ideal body is the health club, and millions of Americans have become members of thousands of spas with such features as swimming, squash, racquetball, weight-lifting, sauna, whirlpool, massage, and aerobics. This injunction to exercise is especially intense among the upwardly mobile middle class, although it also has become part of the life-style of the working class. None of this is to deny that exercise is good and healthful. What interests the anthropologist, however, is that its practice in contemporary America extends beyond rational self-interest to zealotry. And the pursuit of the slim, well-muscled body is not only an aesthetic matter but also a moral imperative.

The morality of the good body is manifest in the message pounded out daily in television commercials that "self-improvement" means attaining physical fitness, an even more mindless activity than the transcendental meditation of the 1970s. Obesity is regarded as punishment for sloth and weak will, and this is nowhere more evident than in the American preoccupation with the diet. "You are what you eat" and "the body is the temple of the mind" are among the platitudes by which we live, although to the extent that one can fathom their meanings, both are nonsense. Nonetheless, if the body is a sacred zone, one must be careful about what one puts into it. Health-food stores now abound, organically grown products are popular, and vegetarianism is on the rise. Fasting and self-inflicted physical punishment are the modern-day equivalents of medieval flagellantism. They are religious rituals, part of the immortality project of a secularized middle class that no longer believes in redemption of the soul and has turned instead to redeeming the body.

Both men and women have found that a youthful appearance is a considerable asset in the business world—quite the opposite of the situation in Japan, where maturity commands respect. In the United States, cosmetic surgery for women has been on the increase in recent years, but even more dramatic has been its exponential growth among men. The emulation of youth has extended itself to fashion as well. During the 1960s, young people began to let their hair grow long as an act of separation and defiance—only to find that in a few short years, long hair had spread to stockbrokers and advertising men, who now have their hair cut (or, rather, "styled") at exclusive salons. Clothing has become more youthfully casual, too. Teachers wear the same blue jeans as their students and suits have a less severe cut. To accentuate youthful beauty, men now use cosmetics, something that would have cost them their masculine credentials in my benighted era. But *these* are he-man products. To cite just one example, the designer Ralph Lauren has "designed" a men's cologne called "Chaps" (as in the chaps worn by cowboys), a concoction, the TV commercial assures us, that expresses the masculine values of the Old West. It's grand hokum like this that makes the present day and age so delicious for us anthropologists.

Much of the ideal American purveyed by the mass media applies only to the upwardly mobile, but on close examination it distorts even their circumstances. In reality, this is a country in which the gulf between the haves and the have-nots is large and growing, and in which the general standard of living has been inching downward ever since the mid-1960s. This stark truth is based on ample evidence that the purchasing power of the average family has declined almost five percent since 1971; the drop would have been far steeper but for the dramatic increase in the number of working wives. The country, however, operates under the illusion that we are living better. After all, secretaries and factory workers travel to Europe on vacation now, something that once only the wealthy could do. But this is merely because jet aircraft—flying cattle trucks carrying nearly four hundred heads per trip—now make the fare to London as cheap in constant dollars as a trip to Niagara Falls was in 1950. But most of today's younger tourists in Europe cannot afford to buy a house or have more than one or two children, something their parents were able to do in 1950. And they did so on one income. Are we really living better?

America is a land of shrinking resources and families, a society whose culture glorifies the body beautiful and youthfulness, while barely tolerating youths. It is small wonder that it harbors people increasingly turned in on themselves in rampant narcissism. To make matters worse, the increased affluence of the upper middle class and upper class is offset by the growing despair of the lower class. The economic plight of their men is eroding the black family, and once proudly independent blue-collar workers now line up in soup kitchens, their jobs sent overseas by American capital. Our cities are littered with homeless people sleeping in bus stations and doorways, rummaging for food in garbage cans, abandoned by a society that dodges responsibility by telling itself that such people choose to live that way. The successful simply shrug their shoulders and say, "I'm all right, Jack." Our cities present scenes that are almost reminiscent of Calcutta, but to most urban Americans the homeless have become invisible. They walk around the human rag piles, they avert their eyes, and they maintain the myth that they dwell in what some politicians have called "a shining city on a hill."

They do the same thing with the disabled.

The kind of culture the handicapped American must face is just as much a part of the environs of his disability as his wheelchair. It hardly needs saying that the disabled, individually and as a group, contravene all the values of youth, virility, activity, and physical beauty that Americans cherish, however little most individuals may embody them. Most handicapped people, myself included, sense that others resent them for this reason: we are subverters of an American Ideal, just as the poor betray the American Dream. And to the extent that we depart from the ideal, we become ugly and repulsive to the able-bodied. People recoil from us, especially when there is facial damage or bodily distortion. The disabled serve as constant, visible reminders to the able-bodied that the society they live in is shot through with inequity and suffering, that they live in a counterfeit paradise, and that they too are vulnerable. We represent a fearsome possibility.

What makes the disabled particularly threatening are the psychological mechanisms of projection and identification by which people impute their feelings, plans, and motives to others, and, in turn, incorporate those of others as their own. Through these processes, the disabled arouse in the able-bodied the fear that impairment could happen to them and, among relatives and friends, the guilt that it hasn't. In their excellent book *The Unexpected Minority,* John Gliedman and William Roth write that the disabled person becomes the Other—a living symbol of failure, frailty, and emasculation; a counterpoint to normality; a figure whose very humanity is questionable (Gliedman and Roth 1980). So prevalent is the dehumanization of the disabled that I have heard it inveighed against repeatedly by disabled people. The fact that it is not just an American trait is bespoken by the title of Norwegian author Finn Carling's book *And Yet We Are Human* (1962).

It is clear that the disabled arouse primordial sentiments in people throughout the world, but lack of comparative data makes it difficult to say where, how, and why.[1] We do know that the stigma of disability is much worse in Japan than in the United States, and that the aura of contamination that often surrounds the disabled becomes attached to other members of the family. In an article published in 1977, Japanese author Yoko Kojima has written of the mother of a congenitally deformed child who felt such shame and despair that she attempted suicide. The author attributes this severity to a Japanese belief that the individual is somehow to blame for his or her own misfortunes, and to the cultural and ethnic homogeneity of the population. In contrast, northern European attitudes toward the disabled are more relaxed and positive than Japan's or America's, and their rehabilitation programs are correspondingly more advanced. Similarly, my Columbia colleague Morton Klass watched one day as a group of men in India teased a blind man. Klass at first thought this to be cruel, but then he realized that the banter was a way of including the blind man in the group; it was a joking relationship of the same type that anthropologists have found among in-laws in some primitive societies. Significantly, this usually takes the form of avoiding the parents-in-law and joking with brothers- and sisters-in-law, people one may marry; the banter thus can be seen as an alternative way of putting distance between people. In this light, the Indians' relationship with the blind man is a simple transposition of the American avoidance of them. I suspect that future studies will reveal that in lands where poverty and disease are rampant, the disabled will not be as excluded from social life as they are in the United States, but it probably will also come out that they always receive special treatment.

Returning to American culture, there is deep and uneasy ambivalence in relations between the able-bodied and the disabled, for how is one supposed to act toward a quasi-human, a person who literally arouses fear and loathing? While at the same time, these are sentiments that must remain hidden at all costs, for they fly in the teeth of values that dictate concern for and kindness to the handicapped. Social encounters are always tricky games, sparring matches in which each party tries to guess what the reaction of the other will be, and the game is made more difficult when one person has no inkling of what the other is like, such as in the case of a foreigner— or a paralyzed person. To the extent that people look on the disabled as an alien species, they cannot anticipate their reactions; the disabled individual falls outside the ken of normal expectations, and the able-bodied are left not knowing what to say to him or her. One way out of the dilemma is to refrain from establishing any contact at all. This can be done with people in wheelchairs simply by physical avoidance, an easy solution for a person with two working legs.

So pronounced and widespread is the way that people avert their eyes or physically distance themselves from disability that I have never met a disabled person who has not commented on it, and the literature on disability is too replete on this point to be worth citing. The disabled often say, "People act like it was catching." This exact expression was uttered by a Japanese woman, maimed by the atomic bomb at Hiroshima, in describing the fact that nobody ever visits the victims. It is worth noting that people with cancer and those suffering loss through death or divorce are similarly given wide berth; they have all suffered a contamination of identity. Malignancy and mourning are, however, transient conditions. Paralytic disability is not.

Erving Goffman, who was a sociologist by training but an anthropologist in practice, wrote in 1956 that the very core and starting premise of all social interaction is the establishment by the people involved of stances of deference and demeanor. Each party must comport himself or herself as a person of worth and substance, and each must put social space and distance around the self. The other, in turn, respects this demeanor by according it deference. The extent of this mutual respect varies, of course, with the situation and the people involved, and the way in which it is expressed is an artifact of culture. It occurs through a subconscious grammar of gesture and verbal nuance, a language so subtle that it escapes the awareness of both user and listener, except when it is withheld—as it so often is for the physically impaired.

Whatever the cultural and situational variations, a broad segment of the general public handles relations with the disabled by partial withdrawal of deference. They do this unconsciously and in a variety of ways. The violinist Itzhak Perlman, who suffers from the after-effects of polio, says that when he is pushed up to an airline counter in a wheelchair, the clerk commonly asks his attendant, "Where is he going?" This has happened to me on numerous occasions, and I was reminded again that it is not just an American phenomenon when a waiter in a Korean restaurant handed out three menus to our party of four; I called him back and told him I too knew how to read. It did little good, for he did the same thing two months later. People also speak loudly to the blind on the assumption that they are deaf as well. Most disabled people can swap endless anecdotes on this theme.

This kind of denigration is a universal complaint of the handicapped: "You'd think I was retarded, too." When the able-bodied are forced into confrontation with the disabled—that is, when they cannot escape—they often cope with the threat by treating the disabled as minors or as incompetent, withholding deference and thereby depriving them of their due as fellow humans. They are also differentiating themselves from the disabled person by asserting their superiority, as if this would somehow make them less vulnerable to a similar fate. To make matters worse, the disabled, particularly the deformed, are sometimes seen as evil, as in Shakespeare's *Richard III* or Victor Hugo's *Hunchback of Notre Dame*. This may well be a projection of the inner hostility of the able-bodied toward the handicapped, a sentiment that surely exists, however seldom it is shown. And so it is that physical impairment is generalized to the extent that it even includes character, a process called "spread" by social psychologist Beatrice Wright (1960).

Most Americans, including medical people, carry around inside their heads a set of notions about the social position of the handicapped. Whatever its other qualities, this attitude places the disabled not in the social mainstream but on the periphery, pensioned off and largely out of sight. During my periods of hospitalization, even the hospital personnel found me anomalous, for not only was I fully employed, but also doing research in their own area of expertise. One social worker asked me, "What *was* your occupation?" It is not that they begrudged me my ability to keep working. Quite to the contrary, they were honestly pleased by it. It simply made me a very different social type, a special case. My own doctors know this, of course, and they have often corrected a medical colleague's recommendations by saying, "He can't do that, he's a working man." But he's a quadriplegic working man, and this one trait now defines me. It need not always be so, however. Consider Franklin D. Roosevelt's triumph over such total categorization. He muted his disability by always standing to deliver speeches and never allowing himself to be photographed in his wheelchair.

The disabled person must make an extra effort to establish status as an autonomous, worthy individual, but the reaction of the other party may totally undercut these pretensions through some thoughtless act or omission. Even if the able-bodied person is making a conscious attempt to pay deference to the disabled party, the able-bodied must struggle against the underlying ambiguity of the encounter, the lack of clear cultural guidelines on how to behave, and perhaps his own sense of revulsion. This often lends an atmosphere of forced artificiality to an occasion. It can go flat through the need to resort to formality, hyperbole, and fake joviality, attempts at humor or effusive friendliness. Meetings between the able and the disabled can indeed be awkward, tense, and indeterminate affairs.

The distortion of social scenes by some salient and anomalous trait of one of the parties is not limited to the handicapped. A friend once told me of a party he attended at which a female guest wore a wide-mesh net dress and nothing else. She was, for all practical purposes, naked. Now there are some social circles in which the young woman would have been at serious risk— if not from the men, then from the other women. This, however, was a gathering of middle-class intellectuals, people who pride themselves on their urbanity and sophistication, and their lack of sexism. Nobody spoke of the dress or its wearer, and the men took care not to look at her. When a man conversed with her, he would train his eyes on her face in a deliberate effort to keep his glance from dropping to where it wanted to go. Not surprisingly, nobody spoke to her much. My friend commented that the party was a flop. Its tone remained formal, its conviviality was forced, and it broke up early.

The woman's see-through dress became the unspoken center of social dialogue, it subverted all other party activity, and it distorted all other relationships. Small wonder that people fled. In what I believe is the best essay on the sociology of disability yet published, Fred Davis wrote that the same thing happens during encounters, especially initial ones, between the able-bodied and the handicapped (1961). My own research and personal experience confirm his thesis. Just as one's identity as a disabled person is paramount in one's own mind, and the impairment an axiom for one's actions, so too is the other's reaction to the handicapped person overwhelmed by the flaw. This one obvious fact, the disabled person's radical bodily difference and departure from the human norm, dominates the thoughts of the other and may even repel him or her. But these are thoughts that can barely be articulated, let alone voiced.

The disability—paraplegia, blindness, or whatever it may be—is at center stage, in the forefront of the consciousness of both parties, and both must take steps to normalize the meeting, a process that Davis calls "deviance disavowal." The participants try to conduct themselves as if nothing were amiss, as if there were no hidden agenda. Several different scenarios are possible aside from avoidance and patronization. One technique is to make a brief allusion to it at the outset, as if to say, "There, that's on the table and out in the open; now let's get on with our business." This line of action is usually set in motion by the impaired person, who has to become an expert on putting others at their ease. He does this, as I have said, by his cheerful demeanor; anything else would make the other person run away. But every now and then the disabled party lets the other one writhe. It's a good way of getting rid of unwanted company.

Davis correctly states that in these primal scenes the hidden agenda, the dominant yet unspoken flaw, distorts sociability. The able-bodied person is worried about saying something hurtful and tiptoes into the encounter as if walking through a mine field. The disabled person knows what the other is thinking about, and the other knows that the disabled one knows that the other knows . . . as in a hall of mirrors. But these, again, are crazy mirrors, which both reflect and distort, and the normalization process operates on a bed of quicksand, since it is always in danger of being engulfed. Georg Simmel, one of the founders of modern sociology, once wrote that all social encounters threaten imminent disaster, and those with the handicapped are extreme illustrations of this general truth. Simmel also wrote that social action is predicated upon a "teleologically determined nonknowledge of one another" (1950:312), meaning that if people had clear, accurate personal information about one another and observed total honesty, it would destroy sociability and make human society impossible. We can add that not only does each party withhold information from the other, but also each distorts and embellishes those nuggets of fact that are released. And each suspends disbelief and half-accepts these little white lies as a necessary price for getting along. What makes the interaction of the disabled with the able-bodied so fascinating is that it rests not only on little fibs, but also on a big lie—that the physical deficiency makes no difference. It does, and in the uneasy interaction between the two people, misunderstandings become magnified and sociability inverted.

The underground salience of disability was neatly illustrated by a friend of mine who uses crutches because of childhood polio. He boarded an airplane, settled in a seat, and gave his crutches to the flight attendant. A woman sat down beside him, and the two started a friendly conversation that lasted until they landed. When the plane reached the terminal, the attendant returned with his crutches. Seeing them, the woman became flustered and embarrassed, muttered a quick good-bye, and disembarked hastily. She had not learned of the great mortgage on his identity until too late. I am sure that she wondered for the rest of the day whether she had said something "wrong," and it is clear that she would have behaved differently had she known. Her solution was to flee.

Davis was concerned primarily with initial encounters, occasions when, as one able-bodied informant said, "The first problem is where to direct your eyes." Davis's observations also apply to meetings with old associates, however. These can be more trying than encounters between strangers, because a conscious effort must be made to maintain previously established social roles, an attempt that runs foul of the disabled person's new identity and the other's aversion, guilt, and fear. The former is aware of the friend's inner turmoil, and the latter feels a sense of estrangement, as if the old associate, now stricken, had gone somewhere else—which he or she has. Their relationship must be redefined, which is often a harder job than forging a new one. As a result, the recently disabled often drop, or are dropped by, their old friends, kinfolk, and even their spouses.

The social circles of the disabled are foreshortened and shrunken, their associates diminished in number and often drawn from different social strata. Because of my shortened social world, I no longer go to anthropological conventions (which I have regarded as a waste of time ever since I gave up drinking), and consequently the professional circle I move in is smaller, just as my withdrawal from general university life has embedded me in my department and intensified my relations with more immediate colleagues and students. The same thing has happened in my suburban community, where I had made a hobby of local politics and had a large circle of friends. At first they rallied around me, but later they began to drop out of sight, which was partially my fault, for I seldom invited them to visit me. Isolation is a two-way street.

The fact that my isolation was not solely my fault, however, was brought home forcibly when a friend with muscular dystrophy and I organized a well-publicized program on disability at the town library. Naïvely, I had expected a large crowd of friends, neighbors, and political cronies, but only eight people turned up. I had completely failed to realize how much people were repelled by the subject, and how ambivalent their feelings had become toward me. The incident made me resentful, however, and I withdrew into a small circle of close friends who have become at ease with my disability. I realize now that in doing so I cut myself off from a number of other good people who are honestly puzzled about how to approach me. Some admit that they cannot stand what has happened to me, so they stay away. One not-so-close friend reportedly said, "What a shame. He *was* such a nice guy." The speaker's use of the past tense was not just an accident, for rumors surface every now and then that I am at death's door. I savor these incidents as raw data, for they harbor a metaphoric truth: what died was the old social me.

Avoiding the disabled cannot be said to be merely a result of ignorance and fear of the unfamiliar. The equanimity of the American medical profession was sorely strained in 1982 by a paper in the prestigious *New England Journal of Medicine* by Dr. David Rabin, at that time a faculty member at the Vanderbilt University Medical School (D. Rabin, P. L. Rabin, and R. Rabin 1982). Rabin, now deceased, had amyotrophic lateral sclerosis, which is always fatal, and this became widely known. He expected sympathetic understanding from his colleagues, but instead he found that they were avoiding him. This became more marked as the disease progressed, until one day he slipped and fell in the hospital, at which point a nearby doctor looked away. In general, he received more support and assistance from subordinates than from his peers. A great barrier separates physicians from their terminally ill patients, and Rabin had breached this wall. The profession consolidated ranks and, by isolating Rabin, sealed off the mixing of healer and doomed. My anthropological colleagues have behaved much better than that, but then human variety is the stuff of their craft.

The reduction of one's social universe is a qualitative matter as well as a quantitative one. The handicapped often go on to make new contacts, and researchers uniformly report that these tend to be with people of lower social standing than the old peer group (see Cogswell 1968). They befriend other disabled people whom they meet through clubs and church organizations, they associate with other unemployed people, and they feel ill at ease with the affluent—who are also among the first to avoid them. One of Fred Davis's able-bodied, upper-middle-class informants said that it was hard to assimilate serious impairment happening to "people of our status" (Davis 1961). This echoes a small episode in my own experience. I was attending a meeting of a disability rights organization and spotted across the room a state legislator whom I knew from my pre-wheelchair politicking. He at first didn't recognize me, for the chair served as a kind of disguise, but after he had placed me personally, and socially, he said that he hadn't expected to find "a person of your quality" at such a gathering. Such things are supposed to happen only to life's losers.

Owing to my age and long-established position, I was able to maintain my closest and most valued ties, although I attenuated some peripheral ones. I did not shift my associations down the social scale, although my research between 1980 and 1983 on the social relations of the disabled did bring me into association with many economically marginal people. I must admit, however, to feeling more uneasy in the first stages of this research than among Amazonian Indians—not *despite* the fact that I too am disabled, but *because* of it. I coped with the rather unexpected discomfort I felt when among others in wheelchairs by assuming the investigator's front that he is an independent and objective observer, *in* but not *of* the group he is studying. This neat separation of subject and object is never valid, and it was doubly false in my case. I had cherished a personal myth of almost-normalcy and took pride in my productive life; I was not yet ready to identify fully with the disabled. The same reaction was reported by Carling, who wrote, "As far back as I can remember, I withdrew very sharply from any contact with other cripples" (1962). Research among the motor-handicapped and participation in their organizations forced me to see myself in their lives, and this left me feeling that my own status was insecure and threatened. The research was too close to home for comfort—and I had learned a valuable lesson about the relationship between social standing and disability. I also learned a great deal about myself. All anthropological research involves a process of self-discovery, and my experience among the disabled was often painful.

Not long after I took up life in the wheelchair, I began to notice other curious shifts and nuances in my social world. After a dentist patted me on the head in 1980, I never returned to his surgery. But undergraduate students often would touch my arm or shoulder lightly when taking leave of me, something they never did in my walking days, and I found this pleasant. Why? The dentist was putting me in my place and treating me as one would a child, but the students were affirming a bond. They were reaching over a wall and asserting that they were on my side. I was a middle-aged professor and just as great an exam threat to them as any other instructor, but my physical impairment brought them closer to me because I was less imposing to them socially. As for the graduate students, it was not until after the onset of my disability that many began calling me by my first name, which was also a demonstration of closeness, rather than overfamiliarity.

The same thing happened in my contact with black people. I used to be invisible to black campus policemen, who often greeted a black colleague with whom I was walking by saying deliberately and clearly in the singular, "Hello, Professor, how are you today?" They now know who I am and say hello. I am now a white man who is worse off than they are, and my subtle loss of public standing brings me closer to their own status. We share a common position on the periphery of society—we are fellow outsiders.

During my first couple of years in the wheelchair, I noticed that men and women responded to me differently. My peer group of middle-aged, middle-class males seemed most threatened by my disability, probably because they identify most closely with me. Yet I found that generally my relations with women of all ages have become more relaxed and open; they are at once more solicitous than men and more at ease in my company. I noticed, too, that when I got in the elevator with a woman, she often would greet me or start a conversation; in my walking days, we both would have stared silently at the floor indicator. The same thing would happen when I was being wheeled across campus. As a little experiment, I would look at the face of an approaching woman until I caught her eye. At this point, the woman would ordinarily look away, but in most cases she would instead lock glances and nod or smile. The exchange of eye contact was an opening of the self, an acknowledgment of the other, a meeting without closure.

I found this new openness refreshing and agreeable, for despite being totally monogamous, I have always enjoyed the company of women. They are generally nicer people than men, although I should note quickly that there are many exceptions to this blatantly glib and unanthropological generalization. But what did this reaction tell me about relations between the sexes? It confirmed Freud's thesis that men and women are separated by a wall of antagonism, and that both sexes have elaborate, largely unconscious, mechanisms of defense against the other. And this was not merely a feature of Freud's Vienna. Yolanda and I found vivid evidence of this antagonism among the Mundurucu, where it was embedded in a living arrangement in which men and women slept in separate houses (Murphy and Murphy 1974). I argued in another paper that women everywhere commonly defend themselves by observing decorum and restraint; they are trained from childhood to say no, and to see every male as a potential threat (Murphy 1977). And despite all the recent changes in sexual standards, I believe that this is still the prevailing attitude.

The reason, then, for my new ease with women was that I was no longer a source of danger. After all, even if I wanted to pursue a woman, she could easily outrun me. Women were in total command of this aspect of our relations. One might protest that an aging, respectable professor is not much of a threat anyhow, except to himself, but this would overlook the fact that female defensiveness is based on a deeply ingrained, largely preconscious anxiety. It is less an active element in gender relations than an unspoken premise. Most of us do not realize the depth of this disposition, and I became aware of it only because my position as a man had been submerged by my new identity as a paraplegic.

Other researchers have also noted that women relate more easily than men to the disabled (see English 1971), and some have attributed this to the traditional female role in nurturing and in the care of the ill. This may indeed be a factor, but I doubt whether it is the major one. Women went into the nursing field in the past because it was one of the best jobs open to them. Now they prefer to become physicians or bankers. As for their having a special affinity for nursing, I can only remark that some of the finest nursing care I have received has been from men—and some of the worst has been from women. Rather than impute some kind of mothering instinct to women, it is much more to the point to note again that disability is a great leveler. It forecloses an ancient power struggle and puts an end to "male superiority."

Goffman's *Stigma* (1963) had great influence on the sociological study of disability by providing a common framework within which the handicapped, criminals, and certain minority groups could be seen as sharing a common lot: they are all outsiders, deviants from social norms. There are, however, problems with this framework. First of all, it throws into one pot people who have deliberately violated legal or moral standards, and persons who are in no way to blame for their stigmatized state. A person chooses to follow a life of crime, but nobody asks to be born a black, and certainly nobody wants to become a quadriplegic. These stations in life are visited upon people by inheritance or bad luck, not through choice. This, of course, does not prevent others from blaming the victim, and all too many benighted whites look on blacks as lazy and unintelligent people who prefer welfare and crime to working for a living. Even the disabled are often vaguely blamed for their condition, or at least for not achieving maximum recovery. And as sure proof that they bear stigmatized identities, physical impairment is looked on as something that does not happen to respectable people. The blind are folks who make brooms in sheltered workshops, or who sit on street corners with tin cups. They certainly do not belong among the upwardly mobile.

The handicapped and the dark of skin differ from the felon in degree of culpability, but they differ from each other as well. In the United States, racial prejudice has deep historic and economic roots, for blacks and Hispanic migrants have served for centuries as a pool of cheap labor, a position they now share increasingly with women—who could well be included among the stigmatized. It pays to keep them down. There are, however, no strong economic reasons for systematically excluding and abasing the physically handicapped, except for the minor fact that they are often supported and cared for at public expense. Otherwise, it is difficult to understand how discrimination against them can serve any significant social function. Nonetheless, research indicates that people who harbor hostility toward the disabled are statistically more likely to be prejudiced toward minorities (Chesler 1965). There is an element of plain nastiness in all this; bigotry observes no boundaries.

In addition to the structural differences between race and handicap, a different scale of values and emotional responses applies to the disabled. People are socialized to racial prejudice—they are taught to hate Jews and blacks—but not to discriminate against the disabled. Despite this, the physically impaired often arouse, in varying degrees, revulsion, fear, and outright hostility—sentiments that appear to be spontaneous and "natural" because they seem to violate our values and upbringing. But *do* they? Children are quite understandably curious about disabled people and often stare at them, only to have their parents yank their arms and say, "Don't look." Nothing could better teach a child to be horrified by disability; that the condition is so terrible that one cannot speak about it or even look at it. Children are in many such ways taught to regard impairment with a loathing far beyond that of racial prejudice. It is a sentiment that reinforces the fear that this could happen to them.

As for the injunction that the handicapped should be helped, we do this from a safe distance, by contributing to charities or by dropping coins in a beggar's cup. In this way, the able-bodied lull their consciences without getting too close; they stress their own separation and wholeness by an act of charity. These contradictory reactions of kindness and rejection help make the treatment of the disabled an arena of enormously conflicting values.

Seeing disability as a type of social deviancy confuses many issues, leading to a theoretical dead-end for social scientists. During the course of our research, my associates and I found it much more profitable to look upon disability in a different framework, one that simultaneously universalizes the condition and preserves its uniqueness. We treated disability as a form of *liminality*—a concept closely related to rites of passage. Initiation rituals have the purpose of involving the community in the transformation of an individual from one position in society to another. They typically do this in three phases: isolation and instruction of the initiate, ritual emergence, and reincorporation into society in the new role. It is during the transitional phase from isolation to emergence that the person is said to be in a liminal state—literally, at the threshold—a kind of social limbo in which he or she is left standing outside the formal social system.

We owe a great deal of our understanding of ritual to Arnold van Gennep and Emile Durkheim, and to Durkheim's students Henri Hubert and Marcel Mauss, but it is the anthropologist Victor Turner who has done most to bring their ideas into line with modern cultural and social theory. The title of one of his essays, "Betwixt and Between," is actually a neat description of the ambiguous position of the disabled in American life (Turner 1967). The long-term physically impaired are neither sick nor well, neither dead nor fully alive, neither out of society nor wholly in it. They are human beings, but their bodies are warped or malfunctioning, leaving their full humanity in doubt. They are not ill, for illness is transitional to either death or recovery. Indeed, illness is a fine example of a nonreligious, nonceremonial liminal condition. The sick person lives in a state of social suspension until he or she gets better. The disabled spend a lifetime in a similar suspended state. They are neither fish nor fowl; they exist in partial isolation from society as undefined, ambiguous people.

This undefined quality, an existential departure from normality, contributes to the widespread aversion to the disabled reported by researchers. The anthropologist Mary Douglas wrote in her 1966 book *Purity and Danger* that cultural symbolism sorts out conventional reality into tidy categories, and that departures from these neat classifications are regarded in many cultures as dangerous. She argues that the anomaly posed by the pig, an animal with cloven hoofs that doesn't chew its cud, is the reason for the Hebrew taboo on the eating of its flesh. Lack of clarity means lack of cleanliness—pork, therefore, is polluting and must be avoided. The permanently disabled also fall into the category of the contaminated—and for much the same reason. They are anomalies, like deeply spastic people or the so-called Elephant Man, who had the dubious honor of being the most facially deformed person of his time. In the often-brutal argot of our own age, the severely disabled are "downers"; they depress people and are best kept away from places of relaxation and enjoyment. They also "gross out" ordinary folks, meaning that they cause disgust or revulsion. Not everybody reacts this way, of course, but it still is quite common. Until very recently, restaurants occasionally turned away the obviously handicapped, an attitude that changed only after concerted efforts were made to reeducate the public. Some disabilities disturb the able-bodied more than others. There is a hierarchy of devaluation that varies with severity and type of disability. At the bottom of the scale are persons with facial disfigurement or marked body distortion; wheelchairs are somewhere in the middle. The main criterion seems to be based on the extent to which one differs from the standard human form.

One can add to Douglas's theory Claude Lévi-Strauss's idea that the greatest of all binary distinctions in human thought is the separation of nature and culture. Placed in the framework of this grand dualism, the physical impairment is an infringement by nature, an intrusion that undercuts one's status as a bearer of culture. This same process is at work in societies that isolate women during their menstrual periods or after childbirth. This, finally, is what makes disability so different from other kinds of "deviance." It is not just a departure from the moral code, but a distortion of conventional classification and understanding. The contamination of the handicapped by nature joins with the logical anomaly posed by their bodies to compromise their very humanness.

Turner writes that persons undergoing ritual changes of status "are at once no longer classified and not yet classified" (1967:96). They have lost their old status and have not yet acquired a new one. This leaves others uncertain about how to act toward them, and here we have an echo of the recurrent quandary of what to do about the disabled. This indeterminacy can be resolved by segregating or avoiding such liminal people—they become ritually polluted in Douglas's sense. In simple, primitive societies, puberty-rite initiates may be sequestered for weeks, months, or even years, a removal that in modern, complex societies is accomplished by such mild measures as after-school religious instruction and the honeymoon. A far more severe form of isolation is effected by the confinement of the disabled to hospitals and nursing homes, or by their inability to leave their dwellings because of the physical barriers of curbs, steps, and inaccessible public transport.

There are other striking parallels between the disabled and initiates. Turner writes that "between instructors and neophytes there is often complete authority and complete submission; among neophytes there is often complete equality" (1967:99). This certainly describes the authoritarian and tutelary role of medical people, who serve the same purpose in rehabilitation wards as do tribal elders in bush schools. The equality of the neophytes is also present. Hospitals strip people of their previous identities and reduce them to the amorphous status of "patient," and anyone who has spent long spells in these establishments knows that the patients usually interact as equals, ignoring one another's prior social distinctions.

This parity of rank also occurs outside the hospital among the disabled. During the past ten years, I have participated in a number of organizations of the handicapped and attended countless meetings, and I have been struck with the egalitarian atmosphere that prevails. This equality has been extended to me despite the fact that I have often been the oldest person present and almost always the holder of the most prestigious professional position. Nobody, however, has called me "doctor" or "professor" or even "mister"; they have used only first names. There has been some deference to the fact that I was more informed about disability than most of them, but it has given me little authority. In fact, I have often been chagrined to find that many of my opinions have been shrugged off—a blow to the ego of somebody accustomed to having his audiences take notes on everything he says. What was even more threatening to my professional stuffiness, however, was the fact that much more serious attention was paid to able-bodied, outside "experts." The disabled thus engage in the same invidious distinctions and practices they ostensibly deplore.

Our shared identities as disabled people override the old hierarchies of age, education, and occupation, and they wash out many sex-role barriers as well. I first noted this when undergoing physical therapy in 1976. Immediately after being introduced to a young woman with a partially paralyzed leg, I asked her, "How is your therapy going?" She replied, "I cry a lot lately." And I responded, "I can't cry at all, and that's worse." It was a totally spontaneous exchange, and afterward I thought what an unusual conversation it had been. Did I really say that to a woman I had just met? During a later hospitalization on a rehabilitation floor, I was placed in a room with three women. This departure from customary hospital procedure was necessitated by crowding and scheduling problems, but it did not bother us occupants. None of us could get out of our beds, and an attempted molestation by me, or by one of the women, would have been hailed as a miracle.

As liminal people, the disabled confront each other as whole individuals, unseparated by social distinctions, and often they make strikingly frank revelations to one another. I have had informal conversations with paraplegic women that gravitated without direction to bowel and bladder problems. And one multiple sclerosis researcher, who has the disease herself, says that male informants usually tell her voluntarily about their impotency problems. This openness facilitates fieldwork among the disabled by disabled researchers, although one must be careful not to assume that one's own experience of impairment is the same as an informant's. Another result of this democracy among the disabled is that, after they have got over their initial aversion—which only adds to their isolation—many seek one another's company, often through membership in disability organizations. There they find fellowship and refuge from a world that commonly relegates them to its margins.

The disabled person fits into the mold of liminality far better than into the model of social deviance followed by sociologists. Writing about ritual process in primitive societies, Turner says "liminality is frequently likened to death, to being in the womb, to invisibility, to darkness, to bisexuality, to the wilderness, and to an eclipse of the sun or moon" (1967:95). How well this fits everything we have discussed: the occasional rumor of my death, the social invisibility of the disabled, the attribution of asexuality in the popular mind, the unisex hospital room, and the blurring of sex roles within the fellowship of the handicapped. The disabled are more than deviants. They are the Other.

Just as the bodies of the disabled are permanently impaired, so also is their standing as members of society. The lasting indeterminacy of their state of being produces a similar lack of definition of their social roles, which are in any event superseded and obscured by their spoiled identities. Their persons are regarded as contaminated; eyes are averted and people take care not to approach wheelchairs too closely. My colleague Jessica Scheer refers to wheelchairs as "portable seclusion huts," for they are indeed isolation chambers of a sort (Scheer 1984). So, too, are the dwellings of the handicapped, and my associate Richard Mack reports on the plight of many poor, black paraplegics who live in New York City walk-up apartments that they can leave only when they are carried down several flights of stairs—which means seldom (Mack 1985). They are prisoners.

The disabled in America are pulled back into themselves by their own sense of loss and inadequacy, an impulse to withdraw that conspires with their devaluation by society to push them further into isolation. Add to this the fact that they confront a physical environment built by people with whole bodies for people with whole bodies, and one may well wonder how any of them manage to break out into the world. But they do, and in increasing numbers.

NOTE

1. For a cross-cultural survey of attitudes toward the disabled, see Hanks and Hanks 1948.

REFERENCES

Carling, Finn
    1962   *And Yet We Are Human.* London: Chatto and Windus.
Chesler, M.
    1965   Ethnocentrism and attitudes toward disabled persons. *Journal of Personality and Social Psychology* 2:877–882.
Cogswell, Betty E.
    1968   Self-socialization: Readjustment of paraplegics in the community. *Journal of Rehabilitation* 34:11–13, 35.
Davis, Fred
    1961   Deviance disavowal: The management of strained interaction by the visibly handicapped. *Social Problems* 9:121–132.
Douglas, Mary
    1966   *Purity and Danger: An Analysis of the Concepts of Pollution and Taboo.* London: Routledge and Kegan Paul.
English, R. William
    1971   Correlates of stigma towards physically disabled persons. *Rehabilitation Research and Practice Review* 2:1–17.
Gliedman, John, and William Roth
    1980   *The Unexpected Minority: Handicapped Children in America.* New York: Harcourt Brace Jovanovitch.
Goffman, Erving
    1956   On the nature of deference and demeanor. *American Anthropologist* 58:473–502.

1963 *Stigma: Notes on the Management of Spoiled Identity.* Englewood Cliffs, N.J.: Prentice-Hall.

Hanks, Jane, and L. M. Hanks, Jr.
1948 The physically disabled in certain non-Occidental societies. *Journal of Social Issues* 4:11–20.

Kojima, Yoko
1977 Disabled individuals in Japanese society. *Rehabilitation World* 3:18–25.

Mack, Richard
1985 Manuscript.

Miner, Horace
1956 Body ritual among the Nacirema. *American Anthropologist* 58:503–507.

Murphy, Robert F.
1977 Man's culture and woman's nature. *Annals of the New York Academy of Sciences* 293:15–24.

Murphy, Yolanda, and Robert F. Murphy
1974 *Women of the Forest.* New York: Columbia University Press.

Rabin, David, with P. L. Rabin and R. Rabin
1982 Compounding the ordeal of ALS: Isolation from my fellow physicians. *New England Journal of Medicine* 307(8):506–509.

Scheer, Jessica
1984 They act like it was contagious. In *Social Aspects of Chronic Illness, Impairment, and Disability,* ed. S. C. Hey, G. Kiger, and J. Seidel. Salem, Ore.: Willamette University.

Simmel, Georg
1950 *The Sociology of Georg Simmel,* ed. Kurt Wolff. Glencoe, Ill.: Free Press.

Turner, Victor
1967 *The Forest of Symbols: Aspects of Ndembu Ritual.* Ithaca, N.Y.: Cornell University Press.

Wright, Beatrice
1960 *Physical Disability: A Psychological Approach.* London: Harper and Row.

EIGHT

Sighted Lovers and Blind Husbands: Experiences of Blind Women in Uganda

Nayinda Sentumbwe

During eleven months of fieldwork in 1987 and 1989 I examined the social and economic experiences of informants who, with varying success, had participated in the education and/or rehabilitation programs available to blind people[1] in Uganda. I did not specifically collect data on the conjugal experiences of informants. Nevertheless, I became aware of the disparities between the marital patterns of female and male informants and inquired about them at opportune moments. The study covered thirty blind informants, including twelve women. Five women were married or cohabiting and one was separated; of the remaining, five were still at school and the sixth one employed and not involved in any steady relationship at the time. The five women who were married or cohabiting had blind husbands or cohabitants, and even the separated one had been married to a blind man. Moreover, a number of these informants had been involved in various sexual relationships with blind men.

I will attempt to scrutinize the sexual and marital opportunities of blind women in Uganda in terms of the experiences of these female informants. Most blind people in education or rehabilitation programs expect to lead lives that are not too dissimilar to those of their "educated" sighted kin and peers, including marriage and child rearing. "If I am lucky enough to complete my studies, I am certain of a bright future. I expect to get a good job, to marry and to set up house. . . . I hope to be a useful citizen of my country," said one blind secondary school student, for example. Although only an insignificant number of the estimated three hundred thousand blind Ugandans currently benefit from education and training programs, their role and influence as representatives of blind people is significant.

DEFINITION OF THE PROBLEM

According to my data, the marital opportunities of blind women in Uganda are limited. All married female informants had blind spouses, while such was not the case for the males. For want of a better term, I refer to the practice of marriage between disabled persons as *in-marriage*.[2] My research showed that blind Ugandan women are more prone to in-marriage than blind men are. In-marriage for blind women results from sighted men's lack of desire to enter into legitimate marital relations with them. Explanations for this lack of interest can best be understood through an analysis of two patterns: people's perceptions of blindness and blind people, and gender relations, particularly as they are manifested in the roles of a housewife in the Ugandan household.

The above analytical approach does not overlook the fact that in-marriage is generally facilitated by the provision of education and rehabilitation to the blind. One aspect of such normally institution-based education or rehabilitation is that it often provides the arena for the first social contact between individuals having a similar physiological impairment. Such institutions, therefore, have the significant function of initiating and forging social relationships, which, as substantiated by my data, become long-term. All the in-married couples in my 1987 study and those I heard about elsewhere met their spouses at institutions of training. Nevertheless, we still have to account for the fact that females tend to be more prone to in-marriage than blind males are.

Schooling and training programs for blind people can be seen as measures taken to enhance their social and economic opportunities because such programs tend to transform the coping prospects of the blind and, hence, their *life space*. Life space can be described as the type and character of social and cultural fields of relations in which people operate, or to which they are confined. "Coping" primarily refers to an individual's ability to function in everyday life situations. For the disabled person such functioning entails the strategies applied in performing daily routines of life, including management of social relations. Education and rehabilitation programs support coping in the sense of the ability to organize life in a manner that minimizes patron-client patterns and maximizes relative independence so that one's life space is enlarged.

PERCEPTIONS OF BLINDNESS

Most sighted Ugandans, including close kin of blind people, consider blindness to be problematic to normal social interaction. Loss of sight is believed to be the most incapacitating and, therefore, the worst of all physical disabilities. Nineteen-year-old Lekuro explained, "As a blind person many people have given me the impression that being blind is the worst thing that could have happened to me. I have, for example, heard people in my village say that it would have been much better if I had lost a leg or become deaf." Blind from the age of five, Lekuro was the only blind female student at the annex Senior Secondary School she attended then.

Martin, a thirty-year-old partially blind informant, married to a sighted wife with whom he had four children, remarked with bitterness:

> Most people are not aware of the fact that given the chance, blind people can do almost anything. They see a blind person as useless; as one who is a loss to his family and society. . . . The worst thing is that in most cases, persons with the preferred handicaps are treated no better than we the blind are.

Thirty-two-year-old Akello, who became blind when she was one year old and is now a single mother of four, puts the problem more empirically:

> My parents have just realized that a blind daughter can be useful, too, simply because I am educated; otherwise their understanding has been very discriminative where I am concerned. For example, I have no share when my sisters get land in which to do their gardening activities. Nothing is allocated to me, simply because I am blind.

This parental prejudice was also noted by an official of the department of special education:

> To begin with, not many parents saw the purpose of educating a blind child. They considered it a waste of money since God had cursed them by giving them a blind child. That blind child had to be kept at home until he or she died a natural death. Also, because of the usual sexist traditional beliefs that men are more important than women, parents are not very keen to help their blind daughters because they think they are more helpless than the blind boys.

The preceding statements point to beliefs and attitudes about blindness that generate negative perceptions and behavior toward the blind. Such negative perceptions are, for the most part, due to the functional attributes associated with sight. Loss of sight is, therefore, perceived as leading to defects in other basic physical functions. This phenomenon is what is generally referred to as *spread*. We might define spread as: the assumption that loss of one function leads to a decrease of capacity in other physical functions. Such an assumption can be the cause for inhibitions on the disabled person's participation in certain activities, as in Akello's case. Beatrice Wright has pointed out that "spread not only affects additional physical areas, but also involves social abilities and events as well. Others may look upon the person as less worthy, less acceptable" (1960:118). Spread must, therefore, be seen in relation to aspects of coping and one's life space. Particularly significant as we attempt to grasp the seeing public's attitudes and behavior toward the blind are situations of primary social interaction that call for face-to-face encounters between actors. In such situations, many sighted people imagine themselves in the blind person's position and, more often than not, envisage only incapacity and hopelessness. This is evident in such common emotionally expressed clichés as "I cannot imagine how you can . . . when you can't see."

THE VULNERABILITY OF BLIND PEOPLE

Ann Goerdt (personal communication) observed in her study of physical disability in Barbados that the assumed vulnerability of blind people contributes to the negative perception of their disability. In spite of being aware of what blind people were capable of doing, most Barbadians named blindness as the worst handicap one could have. They made references to the blind person's lack of function and, in particular, to the vulnerability of the blind. "Hence, when Barbadians identify the worst handicaps one could have, they reveal their concern with the control of self and the fear of being vulnerable to the control of others" (Goerdt 1984:13).

In Uganda, the helplessness and implicit vulnerability of the disabled and the blind in particular are manifest in the terms *kateyamba* and *agoro,* which the Baganda and Acholi ethnic groups respectively use to categorize the physically disabled. *Kateyamba* means unable to help oneself, and *agoro* may be translated as frail or helpless person.[3] The perception of the blind as "useless" implies that they are often regarded as the most helpless of those believed to be unable to help themselves. As will be shown in the next section, this becomes social reality in a variety of ways.

THE PERSISTING SICK ROLE

In Uganda blindness is frequently seen as sickness requiring corrective therapeutic action. This phenomenon of being persistently perceived as *sick* is often experienced in situations of social interaction involving both relatives and new acquaintances. People frequently ask me, as part of the usual friendly greeting in Luganda, "How is *sickness?*" (*Obulwadde butya?*). Believing themselves to have knowledge about hitherto untried remedies, well-meaning people offer information about possible cures. During a visit to one of my brothers, I happened to screw off the tip of my white cane. Surprised that a bit of the cane could so easily be taken off, my sister-in-law confessed her concern for "my situation." She revealed that she had consulted a folk healer about my blindness, during one of my previous visits. Her attempts to do something about my lost sight were thwarted: "The doctor could assist only if he got the tip of your walking stick. Your stick was made of metal so I simply had no way of chopping a bit off it without you knowing."

Combined with spread, the sick-role phenomenon can have significant social ramifications for the person so perceived. Illustrative of this is the case of a couple who, having agreed on marriage and gone through most of the relevant rites leading to marital status, had to end their relationship. The man was blind, and they were pressured by the girl's relatives who had been unaware of the impending marriage. These relatives could not envisage "their child" married to a blind man, a sick man. "Uganda is full of healthy men who will fight to have a beautiful girl like you. If you can't find one to marry you, tell us and we will get you as many as you want," one disbelieving paternal aunt (*senga*) is reported to have said. Marriage of a daughter should, preferably, be to in-laws with potential to help in times of need. The paternal aunt assumed not only that the blind fiancé was sick but that his impairment spread to all his faculties so that he would be unable to play even roles not dependent on sight.

One aspect of the sick role and spread which also contributes to the negative perception of the blind is the believed cause of disability. Where sinful or socially undesired acts such as witchcraft by the victim or parents are suspected, the blind person and the whole family might be permanently stigmatized. This form of spread will affect the life space of the people concerned because social interaction with them becomes limited to the minimum. This is so because many Ugandans dread sorcery.

We must note that positive perceptions are also experienced by blind people in the course of social interaction. My own material and studies on social perception by researchers such as G. Roger Barker (1948) indicate that intimate interaction between disabled and nondisabled individuals normally leads to changes in the way the latter perceive the former. Closer acquaintance leads to judgment of the disabled person on the basis of personality characteristics other than disability.

With respect to marital relationships, however, factors that evoke negative perceptions of the blind woman must be grasped in terms of the roles of a housewife in the Ugandan household and, in relation to the cultural values, beliefs, and practices that sustain them. Such factors, in most situations, preclude judgment of the blind woman on the basis of personality characteristics independent of her physical defects.

THE DOMESTIC ROLES OF UGANDAN WOMEN

In Uganda, as elsewhere in male-dominated societies, women are expected to satisfy men's sexual needs. However, which females it is permissible to have sexual intercourse with and/or to marry varies in accordance with the cultural beliefs and values of the various ethnic groups in the country. Like most women in other societies, Ugandan housewives are obliged to carry out household roles: mother, hostess, house- and homestead-keeper, provider of meals, provider of home-grown food, and so on. Even when most of the household tasks are performed by others, credit and/or criticism will be given to the housewife.[4] She is also the "social contact" between her own and her husband's family and is supposed to keep good and cooperative relations with neighbors. A woman's ability to fulfill these roles is always tested at times of celebration or crisis—occasions like weddings or funeral ceremonies, which prompt neighborhood and family gatherings. It is at such events that criticism of a woman's physical appearance and ability to perform tasks expected of a housewife is expressed. Such criticism is an evaluation of the man's choice of a wife: she is, for example, beautiful, charming, hard-working, ugly, lazy, and so on.

The status of wife involves economic and social aspects so important that among most ethnic groups in the country a household in which there is no wife is not considered to be a respectable home for the male owner. This socioeconomic dependence of men upon women is, for example, the theme for many folk and pop songs and jokes that lament the ills of bachelorhood. According to H. M. K. Tadria, even in recent years, the roles of Ugandan women as described above have not diminished in importance or changed in nature. However, "their social interpretations have changed and women's tasks are now conceived of as subsidiary to the tasks of men, not as complementary or crucial to survival and development" (Tadria 1987:79).

As a result, such tasks are often performed under stifling circumstances, with women frequently left open to the possibility of further exploitation and oppression. In a study of a Kampala suburban area, Christine Obbo (1980) found that women from all over the country migrated to the city in order to seek their social and economic independence.

Thus we see how important it is for men to get married and why they seek out competent women as wives. And we can better understand why blind women are not perceived as attractive marital partners for sighted men.

In spite of what would appear to be a life of wearying chores, most Ugandan women aspire to marriage. This is because in social terms, womanhood is signified by (1) matrimony, which implies (2) having a home, (3) motherhood, and (4) ability to fulfill specific domestic roles. Parents see marriage as the fulfillment of dreams for their daughters, particularly when celebrated with a wedding. A girl who seems to be turning into a spinster will be cajoled if not coerced into it as efforts at matchmaking are stepped up. Among other things, the girl's desire for marriage might be partly related to the expected *independence* (having a home of her own where she can enjoy some social status) and partly to the social security envisaged. Parenting children is part of the process for ensuring continuity of such security after the husband dies.

SEX AND MARITAL RELATIONSHIPS

Until the recent scare from AIDS, sexual promiscuity, especially on the part of males, has been common though not condoned. For women, particularly adolescent girls in urban areas, such casual relations often become the means for obtaining consumer goods that close kin cannot afford to provide.

Such sexual relationships as are permissible between male and female normally receive varying social definitions and legitimacy, not only according to the social relations between the parties involved but also depending on whether the relevant rites have been performed. Such rites may be religious (i.e., Christian, Islamic, etc.) or ethno-traditional (so-called customary). These, in addition to marriages contracted by the Registrar of Marriages, are given legal status in accordance with the country's Marriage Act. However, in everyday talk, even when no co-residence is involved, partners in any steady sexual relationship are normally spoken of as husband and wife, even though no rites have been performed. Even when marriage is legitimized by any of the other forms, customary obligations are expected to be fulfilled, particularly by the prospective wife and her family. These include the formal presentation to the prospective affines, payment of the bridewealth, a wedding ceremony, and so on. Either partner, particularly at times of disagreement, may refute the marital status with reference to any unperformed rites. Indeed, failure to observe certain rites may deprive the male partner of particular rights. For instance, until the necessary bridewealth has been paid, Akello's children belong to her clan, according to the customs of her ethnic group. However, marital processes have become flexible though confused. Rwama, blind and married to a sighted wife, informed me, for instance, that he paid the bridewealth for his wife in 1974. Eight years later, in 1982, they sanctified the marriage with a church ceremony. By then the couple already had several children.

In spite of this web of rights, rites, and different forms of legitimacy surrounding sexual relations, it is possible to categorize such relationships as follows:

1. *Lover:* Relationships that belong to this category include casual affairs by all age-groups and people of varying social statuses, including those already married. There is normally an element of secrecy in such relationships, though several trusted persons might know about the affair and may act as go-betweens for the sometimes clandestine meetings. For the unmarried or where polygamy is permissible, this relationship may eventually develop into legitimate marriage, particularly where pregnancy or elopement occurs.

2. *Mistress:* This is an informal relationship in which the man has economic responsibility for the woman's needs in return for her sexual and other services (such as doing his laundry). In this case, none of the rites are performed. Cohabitation is not entailed nor is procreation usually desired in such a relationship. The relationship can,

however, be turned into a concubinal one or into full marital status by the performance of the relevant rites.

3. *Wife:* Marriage is traditionally acknowledged as the most legitimate of all relationships involving sexual relations. It is consummated after the rites pertaining to at least one of the three legally accepted types of marriage have been performed.

4. One other relationship worth mentioning is one in which an economically independent female as household head keeps a male partner in return for his sexual services. Among some Bantu groups of Uganda, this *kweyombekera, nakyeyombekedde* status implies that the woman built her house.

Whichever of the above relationships is entered into, both the female and male parties to it often hope for approval of their partner from relatives and friends. As was exemplified by the case of the rejected blind husband-to-be, it is traditional practice, in fact, for a prospective spouse, particularly the female, to be "commended," "seconded," and finally "approved" by close kin and friends. Such kin and friends, including neighbors, normally contribute materially or otherwise both to the bridewealth and wedding ceremonies. Furthermore, as an addition to the family, the prospective spouse has to be acceptable in most physical and social aspects to the future in-laws, who expect to receive various services. How far a blind woman can be acceptable or participate in any of the above relationships and with what kind of males is significant for her life space and her achievement of full womanhood.

THE SEXUAL AND MARITAL OPPORTUNITIES OF BLIND WOMEN

We must take into consideration the differences in opportunities created by social, physiological, and other factors in the relationships of blind women. Whether a woman is totally blind or not will, for instance, often influence her coping and, subsequently, how she is perceived by others. Parents of a partially blind girl will, for example, be less protective of their daughter than will those of a totally blind one. Forty-year-old Mrs. Malitini, totally blind from the age of one and a half years, explained: "Those women who still live with their parents or other relatives are highly overprotected. Because the parents are oversympathetic and prevent their blind girls from doing anything in the home, others seeing that girl passive and unable to participate in any work see no use in marrying her."

Mrs. Malitini's observations, which are partly based on her own experiences prior to joining a vocational institution for the blind where she met her blind husband, exemplify how people's perceptions of the blind can become social reality. In the attempt to protect their daughters from assumed danger, parents neglect the traditional socialization processes that are intended to transform girls into competent housewives. Thereby, the stereotypes about the blind are reaffirmed. Even when she has received some education, a blind girl still has reduced marital opportunities because of the endorsement practice alluded to previously. Hence, although sexually attractive and able to participate in category 1 (lover) sexual relationships, a blind girl will normally not be socially acceptable as a potential housewife.

> Sighted men fear the reactions of others, mostly their relatives, [too much] to get too involved with blind women. For instance, it is difficult for a sighted man to introduce a woman who cannot see to his relatives and friends. He would feel ashamed, as, in our culture, marriage is not a thing between only two persons. Even if a sighted man makes you pregnant, he would not like it to be known that so-and-so has a child with a handicapped woman.

This was Mrs. Malitini's explanation when, in the course of one interview session, we touched on the subject of marriage between sighted and blind people.

Mrs. Malitini's observations are confirmed by the experiences of Judith and Juliana, who were once involved with sighted men in relationships of type 1 and 2, respectively. According to Judith,

> the boy lived near us in our village. He was my first boyfriend and used to tell me that he loved me very much and that we would get married when I completed school. Peter had already dropped out of school by then. . . . As I was at boarding school, I only used to meet Peter during my holidays. At school, we used to talk with the sighted girls about sex, but I think I was the only one among the blind that had a boyfriend. . . . I don't think that anyone else suspected us, though our affair lasted for over a year. . . . When the teachers discovered that I was pregnant, my parents were called in and I was expelled. At first I was afraid to tell who had put me in the situation, but eventually I did. . . . I don't recall the reaction of my parents, only that they were furious with Peter's father when he insisted that there was no way his son could have become involved with a blind girl. . . . To tell you the truth, in the beginning, not even my own family would believe that I was pregnant. . . . Nobody talked about him marrying me although I had told mother about Peter's promises.

Judith married a blind man later. In 1987 they had lived together for over twenty years and had seven children. Judith's case also illustrates the ambivalence and resignation of most parents to the destiny of their blind daughters.

Juliana's experiences illustrate the problematic nature of relationships between blind women and sighted men from a different perspective. Juliana, thirty-six and now almost blind, has had various sexual relationships, one of which was with a sighted man.

> I think it was easy for Lutta to like me because I was not totally blind, had employment and my own accommodation. Some sighted people don't usually

pay attention to your handicap, especially when you do most things well, you
know. . . . Lutta and I stayed together for maybe three years. . . . I am not certain of why we broke up, but it could be that when my sight started to deteri-
orate, I started doing things haphazardly, like a blind person, according to
those who see well.

Since the termination of her relationship with Lutta, Juliana has been involved with a blind man. She still has her job and with assistance from her
mother has raised six children, one of whom is from the relationship with
Lutta. Lutta's reasons for disengagement from the relationship are probably not so different from those of other men who reject marriage with blind
women. With Juliana's deteriorating eyesight and hence his fear of being
with a *blind* woman, with whom he could not get properly married, Lutta
had to terminate the relationship.

THE SOCIAL RELATIONS OF SEXUALITY AND DOMESTICITY

By analyzing the type of social relations and kinds of tasks involved in the
two dimensions, sexuality and domesticity, we can, to a certain degree, grasp
why sighted men are usually willing to have casual sex with any category of
disabled women but see them as unsuitable spouses. Three concepts—life
space, coping, and spread—are useful tools in such a task.

Sexual intercourse is an activity of the *private sphere* which generally requires no more than the two participants and an occasional go-between for
its consummation. Its life space aspects are thus circumscribed by the nature
of the relationship and its objective, namely sexual satisfaction. Other physical abilities or approval of the disabled partner by others are not required
for its realization. Consequently, a blind woman in the right place at the
right time is not disqualified as a possible sexual partner by factors normally
attributed to her disability. She is, therefore, not perceived as too incapacitated to *satisfy the sexual needs* of sighted men. This implies that relations
based on the sexual gratification of the sighted partner have the potential
for under-communicating factors that govern "normal" social interaction.
These sex-based relations are distinct from ordinary love relationships,
which involve a multiplicity of genuine emotional and other social considerations. We may correctly assume that some sighted men perceive disabled
sexual partners as "sexual objects." In this case, however, the physical and
other feminine attributes men usually pay attention to in their choice of sexual partners might not count for much.

In contrast, a Ugandan homestead is a relatively public sphere in which
domestic relations are intertwined with others in the social structure, all of
them sustained by cultural values and practices. Relationships of the *domestic sphere* thus involve more people than the spouses themselves, such that,
as suggested earlier, there is more room for evaluative criticism in the

course of social interaction. The public nature of almost all of the domestic roles of a housewife is more likely to evoke a linkage between physical impairment and other physical attributes than does her purely sexual role. Hence, coping in one sphere or field of social relations does not imply recognition of coping potential in the other. The management of a home requires sight and complete physical functioning, most people presume.

Judith's and Juliana's experiences illustrate the kind of relationships sighted men are willing to engage in with blind women. Juliana's case illustrates further that partially blind women have a greater scope of participation in such relationships. However, these relations are normally casual and less socially acceptable than others. In-marriage remains the viable alternative for blind women interested in long-term and *socially correct* relationships.

BLIND WOMEN AS EXAMPLES OF
THE COMPETENT UGANDAN WOMAN

According to my data, assumptions about the inadequacies of blind women are not wholly true. As exemplified by both the in-married, cohabiting, and other female informants, blind women are capable housewives and housekeepers who can successfully fulfill the various domestic roles assigned to Ugandan women. Some blind women are in situations typical of other Ugandan women:

1. Married, full-time housewife, staying at home to mother and bring up children, responsible for the household including food production (Judith)
2. Married and out in fixed-income employment, but still responsible for the domestic tasks (Mrs. Malitini)
3. Cohabiting and expecting to marry, with children from several different relationships (Juliana)
4. Single mother of children from several relationships (Akello)

Some of these women are well integrated in their communities and participate in intricate social relations, some of which include clandestine sex-related activities. This management of neighborhood and other social relations by blind women was, for example, once brought to my attention when what I had intended to be a facetious remark between former schoolmates was misunderstood. Being well acquainted with one Mrs. X, a blind lady, I once said jokingly that she should introduce me to any suitable women friends of hers since my wife was far away. That evening Mrs. X brought two friends of hers to see me. Both were sighted neighbors, and I had earlier been to the home of one of them, Mrs. Y, on a casual call on the neighbors of my informants. After Mrs. X had seen the visitors off, she returned and said with great satisfaction that she had accomplished her part.

Her friend Mrs. Y, she explained, was very much interested in me and since her husband was away visiting his second wife, all was clear for me to start a casual affair with Mrs. Y.! That personal experience clearly illustrates aspects of coping and life space, especially those concerning the management of social relations. What Mrs. X did was to play the normal social role of go-between in sexual intrigues, particularly the casual ones of the lover type.

THE SOCIAL IMPLICATIONS OF SEXUAL RELATIONS WITH SIGHTED MEN

Sexual relationships with sighted men have certain noteworthy ramifications for the blind female partner, particularly when motherhood is the result. Children have value as future providers of social security. Not only is the child expected to provide for the blind mother when the child is grown but often the child is brought up as the helping hand and companion, expected to be dependable and uncomplaining, and relieving other family members of such tasks in the process.[5] Furthermore, being a mother elevates the blind woman socially, for not only has she proved her womanhood by going through the experiences of childbirth and motherhood but also she has proved her fertility; childlessness is traditionally associated with barrenness. In the process of fulfilling the mother role, the blind mother also improves her coping and life space. In raising the child, she learns new techniques for care and survival, develops new values, and interacts with different categories of people, some of whom perceive her in a different light relative to their previously held perception of her and her lot. Moreover, a child of her own on whom she believes she can rely gives her feelings of independence.

Because most men fathering children with disabled women leave them in the sole care of the mothers, a blind woman, even when employed, may have difficulties meeting the needs of her child, such as school fees.[6] Because of the changes in the work, economic, and social patterns brought about by years of political and economic turmoil, she may no longer take it for granted that her kin will provide the necessary support either. (See, e.g., Banugire 1987; Harmsworth 1987.)

CONCLUSION

Sighted men in Uganda perceive blind women as possible sexual partners but not normally as suitable housewives. People's perceptions of the blind (as helpless, useless, vulnerable, and sick) and the culturally determined domestic roles of women are significant factors that determine the nature of such relationships. Because of the functional characteristics attributed to sight, so-called normal people associate loss of sight with lack of physical functions. This has been referred to as spread. Because of it, men envisage only obstacles and lack of coping in the everyday life situations of a blind woman. In the public sphere of the Ugandan household, in which members of the extended family, neighbors, and friends actively take part, participants cannot envisage housewife roles for blind women. Nevertheless, sighted men and blind women do engage in sexual relationships, which are considered less legitimate and therefore of a lower social status. If, as often happens, pregnancy results, the social status of the blind mother is positively changed because of the cultural values and practices pertaining to motherhood. These will entail involvement with wider social networks that engender new coping skills and changes in her life space.

As is apparent from the in-marriage cases, blind women can successfully fulfill the domestic roles traditionally expected of Ugandan housewives. However, if sighted men are to be made aware of such success and, thereby, the plausibility of marriage with blind women, the equation of visual impairment with physical incapacity has to be refuted. This can, to a certain extent, be done through education for the blind themselves so that they do not become the living example of stereotypes about the disabled. On another level, education and information must be targeted at parents of blind children and the general sighted public. Through such public education, the sighted might come to see the blind as persons with a visual impairment rather than as people who are blind and therefore socially and physically handicapped. This would be in line with the experiences of many informants and scientific studies indicating that closer acquaintance between the disabled and the nondisabled normally leads to judgment of the disabled person on the basis of other personality characteristics. Nevertheless, studies concerning the employment opportunities of the physically disabled indicate that they normally have to show greater ability than their nondisabled rivals; it will therefore take more than programs of public information and close contacts between sighted and blind for blind women to become perceived as desirable wives in the homes of Ugandan sighted men.

Cross-cultural observations confirm the problematic marital experiences of blind women. From Nicaragua, Frank Bruun (personal communication) reports tendencies toward in-marriage similar to those in Uganda. Bruun's observations are supported by Constance Buvollen (1983) in a report on visually handicapped women in Managua submitted to the Norwegian Association of the Blind. Even in Norway, where the levels of sexual equality and technological advancement are claimed to be high, E. M. Haugann (1989) suggests that traditional gender roles, among other things, hamper marriage between sighted men and blind women. Shlomo Deshen (1987) reports similar problems from Israel. Ann Goerdt (personal communication) maintains that it is a general phenomenon among most categories of disability that women experience "problems" with finding nondisabled husbands.

For the blind woman in Uganda to improve her marital prospects, measures designed to alleviate the socioeconomic factors that, together with certain cultural practices and values, circumscribe her life chances and her life space have to be given priority. The self-reliant "normal" woman always has the potential to attract men because of her socioeconomic status; self-reliance might provide the same opportunities to a blind woman. The capacity for self-reliance is, for example, among the main reasons for the relatively common phenomenon of marriage between blind men and sighted women. Sighted women participate actively in income-generating activities and have, with increased education and other social and economic changes, progressively embraced male-dominated activities. Therefore, they do not have to depend totally on the blind spouse or on the goodwill of their kin for survival. In contrast, most men refuse to take on any "woman's activities"; consequently, men still need competent housewives who can carry out the domestic roles that make a Ugandan household a good home.

This work raises important questions for further research. What of the blind women who, living all their lives in their home surroundings, get no opportunity to meet blind men? What of the school dropouts and those who, on completion of education or rehabilitation programs, return to their home villages with little or no opportunity for social contact with blind friends? What happens in cases where married women acquire visual impairment?

Although it is possible to make certain assumptions regarding such questions from the perspective taken in this article, comprehensive studies about the sexual and marital opportunities of blind Ugandans are needed. Because both activities are transactions normally entered into on the basis of important cultural, economic, and social considerations, such studies would elucidate patterns fundamental for all Ugandans, and they would also contribute toward a better understanding of the particular life situations of Ugandans who are visually impaired.

NOTES

1. I will henceforth use the term *blind* instead of the more encompassing but cumbersome *visually impaired*. In Uganda, the popular usage of the former term is much broader than the biomedical definition. According to Dr. Mutambo of Jinja Hospital, and in line with the WHO, the medical profession in Uganda defines one as "blind" who cannot count fingers at a distance of six feet.

2. Not to be confused with the endogamous practices anthropologists usually associate with "in-marriage."

3. As designations for disabled persons, the terms are apparently of recent origin, necessitated by the introduction of institutions for the disabled.

4. Other members of the household such as children, female kin, and house girls/boys (usually found in well-off families, particularly in urban areas) are obliged to assist the housewife in most of her domestic duties.

5. The value of children to their blind parents, even in mixed marriages, cannot be emphasized enough. This is exemplified by fifty-six-year-old Tirigana, blind since 1968. When I asked him whether he felt bad about having his twelve-year-old son for a guide instead of letting him return to school, he replied: "Ah! I do feel that and he has lost a lot, but he is the only dependable person./ . . . I can't rely on any other person to the extent I do on my son."

6. The problem of these children, born into lives of deprivation, was raised by a representative of the Uganda Foundation for the Blind. Blind informants referred to it repeatedly as well. Several families are receiving educational assistance for their children from foreign Christian organizations.

REFERENCES

Banugire, Firimooni R.
    1987   The impact of the economic crisis on fixed income–earners. In *Beyond Crisis: Development Issues in Uganda,* ed. P. D. Wiebe and C. P. Dodge. Kampala: Makerere Institute of Social Research.

Barker, G. Roger
    1948   The social psychology of physical disability. *Journal of Social Issues* 4(4):28–38.

Buvollen, Constance R. A.
    1983   Blind women in Managua: A field study. Report to Norges Blinde-forbund, Oslo.

Deshen, Shlomo
    1987   Coming of age among blind people in Israel. *Disability, Handicap and Society* 2(2):137–149.

Goerdt, Ann
    1984   Physical disability in Barbados: A cultural perspective. Ph.D. thesis, New York University. Ann Arbor: University Microfilms.

Harmsworth, Josephine Wanja
    1987   The Ugandan family in transition. In *Beyond Crisis: Development Issues in Uganda,* ed. P. D. Wiebe and C. P. Dodge. Kampala: Makerere Institute of Social Research.

Haugann, E. Momrak
    1989   Synshemma kvinner i eit feministisk perspektiv [Visually impaired women in a feminist perspective]. *Norges Blinde* 24:5–13.

Obbo, Christine
    1980   *African Women: The Struggle for Economic Independence.* London: Zed Press.

Tadria, H. M. K.
    1987   Changes and continuity in the position of women in Uganda. In *Beyond Crisis: Development Issues in Uganda,* ed. P. D. Wiebe and C. P. Dodge. Kampala: Makerere Institute of Social Research.

Wright, Beatrice A.
    1960   *Physical Disability: A Psychological Approach.* New York: Harper and Row.

NINE

Public Discourses on Rehabilitation: From Norway to Botswana

Benedicte Ingstad

In recent years the adoption of a rehabilitation program in a developing country has most often taken place in one of the following ways:

A nongovernmental organization (NGO) from a developed country wants to establish a rehabilitation activity in a developing country and approaches the government for permission. Sometimes it also links up with a local sister organization or helps one to be established. Money for setting up the rehabilitation activity is brought in from the North (i.e., North America or Europe), most often with the expectation that it will eventually be sustained locally through fund-raising and/or government support. Rehabilitation projects established in this manner usually take the form of a center or a special school, catering mainly to clients from one limited area, often with only one type of impairment. In recent years, however, some NGOs have tried to reach a larger population, usually through some sort of community-based program.

Alternatively (or sometimes simultaneously), a government from a developing country has identified rehabilitation as a need and approaches other governments or NGOs for bilateral aid in setting up a program. This pattern of establishing rehabilitation was seen quite frequently in the time immediately before and after the International Year of Disabled Persons (1981). The conscience of the international community was stirred, and in many countries disabled people were for the first time officially defined as a group with certain rights. Programs established through the government usually aim at (eventually) reaching the whole population of disabled people. There are, however, recent examples of governments building rehabilitation centers, especially following wars.

This chapter is concerned with the transfer of discourses about rehabilitation from the North to the South. It deals with historical transformations in which popular perceptions of disabled people as persons relate to ongoing processes of change in society at large.

Two countries—Norway and Botswana—and the relationship between them are used as examples. Norway has for many years been one of the main supporters of the development of the Botswana health care sector, of which rehabilitation is supposed to be an integrated part. Thus, discourses in the form of programs are carried over from North to South in the name of "development."

Although influenced by the development in other European countries, and similar in many ways to the discourses in the other Scandinavian countries, the present Norwegian public discourse on rehabilitation has its own history. It has sprung from the development of a particular state structure based on concepts of the equality and welfare of all citizens. Present-day rehabilitation programs thus define disabled people as equal citizens, as individuals enjoying certain rights and for whom the state and the community have responsibility. But it has not always been like this. I will describe the emergence of the key elements in the Norwegian public discourse on rehabilitation in order to contrast the Norwegian situation with that of Botswana, where some of these elements have been exported to form part of a very different history. In recent years Norway has stood as one of the pioneers (together with Sweden and Denmark) in establishing the principles of *integration* and *normalization* as a goal in the rehabilitation of disabled people, and these are the main premises on which their aid to rehabilitation in Botswana is founded.

The history of rehabilitation discourse in Botswana is much shorter. Only in recent years have people with various types of disabilities been recognized as persons with potential for improvement, and they are still seen as being mainly the responsibility of their households and extended families. Discourses on "what is best for the disabled person" imported from England and Germany and later from Norway and Sweden do not fit with local concepts and social organization. They take time to be internalized among the people and to be given priority at the national level. Rehabilitation workers coming from the North, like other development "experts," tend not to be aware of this. Thus when programs fail to live up to expectations, which has been the case in Botswana, this tends to be blamed on the recipients and not on the planners and implementers (see chap. 13).

In focusing on public discourses on rehabilitation we have to remember that these do not necessarily reflect how all or even most disabled people are treated. Discourses include stereotypes, in some cases negatively loaded, in some cases idealized pictures, in some cases "recipes" for action. The real life situation of the disabled people and their family members can only be explored by listening to their own voices telling about their own experiences. Still, an understanding of the generation of public discourses is important in that they represent constraints and possibilities for the choices disabled people can make and their chances of leading a meaningful life in their particular sociocultural setting.

NORWAY

Public Responsibility, Education, and Protection

For almost four hundred years Norway was a colony of Denmark, and for almost a hundred years it was in union with Sweden, gaining independence in 1905. Like colonies elsewhere in the world, it was largely a rural society with little input of investments and large values in the form of lumber, minerals, and fish going out of the country. The best farmland and forests were in the hands of a few (sometimes foreign) owners passing down undivided from father to eldest son. This produced a system of landless farmers who gave free labor, and sometimes also paid, for the right to cultivate a small plot of the landowner's soil, and it laid the ground for extensive rural poverty and eventually also for large-scale emigration to America.

Before the latter part of the nineteenth century, "disability" does not seem to have provided a specific identity in Norwegian society. People with impairments were members of families and participated in the lives and tasks of their households according to their abilities. However, in the poor families at least, there would have been little time or human resources to spare in order to give a severely impaired person sufficient stimulation to develop his or her potential. And in the population at large there was probably little idea that improvements could actually take place in some cases.

At the bottom of the social hierarchy were those who had no access to land and no means of support: the extremely poor, the orphans, and the aged without families to care for them. Among these there were certainly also some disabled people, although as in other parts of Europe (Stiker 1982; Stone 1984) they were not at this time singled out as a special category but grouped with others as *verdig trengende* (worthy needy), in contrast to those considered less worthy such as petty thieves and other criminals as well as some ethnic minorities. They were assigned to the poorhouse or they drifted along from farm to farm begging for work or charity (Sundby 1981). A system in which the farmers took care of a certain number of drifters for a limited time was developed, thus sharing the burden of support between the landowners. Much later, as the government came to take more responsibility for disabled persons, remnants of this tradition survived: farmers were paid for giving food and lodging to special types of "patients" (mainly the mentally ill and mentally retarded), providing an additional income to some marginal farming districts. The possibility for exploitation of labor that this allowed was largely undercommunicated.

Following the adoption of a new constitution in 1814, a major effort was made to establish free and compulsory basic schooling for all children. It soon became clear, however, that there were some children who could not follow the ordinary classes. Schools for the blind and the deaf were founded around 1870, patterned after similar schools elsewhere in Europe, and public education of children with mental retardation started soon thereafter. In 1881 a law was passed that established compulsory education for children who were blind, deaf, and mentally retarded.

Education of the mentally retarded, or "idiots" or the "abnormal" as they were then called in public documents, posed particular problems. The purpose of the special education was "to relieve the public school system of this burden and through intensive training eventually to bring these children to a stage where they may return to and profit from the public school system" (NOU 1973:11, my translation). We see that this quotation from one of the pioneers in special education for the mentally retarded in Norway reveals a great deal of optimism: Mentally retarded children, given the right amount of training and stimulation, would eventually become "normal." This necessarily led to a certain amount of disappointment. After special classes had been started in several major towns, it was found that, although training brought amazing results in some pupils, they still lagged behind their age-mates and many of them were never able to profit from "education" the way the term was understood at that time.

Special education was continued for the deaf and the blind and the mildly retarded along the lines laid out by the first educational pioneers, through special classes and, later on, special schools. However, for the more severely mentally retarded the developments eventually led to efforts aimed more at protecting the weakest.

Following the realization that the special classes had not reached the moderately and the severely mentally retarded children, voices were heard in favor of building homes for the "untrainables" (as they were called in public documents). The purpose of these homes was partly to relieve the families of their heavy burden, partly to give care and protection. The first "home" of this kind was established in 1907 on a private basis, and a few more were to follow shortly. However, most of these were taken over by the government within the next decade, which shows us that already in these early years there existed an ideology that care for disabled people should be a public responsibility. However, the spirit of voluntarism and charity continued to play an important role up into the 1970s in the form of "support groups" (*støttelag*) of dedicated people (mainly women) who in various ways collected money for extra-budgetary expenses benefiting the inmates of these "homes."

Although these "homes" for disabled people were started with the best intentions of being a positive substitute for living with their families, their mere existence created a demand that soon led to overcrowding. The good intentions were increasingly hard to realize, and the main effect of these places was to segregate the retarded from mainstream life. A similar pattern was evident in the development of institutions in other European countries, the extreme of which we have recently seen in Rumania. Still, the idea that this was a good solution for everyone concerned remained, partly kept alive by the fact that few people had actually been inside such institutions. Only one or two decades ago some pediatricians at the birth of a Down's syndrome child would advise the parents to send it to an institution and to forget about it.

Although by nature somewhat different in their scope, the special schools for blind and deaf children also tended to segregate their pupils from society. Because these schools were established in a few dispersed places, they tended to accommodate many students, who often had to travel long distances, and then were able to see their families only once or twice a year. I grew up very close to such a school for the deaf. Not once can I remember the deaf children being let out to play in the neighborhood. The closest we came to interacting was throwing snowballs at each other from either side of the hedge surrounding the school. This may reflect a policy of protection of the deaf children; it certainly did not make integration of these children into society easy.

The Welfare State, Integration, and Equality

To understand further developments in the perception of disabled people in Norway we have to examine what took place in the society following the Second World War. With the Labour Party continuously in power for the next twenty years, the "welfare state" found its form; the state took on the main responsibility for health care development and the support of needy groups through various types of pension schemes.[1] The main aim was to achieve as much equality in the population as possible. The notion of "rights" was developed simultaneously. Support in times of need was no longer seen as a question of charity, but as a *right* to protection and a minimum standard of living that people had as a result of their citizenship (and payment of taxes).

It was probably inevitable that these ideas eventually should reach the area of care for—and rehabilitation of—the handicapped. In 1965, Arne Skauen, a well-known author and journalist and the father of a mentally disabled child, wrote three flaming articles in the national newspaper *Dagbladet* (5, 9, 12 June). In these he accused the government of not providing mentally disabled people with equal rights, and he criticized the parents of the disabled

for not standing up and fighting for these rights. This and the following public debate provoked an uproar from those working in institutions and special schools who felt their position threatened, as well as from the "charity
ladies" in the organizations for the disabled whom he accused of wanting to
keep the mentally retarded as "lollipops" to boost their own egos. The negative aspects of institutions and special schools were further illustrated by the
same newspaper in the following years, as it brought forward cases of abuse
of disabled people in state institutions for the mentally retarded.

It was significant that the seed of this change in the public perceptions—
from the disabled as people to be protected and treated/trained separately
to citizens with equal rights—should come from a parent of a mentally disabled person. People with physical, visual, or hearing impairments would to
some extent be expected to represent themselves, although they may find it
hard to do so because of their often underprivileged position. People with
mental retardation necessarily have to be represented by their parents or
close kin, some of whom are influential as lawyers, doctors, teachers, and so
on. The same thing has been known to happen in developing countries. The
birth of a mentally retarded child to a politician or other influential person
greatly strengthens the cause of disabled people.[2]

As the snowball continued to roll, an association called Justice for the
Handicapped was formed, mainly consisting of parents of mentally retarded
persons.[3] Thus the first interest group by the people concerned (and their
families) came into existence, empowering the weakest of the weak. After
some hesitation, groups representing other types of disabilities followed
with their demands for equal rights, and today an umbrella organization
representing all these groups is in direct dialogue with the government in
matters concerning disabled people.

The main problem has been how to make the notion of "equal rights for
the disabled" operational. One of the first themes to be emphasized was that
growing up in the family and local community was best for any disabled
child. Actually this was probably what many parents had always felt. For example, when the writer Sigrid Undset, herself the mother of a mentally retarded child, got the Nobel literature prize in 1928, most of the money was
placed in a fund to make it possible for parents to keep their mentally retarded children at home.

What was new after the institutional scandals and public debate of the
late 1960s was that these ideas had gradually become part of the public discourse on rehabilitation. People no longer believed that it was best for severely disabled children to be left in an institution and "forgotten." The key
words for this new discourse came to be *integration* and *normalization:* integration meaning that disabled people should participate in society on their
own premises and on an equal basis, normalization meaning that the vari-

ous sectors of society should also take responsibility for the needs of disabled people (health sector for health, transportation sector for transport, educational sector for schooling, etc.)—there should be no special department or institution taking care of these matters, and those specialized services existing, especially those for people with mental retardation, should be closed down within a ten-year period. This policy (for the mentally retarded) was finally confirmed in a proposition presented by a working committee (in which the association formed by parents of the mentally retarded played a strong role) to the government in 1973 (NOU 1973).

One of the main issues was how to solve the problems of education under this new policy of integration and normalization, and another key word soon appeared, that of *decentralization*. Norway is a long and fairly sparsely populated country;[4] although it was part of the ideology of normalization and also most practical to place the responsibility for giving special education with the local schools, they often had little or no previous experience with special children. Besides the economic problems many school districts were facing in living up to these expectations, there was a lack of expertise in special education in the more remote areas, and it was not always easy to get special education teachers to move there even if a job was advertised. The greatest worry, however, was how the integration of disabled children, and especially those with moderate to severe mental retardation, in ordinary schools would affect the education of children without impairments. Parents protested and claimed that their children would get less attention from their teachers if they also had to attend to a special child.[5] Perhaps more surprising was the fact that some parents of disabled children also protested, fearing (sometimes rightly) that their children would get less attention than in a special school.

The second important issue under the new ideology was that of housing for those disabled people who were living in institutions and those living at home past the age when this is normally expected.[6] The problem was particularly pressing for the moderate and severely mentally retarded who up until then had been living in institutions or with parents, and for whom a model of independent living was hard to visualize. According to the proposition (NOU 1973) they should be the responsibility of—and be integrated in—their home communities (i.e., the community where they had lived with their parents), where many of them had few or no connections after years of living in an institution elsewhere. Some parents feared that the county would not allocate enough money to provide satisfactory solutions and that they would again be made responsible. Others feared the loss of the safe haven that they had come to see the better-functioning institutions to be, and feared that the disabled inmates would be isolated, living alone or in smaller units. Some parents of mentally retarded persons in institutions even went as far as to establish an alternative parent organization advocating the right to choose for their children not to be "integrated."[7]

Ten years after the first proposition, a new committee was appointed in order to evaluate the progress according to the recommendations given by the first one. It was found that although integration was well on its way and many disabled people had been "relocated to their home communities,"[8] most institutions and special schools were still operating more or less as before. It was concluded that the mere existence of these institutions was hampering progress on the road toward integration (Odelstingsproposisjon 49, 1987–1988). Following this, a bill was passed through parliament confirming that for "integration" and "normalization" of the lives of mentally retarded people to be achieved, all state institutions and special schools must be closed down within a few years. The responsibility for education was to be taken over by the mainstream school system and for housing by the municipalities (Stortingsmelding 47, 1989–1990).

Although no parliamentary committees and propositions have been made for the other types of disabilities, the trail of "rights for the handicapped" once staked out by parents of the mentally retarded has strongly influenced the perception of, and actions for, the other categories of impairments.

Changes in the perception of disabled people as persons have also been reflected in the official language throughout the periods described. *Idioter* (idiots) became *åndssvake* (weak in the mind) and finally *psykisk utviklingshemmede* (mentally retarded) in order to avoid stigmatization. The physically impaired have passed from *krøplinger* (cripples) via *vanføre* (movement hampered) to *fysisk funksjonshemmede* (physically disabled) for the same purpose. Hearing and seeing impairments have not undergone the same changes (perhaps indicating that they may have been perceived as less stigmatizing), but during the past decades the word *handicapped* has been used as a term covering all disabilities, lately replaced by *funksjonshemmede* (lit., "function restricted").

Since the early 1970s Norwegian organizations *by* the disabled had more or less banned any form of charity and private contributions to their cause as a matter of policy, to make the government take more responsibility. Yet three of these organizations in cooperation with Norwegian Red Cross launched a nationwide fund-raising campaign through television in 1981. This brought in more than ninety million Norwegian kroner (approximately $12 million U.S.) under the heading "Et Nytt Liv" (A New Life), and it was repeated with similar results in 1991. The money was to be used for projects to provide services to disabled people in developing countries—an objective that became significant for the development of rehabilitation in

Botswana. It was also clearly stated that the projects should promote the issue of equal rights for disabled people and, when possible, support groups *by* the disabled themselves.

BOTSWANA

Background

We know very little about how people with disabilities were perceived and treated in Botswana in the early days. One folk tale tells about an albino girl, initially chased away by her family because of her looks, who managed to be accepted and actually take the place of her lazy normal sister as the parents favorite when she proved herself to be hardworking and useful around the compound. This seems to reflect the still dominant view among rural Tswana (Ingstad n.d.) that the contribution someone can make to the household and community is more important for how he or she is evaluated as a person than the actual physical appearance.

A common myth (especially among Europeans) seems to be that in the old days disabled children were killed or left to die. Yet when present-day old people are asked about this they claim that it was not the case. Also, when in 1992 Botswana changed the law that previously punished all abortion by up to eight years of imprisonment to a law allowing abortion in cases of (suspected) impairment of the fetus or when the mother's life was in danger, this caused a vigorous debate. The newspapers printed letters from readers stating that it had always been Tswana tradition to accept and care for disabled family members. The idea of a more liberalized abortion law was interpreted by many rural elderly as Western imperialism wishing to weaken the Tswana family system by forcing them to have fewer children. In the Tswana culture *all* children were welcome, they claimed.[9]

The missionaries and the British protectorate administration found a fairly easy foothold in Botswana. The British introduced the English legal system, which has coexisted up until today with the tribal law. The missionaries, who came first from Britain and later from several other European countries, gave their God the name for the old Tswana God, Modimo (Comaroff and Comaroff 1991). To what extent these two agents came to influence the perception of disabled people we can only guess. If the myth of the killing of children born disabled had any core of truth, the administration would certainly have tried to counteract this practice when possible. More important however was the Christian credo of "thou shalt not kill" and "love thy neighbor" in motivating people toward mercy and charity toward their less fortunate relatives and neighbors.

However, charity is not necessarily a foreign concept in Botswana. The idea that the wealthy (especially the chiefs) should share with the less fortunate is a deep-rooted Tswana value expressed especially in distribution of cattle and food. In principle, however, care for disabled people has always been, and still is considered, the responsibility of the family. The government is very reluctant to initiate any policies that may weaken the family as a support system. For example: To qualify for destitute support (the only regular state support to people in need),[10] which is distributed according to the criteria of extreme poverty, one has to be without any close relatives whatsoever. Whether or not relatives actually contribute or their whereabouts are known is not relevant. Impairment and old age are not seen as criteria that in themselves should qualify one for public support because "what if the family is well off?"

Health Services and Education

At independence in Botswana (1966), modern health care was to a large degree centralized in a few hospitals run by missions, and the majority of the rural population had little or no access to modern medical care. Thus one of the first tasks for the new government was to plan for development of a health service that could reach out to people in the remote corners of the nation. This was also the time for new ideas about primary health care in the rest of the world. Strong donor support for development of the health sector (with Norway as one of the main donors)[11] made it possible for Botswana to be ahead of most developing countries at the time of the Alma-Ata declaration (WHO/UNICEF 1978) in planning for "Health for all by the year 2000."

The government takeover of the mission hospitals was part of the realization of this new health plan. However, some missions have continued to send personnel for some key positions. Special educational services for the visually and hearing impaired were established as an extension of such (German) missionary activities. Also during those early independence years, a German couple inspired by the Waldorf principles[12] established a training center (boarding) for mentally retarded children. All these centers were located in larger towns, with a limited number of trainees who were boarding. Thus they came to take on some of the qualities of small institutions, taking people away from their local communities for longer periods,[13] but catering only to a fraction of the children in need of special education.[14]

A national system of primary education was established after independence. Although the aim has been to reach all children, no provisions were initially made to include those who were disabled, and schooling has not been made compulsory.[15] Among the 15 percent who are not yet in school, disabled and ethnic minority children probably make up the majority (Kann et al. 1989). The Unit for Special Education was established under the Ministry of Education in 1984 to facilitate the teaching of disabled children in mainstream schools. This unit was strongly supported financially by the Swedish International Development Agency (SIDA), with a Swedish special education teacher as advisor to the unit head for a period of two years. A few years later the Swedes supported the building of a training center for special education teachers in mainstream schools, a project that so far has had very limited impact in the educational system.

Community-based Rehabilitation

The Botswana National Development Plan for 1973–1978 stated that insufficient attention had so far been given to the problem of disabled people. The plan recommended that the government should seek assistance in the preparation of a program for detection, care, training, and rehabilitation of disabled people. In 1977, Dr. Einar Helander, as a consultant, gave inspiration to the development of the WHO Community Based Rehabilitation Programme.[16] The inspiration for the CBR program seems to have come partly from the ideologies of the Alma-Ata declaration, which asserted the need for accessible services for everyone, utilizing simple and affordable technology. We can also read the Scandinavian influence between the lines of the training manual,[17] and although the question of *rights* is strategically toned down, it is definitely implicit.

By 1979 the CBR program was ready for field testing in nine developing countries, among them Botswana. Initially there was debate about whether CBR should be placed under the Ministry of Health or the Department of Social Services.[18] The choice of the Ministry of Health determined that disabled people were to be perceived as people with a health problem.[19] The decision led to the Department of Social Services more or less discontinuing its engagement in the cause of disabled people, at least during the initial years of CBR.

A pyramidal structure was set up, headed by a commissioner for the handicapped, with special social workers for the CBR program placed as part of the district health teams in all fifteen health districts, thus integrating it in the primary health care system.[20] The district medical officers, several of them Norwegian expatriates, were to be the immediate supervisors of the CBR program. In order to reach the communities, each CBR social worker was to cooperate with the local clinics, and especially with its family welfare educators,[21] who were to be the field-workers of the CBR program.

Some years later, in 1981, another nationwide CBR program was set up by the Botswana Red Cross (BRC), sponsored by the Norwegian Red Cross (NRC) through money gathered in the televised fund-raiser "Et Nytt Liv" (see above). BRC had previously been involved with rehabilitation by running a training center for physically handicapped people on a two-year boarding basis, financed through fund-raising and based on a spirit of charity and voluntarism. However, with the coming of the International Year of Disabled People, BRC had been inspired by the joint efforts of WHO and NRC, and a promise of generous financing for a five-year period, to try the

CBR ideology. Another pyramidal structure was set up with a program coordinator on top and two senior district officers, one for the south and one for the north, supervising seven district officers. One Norwegian physiotherapist was assigned to the program for two years as an advisor. The fieldworkers of the Red Cross Program were to be the volunteers of the local Red Cross branches.

Both CBR programs soon ran into trouble. Although the BRC program on paper was supposed to be supportive of the government CBR effort, an effective cooperation was never established. On the contrary, being better funded and better equipped with vehicles, the BRC district officers had a much better chance of getting out in the field, leading to a feeling of hopelessness and unfair competition among the government CBR social workers.

Neither program was able to fully implement the CBR ideal of reaching all disabled people in their own homes and communities. Both faced problems in getting their field-workers to do the job of identifying and following up the families with disabled members. For the Red Cross, the spirit of voluntarism proved not so strong as originally anticipated, especially since these were years of severe drought and poverty. A failing subsistence economy made people rely more on cash than ever before, and they were reluctant to do any work that they were not paid for. In the government program the family welfare educators did not embrace CBR with the enthusiasm that had been hoped for. They felt that this was just an additional burden placed upon them without sufficient instruction and follow-up and with no extra pay. Also, their immediate superiors, the clinic nurses, did not embrace the CBR idea, and in some instances even opposed it, resenting the CBR social workers making claims on the family welfare educator's time.

Faced with these problems, both programs soon ceased to be truly community-based and took the form of outreach programs in which a few field officers struggled to follow up a limited number of disabled people and their families in a large district. For the Red Cross field officers this was to some extent possible since they had been given cars from Norway. For the government CBR social workers who had to compete for scarce transport with other members of the health team it became almost impossible.

Following an evaluation (Ingstad and Melsom 1985), the Red Cross CBR program was consolidated. After assessment of the problems of the past years and visualization of the economic problems that would come when the Norwegian Red Cross support was stepped down, it is now limited to one relatively small region in the North where it has been operating quite successfully for some years with the support of physiotherapists from Norway. Such concentration of development efforts in one limited area is not unusual among donors, who want showcase successes (which may be referred to as "pilot projects" in the often unrealistic expectation that they will later be expanded to the whole country). However, regionalization is incompatible with the ideals of disability programs in the donors' own countries.

For the government CBR program, which still exists nationwide in principle, the problem basically boils down to that of resources. Positions of CBR social workers have been difficult to fill because they are low on the salary scale. Long vacancies mean no CBR activities in that particular district, and when the position is finally filled, a new employee has to start more or less from scratch. Rapid turnover in the positions makes it difficult to follow up with proper training of new staff, and several of the social workers functioning over the years have not received any formal training in CBR. Transport is still a major problem, and once a need has been identified for a disabled person, there are few or no resources to alleviate it.

CBR was "marketed" by WHO as a cheap program because it was supposed to be integrated in the existing primary health care system (or any other preexisting structure). It now seems clear that although setting up the government program in Botswana may not have involved major costs, its sustainability depends on the willingness to invest continuously in training, transport, and those sectors of society in which the disabled people should have their share (education, employment, referral health services).

In an effort to consolidate and strengthen the government CBR program and to clarify the divisions of responsibility between the government and the NGOs, the Norwegian Agency for Development Cooperation (NORAD) offered to pay for a consultancy to make a national plan for rehabilitation (Omphile et al. 1987).[22] The plan came up with several suggestions for increased government involvement in order to strengthen CBR, the need for extensive training of a new cadre of middle-level rehabilitation workers being one of the most important ones. Unfortunately, the movement of this plan through various ministries has led to even fewer CBR activities—most requests for resources seem to be met with the response, "wait for the plan to be approved."[23] The difficulties in passing the plan probably reflect the fact that CBR is no longer an area of high priority now that the International Year of Disabled Persons has passed. It is merely one of many that have to compete for government attention and scarce resources.

Withdrawal of the State?

The first signs that government was tapering off its CBR involvement may be traced back to the informal competition with the Red Cross program. Although there was no declared withdrawal from the CBR program, there was evidence of a certain tiredness among its executors, who seemed to feel that they were struggling in vain.

In the empty space left by the shrinking of the Red Cross activities and the near death of government CBR activities, there was a niche for a new initiative. Backed by an English charitable organization, the Cheshire Homes Foundation, with strong support from the Catholic church, a physically disabled European who was a long-time resident of Botswana built a modern rehabilitation center just outside the capital, Gaborone. The center provides assessment and short-term training for physically disabled people from all over the country and has also embarked upon a CBR program in the area nearby.[24] This man has himself made many "walks" through several African countries in order to raise money for the cause of disabled people and to raise awareness about their often hidden resources. The money for the running of the center comes from these walks and from more recent local ones in which even the president has participated. The spirit of the venture is that of private initiative and to some extent charity; the message conveyed is that of ability (in contrast to disability). The issue of "rights" comes out less clearly—if at all.

Not surprisingly, this initiative has been officially praised as an example of how disabled people and communities can help themselves. It seems now that some of the activities proposed for the government in the rehabilitation plan (such as the training of CBR workers) may be taken over by this center. Whether this marks the beginning of government disengagement from CBR in favor of the NGOs remains to be seen.

Other new actors in the field of rehabilitation today include a Lutheran mission responsible for a somewhat similar rehabilitation and assessment center in the north and two small NGO day-care centers for mentally retarded children in two of the larger villages. Both of these day-care centers were established with strong support from the Norwegian Agency for Development under the condition (which has never been confirmed by the government) that the local councils should take over the responsibility after five years. However in the opening speech for one of these day-care centers the president's wife stated clearly that families and communities with disabled members should contribute themselves (the type of contribution was not made clear) and not rely on the councils to provide everything.

A Botswana Council for the Disabled, originally established to coordinate all government and NGO activities, has more or less ceased to function, awaiting the finalization of the national plan for rehabilitation.

In the latest National Development Plan (1991–1997) disabled people and their needs are still mentioned as a priority. CBR, orthopedics, and audiology are mentioned as areas of focus. NGOs, especially rehabilitation centers, are expected to play a major supportive role and receive government subventions (Government of Botswana 1991). However, the relative importance of NGO versus government activities is not made clear.

TRANSFERRING REHABILITATION DISCOURSES

The examples of Norway and Botswana have shown us the importance of seeing the process of transferring rehabilitation discourses from countries of the North to those of the South in terms of different historical, cultural, and social contexts. A historical perspective has provided us with an under-standing of how such discourses are generated and changed over time, and thus gives a better understanding of the problems involved when such a transfer is made in the name of "development."

Characteristics of the Transfer Process

The transfer process described in the preceding sections is characterized by a very short time span. In less than thirty years Botswana has been expected by the international community (WHO) and several donor countries to adopt discourses on rehabilitation which it has taken Norway (and other European countries) more than a hundred years to develop.

In Norway the changes in people's perception of disability have developed from within, closely linked to other changes in society and sustained through internal economic sources. Botswana has received different and sometimes even contradictory discourses from outside, linked to fairly generous contributions of money from various donor countries and organizations. Botswana was expected to follow the often invisible premises from which these discourses have been developed.

The initial willingness by the Botswana government to accept CBR partly had to do with the fact that it was supposed to be cheap and was to a large extent financed from the North in an initial phase. When it became clear that the sustainability and development of support services were not so cheap after all, the interest seemed to fade, although it is still part of the official policy. However, Botswana is no longer a poor country as far as the national economy is concerned (although there is still extensive poverty in some rural areas), and it could sustain CBR at an acceptable standard if it were given priority.

Rehabilitation in Botswana has been accepted without major political controversies, but (so far) without an accepted plan to guide the development, and in particular the relationship between the government and the NGOs. Interest groups formed *by* disabled people themselves have played a very minor role and have not been able to consolidate themselves to find a common platform or to influence government policies. In contrast, rehabilitation in Norway became politicized at an early stage, with educational pioneers and parents of mentally retarded children acting as entrepreneurs (Barth 1963), combining existing resources in new and ingenious ways (school laws, welfare state ideologies, the press) to improve the quality of life for disabled persons and promote equal rights.

The closest Botswana has come to an entrepreneur in this field is the disabled man who through his "walks" and connection with the Cheshire Homes managed to raise considerable awareness for the cause of rehabilitation as well as money to run his center. Although embraced by the government as an example of what private initiative can lead to, as a *lekgoa* (white man) he can hardly be said to represent the ordinary disabled person in Botswana.

The lack of public debate on rehabilitation in Botswana has deprived people of an opportunity to internalize the rehabilitation discourses in the Tswana value system. However, the process of transfer has succeeded in establishing some principles of rehabilitation on which most influential actors in the arena seem to agree (i.e., integration, normalization). While in Norway these principles reversed a tendency of separation and brought disabled people back to the communities, they have little meaning to the ordinary Batswana, who always have practiced some form of "integration" in the family and local community.

Through this process of transfer of discourses, "disability" has become a unifying category, most often using the Tswana word for physical impairment, *digole,* to cover all types of disability. For the ordinary Batswana, however, *rehabilitation* still has hardly any meaning at all. Impairments are dealt with on the basis of their perceived origin (e.g., witchcraft) and appropriate cure. The idea of improvement in isolated skills and quality of life as a value in itself has not quite settled in. Many feel that help to the disabled person should mean help to the care-giving family in the form of food and clothes, and they feel cheated when such help does not appear.

The Priorities of Recipient Governments and Donors

The decision by the world community to introduce a year—and a following decade—for disabled people and the attempt made by WHO to construct a rehabilitation program to be applied worldwide have illuminated a fundamental priority dilemma for both donors and recipients. Should we try to reach as many as possible of the world's more than 100 million disabled with at least some sort of basic rehabilitation services? Or should we aim at providing services that we in the North would consider the best, accepting that in this way we will only reach a minority of those in need? And who is to decide what is sufficient and what is best anyway? These are all questions to which there are no easy answers. Responses reflect the position of the respondent, the perception of disabled people as persons, and the sociocultural context in which choices are made.

In Botswana the problem is not so much disagreement about rehabilitation as it is a variety of approaches that are largely uncoordinated. Each of these approaches has implications for the level of expertise at which help is to be given, and to whom. These consequences have not yet been subject to serious public debate. While wanting to embark on CBR as a way to reach all disabled people in the same way that primary health care is (at least in principle) available to everyone, the government has been reluctant to make the necessary investments (manpower, vehicles, etc.) to succeed in this, and thus it welcomes private and NGO initiative that may alleviate the problems.

Special schools and centers of various kinds are sought after as visible proof for the donor (and the government) of activities in the field of rehabilitation.[25] They can be shown off to the many visiting delegations and can serve as targets of local fund-raising. They do however run the risk of becoming white elephants when expectations for various reasons cannot be fulfilled, or they may run into serious difficulties when the time for donor support comes to an end.[26] Donor withdrawal may mark the end of an agreed-upon period of support with the expectation of self-sustainability in the form of production or local fund-raising and/or government support. It may also be a way of getting out of something that is not considered good enough or is no longer the "fashionable" way of supporting this field in the donor country. Such a project most often will remain (at least for a while), with its clients and staff struggling along on their own.

CBR programs, on the other hand, do not have the same visual appeal, even when they succeed, and if they fail, there is nothing left but disappointed families and frustrated field-workers.

Cultural Differences

The government initiative in promoting CBR seems (so far) to have more or less failed in Botswana because the ideology of equal rights and state responsibility for the weak does not have the same power behind it in Botswana as in the Scandinavian welfare states. While these ideologies are built on a strong concept of the equal individual, Tswana society was always *hierarchical*, with some people being ranked higher than others by virtue of descent and wealth. Tswana values stress the collective before the individual, and to contribute to the family is considered one of the highest virtues. As pointed out by Jean Comaroff and John Comaroff (1991:144), this is "a far cry from the ontology and base of the modern Western individualism, in which spirit and matter, people and objects, were definitively set apart, and in which every man and woman [is] responsible, on their own account and in their own right, for their spiritual, social and material situation in a radically disenchanted universe."

While "equality" for the disabled individual became a powerful tool in the hands of political advocates in the North, it has less relevance where the disabled person is seen primarily as part of a larger whole—the care-giving family. Thus the question of input of public resources in a CBR program becomes not only a question of the allocation of scarce goods and giving priority to one type of need before others, but more a fundamental question of not taking responsibility away from the (extended) family and thereby weakening it as the main source of social security. We see this clearly in the public support given to destitutes. While it is designed to meet *individual needs* (extreme poverty), the criterion for receiving it has to do with qualities of *the family*.

Basically we have to do with two different cosmologies, two different perceptions of the disabled man, woman, or child as a person. But such perceptions are not static, and we can foresee that as "development" proceeds and people in general become more concerned with their own profits than with the well-being of their extended family (Ingstad et al. 1992), the question of individual rights may become more of a political issue.

Important parts of the integration ideology have been difficult to realize in Botswana because primary education is optional and not compulsory. It was precisely the *right* to education for everyone in Norway that provided a weapon with which to pressure the government into educational options, even for the more severely mentally retarded children. Botswana aims at universal education and has come very far in achieving it compared to many other developing countries. But disabled children are still seen as different from other children of school age, and it remains an unsolved question whether or not the district councils (who are responsible for education at the local level) should pay salaries for teachers in special schools and training centers (the principle of normalization).

The Transfer of Rehabilitation Discourses

As mentioned previously, the transfer of European discourses on disability to Botswana involved a very short time frame. With more time to create Tswana priorities and more consideration of how the CBR program could be adapted to the unique Botswana situation, it might have been more successful. However, with the coming of the International Year of Disabled Persons, everyone, including the Batswana themselves, seems to have been in a hurry to get the program going.

It also seems to be a general problem that fewer questions are raised about the cultural appropriateness of medical programs than those in other sectors of society. This holds for rehabilitation programs, which, although they are not always defined as "medicine," tend to carry with them some of the qualities of absolute truth and simple technical solutions that characterize biomedicine. This is illustrated at its most extreme by Frank Bowe (1990), when he suggests that the integration and normalization of people in third-world countries (even the remote rural areas) can be achieved through the transfer of advanced tele-technology and computer technology.

Botswana paid a price for being one of the first countries to apply the WHO CBR model. With no previous experience in implementing the program, they had to rely mainly on their own judgment and were not able to profit from the experiences of others.[27]

CBR is no longer simply a WHO model but has become a *concept* that has been applied differently in different projects. WHO designed a culturally neutral model that was supposed to be applicable with only minor adjustments in all developing countries. Other countries have tried to build on the same ideas but have transformed the model into something culturally more specific, for example by linking the CBR activities to already existing and culturally integrated support systems. If CBR can be perceived not as something *new* that mainly needs expertise from outside but as a way of mobilizing the community itself, it stands a much better chance of being sustained. This is the way the model is intended to be used, but because insufficient effort is usually put into examining these local communities *before* a program is started, it does not always turn out this way. Instead, as in Botswana, the model becomes an outreach instead of a community-based program.

I have shown the importance of a historical perspective on the transfer process. In planning or analyzing any type of rehabilitation program, we need to ask ourselves what is politically, economically, and culturally appropriate. These considerations are as necessary in examining the transfer of rehabilitation discourses and programs as in analyzing any other type of development practice.[28]

NOTES

1. Some of these schemes had been started before the war but were developed further during the postwar years.

2. Kenya and Nicaragua are two such examples.

3. This society later changed its name to Norsk Forbund for Psykisk Utviklingshemmede [Norwegian Association for the Mentally Retarded] and became the main interest group representing mentally retarded people.

4. The distance from Oslo to North Cape is the same as from Oslo to Rome. The population is 4 million.

5. In most places this problem seemed to have been solved by hiring special helpers for the disabled children to sit with them in the class. Sometimes small groups for disabled children were made so that they could sit by themselves with their helper for some subjects and be with their class for other subjects.

6. The integration/normalization discourse frequently asserts the right of the individual disabled person to independent living. The "right" of parents to get their children out of the house at a certain age is seldom mentioned.

7. This organization was an alternative to the one that had been instrumental in developing the integration proposition.

8. This had sometimes happened against their own wishes and those of their families, which was not the intention of the proposal.

9. I was at the time doing a study of aging in Botswana, thus interviewing many elderly people.

10. In times of severe drought, food rations are also given to pregnant and lactating mothers, malnourished children, and tuberculosis patients.

11. A major part of the Norwegian aid to the development of the health sector in Botswana was in the form of technical assistance. Norwegian ideas about decen-

tralized health care, developed under the "welfare state," were brought to Botswana by advisers to the Ministry of Health.

12. Based on the ideas of anthroposophy laid down by the German philosopher Rudolf Steiner. The Waldorf schools base much of their teaching on the development of each child through artistic creativity.

13. In later years the centers for the blind and deaf have had classes for their students in mainstream schools. However, the majority of their students still come from other towns and are boarding at the school. The Waldorf center has responded to the question of integration (and also the need to make money) by taking in craftsmen from the neighboring village to train and work together with the mentally retarded students.

14. In later years some of these centers have taken on outreach counseling, but still the main activities take place in the centers.

15. Although in principle schooling is free, uniforms, shoes, and various smaller fees still add up to quite a large amount per child for a poor family.

16. Personal communication, 1987, Dr. Einar Helander.

17. Two of its authors come from Sweden, which has had a history of development of a discourse on rehabilitation very similar to that described for Norway.

18. The Department of Social Services is under the Ministry of Local Government and Lands and Housing.

19. The fact that CBR was a WHO program was probably an important factor in this choice.

20. Some of these positions have never been filled, and some have been vacant for long periods.

21. People elected from the village and given three months of training in basic health work.

22. Two of the team members were Norwegians; one of them had several years experience from an organization formed *by* disabled people.

23. In February 1994 the plan was still not approved.

24. This area was supposed to be covered by the government CBR program and previously also by the Red Cross program.

25. In 1984–1985, I attended some initial meetings with people from the Cheshire Homes foundation when they made their first approaches to start a project in Botswana. It was then clearly stated that what they wanted was an institution or center that they could put their name on, rather than to contribute to already existing CBR activities.

26. This was recently the case with a workshop for the blind that was saved at the last minute by donations from a local business after the German mission decided it was time to withdraw.

27. One example is the translation of the CBR manual to Setswana, which took quite some time because of shortage of funds and general delays. By the time Botswana had completed the translation of the first WHO CBR manual there was already a new and improved one out, and since then still another one has appeared.

28. I am grateful to Susan R. Whyte, Michael Whyte, and Hans Christian Sørhaug for valuable comments on this chapter. I am also grateful to Vigdis Christie, Frank Bruun, and Inger Buskerud for help in collecting literature.

Fieldwork in Botswana was made possible through grants from the Norwegian Ministry of Foreign Affairs/NORAD and WHO. The University of Oslo generously gave me sabbatical with half pay for 1984–1985. Return visits for various purposes almost every year since the first fieldwork have made it possible for me to follow up on the developments on rehabilitation in Botswana.

REFERENCES

Barth, Fredrik
    1963   *The Role of the Entrepreneur in Social Change in Northern Norway.* Bergen: Universitetsforlaget.
Bowe, Frank G.
    1990   Disabled and elderly people in the first, second and third worlds. *International Journal of Rehabilitation Research* 13:1–14.
Comaroff, Jean, and John Comaroff
    1991   *Of Revelation and Revolution: Colonialism and Conciousness in South Africa.* Vol. 1. Chicago: University of Chicago Press.
Ingstad, Benedicte
    1991   The Myth of the hidden disabled: A study of community-based rehabilitation in Botswana. Working paper. Oslo: Section for Medical Anthropology, University of Oslo.
Ingstad, Benedicte, and Turid Melsom
    1985   *An Evaluation of the Botswana Red Cross Society Primary Health Care and Community-based Rehabilitation Programmes.* Gaborone: Botswana Red Cross Society.
Ingstad, Benedicte, Frank J. Bruun, Edwin Sandberg, and Sheila Tlou
    1992   Care for the elderly, care by the elderly: The role of elderly women in a changing Tswana society. *Journal of Cross-Cultural Gerontology* 7:379–398.
Kann, Ulla, D. Mapolelo, and P. Nleya
    1989   *The Missing Children: Achieving Universal Basic Education in Botswana. The Barriers and Some Suggestions for Overcoming Them.* Gaborone: National Institute for Development Research and Documentation.
Ministry of Finance and Development Planning
    1991   *National Development Plan 7, 1991–1997.* Gaborone: Government Printer.
NOU
    1973   *Omsorg for psykisk utviklingshemmede* [Care of the mentally retarded]. Norges offentlige utredninger 25. Oslo: Sosialdepartementet, Universitetsforlaget.
Odelstingsproposisjon
    1987–1988 Midlertidig lov om avvikling av institusjoner og kontrakter om privat pleie under det fylkeskommunale helsevern for psykisk utviklingshemmede [Provisional law on the discontinuation of institutions and private care contracts under county health service for the mentally retarded]. No. 49.

Omphile, C., B. Bertrancourt, P. Mokgadi, V. Hoel, and L. Richter
1987   *Proposals for a National Plan for Services for Disabled People.* Gaborone: Ministry of Health Botswana and Norwegian Development Cooperation.

Stiker, Henri-Jacques
1982   *Corps infirmes et sociétés.* Paris: Aubier Montaigne.

Stone, Deborah A.
1984   *The Disabled State.* Philadelphia: Temple University Press.

Stortingsmelding
1989–1990 *Om gjennomføring av reformen for mennesker med psykisk utviklingshemning* [On the implementation of the reform for people with mental retardation]. No. 47. Oslo: Sosialdepartementet.

Sundby, Per
1981   Sosialmedisin: Teori og praksis [Social medicine: Theory and practice]. In *Sosial Velferd og Sosial Omsorg: En Innføring i Sosialmedisin* [Social welfare and social care: An introduction to social medicine], ed. Per Sundby. Oslo: Fabritius Forlagshus.

WHO/UNICEF
1978   *Primary Health Care.* Report of the International Conference on Primary Health Care, Alma-Ata, U.S.S.R., 6–12 September. Geneva: WHO/UNICEF.

TEN

Hero, Beggar, or Sports Star: Negotiating the Identity of the Disabled Person in Nicaragua

Frank Jarle Bruun

His mother did not want anyone to see him without his left leg. But he himself proudly states: "I don't feel ashamed, my friends come to visit me with a great deal of respect."

—*LA BARRICADA*, 12 AUGUST 1987

From 1979 when the Sandinistas came to power until 1990 when they lost the parliamentary election, Nicaragua was the scene of a struggle to change the identity of disabled people.[1] I am not speaking of identity in the strict psychological sense, but of the social identifications continuously made by disabled people themselves and by others around them. In the new political situation created in the 1980s, an attempt was made to turn the stigma of a handicap into a leverage point for redefining all disabled people as valuable members of society. New social identifications were proposed and contested.

The tools used in this struggle were both old values that already had meaning in the society and new foreign ideas. Among the former was the "macho" ideal of the heroic man willing to give his life or part of his body for a political cause. The Christian notion of charity was also a long-standing theme in Nicaraguan tradition. The new element was the Northern (i.e., European and North American) ideal of equal rights for disabled people to participate in society, support themselves, and bear the same responsibilities as everyone else.

Attitudes toward meanings asserted in a struggle for dominance depend on interests and knowledge that are unevenly distributed and controlled. As Roger Keesing says, "We need to ask who creates and defines cultural meanings, and to what ends" (1987:161). Thus, the results of a contest depend to a great extent on each party's power to present a view that will be accepted by the public. The Nicaraguan situation exemplifies these political aspects of the social construction of disability and personhood.

The point of departure for the study was the alleged tendency to overprotect disabled people in Nicaragua. Overprotection—as my informants stated, and I myself observed—was a problem for the personal progress of the disabled individual. However, in the new social context emerging after the revolution, severely wounded soldiers were getting new roles due to their political importance as symbols of the revolution. Other disabled people were also facing new possibilities with the help of organizations of or for disabled people, a situation that was quite new in Nicaragua.

In focusing on this marginal group's struggle for new identity, I will portray some important Nicaraguan cultural values, such as heroism and martyrdom. In so doing, I will try to analyze to what extent these values were used or whether foreign values were called upon to promote the group's goals. Thus the study of disabled people leads to better understanding of Nicaraguan society and the development it was going through while the Sandinistas were in power.

To analyze this process I will treat the problem of disabled people as a problem of defining a new identity. The war heroes did this with greater success than did the other disabled people in Nicaragua. What I will describe contrasts with what Robert Murphy and his coauthors saw as the disabled people's dilemma of not being able to get out of their "socially ambivalent and ill-defined" situation (Murphy et al. 1988). In Nicaragua some disabled people achieved a well-defined position thanks to the political context created by the left-wing movement.

Since my main concern is to understand how the struggle for a new social identity is manifested, I will focus on the positioning of the different actors involved, and what was at stake for them. With this in mind, I will describe the homecoming of a mutilated soldier and make an analysis of three views that were common in newspaper presentations of disabled people.

BACKGROUND

In 1979, a long struggle in Nicaragua ended with the overthrow of the Somoza dictatorship, which had lasted for about forty years. The new Sandinista regime was socialist. According to the new ideology, health services should be free and equally accessible for the whole population (Guido 1982). However, later political decisions ensured the war victims priority in access to the resources available.

No statistical material on disability existed in Nicaragua at the time of this study (1987–1988) with the exception of that on the war victims, who were all registered. The authorities seemed to be reluctant to invest resources in a survey to assess the number of disabled people, because this might have raised expectations for treatment that could not be met.

However, a rough estimate can be made using the World Health Organization's formula. According to Einar Helander (1984:26), 7 to 10 percent of the total population in developing countries can be defined as disabled, and 3 percent can be defined as needing rehabilitation that includes training, schooling, or job placement. (For a discussion of the problem of estimating the prevalence of disability, see Helander 1993:20.) For Nicaragua, with an estimated population of 3.5 million in 1987, this would mean that about 105,000 people were in need of rehabilitation. In fact, the real number must have been far higher, for the WHO estimate assumes normal, not wartime, conditions.

The fighting after the revolution produced many severely wounded and disabled persons. The Sandinista regime introduced two years of compulsory military service for men from the age of seventeen. During the service period, one could expect forty to fifty confrontations with the Contras.[2] The chances of getting killed or mutilated were fairly high. "Es una cita con la muerte" (It is a rendezvous with the death), one mother put it. One estimate was that there were between three and four thousand severely disabled ex-soldiers in 1989 (*La Barricada,* 28 March 1989).

The research on which this chapter is based was done both in organizations of and for disabled people and among disabled people with no relationship with these organizations. Fieldwork, which mainly consisted of participant observation, was done in the capital and in a village, from September 1987 to July 1988. The net time in the field was seven months. The majority of the population in this area is mestizo and Spanish-speaking.

REVOLUTIONARY HEALTH CARE

In spite of a prospering national economy in the 1950s and the 1960s, there was little governmental involvement in work for disabled people before 1979. Lea Guido criticizes the Somoza regime for leaving health questions very much to religious and charitable groups (1982:55–63). Immediately after the revolution, although the economic situation was extremely bad, the Sandinistas took steps to create a health service that would be available for all (ibid.). Here I will not go into the numerous problems hindering the fulfillment of this ideological goal but will note that a change in Sandinista policy from reconstruction to politics and to an economy geared toward survival also influenced the health sector. Consequently a law was passed which would give preference to war victims and secure for them all the support the state could give.[3] This law reflected the general change from ideology to pragmatism in Sandinista politics at the time, a change that resulted from the economic crisis. With a deteriorating economy, survival, not progress, had to be emphasized. Concerning the disabled, this meant that the country could not afford to provide rehabilitation services for everybody, and the state decided to concentrate all efforts on the ones who had been wounded in the war. As a result the National Commission for Help to the Fighters (CNAC) was created in 1984 to supervise the fulfillment of all the governmental programs designed for the *combatientes,* the fighters. The commission worked to coordinate all ministerial departments that had obligations toward the ex-soldiers: Ministry of Health, Ministry of Labour, and Ministry of Social Services. The Organisation of Revolutionary Disabled, Ernesto 'Che' Guevarra (ORD), which was the biggest organization of disabled in Nicaragua, was also represented in the commission. In the Law of August 1984, the disabled fighters were given preference at hospitals and health centers and priority for employment, education, housing, and social security.

COMING HOME FROM THE MOUNTAINS

The village this example is taken from has about eighteen hundred inhabitants in its urban section. Among the disabled people were three who were blind, one wheelchair user, two with mental retardation, two with polio, and one with epilepsy. One man's right hand had been mutilated during the insurrection and another had been wounded in the foot, but during the time I was there, no one became severely disabled because of the war. That is, until the day Carlos[4] came back from the mountains with both legs amputated above the knees and one hand seriously injured.

Everybody came to see the war hero and welcome him home. The school children came, one class after another, with their teachers. Carlos had been slightly injured before and was then received with joy—this time the school classes came in silence. Each class went into the house and stood for a while around him. There was not much talk, only a few questions uttered in low voices. It was very hot and quiet in the small tin-roofed house. The sun was strong on this day in April just before the rainy season started. The hero himself appeared to be a bit bothered by all the attention, but a faint smile could be seen now and then on his face as he answered the questions from the visitors.

Carlos talked about his comrades and their life in the mountains when they hunted Contras. "I was about to cross a road after we had pursued the enemy [el enemigo] over a big river. Suddenly I was floating in a cloud of dust, didn't hear any noise, and felt no pain. Two days went by, from the moment I stepped on the mine, until my comrades [compañeros] got me across the river again and into a field hospital. Later, I was transferred to the Aldo Chavarría hospital in Managua for physical rehabilitation. There the minister of defence personally came to see all twenty of us who were severely injured during this offensive. He promised us that we would get the best treatment the country could offer. Now I'm fine, my morale is high, but at night I sometimes wake up searching for my gun."

Previously he had worked as a lathe operator. This was a popular vocation among young men, as it was relatively easy and one made good money. With no legs and only one hand functioning well, this would now be difficult for him. In this village, people work with handicrafts and/or small-scale farming. The use of hands and legs is essential in both these fields. In Managua, there was a vocational school[5] for disabled people like him, but this school did not have the capacity to take care of everybody. Thus, many were sent abroad, especially to socialist countries.

Carlos was ensured a small pension from the state, and also free entrance to cinemas and on buses. During his physical rehabilitation he was also helped with transport, so that he could go home some weekends. Transport was very expensive and difficult to get at that time. For his mother to pay for it would have meant a cost equal to what she earned in a month for only one visit. She was a widow with five children, the youngest of whom was disabled by polio and could hardly walk. The family was maintained by what the mother earned from selling bread and cookies in the street.

What the missing legs and the destroyed hand meant for Carlos and the villagers who came to see him is hard to tell exactly. However, six weeks later when I spoke with him again, Carlos said he was very optimistic about the future. The physical rehabilitation training at the Aldo Chavarría hospital helped him to progress, and he was now practicing walking with prostheses. About his job plans, he expressed hopes of going to Bulgaria for vocational training, as there was no place for him at the Gaspar Garcia Laviana rehabilitation center. All in all he seemed to be positive and to have "a high morale," as he himself said. The villagers expressed themselves more carefully about Carlos's situation. Some worried that it would be difficult for his mother to take care of him. Others stated that probably not so many would come to visit him when life was back to normal and he needed to be pushed around in a wheelchair. However, it is possible to analyze the homecoming of Carlos as an initiation into a new identity. Before he left for the mountains, his identity comprised being a lathe operator, an oldest son, a friend, a drinking partner, a provider for his mother and brothers and sisters, and so on. As far as I could ascertain, he had been quite an active boy in the village. After being away for a long period, he then came home mutilated, making it in many ways impossible for him to resume his previous activities, such as his vocation. His old identity was reduced by his inability to fulfill all his former roles. But as a soldier wounded in battle he got a new identity as a hero, an identity consciously created by the authorities. This identity was first affirmed by the treatment he received from the state— the very best rehabilitation the country could offer—and by being given preference over other disabled persons and having the minister of defence visit him. Later, while in the rehabilitation hospital, he was helped to visit his home. At home he was also treated as a hero, as exemplified by the school children who came to pay their respects.

One might say, with Erving Goffman, that his handicap was a stigma because his body was marked and he could not escape from the handicap

(Goffman 1963). However, Goffman's stigma and deviance model, with all its negative connotations, does not give us the tools for understanding what happened when the actual reason for the stigmatization worked to give the person a new status. Murphy and his coauthors have interpreted the situation of the disabled person as one where the "lack" of an identity is the real problem (Murphy et al. 1988). The disabled person is "considered to be in a 'liminal' state . . . socially ambivalent and ill-defined, condemned to a kind of seclusion no less real than that of the initiate in the puberty rites of many primitive societies" (ibid.: 235). This may be true in some cases. However, while Murphy's cases showed stagnation, this Nicaraguan case shows that the disabled people actually were achieving a new identity through the help of the social ritual that was a consequence of their being war victims. The ritual marked the change from one status to another. When Carlos came back from the mountains, he was given a lot of prestige and recognition, both by the villagers and by the authorities. With his handicap Carlos had succeeded in gaining a new position or identity, that of a hero of his country. What really made this change of identity possible was the political context of his trauma, which made him more special than he would have been if he had been born disabled.

Following this line of thought, I wanted to find out if there were any way of generalizing about what was being expressed about the disabled victims of the war. Therefore, I went to the organizations of and for disabled persons and also searched the newspapers for similar cases. Very different tendencies were found, as I will show in the next examples.

NEWSPAPER STORIES OF BEGGARS AND HEROES

Nicaragua in 1989 had three daily newspapers. *La Prensa* represented the opposition, *La Barricada* was an organ for the Sandinista party, and *El Nuevo Diario* was also sympathetic to the Sandinista government. These newspapers used all their material in a symbolic way either for or against the government. This affected what and how they wrote about the war victims, as we will see below.

Juan was a blind young man whom I met during my visits to the rehabilitation center. He was always one of the first to stand up and shout slogans at meetings. He gave the impression of being a true follower of Sandino. Great was my surprise when one day he appeared in the opposition newspaper, *La Prensa,* under the headline "Drama de un joven SMO" (A young soldier's drama).[6] In the article Juan described how he was forced to do military service and lost his sight in combat. "In this situation where I, thanks to the Sandinista government who sent me to the war, feel ruined, frustrated, and without a future, I beg that someone will help me to get some kind of work. . . . I am not in favor of the demonstrations outside the American Embassy nor the marches organized by the Sandinistas" (*La Prensa,* 21 June 1988). This is an example of the presentation the opposition newspaper made of the war victims. What Juan really meant is not the issue here. What is of interest is the way the newspaper chose its story, and the manner in which it was presented. This revealed the newspaper's position in relation to problems of the disabled. *La Barricada* had quite another attitude than *La Prensa,* as we see in the *La Barricada* headline "Liciados de guerra—Cachorros de acero" (War victims—steel soldiers) (*La Barricada,* 7 December 1987).[7] These soldiers are pictured smiling as they tell their story about what happened when they trod on the Contra's mines. What is interesting for us is what is being emphasized in the article. Fredy: "I feel OK. My social integration and political activity are normal. I am a militant in the Sandinista youth organization, I have work and I am helping people in the neighborhood [*barrio*]." Another said he felt proud because he "gave a part of his life."

Presentations like these were frequent in Nicaraguan newspapers in 1987 and 1988. The disabled people were being used as symbols in the struggle for political support. The Sandinistas used the term "heroes and martyrs" about those who had fallen in battle. The connotations of this symbol are many and strong. In Victor Turner's terms, these were "dominant" symbols, which are symbols "regarded not merely as means to the fulfillment of the avowed purposes of a given ritual but also and more importantly [these symbols] refer to values which are regarded as ends in themselves, i.e., to axiomatic values" (Turner 1964:21–22). The Sandinistas used heroism and martyrdom to bring together connotations of religion and machismo, two important aspects of Nicaraguan daily life, with the values of the revolution. The war victims proved that they were willing to live up to the standards of what is required, both for martyrs and for heroes. The Sandinista presentation of the disabled victims of the war evoked feelings that were important both for the disabled persons themselves and for the revolution. The revolution needed to show again and again that it was a worthy cause; the heroes needed the psychological support such a recognition could give and also all the practical help this could bring.

The political opposition presented the martyr aspect but not the heroism. *La Prensa* presented the war victim as a victim of the Sandinista policy and as one who suffered for a lost cause and who was therefore liable to pity and charity.

Thus we see that these newspapers based their widely different presentations on criteria other than pure concern for the disabled soldiers. Both newspapers used the disabled people in a political struggle, but regardless of their hidden agendas, what these newspapers wrote probably had strong impact on the public's perception of disabled people. It follows that it was important for the disabled people themselves to participate in this media struggle. Below we will see an example of how they were able to present a third view in the debate.

ORGANIZATIONS AND DISABLED SPORTS STARS

One of the drastic means the government introduced in February 1988 to control the economy was a devaluation of the currency. The effect was less money in circulation and a very difficult time for everybody, but inflation was curtailed for a time. In response, *La Prensa* featured two beggars in its attack on governmental politics, claiming that because of the government, people did not have any money to give to the blind beggars (the persons in question were not war victims). The headline was: "No videntes resienten cambio de moneda. Por favor . . . una limosna por Amor a Dios" (The blind feel the impact of the monetary change. Please . . . a donation for the love of God) (*La Prensa,* 23 February 1988). This article also has its political message: all misery could be blamed on the Sandinistas. The readers also got an impression of the blind beggars as childish clowns who are in the hands of charitable people. The Organization of the Blind used this opportunity to present its view on begging under the following headline in *El Nuevo Diario:* "¡¡¡Por el amor de Dios! Ciegos no deben pedir limosna!!!" (For God's sake! The blind ought not to beg for alms!!!) (*El Nuevo Diario,* 28 February 1988). In this article the president of the organization emphasized that more than one hundred blind people were working in the civil service, many were working at home, and others were studying to get a good education so that they could support themselves and their families in a dignified way. This was what they wanted the public to recognize—the beggar stereotype was something the organization was fighting to get rid of. So blind people, too, tried to evoke heroic connotations about those who had overcome their handicap and become valuable citizens, but not out of a purely party-political concern.

In line with its political inclinations, the newspaper *La Prensa* expressed a particular attitude both toward disabled people and to their rights and possibilities in the society. *La Prensa* presented the war victims and other disabled people as people who were begging for help and for whom the public should feel pity and to whom they should give charity. This, I think, was not a policy but rather the result of trying to use any argument whatsoever in their efforts against the Sandinista regime. The Sandinista organ *La Barricada* emphasized war victims as heroes who still were fighting for the revolution and in that way were integrated in the society. The third view, here exemplified by the Organization of the Blind (OCNMT), was that of the organizations of and for the disabled, who were working to achieve rights and measures that would enable them to participate in normal work and social life. However, what the different organizations regarded as normal work and social life was a matter of definition. The organizations may be said to be divided in at least two groups: those who took a clear and active political stand like ORD, and the ones who wanted to be apolitical, like OCNMT.

It was difficult for an organization to be apolitical in Nicaragua at that time. One that tried to be politically neutral would be considered, by the people, to be against the government. This did not mean, however, that only some organizations received governmental support. I saw on several occasions that the Sandinista government was positive to all initiatives that aimed at supporting the disabled people. The help the organizations got from the government could be land for cultivation, transportation, or help with administration. But because of Nicaragua's strained economic situation, no direct financial support was given. While it certainly was a support to the government to be an active member of the ORD, it could be interpreted as being against the Sandinista government if you were a member of an organization that was not actively engaged in politics. Thus, for the Organization of the Revolutionary Disabled (ORD), the word *integration* meant active political work in support of the Sandinista government, while for the blind people's organization (OCNMT), *integration* meant education and work to become economically independent.

In Nicaragua it was obviously a select group that was taking the lead in controlling this process of change in attitudes toward the disabled people. The fact that the war heroes were young, most often men in their twenties with some type of education, made them stand out as individuals with more personal resources than the average disabled person. They and other supporters of the Sandinista party formed a political elite that attempted to define an identity for disabled persons.

Of the five organizations I had contact with, the four most important ones had war heroes or persons wounded during the insurrection as leaders. It was typical of the Nicaraguan society in general that many of its leaders earned their reputation "in the mountains," that is, fighting for the overthrow of Somoza. This was also the case for the organizations of and for disabled people. The fastest growing of them all was Los Pipitos, an organization for parents with mentally retarded children. The president of this organization was himself a *comandante,* a military leader from the revolution who had a lot of prestige. He took the initiative to form the organization after his twins with Down's syndrome were born.

Of other types of activities in which these organizations were getting involved to promote the cause of their members, sports were perhaps the most visible. Sports were important in the rehabilitation centers, and the organizations were interested in promoting these activities. Therefore, in November 1987 the first national sporting event for disabled people was arranged in Nicaragua. There were four days of competitions for the blind, the deaf, the amputees, the wheelchair users, and the mentally retarded. The event was organized by ORD, CNAC, the Ministry of Health, the Nicaraguan Sport Institute, and the Ministry of Social Welfare. The Sandinista army provided food, transport, and housing. Competitors came from schools, organizations, and rehabilitation centers. The competition was repeated in 1988, this time with participants from El Salvador and Panama. The competition was amply covered by mass media, and various issues besides pure sports results were brought before the public. For example, one participant, Tomás Alvarado, was quoted after winning the wheelchair race, saying, "We disabled are not incapable persons, the blind, the war victims, and the amputated; we are able to do what we put our minds to." From Fernando López, national coordinator of ORD: "International participation is one way of showing that the fight of the disabled is the same everywhere, [namely] to consolidate the opinion that the disabled form a part of society." In the same interview López called for sports budgets to include funds assigned for disabled people's sporting activities.

The arrangement brought the disabled into the public's eye in a positive way, something that had not happened previously. People were amazed, for until recently, one never saw disabled people outside their homes, and now they raced with wheelchairs in the streets!

The press coverage the disabled people received in this sporting event and other situations arranged by their organizations also made it clear to the public that disabled people can contribute to the support of their own family by decent work, as well as take part in social life and make progress in spite of their handicap.

HEROES AND MARTYRS

"Heroes and martyrs," the term the Sandinistas used for those who had lost their lives in the war against the Contras, had such strong connotations that it also justified the situation of those who had almost given their lives—the living war heroes.

The Sandinista government's favored treatment of the war victims (instead of equal treatment of all disabled) and presentation of them as heroes can be seen as a political gesture used to gather support for the Sandinista policy. In a society that had experienced violence, guerrilla warfare, and revolution, one in which everybody faced a daily struggle for survival, it was of utmost importance for the leadership of the country to remind all the people who were suffering of the value of their sacrifice. Again and again Sandinista leaders made a point of the revolution as an ongoing process and not as a battle that was won in 1979. Thus they showed that people were actually still sacrificing themselves for this cause. Presenting the disabled soldiers as heroes to the public may have served as a proof of how worthy the revolutionary process was. Another intended message might have been that in the light of the sacrifice the war heroes had made, the daily problems a lot of people were experiencing should pale in comparison.

But where did the hero symbol get its power? How did the Sandinistas get followers by showing mutilated soldiers in public, and how could the sight of the disabled persons give relief to others who suffered? The explanation could be that Nicaraguan society to a large extent may be seen as a "macho society." Here the hero as a symbol is of real value because heroism can be connected to the values of machismo. Machismo is perhaps the value set that is most often thought of, at least by Westerners, in connection with Latin America. Evelyn P. Stevens calls it "a cult of virility," where the "chief characteristics . . . are exaggerated aggressiveness and intransigence in male-to-male interpersonal relationships" (1973:90). Other researchers have pointed out that Nicaraguans both talk about and believe in their own "violence" (Ekern 1987:95). The Sandinistas were appealing to these values in their use of heroes and heroism as something with a value in itself.

The political opposition, however, used the disabled persons in the ex-amples mentioned to make attacks on the Sandinista government, thus pre-senting the disabled persons as victims of Sandinista policy. The La Prensa article about the blind soldier Juan used such phrases as "against my will" and "thanks to the government." The reader is led to feel sympathy for Juan and antipathy toward those responsible for his situation.

In the political debate between the Sandinistas and the opposition, the disabled people tended to be presented in two extreme ways, almost as dif-ferent as black and white. One presented only the war hero, a victim for a just cause. The other presented the disabled as a victim, or the martyr of an unjust policy. Both were using the disabled as symbols in a political rhetoric.

The organizations of and for disabled persons, which were influenced by Western ideas, also present their more successful members in a heroic way, as in the article by the president of the blind people's organization, OCNMT. But this was another type of hero, a hero who was struggling to be as normal as possible in everyday life. This last view was made available to the public when disabled people became able to organize and speak for themselves. Their view made the situation less black and white, more diver-sified, than before the revolution of 1979.

The high number of war victims combined with the Nicaraguan society's ability and will to do something for them can be compared with the situa-tion in Europe and the United States after World War I. After that war a ris-ing social consciousness led to the introduction of pensions, integrated rehabilitation, and the formation of a variety of interest organizations of and for disabled war victims. The present development in Nicaragua also creates a spillover effect for the rest of the disabled population, which I observed in the organizations of and for the disabled. However, the actual extent of this effect cannot yet be assessed.

CONCLUSION

Making political use of disabled people created a situation where there was room for negotiation to define a new identity for disabled people, one different from that of helpless persons who needed charity and protection. In this negotiation the disabled people themselves have played an important part, especially through their own organizations. The negotiation for a new identity to a large extent went on in the mass media, for example, the newspapers. The recognition of the disabled war victims as important members of society may have been an advantage for disabled people in general if it made a handicap a more normal thing to see.

The situation for disabled persons in Nicaragua had in fact already changed to some extent at the time of this study, because previously they had rarely been seen in public places (personal communication, ORD and OCNMT). Some had jobs, others used public transportation, and some were involved in sports and were written about in the newspapers.

The mass media, in this case the newspapers, demonstrated the variety of concerns and emotions found among the population in regard to disabled persons. The media may also have generated new attitudes by what they wrote about disabled people. That disabled people had been officially put on the government's agenda as a state concern, that the country had been experiencing a revolutionary process for a decade, and that new ideas from abroad had been made available had changed the entire social context. In this new context many new organizations of and for disabled persons were created. These were now making their own views heard.

Based on the data gathered in urban and semi-urban areas, and from which the examples presented here are taken, I think the public was changing its attitude toward disabled persons, and the disabled themselves were gaining new self-confidence in the 1980s.

In this chapter, I have not dealt with possible conflict of interest between war victims and other disabled people. Nor have I mentioned conflicts between the Sandinista war heroes and the disabled Contra soldiers. These may become more pressing issues in time to come. One might anticipate a difficult relationship between the war victims who have gained new identities as heroes and those born disabled, who still are working to achieve a position as valuable citizens.

An important issue for the continuation of the work that the disabled themselves are doing to achieve an identity of respect and worthiness is the kind of role the war heroes will play in the future. Can we expect new governments to continue the active support of this group? Or will other qualifications like civil achievements by the disabled be more important? The work of the blind people's organization, as reflected in the article by its president, can be a signal of what disabled people themselves and their organizations will try to emphasize in their future work.

Although I cannot answer all the questions raised here, I have tried to show how social and political changes in the 1980s produced new identities for disabled people. For the first time, many became aware of their rights and possibilities for participation in Nicaraguan society.

NOTES

1. This is a revised version of a paper presented at the Oslo Workshop on Disability and Culture, 5–6 October 1989, in response to which I received many valuable comments. Especially, I want to thank Benedicte Ingstad and Susan Whyte for their support and encouragement. I also owe thanks to Group 3 at the Institute and Museum of Social Anthropology, University of Oslo, and to Ånund Brottveit and Gerd Holmboe Ottesen for constructive critique in respectively the first and the last phase of the writing. All translations from Spanish to English are my own.

2. The Contras were the counterrevolutionary guerillas fighting to overthrow the Sandinista regime.

3. Instituto Nicaragüense de Seguridad Social y Bienestar (INSSBI), Resolución No. 58. Managua, 12 Junio 1984. And Decreto No. 1488, "Ley que concede beneficios a los combatientes defensores de nuestra patria y su soberania." Managua, 6 Augusto 1984.

4. Some names have been changed to give the persons anonymity.

5. Centro de Rehabilitación Psicosocial Vocacional Gaspar Garcia Laviana.

6. Servicio Militar Obligatorio (SMO) (Obligatory military service) was *La Prensa*'s own denomination. The official name was Servicio Militar Popular (SMP) (Popular military service).

7. *Cachorros* is a name used for soldiers; *Los Cachorros de Sandino* (Sandino's puppies, soldiers with go-ahead spirit).

REFERENCES

Bossert, Thomas J.
    1981   Health policy making in a revolutionary context: Nicaragua,
                1979–1981. *Social Science and Medicine* (15C):225–231.
Ekern, Stener
    1987   *Street Power: Culture and Politics in a Nicaraguan Neighbourhood.* Bergen
                Studies in Social Anthropology, no. 40.
Goffman, Erving
    1963   *Stigma: Notes on the Management of Spoiled Identity.* Englewood Cliffs,
                N.J.: Prentice-Hall.
Guido, Lea
    1982   La salud en Nicaragua [Health in Nicaragua]. *Revista Centroamericana de ciencias de la salud* [Central American review of health sciences], January–April:21.

Helander, Einar
 1984   *Rehabilitation for All: A Guide to the Management of Community-based Rehabilitation. 1. Policymaking and Planning.* WHO/RHB/84.1. Provisional version. Geneva: WHO.
 1993   *Prejudice and Dignity: An Introduction to Community-based Rehabilitation.* UNDP Report No. E93-III-B.3. New York: United Nations Development Program.
Keesing, Roger M.
 1987   Anthropology as interpretive quest. *Current Anthropology* 28(2): 161–176.
Murphy, Robert F., Jessica Scheer, Yolanda Murphy, and Richard Mack
 1988   Physical disability and social liminality: A study in the rituals of adversity. *Social Science and Medicine* 26(2):235–242.
Stevens, Evelyn P.
 1973   Marianismo: The other face of machismo. In *Male and Female in Latin America,* ed. Ann Pescatello. Pittsburgh: University of Pittsburgh Press.
Turner, Victor W.
 1964   Symbols in Ndembu ritual. In *Closed Systems and Open Minds: The Limits of Naivety in Social Anthropology,* ed. M. Gluckman. London: Oliver and Boyd.

ELEVEN

Disability and Migration: A Case Story

Lisbeth Sachs

Women from a rural community in Turkey, who perceive and must deal with sickness and disability in a setting that is new to them, a Stockholm suburb, undergo a form of adjustment which to some extent can be described in terms of deviance as a cultural category (Freidson 1970:231–243; Romanucci-Ross 1983:267–281). The women's actions in connection with deviance (sickness and disability) provide a guide to their perceptions and interpretations of the new world around them. In fact, it is their new situation that causes their perceptions of sickness and deviance to change. It is in the process of adapting to a new life in Sweden that the Turkish families become more aware of deviance as mirrored against not only what has been seen as normal in their own world but also what is seen as normal in the new world surrounding them.

In Sweden as in several societies in the West, the biomedical system sees deviance in the form of bodily and mental impairments as technical and economic problems to be overcome. Disabled people and their families, however, do not. It is less common today to exclude deviant children from what is regarded as normal everyday life; children who are blind or deaf are integrated in regular schools; so are children with various other bodily and mental impairments. Obvious disorders, such as a crippled limb, were not remarked upon by Swedes in or out of health care institutions, which surprised the Turkish families. Nurses would greet a mother with a crippled little boy with: "How does this nice little boy feel?" While members of the Turkish group would tend to mock and point at such a boy, the Swedes avoided looking at him or talking about him. In other instances Swedish doctors would be concerned about invisible metabolic changes leading to what they called "mental retardation." Such a diagnosis was hard to accept as deviance for the Turkish families, although it would lead to much active intervention within the Swedish health care system.

SOME CONCEPTS

Given such obvious differences in the interpretation of deviance as those of the Turkish migrants and the Swedish doctors, one may be inclined to use the concepts of "illness" and "disease" in the analysis of various kinds of deviance (Eisenberg 1977; Young 1982). But in my view we may first need to redefine those concepts. Furthermore, the problem of disability as one form of deviance is manifold.

Referring to the WHO definitions of impairment, disability, and handicap, Susan Whyte and Benedicte Ingstad (this volume) point out that such a definition implies a basically medical view of disorders which may be problematic. If we agree that biomedical diagnosis (disease) like any other diagnosis is built on culture, and thus not objective from a universal point of view, we may come closer to making such concepts as illness and disease useful in this case. The biomedical care that the women from the rural villages in Turkey have experienced is very different from that in Sweden (Sachs 1983:58–63), which made many of their expectations of care in Sweden unrealistic from their Swedish doctors' point of view. Biomedical doctors in societies without technical equipment work with criteria that are more visible than those we are used to in Sweden, where advanced diagnostic instruments make it possible to diagnose internal pathological processes, some of which are not even experienced by the diseased (Djurfeldt and Lindberg 1975:158; Horton 1967:50–71; Paine 1989:141–143; Sachs 1983:165). When distinguishing between illness and disease, it is thus important to consider that both categories may be based on cultural symbols and thus perceived or not perceived as deviance from normal by the other. A more fruitful definition than pathology (disease) in one case and emotional experience (illness) in the other (Kleinman 1980) would be to distinguish the two categories as *labels* made from different power positions within society and to look at their impact as *sickness* (Young 1982) or social *stigma* (Goffman 1963). Deviance is what people so label, and we need to describe what the concepts tell us about social life and culture through our ethnographic data.

Social scientists of the symbolic interactionist persuasion have assembled a sound case for the importance of the labeling process in the study of deviant behavior. They have argued that deviance is widespread; that it is relative to time, place, and audience; and that it is diverse as to form, process, and consequence. They assume initially that what is made of the deviance—how it is detected, recognized, defined, and managed—should be the central concern in social science (Goffman 1961; Lemert 1967; Scheff 1967).

Therefore we need to base our discussions in the reality of our subjects. This must be essential within the anthropology of disability as well.

Forms of behavior per se do not differentiate deviants from nondeviants; it is the responses of the members of the society who identify and interpret behavior as deviant that transform persons into deviants. Any definition of the concept must aim at being empirically based in cultural context. All this is also true of disability. In this ethnographic case I want to use the dichotomy made by George Devereux (1963) to analyze the process of defining disability by a group of migrants in Sweden.

Devereux made the distinction between the "non-normal" and the "yes-insane" the negative and the positive classification of deviance. He considered whether a classification is made in terms of the criterion of deviation from the norm (non-normal) or in terms of fitting certain marginal norms (yes-insane) and ruled in favor of the latter. A given individual is not considered insane because he or she does not behave normally, but because he or she does behave the way the insane are known, expected, or supposed to behave. In fact—and this is a key thesis of Devereux—the incipient knowledge of prevailing models of positively named deviance actively influences the formation of symptoms. When it comes to small children, as in the case described below, the interpretation of symptoms made by the adults in the group must be understood and agreed upon in the process of forming a positive classification.

Among Turkish migrant families it seems that when someone is seen as non-normal, there is still the possibility of correcting this state into a normal state, but when the person is classified yes-disabled, it is a permanent state and there is nothing else to do. To classify someone as being yes-disabled means that he or she is within a category that is accepted and defined by members of the social group. As we shall see in the following case, the search for a yes-disabled classification of a child tells us much about emotions in a process of social and cultural change.

My aim here is to give one extensive case story through which the above will become clear. The case illustrates the way that disability is culturally constructed in a situation of social change. The mother in this case sees her child as non-normal, and though she tries to get treatment both in Sweden and in her home village, she seems to be in a process of defining the condition as incurable. The Swedish doctors say the child in the case is sick but not disabled; they believe he could be cured.

BACKGROUND

The case story, involving a young woman, Döne, and her two sons, is one of many illness processes that I followed among Turkish migrant families in a Swedish suburb and in a town in middle Anatolia[1] (Sachs 1983). The reactions of the young woman in connection with her son's symptoms are based on the stock of knowledge that she holds in common with other women of her group. She does what she believes to be right, in the light of her knowledge and experience. This stock of knowledge accumulates from the thoughts and actions of people in a certain sociocultural system. Personal experience may vary, but it is integrated in the shared stock, becoming part of this. Individual experience may also modify the common stock in time, though this is usually a slow process. In a situation of migration, however, this process may be accelerated by various unpredictable experiences.

The Turkish migrant families perceive deviance from normal, be it illness or other afflictions, as caused by powers outside of the human will. God's will is the ultimate answer or cause of everything that happens in life. God has a meaning for everything. Agents of evil are jinns (demons living in close contact with humans) or the evil eye (Sachs 1983:75–79). The Turkish villagers commonly believe that mental illness and mental disability are a result of being possessed or "mixed up" by the jinns. Possession is believed to occur usually by accident but sometimes as punishment for violation of certain taboos or for performing daily activities without ritual precautions against the jinns. The result may be aphasia, strokes, epileptic attacks, or certain "mixed up" states known in psychiatry as schizophrenic reactions, manias, and severe delusional depressions (Özturk 1964). The village women have observed people with anxiety who have been, as they say, "frightened by the jinns."

The Turkish migrants see evil eye as another cause of illness and failures in life (Flores-Meiser 1976). Certain people (especially those with blue or green eyes) are believed to have the capacity to look with evil eyes. Successful, progressing, healthy, and attractive people are particularly vulnerable to the evil eye. Such people are believed to arouse envy and hostility in others, whose eyes have the power of inflicting various afflictions by a mere glance (Foster 1972). It is sometimes believed that the eyes of the closest and dearest person may have an evil influence. For example, some people believe that mothers should not praise or look at their children with admiration. Villagers usually hide their babies from the eyes of other people in order to protect them from evil influences.

In Sweden the ideas that the Turkish women share about illness, deviance, and disability are exposed to many influences, not least in encounters with Swedish health care. This is a collective process. Everything that happens to the woman and her children in our case story is discussed in her group and may either reinforce or weaken their ideas and attitudes. One may ask what it is that causes the system of ideas of these women to survive and be reinforced and what causes it to be perceived as a failure.

THE ENCOUNTER WITH WESTERN BIOMEDICINE

The young Turkish woman Döne has been called to come to the well-baby clinic in a Stockholm suburb for a checkup of her four-year-old son, Ali. She has come with him and her infant of six months. The doctor has just finished examining the elder boy and transfers his interest to the infant in the mother's arms.

The mother now hesitates, looks anxious, and tells the interpreter that she is here just for Ali's checkup. The interpreter replies that, having come to the center, she must let the doctor take a look at both children. The mother then places the child in its blanket on an extension of the doctor's desk that serves for examinations. Having washed his hands, the doctor removes some layers of blanket and clothes to reveal a small boy lying motionless, neither asleep nor awake. The doctor cups his hands around the tiny head, examines the neck and ears and tests reflexes. Instead of addressing the mother, he now puts his questions to the interpreter and asks for how long the boy has been like this. The mother replies that he has always been that way.

> "What does he get to eat?"
> "I nurse him; he gets a bottle at times but spits it out."
> "Why haven't you come here with this boy? He is not well."

At that the mother goes up to the table and starts to dress the child, saying there is no point in going to a hospital with this boy because doctors do not understand what the matter is. The doctor then asks the interpreter to explain that the child is in need of immediate care at a hospital. He sits down, writes out a referral, and says that the mother is to take the baby at once to one of the major hospitals in Stockholm: "The boy ought not to be so listless and uninterested."

The mother dresses both children and moves toward the door while the doctor explains how to get to the hospital and stresses that she must go today. When the mother has gone, the doctor says that he thinks the child has had diarrhea for a long time with consequent dehydration, plus an upper respiratory infection that has developed complications. What he fears is meningitis.

What has taken place at the child health center? To elucidate this we have to sketch the young mother's background and accompany her to the apartment of her parents-in-law, with whom she is living, as well as on the journey she undertakes with her father-in-law to her home village in Anatolia so that a folk healer can treat the child for the deviance that she and her family suspect he is suffering from.

THE STORY OF DÖNE

Döne was born and grew up in a small rural village in middle Anatolia. She has a sister and two brothers, all younger than herself. Her father died when the children were quite young, and since then her mother has managed on her own, continuing to breed sheep and till the soil, chiefly as a market gardener. The mother is a notable person in the village, a deviant woman who drives a horse and cart, does business, and goes her own way. Men have lived with her at times but she has not remarried. In recent years some of the farmwork has been taken over by the two sons, but the mother is still to be seen at the reins on the dusty roads around the village.

As the eldest child, Döne had to manage the youngsters and do housework from an early age. Her mother and a paternal aunt had been pregnant together and had planned that the children would marry. Döne accordingly grew up in the knowledge that her cousin was to be her husband. This did not happen, however, because Döne's life changed in many respects after the death of her father. Döne's mother refused to submit to her mother-in-law and the relationship broke down. The cousin subsequently married another young woman; Döne's mother had other plans for her daughter.

When Döne reached puberty she stayed for some months with a maternal aunt in Ankara. There she was attracted by clothes and makeup and wore what was fashionable in the city. She was thirteen years old and caused a stir on her return to the village. Becoming interested in a young man, she asked her mother's permission to marry him. The mother did what she could to comply; Döne's future family had already migrated to Sweden, and after the wedding she started her life as a young in-law in a suburb of Stockholm.

Her father-in-law had been against the marriage from the start, on account of Döne's family's reputation in the village, but the son was so insistent that in the end he gave way. Döne arrived in Sweden and was ranked lowest in her new family. She did the domestic chores that were imposed on her and continued to function as a daughter, albeit in a household of strangers. When Döne joined the household it consisted of her parents-in-law and their five sons, plus the eldest son's wife and small daughter. The youngest son was only five years old and two of the others were of school age.

During the day there was no one at home. The father-in-law washed dishes at a restaurant in Stockholm, accompanied by the eldest son when there was a lot to do. Döne's husband tended the paths and flowers in a churchyard outside Stockholm in the mornings and worked at a pizzeria in the evenings; he came home after Döne had gone to bed and left before she got up. Döne's sister-in-law had a job as a nursing aide at a Stockholm hospital, where she had worked ever since her arrival in Sweden.

Döne became pregnant quite soon and a son was born after barely a year in Sweden. To start with she stayed at home, doing the housework and minding the children. She received the one-year maternity allowance, which she handed over to her father-in-law. It astonished her that one could earn money without doing anything. With the birth of her son, things started to change for Döne. The baby was the first grandson for her parents-in-law, who were proud of it and looked after the boy as they thought best. But the baby also led to growing tension between the two daughters-in-law.

Döne's sister-in-law is the daughter of a respected, big landowner in the home village. Many members of her father's family have migrated to Sweden, and she has spent a lot of time with them right from the start. She maligned Döne to her parents-in-law, as well as among her relatives and friends.

When the boy was one year old, the father-in-law decided that Döne should go out to work in order to bring in money. One of his brothers arranged a job for her at a Stockholm hotel where the brother washed dishes and other women from Turkish villages worked as cleaners. Döne handed all her pay to her father-in-law, who managed the finances and gave his wife money for household expenses.

When Döne had been in Sweden for just over two years her husband returned to Turkey for twenty-one months of military service. Döne's second pregnancy had started; she continued to work but developed back trouble, whereupon a Swedish doctor certified her for sick leave for the last four months of pregnancy. She stayed at home to look after the family's three small children while her mother-in-law worked as a school cleaner in the afternoons. The three children were the youngest son of the mother-in-law, Döne's son, and her sister-in-law's daughter.

Döne felt unwell during the pregnancy, and she disliked being alone in the daytime and felt threatened, uneasy. When her time came she was very frightened, and it seemed to her that something was wrong with everything to do with her delivery. Although she got a second son, it did not make her at all happy. The baby was small and thin, too weak to suck her milk, and he fretted constantly. For her stay at the maternity clinic she had taken a copy of the Koran, her amulets, small scissors, and one of her husband's pullovers. When the lights were turned out at night she was frightened and turned on her bedside lamp, at which the other women in the room complained. Döne was convinced that she saw Alkarisi (a demon who haunts newborns and their mothers) outside the window; she felt hot and could not breathe normally. She lay awake in fear the whole night. When her baby was brought in by the nurse in the morning, he had scratches on his face, so she knew that Alkarisi had attacked him. She decided to go home immediately. The doctor at the clinic said she had a slight fever and would not be allowed home until it had subsided. She then phoned her mother-in-law to get the family to fetch her. She related that Alkarisi had been there, that the room had to be in darkness at night, and she did not dare to keep the Koran under her pillow when the staff came round to make the beds. She was certain to get *albasmisi* (a folk term for childbed fever) if they did not fetch her, so that she could be treated as necessary.

The father-in-law came to fetch Döne, accompanied by his wife. This caused a commotion because the baby had not been examined by a pediatrician and could not be discharged before it was clear that everything was in order. The doctor told the father-in-law, with the aid of an interpreter, that the staff would talk with Döne and calm her down; he explained that she had a slight temperature, possibly due to milk congestion, and she would definitely get the best care and rest at the hospital. The father-in-law rejoined that she should return home and would be cared for better there, whereupon the doctor allowed Döne to leave, alone and at her own risk. The baby had to stay at least until the following day to be examined.

Döne's despair at having to leave her son behind was overcome by her fears of what might happen if she stayed in the hospital. Safely home, she received treatment from her mother-in-law and prepared for her son's return the following day. All that night Döne thought she saw Alkarisi; her mother-in-law and sister-in-law sat by her in turns. The sister-in-law had a patrilineal relative who had seen Alkarisi outside their home village one night and managed to grasp her long hair and extract a promise never to strike a member of his family. As the sister-in-law now belonged to her husband's family, however, she was less confident and felt frightened too. Many women in their village had died of the disease that this witch causes after delivery.

The next morning the father-in-law went back to the clinic to fetch his grandson. The doctor repeated that the baby would be discharged at the father-in-law's risk and that a nurse would call as soon as possible to lend a hand.

Döne perceived that all was not well with her baby boy. She was sure that he had been struck by Alkarisi and possessed while he was on his own. He had differed from her other son right from the start. For the first few months he was a poor feeder despite her efforts. He was thin and listless. The nurse from the child health center called and took Döne and her baby to see the doctor; he found the boy thin and suggested that Döne should give him less food more often rather than everything at once.

Döne continued to believe her boy had been possessed and that he was not normal. She did not allow any stranger to see him and kept him indoors. Her mother sent an amulet in an envelope from the village. For five months after the boy's birth, the father-in-law stayed at home on account of protracted headaches so severe that he could not see. He lay in the living room most of the time and was not to be disturbed. Döne supplied him with food and tea and kept the youngsters out of the way. When he occasionally left the flat, Döne was able to smoke, watch television, or listen to a tape of Turkish music that she had received from home. During this period she never left the flat.

Döne and her mother-in-law suspected after some time that the baby was suffering from *kurbagacik*. His fontanel was depressed and pulsated, there were small white lumps on the roof of his mouth and a dark streak on his back, all of which indicated that it must be kurbagacik. He seemed to get smaller and smaller, had continual diarrhea, and was tired and listless, eating hardly anything. Several relatives who saw the boy agreed that it must be kurbagacik. A child who suffers from kurbagacik is extremely vulnerable. The sickness is in itself a condition caused by evil impact, usually a jinn, at an unprotected moment. At a certain point people tend to give up and see the child as incurable and impossible to help. Some children whom one may see in the villages who are marginal in one way or the other are said to have suffered from kurbagacik as infants. These children are all very thin, seem shy, do not speak, and usually mingle with much younger children. They are all children who are considered as "children of God" but who in one way or another have been left as anomalies in society. Kurbagacik is an affliction that indicates the child is possessed. It may be defined as, or lead to, a yes-disabled state.

The father-in-law decided to take his grandson and Döne back to their village in Anatolia to get a treatment. Meanwhile the nurse from the child health center called again and asked Döne to bring her four-year-old son Ali for a checkup. An appointment was arranged, and the nurse phoned in the morning to remind her. Döne took both her children to the center, where she encountered the doctor, as described above.

Returning from the center, Döne was distressed and frightened. She could not forget the blue eyes and the fair hair of the nurse or the latter's admiration of her son. Döne was fearful of the evil eye; the nurse did not know that she ought to have said *masallah* to ward off the evil eye when admiring a child. Having attached amulets to her child, Döne waited for her mother-in-law.

When the mother-in-law came home, Döne showed her the referral from the doctor and related that he had told her to take the baby to a hospital. The mother-in-law replied that her husband would have to decide but added that there was certainly no point in going to see a Swedish doctor, who could not know what was wrong with the boy; in any event, they could not help this boy in Sweden.

A couple of days later the father-in-law left for Turkey with Döne and her son. There they went immediately to the woman who is a specialist folk healer in incisions for kurbagacik. The woman held the boy's head, made small incisions round the fontanel, placed chicken liver on them, and bandaged the head. When she removed the bandage after a time, the fontanel was no longer depressed. Döne could see for herself that the treatment had been effective and relieved her son of his symptoms. She felt happy and grateful to the healer and resolved to bring gifts next time she visited her village. The boy had received an amulet against the evil influence that had come into him at birth. But nothing could help him totally get rid of this influence; he was extremely vulnerable and must be especially protected.

Döne spent no more than a week in Turkey, where she looked after her father-in-law in his house. She managed to visit her mother only once and as her father-in-law was present, there was little she could say. Back in the Stockholm suburb, Döne soon found that the baby's digestion was very poor. After a short time both children got pains in their ears and cried all night. Accompanied by her brother-in-law, Döne took them to the emergency clinic at a hospital in Stockholm; penicillin and nose drops were prescribed and Döne obtained them at the pharmacy. The elder boy took his medicine but the baby refused and Döne did not want to force him, particularly as the medicine would not have any effect on him since his possessed condition was preventing him from getting well.

The elder boy recovered but the little one got worse, and the day came when he could not be aroused. This frightened Döne, who was alone at home with all the children. With the baby wrapped in a blanket, she took the underground to a hospital in Stockholm, leaving the other children behind. At the hospital the doctor told her they must keep the baby for some days to give him nutrition and fluid. They placed him in a bed and attached tubes to his body. Döne returned to the other children and waited, frightened and unhappy, for her mother-in-law, whom she told that she wanted to take the boy back to Turkey.

After a week the boy was fetched by the father-in-law from the hospital, where the doctor said that he had lost fluid, seemed to be undernourished, and must have had diarrhea for a long time. Back at the flat the boy was calm and seemed content but Döne did not think he was any better. The mother-in-law and sister-in-law both considered that he was better than he had been before, but Döne did not see it this way. Her view of her baby son was that he was disabled and that nothing could help him. On no occasion did Döne consider that Swedish doctors or visits to hospitals helped her boy. She interpreted his symptoms differently from time to time but always believed that he had been afflicted at birth by Alkarisi and that he was now disabled for life.

DÖNE'S SON: THE VIEW OF THE VILLAGE WOMEN

For Döne the first sign of her baby's affliction is that he will not eat. As long as a person copes with normal functions and meets the sex- and age-related expectations of those around him, that person is regarded as normal. For the women from the rural village, disability or sickness among themselves is equivalent to being incapable of performing daily tasks, which consist in their village of keeping the house clean, sewing clothes, carrying water, preparing food, minding young children, and so on. Sickness interferes above all with everyday actions and functions; it is such incapacity that reveals its presence to other people.

In Döne's case, several members of the family as well as relatives and friends from her village consider the baby boy to be deviant and not normal, too skinny and pale. The symptoms of a skinny baby may be seen as either a sickness (curable) or a disability (incurable). The symptoms are not interpreted as incurable by all the women in the group. Döne and her mother-in-law identify the disability as having to do with a possession by a jinn (Alkarisi) at birth, but this does not meet with general agreement. Some women are more inclined to see the problems as evidence that Döne, like her own parent, is no good as a mother and lacks the ability to protect her child.

Knowing what is wrong with her son, Döne is unmoved by this slander. No blame attaches to her since she attributes the cause to powers over which she has no control. One woman believes that the baby has been bewitched out of envy by the sonless sister-in-law. Others are convinced that the baby is disabled because it was born in Sweden. They are most upset that Döne left her newborn baby unprotected at the Swedish hospital; this was dangerous because people there do and say things without thinking. The women also criticize Döne's family for not compelling the hospital staff to hand over her baby. The infant is hers, not theirs. How can a hospital hold on to other people's children for no reason?

Some of the women state that children born in Sweden have "less good quality" and are deviant in ways that they have never experienced in their village. They come across children with evident incurable defects, such as not being able to move, eat, or talk. Children who are obviously deformed belong to this category but also children who are perceived as different from what is expected. The subtle symbolic interpretations are based on multifactoral and complex situations. Children who are disabled in this way at birth are "children of God" and should be taken by God to prepare for their parents in heaven. Swedes may think they can oppose God's will, but then they have to take care of the child. Some women from their village who have given birth to disabled children in Sweden have left their children to be taken care of by Swedish institutions.

The understanding of disability held by these Turkish families is that certain signs indicate that a child or a person belongs to a certain category of yes-disabled. The signs may be physical or mental, but they are always ultimately related to a specific evil cause. Some women around Döne say they *know* that her child is non-normal but do not know whether he is incurable or not and have difficulties in categorizing him as yes-disabled. They read the subtle signs and symptoms as they read all other communicative messages, as parts of their cultural grammar. They also consider the ultimate cause as being God's will but argue about what could have been done by Döne. They agree that a person usually cannot be responsible for being struck by a jinn or evil eye herself but may be to blame for not protecting her children. This is one point where their new life situation in a new world may lead to changed ideas. Who is to blame for what happens to their children? Is it Sweden, the Swedes and their institutions, that do not take notice of God's will, or is it the mother of the child and her family who seem to be marginal in some sense in the Turkish village and thus also in their Swedish Turkish community? Do jinns really exist in the Swedish environment? Are Swedes able to transmit the evil eye? Some answer yes and some no to these questions.

Döne is not yet sure what to do, but she is never at a loss to explain failures on the part of the village health care system that was hers in her childhood. Using her combination of explanations, failures of a folk treatment are attributed not only to difficulties in repelling the evil eye but also to the ultimate outcome of a disability being in the hands of God. It is not that she expects her actions invariably to produce the intended result; she simply feels she has done the right thing, even though it does not always work. When it comes to health care in the Swedish system, Döne has no such secondary explanations and blames it accordingly.

The illness kurbagacik is a sign that confirms for Döne that she and her family are pursued by evil: Alkarisi and the evil eye. She uses the illness to account for several features of her life, including her own failed expectations in Sweden: a prosperous life, beautiful clothes, and a Mercedes.

DÖNE'S SON: THE VIEW OF THE SWEDISH DOCTORS

The doctor believes at first that the baby has meningitis and is therefore insistent about hospital care without delay. He also notes that the baby has had diarrhea and is very weak. The symptoms may represent some dehydration, but the doctor cannot tell for certain. Nothing can be established definitely until the diagnostic examinations have been made at a hospital. The doctor never doubts that the boy has a disease. According to the doctor, it is chiefly the mother who is responsible for her son's condition.

> She is too young and immature and has to look after too many children during the day. She is, quite simply, unsuited to look after small children; she is just a child herself. She never takes the children out and somehow lets them get on as best they can. She has come to the child health center several times with various children and has always seemed inaccessible and uninterested, almost furtive.

The nurse who calls on Döne provides the doctor with further information. His opinion about the causes of the boy's condition is strengthened by her reports. During her visits Döne had smoked and read magazines, while the children ran about and carried the baby. The other children had been allowed to hug and kiss the little boy even when they had a cold and appeared diseased. It seemed to the nurse that Döne had a poor social situation. Her children received no stimulation and were left on their own too much. The nurse noted that the children were not undressed at night and had no toys, while the baby had no bath or bed of its own. She described the situation as "real destitution."

The doctor and his medical colleagues at the hospital consider that the boy is not getting the care he needs, particularly for infections. He needs to be fed with a more varied diet to suit a child of that age, and to be treated very patiently. Regular mealtimes would also be desirable. The doctors believe that medically there is nothing fundamentally wrong; it is simply that the boy never recovers properly from one infection before he contracts a new one. All that is really wrong is the boy's management. Steps should be taken to get him into a Swedish day nursery, where he would receive the care he needs.

The doctors are very dubious about the trips to Turkey. A child born in Sweden is less able to stand up to the bacterial flora, infectious diseases, and parasites there. A child in poor condition should definitely not make the trip. Infant mortality is high in the village, and the doctors are in favor of recommending that some mothers leave their infants in Sweden while they holiday in Turkey. It has happened that children who accompanied their parents during summers in Turkey died there.

The doctors are also aware that impaired children from these families are left with Swedish institutions. This is not understandable and quite shocking to the health care personnel.

CONCLUSION

As is true for any person, Döne's sense of reality consists of two parts. There is her "model" of reality, which contrasts and connects the objects that exist in her world, and there is her conviction that these perceptions are true and extrinsic to herself. Before her model of reality can provide her with a sense of reality, she must confirm it through experience; models of reality are simultaneously "models of" and "models for" (Geertz 1967:6–8; Goodenough 1971:36–38). A sense of reality means, then, imposing order through practical activity. This could be any activity that seeks to go beyond the existing situation in order to change it.

The disability of a child always elicits a response, both of actions and of questions, about its significance. Episodes of serious affliction rarely lack compelling motives for action. As we have seen, Döne is continuously trying to find a cure for her son, regardless of her perception that he is disabled. To do something may in any context be psychologically satisfying and a way of relieving anxiety; anything is better than just remaining passive and waiting. Deviance is an event that challenges meaning in this world; beliefs and practices organize the event into an episode that gives it form and meaning.

On the one hand, then, there is the seeking of a remission of symptoms; on the other hand, there is a social motive of seeking exculpation for deviant behavior (Young 1976:12–13). In the case of Döne, the social accountability for her behavior can be transferred onto some agency beyond her own will: evil eye and Alkarisi. Disability of the child may contribute in this way to the orderliness of Döne's life, since it can be used as a vehicle for communicating and legitimizing her relations within the Turkish as well as the Swedish community. She is without guilt but afflicted by external powers.

Döne is adapting to a new situation in Sweden where she is regarded as a "bad mother" by Swedish health care personnel and as "not protective enough" by the other Turkish women and as "alien" in her home community in Turkey. How this influences her translation of "signs" (behavioral and physical expressions of her child) into the category kurbagacik and consequent actions is a quite complex process. She seems to be ambivalent about the question of non-normal or yes-disabled.

According to the ideas of disability in her village, the children who are regarded as non-normal, but who survive, are usually treated as if they were sick until it is obvious that they cannot be cured. Then they are treated as all other children; they have to survive on their own within their social network. There are also children of a different kind, God's children, who are integrated into society as well. They are deviant in a predictable and well-known way; they are yes-disabled. The problem for the migrant women in Sweden is that their children sometimes deviate in unrecognized ways, which means that they are not so easily categorized as yes-disabled and not curable. When this happens they may be left to Swedish institutions for care.

Although Döne's son is recognized in her community as having a folk disease, caused by evil external impact usually leading to incurable disability, the state seems to create ambivalence due to the complex situation and different types of actors who are involved in the migrant situation. The process of classifying and labeling the little boy as yes-disabled seems to have become an endless search for meaning in his mother's new life.

NOTE

1. The fieldwork on which this chapter is based was conducted in Sweden between 1976 and 1981. During that time I also made two trips to Anatolia with migrant families who were going home for visits. The elder women who were my informants in Sweden were illiterate and were offered literacy classes in their own language by Turkish teachers. I learned Turkish during these classes and, with the help of my informants, became familiar with the dialect they used. The younger women like Döne could read and write, even though they did not make much use of these skills in their

daily lives. Döne learned Swedish quite quickly and we spoke both languages together, depending on the situation. I knew Döne from the very beginning of my research, when I made contact with her at the child health center. We became very close, and Döne's family was one of those with whom I traveled to Anatolia.

REFERENCES

Devereux, George
    1963   Primitive psychiatric diagnosis: A general theory of the diagnostic process. In *Man's Image in Medicine and Anthropology*, ed. I. Goldstone. New York: International Universities Press.

Djurfeldt, G., and S. Lindberg
    1975   *Pills against Poverty: A Study of the Introduction of Western Medicine in a Tamil Village.* Scandinavian Institute of Asian Studies Monograph Series, no. 23. Lund: Student Litteratur and Curzon Press.

Eisenberg, Leon
    1977   Disease and illness: Distinctions between professional and popular ideas of sickness. *Culture, Medicine and Psychiatry* 1:9–23.

Flores-Meiser, E.
    1976   The hot mouth and evil eye. In *The Evil Eye,* ed. C. Maloney. New York: Columbia University Press.

Foster, George
    1972   The anatomy of envy: A study in symbolic behavior. *Current Anthropology* 13:165–202.

Freidson, Eliot
    1970   *Profession of Medicine: A Study of the Sociology of Applied Knowledge.* New York: Dodd, Mead.

Geertz, Clifford
    1967   Religion as a cultural system. In *Anthropological Approaches to the Study of Religion,* ed. M. Banton. London: Tavistock.

Goffman, Erving
    1961   *Asylums.* New York: Doubleday.
    1963   *Stigma: Notes on the Management of Spoiled Identity.* Englewood Cliffs, N.J.: Prentice-Hall.

Goodenough, Ward H.
    1971   *Culture, Language, and Society.* Reading, Mass.: Addison-Wesley Publishing.

Horton, Robin
    1967   African traditional thought and Western science. *Africa* 37:50–71.

Kleinman, Arthur
    1980   *Patients and Healers in the Context of Culture: An Exploration of the Borderland between Anthropology, Medicine, and Psychiatry.* Berkeley, Los Angeles, London: University of California Press.

Lemert, E. M.
    1967   *Human Deviance, Social Problems, and Social Control.* Englewood Cliffs, N.J.: Prentice-Hall.

Özturk, O. M.

1964   Folk treatment of mental illness in Turkey. In *Magic, Faith, and Healing*, ed. Ari Kiev. New York: Free Press.

Paine, Robert

1989   Making the invisible "visible": Coming to terms with Chernobyl and its experts, a Saami illustration. *International Journal of Moral and Social Studies* 4(2):141–143.

Romanucci-Ross, Lola

1983   On madness, deviance, and culture. In *The Anthropology of Medicine: From Culture to Method*, ed. L. Romanucci-Ross et al. New York: Praeger Publishers.

Sachs, Lisbeth

1983   *Evil Eye or Bacteria: Turkish Migrant Women and Swedish Health Care.* Stockholm Studies in Social Anthropology, no. 12. Stockholm: University of Stockholm.

Scheff, Thomas J.

1967   Toward a sociological model of consensus. *American Sociological Review* 32:32–46.

Young, A.

1976   Some implications of medical beliefs and practices for social anthropology. *American Anthropologist* 78(1):5–24.

1982   The anthropologies of illness and sickess. *Annual Review of Anthropology* 11:257–185.

TWELVE

Constructing Epilepsy: Images and Contexts in East Africa

Susan Reynolds Whyte

Since the 1960s doctors working in East Africa have published striking accounts of the strange beliefs and lamentable conditions with which epileptics live there. In 1965 Louise Jilek-Aall wrote a long article in *Acta Psychiatrica Scandinavica* describing the "cruelty and neglect" to which epileptics were subjected among the Wapogoro people of Tanzania. Epilepsy was so dreaded and so well known there that she referred to it as their "tribal sickness." She wrote of the conviction that epilepsy was contagious and that it was a punishment for sin or the incarnation of an evil spirit or the result of witchcraft.

> It is very difficult for an outsider to comprehend the ideas connected with it [epilepsy]. Most likely the person questioned will keep many facts secret, partly for fear of the mganga [medicine man] and also of the revenge of the spirits. But the shame of having an epileptic in the family also plays a great part in the unwillingness to give information. The people prefer to hide the afflicted in the hut away from strangers. (Jilek-Aall 1965:63–64)

Nevertheless, once it became known that she was offering treatment, many came forward. The typical new patient presented the following picture:

> An indescribably dirty and timid person comes slowly through the door. On being offered a chair he does not dare to seat himself, but cowers on the floor with downcast eyes, diffusing an odour of filth and poverty about him. At first no words are uttered, the fear and feeling of inferiority are too overwhelming. To give the patient time to accustom himself to the situation a conversation is first carried on with relatives, and after a while the patient is asked some questions with their help. From the coarse and unfriendly manner in which they address him one can sense the entire atmosphere of contempt surrounding him. (ibid.:69)

From Ethiopia, R. Giel presented a similar picture of epileptics as despised outcasts, hanging about churchyards and cemetaries with lepers.

> The epileptics . . . , many of them insane by the time they make a cemetery their home, are feared and almost completely ignored. Aside from the badly smelling sores and the other deformities that they share with lepers, they are often made more repulsive because of their unpredictable and aggressive behaviour. (Giel 1968:27)

From Uganda, John Orley published ethnographically rich descriptions of the ideas and practices surrounding mental illness and epilepsy. He too described the dread of epilepsy and the idea that it was infectious. Epileptics had to eat and sleep separately, and epileptic children could not play with others. The stigma lingered on even after death. No one could inherit from an epileptic, and the epileptic could not have a grave near the homestead like other family members but had to be buried in the bush (Orley 1970:38–39). The fear of contagion was especially great in connection with fits, causing onlookers to run away. "If he should fall in the fire or into water it is quite likely that no one will pull him out and he will be left to burn or drown" (ibid.:35). Indeed, severe burns are a concomitant of epilepsy everywhere in Africa (Swift and Asuni 1975:165), and diagnostically they may serve as an indicator of the disease (Jilek-Aall et al. 1979:614).

Since these earlier publications, a great deal of literature has accumulated on epilepsy in various parts of Africa. As neurology and psychiatry departments have expanded at national hospitals, and particularly as attempts have been made to integrate treatment of common neuropsychiatric conditions into primary health care, the Medline printout has lengthened. (A recent search on epilepsy in Africa yielded 114 titles since 1975.) These studies confirm many of the cultural features outlined in the earlier ones: the stigma of epilepsy, the notion of contagion, the preference for treatment by traditional healers. But the picture is beginning to blur in important ways as well. Some researchers have found that stigma is not as great as they expected; others have questioned whether the "myth of contagion" is actually so widely held. Still others have suggested that treatment preferences depend on what people believe is available. In general it appears that there is now enough research to allow us to question what we actually know and how we know it. Do differences in reports reflect differences in reality due to historical changes and/or regional variation? Or are they due to differences in research methods? Or is the cultural phenomenon of epilepsy in Africa more fluid and complex than originally realized, and are researchers merely grasping limited but complementary aspects of it?

In this chapter I would like to consider some problems of understanding epilepsy in another cultural context by presenting material I gathered during research in Tanzania and drawing comparisons to other studies. My

work was part of a baseline study for the Tanzania Mental Health Programme[1] carried out in the Morogoro and Kilimanjaro regions in cooperation with the Tanzanian Ministry of Health and with the assistance of
Tanzanian health workers and WHO consultant psychiatrists. It involved
nine weeks of fieldwork in 1983 and 1984; in addition to ethnographic interviews of a range of local people, traditional healers, and biomedical
health workers, we carried out an attitude survey of 200 respondents and interviewed 170 families with mentally ill, epileptic, or retarded members.
There were 66 epileptics among them.

EPILEPSY AS A CULTURAL CATEGORY

In Swahili, which is the national language of Tanzania, there is a term that
is usually translated as "epilepsy." *Kifafa* means literally "little death"; in
other East African languages, words meaning "falling sickness" or "chicken
death" are used, emphasizing the grand mal convulsions that are the major
characteristic of this category of sickness. People describe kifafa in terms of
repeated episodes of falling, jerking of the limbs, foaming at the mouth and
incontinence, followed by sleep and confusion. Petit mal episodes alone are
not seen as kifafa, although some persons suffering grand mal convulsions
were said to have absences as well. We can already sense problems of translation here, since the Tanzanian category is more limited than the Western
medical rubric of "the epilepsies."

Kifafa was a very familiar illness in Tanzania; 97 percent of the respondents to our attitude survey had seen or heard of someone having it. It was
far better known than madness or mental retardation, and probably better
known than it would be on a similar survey in Europe. The familiarity of
epilepsy in Africa has been confirmed in other studies as well. In an Ethiopian survey of over fifteen hundred persons, 86 percent had seen someone
have a seizure and 14 percent said that a family member had epilepsy (Tekle-
Haimanot et al. 1991:204). From Nigeria, another study reports that all of
285 respondents had seen a case of epilepsy (Awaritefe 1989:450).

Is this because of a high prevalence of epilepsy in Africa? Our study in
Tanzania did not gather data on prevalence, though our requests to meet
persons with epilepsy always yielded many names, especially in Morogoro
Region, suggesting that it was common. Louise Jilek-Aall's pioneer study
among the Wapogoro took place in this region, and she estimated a prevalence of 20 per 1000 (Jilek-Aall et al. 1979:616). A recent study in Zanzibar,
also part of Tanzania, found a much lower prevalence: 4.9 per 1000 (Bondestam et al. 1990:329). While some figures from West Africa are as high as
38 per 1000, the Ethiopian study mentioned above took place in an area
where the prevalence had been found to be 5.2 per 1000 (Tekle-Haimanot

et al. 1991:206), which falls within the range often reported for developed countries (Schoenberg 1983:337). In general there is so much variation in the African prevalence figures that I would hesitate to use them as an explanation for public consciousness of the disease.[2] Perhaps more important is the fact that very few epileptics are on regular medication, so that convulsions are frequent occurrences.

Epilepsy is not only a familiar condition in Tanzania, it is regarded as a very grave one. The prognosis was grim according to our respondents in the attitude study; most (79 percent) expected that an epileptic would die from the disease, while the rest said it would become chronic or get worse. Some volunteered that epileptics usually die by fire or water. From his Uganda study, Orley described how people expected epilepsy to "spoil the brain." He adds: "There is no doubt that the social isolation which epileptics are subjected to, especially in the case of children, can lead to failure in their social development, so that the brain certainly appears spoilt" (Orley 1970:37).

Epilepsy as a category is distinguished from the fever convulsions common in children. These latter are called *degedege* in Tanzania, and they are regarded with concern because it is said that they can develop into epilepsy.[3] Many people said that fever convulsions should be attended by indigenous healers whose medicine could tie the degedege and prevent it from becoming kifafa.[4] The conceptual boundary between these two disorders is important but somewhat vague. Generally the repetition of fits and symptoms like biting the tongue and incontinence were held to indicate epilepsy. The occurrence of fever in conjunction with the convulsion is not in itself the decisive dimension. To complicate matters further, the term *kichango,* the diminutive form of the word meaning "worm" (which I shall explain in a moment), is sometimes used either as a euphemism for epilepsy or, according to some, to refer to an intermediate condition of "big fever convulsions."

The process by which symptoms come to be identified as epilepsy can be a lengthy and uncertain one. We visited homes that village officials had indicated as having an individual with kifafa, epilepsy. But three of the sixty-six families seemed reluctant themselves to apply this label.[5] Of his six-year-old daughter who was having seizures every night, a father said: "Some people say this is kifafa, but no froth comes from her mouth, so we hope it is not. Though perhaps as she grows, it will develop and become a real kifafa." And the mother of a girl who had had a series of convulsions during which she had bitten her tongue so severely that she could not eat for several days, said that she was not sure whether the girl had kifafa because she was not incontinent during the fits. A five-year-old boy who was having fits twice a month was said by his father to be suffering from fever convulsions; the father knew herbal medicine for that and was treating him himself. Other families told how, after a period of doubt, they had finally decided that a child in fact had epilepsy—sometimes through a therapeutic trial; if the child was treated for fever convulsions and it did not help, then they concluded that it must be epilepsy.[6]

In the process of using available concepts to identify disorder, the deliberations of the family and neighbors are crucial. The construction and evaluation of particular episodes and conditions take place in the popular sector of a health care system (Kleinman 1980:50–53). We caught a glimpse of this actually occurring in one home in Moshi. A mother was explaining that her daughter suffered from a stomach disorder that caused her to lose consciousness. But a neighbor remarked insinuatingly that it was an odd sort of stomach ache that made her fall, roll up her eyes, and urinate.

The process of identification moves into the folk and professional sectors as well. The authority of healers was not uncommonly cited in support of a particular classification of the problem. In a couple of cases considered cured, where children had had only two or three seizures in connection with fever, the healer pronounced that they had indeed had kifafa. The healer's sister and the children's parents pointed to this as evidence that healers can indeed treat epilepsy successfully. One healer in Morogoro had worked out a classification of types of epilepsy. He tested epileptic patients to see whether a seizure could be provoked by staring into a bowl of water on which the light flickered. Although I think it was rare for a healer to focus this carefully on the empirical symptoms, families reported that healers were far more likely than biomedical health workers to discuss the condition with them and to give a comprehensible diagnosis. A consultation with a healer is likely to involve dialogue and negotiation, leading to provisional agreement about the labeling of the problem, as Robert Edgerton (1969) has shown in an excellent article about the recognition and labeling of mental disorders by Tanzanian healers.

Professional practitioners may play a role in moving families to identify a member as epileptic. Giel, a doctor who worked in Ethiopia, wrote:

> Parents sometimes become aware of the true nature of the disease for the first time during history-taking. They suddenly and with great sorrow no longer suppress what they have observed and it dawns on them that their child was indeed making convulsive movements after it had fainted. (Giel 1968:29)

However, many of the families we interviewed in Tanzania asserted that they had never been given any diagnosis, much less explanation, at hospitals. The lower echelon primary care facilities, the dispensaries and health centers, were even worse; in only 11 percent of the treatments there were the neuropsychiatric disorders actually identified as such. One respondent, whose son had been admitted to a health center for four days following a seizure, reported that he had asked about the diagnosis. According to him, the reply from the staff had been, "It is not your business to know." In part, this lack of communication may be due to the fact that paramedical staff at the peripheral health facilities had not been particularly trained to identify and treat epilepsy; that was in fact the purpose of the mental health program. But it was also the case that patients did not expect biomedical workers to discuss their illness with them.

OF WORMS AND CONTAMINATION

Some of our Tanzanian respondents associated epilepsy with a worm (*mchango*). It crawls up the spinal cord to the brain, and when it turns in the brain, the person falls in a convulsion. This idea is rather similar to the notion reported by Orley from Uganda that epilepsy may be due to a lizard that runs round in the head and causes dizziness and then the fit (Orley 1970:38). Such expressions may sound strange, even primitive, in the ears of people who have learned to express themselves in biomedical terms. But it is very common for metaphors and analogies to be used to describe experiences that may otherwise be difficult to understand and communicate (van der Geest and Whyte 1989). The term *aura,* for example, means "breeze" in Greek. A patient in the second century told the physician Galen that his convulsion started in his lower leg and "climbed upward in a straight line through the thigh and further through the flank and side to the neck and as far as the head." What was it that climbed to the head? "It was like a cold breeze," another said (Temkin 1971:37).[7] The parallel to the notion of a worm crawling up the spinal cord to the brain is striking. Lévi-Strauss has taught us to listen for "the logic of the concrete," that is, to appreciate that people use phenomena from their daily surroundings to think about their experiences. In Eastern and Southern Africa, there is often an association between convulsions and particular kinds of birds. Eagles, which circle and swoop upon their prey, should be avoided, say the Wapogoro (Jilek-Aall 1965:71) and Baganda (Orley 1970:10), who see a similarity to the dizziness and falling of persons having a seizure. The fluttering of a beheaded chicken is likewise analogous to a convulsion, and Wapogoro say that epileptics should avoid seeing that.[8] In Botswana the term for fits means "small dove," referring to the notion that children may acquire the condition by eating doves or other wild birds (Ingstad 1991:109). Talk of lizards, worms, and birds does not necessarily indicate superstition or prejudice, as some researchers seem to conclude. A recent article on attitudes toward epilepsy in Ethiopia begins by alluding to Orley's work:

> In central Uganda, epilepsy is attributed to the presence of a lizard in the brain, and epileptic falls occur whenever the lizard moves. Therefore, atti-

tudes toward epilepsy and the person with epilepsy in indigenous Africa are invariably unfavourable, because they reflect the mythical belief about the disease. (Tekle-Haimanot et al. 1991:203)

In my view, this is a too literal reading of a metaphoric mode of expression, from which oversimplified conclusions are drawn.

The issue of the contagion of epilepsy is the cultural theme that has most fascinated researchers. Not only does it seem to represent a misunderstanding of a concept that is central to biomedicine, but it also appears to be the cause of the neglect and isolation of epileptics. Some writers have pointed out that this notion is part of European medical history as well. Owsei Temkin, in his magisterial history of "the falling sickness," traces the notion of the contagion of epilepsy from ancient Greece into the Middle Ages, citing pronouncements about the dangers of "the terrible breath" issuing from the mouths of epileptics (1971:115–116). Learned treatises warned against approaching a person having a convulsion or even bathing with such a person. Various saints were associated with epilepsy, including Saint Valentine, whose appeal to those who had epilepsy may be related to the fact that his name sounded very like the medieval German word for seizure, *fallenthin*. At the Priory of Saint Valentine in Rufach, Alsace, a quarantine hospital was built in 1486 where contagious pilgrims might stay in isolation from the public (Jilek 1979:130).

In a broad comparative article, Wolfgang Jilek (1979) describes the near universality of the notion that epilepsy is a contagious disease, a notion he finds important in explaining the epileptic's "outcast role." He reminds us that it is the saliva that froths from the mouth during a fit that is most feared everywhere, and in an effort to make this fear of froth rational, he argues that epilepsy is conflated with rabies, which is in fact mainly transmitted by saliva (Jilek 1979:31). This explanation is intriguing and original, but again I think we have here an example of "medical materialism" that ignores the symbolism with which people express themselves.

If epileptic saliva were seen as a mode of transmitting neurological disorder, then we would expect to find that specific cases of epilepsy were often explained in terms of contact with someone having a fit. In our Tanzanian study, we found that this was seldom the case. Even though the notion of contagion was often mentioned, almost no one explained particular cases as having been contracted from another epileptic. This same paradox puzzled a Nigerian research team. In 1985 they published results of a study showing, among other things, that respondents did not mention infection from another epileptic as a major cause of epilepsy. They conclude: "These findings do not support the widely publicized view that Nigerians consider epilepsy to be contagious" (Awaritefe et al. 1985:8). In 1989, the senior author reported another study that found that 100 percent of his 285 lay respondents stated that epilepsy *was* contagious, and even a fair number of medical students agreed. Although he tries to explain this by citing differences in the educational level of the respondents in the two studies, it seems clear that the reason for the divergence was that in the second study he asked not about cause but about willingness to touch an epileptic during a fit or eat from the same dish (Awaritefe 1989). The notion of contagion is not primarily about etiology, I would argue.

As early as 1968, W. R. Billington proposed that the African concept was better rendered as contamination than as contagion, and I think this points in the right direction. Contamination suggests that ideas of pollution are involved, and pollution may have a moral and cosmological sense as well as a bacterial or etiological one. A first clue is that not only saliva but also intestinal gas, urine, and feces that pass uncontrolled out of the body during a convulsion are mentioned as dangerous. This was so in our Tanzanian study, and various bodily products are mentioned from other studies as well (remember that it was the breath of the Greek epileptic that was said to be terrible). In her book *Purity and Danger,* Mary Douglas (1966) has discussed the widespread association of uncleanness and danger with bodily exuviae and excretae. In transgressing the boundary between the body and the outside world, these products offend a basic sense of order and are therefore threatening. People in a village near Same in northern Tanzania denied that epilepsy was contagious but formulated the sense of danger another way. They said that one must never cut or wipe away the froth from the mouth of a convulsive person because he or she might die. Bodily products and boundaries are the problem, not infection.

Close inquiry into the dangers of contamination during fits yielded a picture with important nuances in Tanzania. Although many people mentioned it, the families of epileptics stressed that *other* people were afraid of contamination, but not those who knew the person well. Many families believed they needed to protect their epileptic members from what they perceived as beliefs about pollution on the part of other people. Some children were not sent to school or allowed to play away from home because it was thought that no one would help them if they had a convulsion. One mother was even convinced that her son, who was hospitalized for burns in the district hospital, had been isolated from other patients after having convulsions in the hospital because of fear that he would contaminate others. However, we found little evidence that the family itself isolated the epileptic person in the home. Bowls and cups were shared, and family members cared for the person during seizures.

As Douglas has pointed out, it is characteristic of pollution beliefs that they reinforce social boundaries. The danger of pollution is thought to be greatest in interaction with persons outside one's own group. Just as we feel less comfortable about sharing a spoon with a stranger than with a family member, so the danger of contamination is more pronounced from an epileptic outside one's immediate circle. One of the clearest examples of fear came from the mother of an epileptic boy with strange behavior living in the town of Moshi. "When they see him, the Chagga sometimes say 'Pass quickly so he does not touch you.' They think he can infect them even when he is not having a fit—maybe through his saliva." Two points of interest here: the setting was urban, so that passersby did not know the boy as they would in a village, and the mother was from another ethnic group, describing what she saw as a Chagga attitude.

In general, the Tanzanian data suggest that we should be careful not to take the contamination concept as *the* cultural construct that forms the universal perception of epilepsy. Although it has been popular to point to it as an example of an exotic and negative idea, few researchers have taken the trouble to look at it in context, to see when it is expressed and when it is overlooked. The risk is that we may end by drawing stereotypes rather than producing accurate pictures of the lives of epileptic people and their families.

CAUSES AND TREATMENTS

Researchers who have concerned themselves with the social medicine of epilepsy in Africa have described beliefs in supernatural causes and associated these notions with the preference for treatment by local healers rather than biomedical facilities. This fits with classical anthropological research in Africa on the explanation and treatment of misfortune, which has shown the distinctive cosmologies, rituals, and social relationships of African societies. A recent example full of ethnographic detail is a study of epilepsy among the Bamileke people of Cameroon. The authors describe the conviction that witches cause epilepsy, sometimes by casting a spell on stones, old clothes, and especially a particular type of cactus tree common in the area. At one point, when epilepsy was on the rise, the paramount chief ordered a diviner to root out and burn all the cactus trees as a public health measure. Envious co-wives were often suspected of using sorcery to cause children to get epilepsy, thus striking a terrible blow at the child's mother, who will be condemned to "spend the rest of her life looking after her epileptic child and searching without end for a cure to the disease" (Nkwi and Ndonko 1989:441–442).

Diseases caused by spirits or witchcraft are considered especially appropriate for treatment by local healers.[9] A study of 132 epileptics at a clinic in Lusaka found that on average 3.4 years elapsed between the initial attack and seeking biomedical treatment. The authors attributed this to the fact that people seek traditional therapy first (Cardozo and Patel 1976:492). This issue of relation between perception of cause and treatment preference is not so simple, however, as a study from Botswana suggests. There too a preference was found for treating epilepsy by traditional means. In a sample of 171 villagers, only 38 percent said they thought epileptics should be first taken to the clinic for treatment. But this must be seen in the light of the other finding that only 13 percent of the same sample thought that modern treatment was available for epilepsy. One of the conclusions of this study is that health education should stress the availability of modern effective treatment, rather than scientific explanations, "for it was clear that specific aetiological beliefs had little relation to treatment choice" (Dale and Ben-Tovim 1984:191).

Some light was shed on the relation between perceived cause and treatment choice in our Tanzanian study. There we found that sorcery was the most frequently mentioned cause of epilepsy; ancestral ghosts and spirits of various kinds were also named. But other people said that epilepsy was due to heredity or physical illness, untreated fever convulsions or worms. Or they thought that epilepsy was the "work of God," which in East Africa means that it is fate, which cannot be changed (in contrast to the "work of man," such as sorcery, which may be healed by man). Most disturbing to the anthropologist, who wants to ask relevant questions that people can answer, 41 percent of respondents in our attitude survey stated that they did not know the cause of epilepsy; in a Nigerian survey, 26 percent said the same (Awaritefe et al. 1985:8), and in an Ethiopian survey the figure was as high as 52 percent (Tekle-Haimanot et al. 1991:205).

How shall we interpret these findings of variation and uncertainty about the cause of epilepsy? In part they may be a product of the survey method, which is an artificial way of getting people to express complicated or vague ideas. But I believe that the existence of different explanations and incertitude are essential parts of reality rather than failures of the researcher to find a clear conviction in people's minds. If we take this point of view, the question becomes how people proceed to construct an understanding of their experience. We see African people as actors in the process of interpreting their experience, rather than prisoners of a culture that has all the answers.

The quest for therapy was central to that process of interpretation. While people did seek help in terms of notions of cause they had formulated, they also revised those notions if the treatment did not work. Not only does interpretation affect choice of treatment, but outcome of treatment affects interpretation.

As families recounted treatment histories, it was clear that they had considered various causal explanations. One young man I remember well because he had such a puzzled expression and kept repeating "Kwa nini? Kwa nini?" which means in Swahili, "Why? Why?" His family said that he had been a normal, bright boy until he fell ill with a very high fever and went into a coma, after which he became epileptic, helpless, and feebleminded. He had been treated at the hospital, and by about fifteen different healers. One had made the family walk naked by graves at night to get rid of evil spirits; others thought he had been given sorcery medicine. They had sacrificed goats to their ancestors and made him inhale the vapors of herbal medicines. But still he has convulsions. So now his mother doubts all those explanations. "This must be the work of God," she says, "I don't know the cause." The father of a girl in the same town was also uncertain. He had been to several diviners to learn the cause of his daughter's convulsions. Some said spirits, some said sorcery. One hospital said her fits were due to malaria; another gave her pills to take daily but did not explain the nature of her sickness. He was not sure what was wrong because nothing seemed to help.

Of the various neuropsychiatric conditions we studied in Tanzania, epilepsy was the most frequently treated. We found no cases where the family had not sought treatment of some kind among the sixty-six families we visited, and the average number of consultations was five. While forty-three of the families had first sought treatment from a healer, and three had tried herbal medicine at home, twenty had in fact gone to a health facility in the first instance. Others went to a hospital or health center at some point during their quest for therapy, but only five seem to have become involved in a regular treatment program. Many people were given only treatment for malaria or physical symptoms. Three-quarters said that the biomedical facility gave them no explanation of the problem, while only one-quarter failed to get an explanation from the healer.[10]

When effective treatment programs for epilepsy have been established in Africa, they have been heavily used. Given the often desperate search for treatment, people are quite willing to try biomedicine if they are convinced a treatment exists. This was Orley's experience in the 1960s in Uganda. Most people did not believe that Western medicine had treatment for epilepsy, and Orley concurs:

> There is, of course, a certain amount of truth in the idea that epilepsy was not being treated by western medicines if we accept that treating it involves more than just giving a few tablets. Treatment also requires careful explanations about the continuous nature of the treatment, and an effort to ensure that the patient is able to obtain medicine easily over a very long time. Insofar as treatment is not systematic in this way it is not treatment at all. (Orley 1970:46)

Such systematic treatment programs are now in place in some African communities, and though problems of "compliance" exist there as elsewhere, it has proven possible to get epileptics to attend clinics regularly, not only in urban areas like Lusaka (Cardozo and Patel 1976) but also in rural ones in Botswana (Ben-Tovim 1983), Malawi (Watts 1989), and Kenya (Feksi et al. 1991a, 1991b).

The point is that poor biomedical services rather than "strange" beliefs explain the fact that many patients do not seek modern treatment. We have paid far more attention to exotic cultural conceptions elicited from local people than we have to the delivery of biomedical services and the way they are perceived and used.

THE SOCIAL CONTEXT OF EPILEPSY

I have already indicated some of the generalizations to be found in the literature about the social isolation of the epileptic. Yet recent attitude studies and investigations of the actual situations of persons with epilepsy present a considerably more complicated picture. As with any other impairment, it seems that the consequences depend on the person's social background, individual characteristics, and the severity of the condition, as well as on the attitudes and possibilities presented by the local society.

Some of the early studies described people who were severely afflicted physically and mentally and who for one reason or another had little or no support from their families. But the wretched outcasts hanging about the cemetaries of Ethiopia are not representative of people with epilepsy in that country. No more so than the "demented and anti-social groups of epileptics" who accounted for 12 percent of admissions to Tanganyikan mental hospitals in the 1950s (Tekle-Haimanot et al. 1991:206). In contrast, studies like those of M. A. Danesi and coauthors (1981, 1984) of patients attending the neurological clinics at Lagos University Teaching Hospital present a relatively positive picture of people who were almost all educated and employed.

Systematic community-based studies are needed here; ideally they should combine the kind of ethnographic detail that Orley (1970) or P. N. Nkwi and F. T. Ndonko (1989) provide, with more sociological data on the actual situation of *all* the individuals with epilepsy in the community. Our Tanzanian study does not fulfill these criteria, but at least it did represent an attempt to find and interview people with epilepsy in their normal settings.

In two urban and six rural locations we asked local leaders to direct us to people with epilepsy. Of the sixty-six we met in this way, all except one were living with their families, including the 50 percent who were over the age of fourteen; four of the adults had severe mental impairments as well as epileptic seizures. Our conversations with villagers and our attitude survey revealed that families were expected to care for and sympathize with an epileptic member. In fact, the problems of care were seen as the responsibility primarily of the family, and not of the community. Discussions with epileptics and their families confirmed that families directed concern and effort toward their disabled members. In some cases, large sums had been spent on trying to get treatment, and in other cases where impairment was severe, the burden of care on overworked mothers was very heavy. Certainly there were problems; the African extended family is not always able to provide security for weaker members. But the point is that the people with epilepsy were members of families, and that was the single most important framework for their lives.

Families often seemed to overprotect their epileptic members from real or perceived negative attitudes on the part of others. This was clearly seen in relation to education of children. Less than a quarter of those who were mentally normal enough to go to school were doing so. In a couple of cases, the parents claimed that the teachers had advised them to take their children out of school. But in most instances families explained that they were afraid their children would fall at school and no one would help. So they kept them home where they could care for them. We encountered a few instances where teachers had encouraged parents to send their epileptic children to school, and one child was going to a nursery school where her parents had held conferences with the teachers to explain her problems. Even though epilepsy did seem to be a hindrance to children's education, the situation was not simply one of stigma and discrimination. Parents were concerned for their children's safety, at least in part, and some teachers were concerned for the children's education. In Zanzibar, a more urbanized and generally more prosperous area of Tanzania, a community survey found that most children with epilepsy were in school (Bondestam et al. 1990:329).

Even for children who did not attend school, large households and the sociability of village life meant that there were always others to play with. Essentially all of the epileptic children did play with others, though in some cases at least, their playmates were mainly other relatives who could be counted on to help if the child had a seizure. Here we can see an example of how the idea of contamination, expressed as the expectation that outsiders will not touch someone having a convulsion, may be used as a way of expressing not social isolation but social limitation.

For both children and adults, limitations on social interaction were explained as much in terms of the person's behavior as in terms of fear of contamination. Some epileptics had periods of strange behavior, of aggressiveness or withdrawal. A study of epileptics at the neurology unit of the national hospital in Dar es Salaam found that 60 percent had a psychological disturbance serious enough to warrant treatment. Most of these were associated with an organic brain lesion, and the researcher concludes that organic brain disease, rather than social prejudice, is the primary cause of psychological disturbance in African epileptic patients (Matuja 1990:363). Rather than the picture of people developing "spoiled brains" from social isolation, this study seems to be proposing that damaged brains may inhibit normal social interaction. The lesson we may draw is that the nature of the impairment, as well as cultural beliefs and family protectiveness, shape the social situation.

Our attitude survey, as well as Orley's work in Uganda (Orley 1970:38), suggested that epileptics could not marry and would be divorced if they developed the disease after marriage. We found that in fact about half of the twenty-five adult epileptics in our study had not married (not counting the four who were mentally retarded as well as epileptic). Nine were currently married and four were divorced. Of those who married as known epileptics, we had the impression that they were not able to make very good marriages.[11] Of those who developed epilepsy later, it seems that marriage tended to hold in those communities where marriage was generally stable. In Morogoro Region, where divorce rates are higher, epileptics were divorced. In general it is easier for women to marry than it is for men in a polygynous society; they can always become second or third wives. Of the adults with neuropsychiatric impairments in our study, twice as many women as men were married.

Whether or not they were married, people with epilepsy usually worked normally at home and on the family farm. For women there was a concern about the danger of falling in the cooking fire, but the nature of the work for both men and women was such that all could participate. Very few (four out of twenty-five adults) had paid employment, and even these tended to be self-employed or to work for members of the immediate family. In rural areas, most people are farmers anyway and to some extent can set their own pace. They do not have to punch a clock or be approved by a prospective employer in the first place. Since farming is a family enterprise, they do not have to face prejudice at work.

Even though we heard accounts of prejudice against epileptics and expectations of prejudice, seeing people in their social contexts and talking to their families mitigated the impressions I had from reading about conceptions of epilepsy in Africa. The experience of having epilepsy clearly depended on many things. One of the interesting findings of the Tekle-Haimanot study was that negative attitudes toward epilepsy were more pronounced among urban than among rural people in Ethiopia. They suggest that

> the relative negative attitudes of the urban respondents may probably be due to their frequent exposure to the very unfortunate persons with uncontrolled seizures exhibiting unsightly burns and demented states. Such individuals are often seen in the streets of the towns and the compounds of worship places as beggars. (Tekle-Haimanot et al. 1991:207)

I would add that epileptics living with their families among relatives and neighbors have a social identity that is not only that of epileptic. They are integrated in a social unit, even in those cases where their participation in some aspects of social life (school, marriage) is restricted. The horror evoked by the beggars and outcasts is that they *are* their disease. Those who encounter them see them only as diseased, and not as social persons.

The importance of belonging to a social group and not relating to a community as an epileptic beggar emerges from examples given by Benedicte Ingstad (1991:302–305) in her study of disability in Botswana. Two young men in different villages both had marginal positions and little support from their destitute alcoholic mothers, with whom they lived. Although their epilepsies and their characteristics differed in some respects, both followed a similar pattern in that their identities were transformed by integration into local church life. They gave up begging and "freeloading" on the basis of their disabilities, and established relationships to institutions nearly as significant as family in rural Tswana communities.

OUR CONCEPTIONS AND THEIR EXPERIENCES

The study of people's conceptualization and experience of disability is fraught with difficulties and dangers, especially when we are trying to study across cultures. The tendency to distance oneself and to reify what we are examining is common, almost unavoidable it seems. Medically trained researchers looking at the kinds of issues I have discussed here reveal their position when they use phrases like "correct views on epilepsy," "correct attitudes," "ignorance about the disease," or "superstitious beliefs." They are authorities who know the truth, and lay people's interpretations are usually wrong by their standards. I once spoke on epilepsy in Tanzania to a conference of the World Psychiatric Association, and a doctor in the audience rose to point out that my talk was a total waste of time: "Why do we have to hear about superstitions in Africa?" he asked the full auditorium. "I get enough of superstitions from my patients in England." One with this kind of attitude can never take other people's views seriously and is not really interested in listening. Caricatures of people's "magical notions" serve to explain why they do not behave as the doctor knows is best for them.

Anthropologists pride themselves on trying to elucidate other world-views, showing that they are logical in their own terms if we just put aside our own preconceptions. But we anthropologists fall into another kind of distancing and reification. We tend to emphasize the exotic, to show the effectiveness of symbols and the rational structures of other worlds. The term *cultural construction* is popular in anthropology these days. By this we imply that cultures structure experience; they consist of a set of meanings that interpret the world in a particular way. There is a danger here, and it is that we tend to present the cultural construction, of epilepsy for example, as a given pattern of ideas and practices that are consistent and satisfactory for those who use them—as if a culture always provides answers to the questions people have.

What I hope to convey is that cultural constructions of epilepsy are not in fact simple structures with clean lines and clear functions built by an anonymous contractor called culture. Rather, they are homemade jerry-built affairs made of available materials and subject to remodeling by worried parents, curious neighbors, and healers, both traditional and untraditional. In fact they are not finished structures at all, but ongoing processes. Sometimes they are messy—people disagree, or they are unsure or vague, or, worst of all, they don't know. If we listen only to the articulate experts or cut the tails off our curves or describe only the most exotic and dramatic examples, then we as researchers can find distinct structures. If we talk to ordinary people grounded in particular social situations, who are struggling and wondering, then the picture is a lot less clear. But only by doing that can we grasp the way people are in fact experiencing what we call epilepsy.

Our analyses must be built on the assumption that people are actors within social contexts, not prisoners of a fixed cultural construction. When we describe beliefs about epilepsy, we tend to excise them from that context and from the people who have expressed them—and who might have expressed themselves differently in a different context. We need more studies of the ways people adjust their conceptions to the complexities of particular social, cultural, and neurological situations, rather than descriptions of decontextualized beliefs and practices. Culture does not steer people; people create and re-create it from particular positions. Recognizing that, we can begin to understand how varied and changing are the experiences and concepts of epilepsy in East Africa.

NOTES

1. The study was funded by the Danish International Development Agency (DANIDA) and carried out in coordination with WHO support to the program. A description of the Tanzania Mental Health Programme and a report of our findings are available in Schulsinger and Jablensky 1991. This chapter, which is a substantially revised and expanded version of Whyte 1986, was presented as the 1992 St. Valentine Lecture for the Danish Neurological Society and the Danish Epilepsy Society.

2. Nkwi and Ndonko (1989:438) found that 7 percent (35 out of 500 inhabitants) of a village in West Cameroon had epilepsy. Van der Waals et al. (1983:37) reported a rate of 38 per 1000 from Grand Bassa County, Liberia, with an antecedent febrile illness in 38 percent of all cases. Most striking is the variation reported by Osuntokun et al. (1987:18); in a rural Nigerian village they found a prevalence of 37 per 1000, while in a town only 20 kilometers away, inhabited by the same ethnic group, they found a prevalence of 5.3 per 1000 using the same methods. (See also Schoenberg 1987:721 for a discussion of this contrast.) Prevalence studies of epilepsy are fraught with problems in any case (Schoenberg 1983), and more so in developing countries.

3. Osuntokun (1977:28) and Osuntokun et al. (1987:18) point to febrile convulsions as significant risk factors for epilepsy in Nigeria. They emphasize control of

malaria, immunization against childhood diseases, especially measles, and teaching parents how to cool fevers as important prophylactic measures.

4. E. Feierman (1981) mentions treatment to prevent *mshango wa degedege* in the Usambara Mountains, in northeastern Tanzania.

5. In a study of patient perspectives on epilepsy in Lagos, Danesi (1984) found that even though they all admitted having recurrent seizures, 36 percent did not accept that they had epilepsy, and only 30 percent were willing to tell friends and employers that they had it.

6. Orley describes two Ganda illness categories, *eyabwe* and *kigalanga,* which have symptoms that may overlap with epilepsy (*ensimbu*), and he writes that "because of the terrible social implications of epilepsy, the family would always, where possible, prefer to diagnose them as something else such as *kigalanga* or *eyabwe*" (Orley 1970:10).

7. By the eighteenth century, the concept of aura was no longer restricted to "breeze." "Cullen described the 'aura' as the sensation of something moving in some part of the body and creeping toward the head" (Temkin 1971:247).

8. The "sickness of the bird" is a Bamileke (Cameroon) term for the convulsions of small children, the analogy being to the fluttering of a bird's wings (Nkwi and Ndonko 1989:438).

9. Although epilepsy is commonly treated by traditional healers, there is not unmitigated confidence in their ability to cure the condition. The belief that no healer can cure an epileptic who has sustained burns from falling in the fire is widely reported. A study from Kenya found that while 16 percent of healers in a Nairobi survey named epilepsy as one of the three diseases they best could treat, another 16 percent said it was incurable (Good 1987:268).

10. The positive functions that healers may play in the treatment of epilepsy have been recognized in one publication. Not only do they provide some reassurance, but they ensure that people do not use biomedicine when it is not necessary: "For it is certain that numerous epileptics who suffer one single seizure in their whole lives will be declared cured after one visit to a traditional healer, whereas after consulting a doctor they will be caught up in the diagnostic process and become prisoners of long-term chemotherapy with all its attendant secondary effects and constraints" (Ndiaye et al. 1983:351).

11. Jilek-Aall says that Wapogoro women epileptics usually married poor men or other epileptics. Little or no bridewealth was required for them so they were possible partners for marginal men (Jilek-Aall 1965:77). Nkwi and Ndonko (1989:445) note that epileptic Bamileke women were often married to old men, usually without payment of bridewealth.

REFERENCES

Awaritefe, A.
    1989   Epilepsy: The myth of a contagious disease. *Culture, Medicine and Psychiatry* 13:449–456.
Awaritefe, Alfred, Ada C. Longe, and Milena Awaritefe
    1985   Epilepsy and psychosis: A comparison of societal attitudes. *Epilepsia* 26(1):1–9.

Ben-Tovim, David I.
1983   A psychiatric service to the remote areas of Botwana. *British Journal of Psychiatry* 142:199–203.
Billington, W. R.
1968   The problems of the epileptic patient in Uganda. *East African Medical Journal* 45(8):563–569.
Bondestam, S., J. Garssen, and A. I. Abdulwakil
1990   Prevalence and treatment of mental disorders and epilepsy in Zanzibar. *Acta Psychiatrica Scandinavica* 81(4):327–331.
Cardozo, L. J., and M. G. Patel
1976   Epilepsy in Zambia. *East African Medical Journal* 53(8):488–493.
Dale, Jeremy R., and David I. Ben-Tovim
1984   Modern or traditional? A study of treatment preference for neuropsychiatric disorders in Botswana. *British Journal of Psychiatry* 145:187–192.
Danesi, M. A.
1984   Patient perspectives on epilepsy in a developing country. *Epilepsia* 25(2):184–190.
Danesi, M. A., K. A. Odusote, O. O. Roberts, and E. O. Adu
1981   Social problems of adolescent and adult epileptics in a developing country, as seen in Lagos, Nigeria. *Epilepsia* 22(6):689–696.
Douglas, Mary
1966   *Purity and Danger: An Analysis of Concepts of Pollution and Taboo.* London: Routledge and Kegan Paul.
Edgerton, Robert B.
1969   On the "recognition" of mental illness. In *Changing Perspectives in Mental Illness,* ed. Stanley C. Plog and Robert B. Edgerton. New York: Holt Rinehart and Winston.
Feierman, E. K.
1981   Alternative medical services in rural Tanzania: A physician's view. *Social Science and Medicine* 15B:399–404.
Feksi, A. T., J. Kaamugisha, J. W. A. S. Sander, S. Gatili, and S. D. Shorvon
1991a   A comprehensive community epilepsy programme: The Nakuru project. *Epilepsy Research* 8(3):252–259.
1991b   Comprehensive primary health care antiepileptic drug treatment programme in rural and semi-urban Kenya. *Lancet* 337(8738): 406–409.
Giel, R.
1968   The epileptic outcast. *East African Medical Journal* 45(1):27–31.
Good, Charles M.
1987   *Ethnomedical Systems in Africa: Patterns of Traditional Medicine in Rural and Urban Kenya.* New York: Guilford Press.
Ingstad, B.
1991   The myth of the hidden disabled: A study of community-based rehabilitation in Botswana. Working paper. Oslo: Section for Medical Anthropology, University of Oslo.

Jilek, Wolfgang G.
    1979   The epileptic's outcast role and its background: A contribution to
                the social psychiatry of seizure disorders. *Journal of Operational Psy-
                chiatry* 10(2):127–133.
Jilek-Aall, Louise M.
    1965   Epilepsy in the Wapogoro tribe in Tanganyika. *Acta Psychiatrica Scan-
                dinavica* 41:57–86.
Jilek-Aall, L., W. Jilek, and J. R. Miller
    1979   Clinical and genetic aspects of seizure disorders prevalent in an iso-
                lated African population. *Epilepsia* 20:613–622.
Kleinman, Arthur
    1980   *Patients and Healers in the Context of Culture*. Berkeley, Los Angeles,
                London: University of California Press.
Matuja, William B. P.
    1990   Psychological disturbance in African Tanzanian epileptics. *Tropical
                and Geographical Medicine* 42(4)359–364.
Ndiaye, I. P., M. Ndiaye, and D. Tap
    1983   Sociocultural aspects of epilepsy in Africa. *Progress in Clinical and Bi-
                ological Research* 124:345–351.
Nkwi, Paul Nchoji, and Falvius Tioko Ndonko
    1989   The epileptic among the Bamileke of Maham in the Nde Division,
                West Province of Cameroon. *Culture, Medicine and Psychiatry*
                13:437–448.
Orley, John H.
    1970   *Culture and Mental Illness: A Study from Uganda*. Nairobi: East African
                Publishing House.
Osuntokun, B. O.
    1977   Epilepsy in Africa. *Tropical and Geographical Medicine* 30(1):23–32.
Osuntokun, B. O., A. O. Adeuja, B. S. Schoenberg, O. Bademosi, V. A. Nottidge,
A. O. Olumide, O. Ige, F. Yaria, and C. L. Bolis
    1987   Neurological disorders in Nigerian Africans: A community-based
                study. *Acta Neurologica Scandinavica* 75(1):13–21.
Schoenberg, Bruce S.
    1983   Epidemiologic aspects of epilepsy. *Progress in Clinical and Biological
                Research* 124:331–343.
    1987   Recent studies of the epidemiology of epilepsy in developing coun-
                tries: A coordinated program for prevention and control. *Epilepsia*
                28(6):721–722.
Schulsinger, Fini, and Assen Jablensky, eds.
    1991   *The National Mental Health Programme in the United Republic of
                Tanzania. Acta Psychiatrica Scandinavica,* supplement no. 364, vol. 83.
Swift, C. R., and T. Asuni
    1975   *Mental Health and Disease in Africa*. Edinburgh: Churchill Livingstone.
Tekle-Haimanot, R., M. Abebe, L. Forsgren, A. Gebre-Mariam, J. Heijbel, G. Holm-
gren, and J. Ekstedt
    1991   Attitudes of rural people in central Ethiopia toward epilepsy. *Social
                Science and Medicine* 32(2):203–209.

Temkin, Owsei
  1971   *The Falling Sickness: A History of Epilepsy from the Greeks to the Beginnings of Modern Neurology.* 2d ed. Baltimore: Johns Hopkins Press.
van der Geest, Sjaak, and Susan Reynolds Whyte
  1989   The charm of medicines: Metaphors and metonyms. *Medical Anthropology Quarterly* 3:345–367.
van der Waals, Fransje W., Jaap Goudsmit, and D. Carleton Gajdusek
  1983   See-ee: Clinical characteristics of highly prevalent seizure disorders in the Gbawein and Wroughbarh clan region of Grand Bassa County, Liberia. *Neuroepidemiology* 2:35–44.
Watts, A. E.
  1989   A model for managing epilepsy in a rural community in Africa. *British Medical Journal* 298(6676):805–807.
Whyte, Susan Reynolds
  1986   The cultural construction of epilepsy in East Africa. In *Psychiatry and Its Related Disciplines: The Next Twenty-Five Years,* ed. Raben Rosenberg, Fini Schulsinger, and Erik Strömgren. Copenhagen: World Psychiatric Association.

THIRTEEN

Mpho ya Modimo—A Gift from God: Perspectives on "Attitudes" toward Disabled Persons

Benedicte Ingstad

THE CREATION OF A MYTH

The International Year of Disabled Persons (1981) and the following decade dedicated to the same (1983–1992) were intended to draw attention to the situation of disabled people worldwide. As with previous years and decades named for other purposes (women, children, water, etc.), one can hardly note any revolutionary changes in the life situation of disabled people in most places, but perhaps there is an increased awareness about the needs of this underprivileged group of the population, especially in the so-called third-world countries.

Most of the so-called developed countries already had a long history of special education programs and various other forms of rehabilitation. Many "developing" countries, however, got their first incentive and had to start their efforts to improve the lives of disabled people more or less from scratch. With a general shortage of resources (money, skills, manpower, etc.) and often also a problem of getting political support for giving priority to such a nonproductive group, most developing countries came to rely rather heavily on foreign donor agencies and nongovernmental organizations (NGOs) as well as local fund-raising in their rehabilitation efforts.

Much attention in the "developed" countries came to focus on the needs of disabled people in the "developing" part of the world. However, to raise money one has to create sympathy, and thus a picture of disabled people living in a state of utter misery and neglect was presented to the world.[1] Little or no emphasis was placed on poverty, limitation of health care, and so on. This could easily have become politically too controversial. Instead we experienced a massive emphasis on attitudes, and especially the attitudes of the caretaker. A "myth of the hidden disabled" (Ingstad 1991) was brought

246

forward and strengthened immensely through mass media's focusing mainly on cases of misery and neglect. This "myth" was also promoted through prestigious international forums such as WHO and the International Labor Organization, and it soon took on the character of being an "official truth":

> Disability seen as a divine curse "justifies" low esteem for disabled people and their families. . . . Moral trespasses or "sins" and "evil thoughts" may remain hidden, but the appearance of disability in a family will make the "sin" visible to all. In a close knit society, this may lead [one] to rid oneself or [one's] family of such obvious proof of evil-doing. (Helander 1984:35)

> It is a known fact that mortality among disabled children is much higher than among unimpaired children. . . . Similarly morbidity is also higher. Disabled adults have generally lower incomes than able-bodied adults and, consequently, they are more likely to suffer from poverty. Visibly disabled adult women, such as the blind, are often abandoned by their husbands and deprived of their children. Disabled children have less opportunity to attend school than normal children. The presence of one child with visible and stigmatising disabilities in a family has negative consequences for the marriage of not only the disabled child, but also that of the brother and sister. (WHO 1981)

> The treatment of disabled people, even in Sweden, has changed considerably over time. Weak children once were left in the woods to die and old people were pushed from a cliff. . . . This attitude and such rejection are still found in some developing countries. Those who are most neglected, and among whom the highest death rate is found, are disabled girls in the rural areas, especially in Muslim countries. (SIDA/INFO 1987:4, my translation from Swedish)

ANTHROPOLOGIST AND MOTHER

In recent anthropological writings the importance of giving an account of the background of the researcher has been rightly pointed out. R. Rosaldo stresses that the anthropologist is a *positioned* subject, one who "occupies a position or structural location and observes with a particular angle of vision. . . . The notion of position also refers to how life experiences both enable and inhibit particular kinds of insight" (Rosaldo 1989:19).

In my case it was precisely my own experience as a mother of a disabled—now adult—son, combined with my professional background as a social anthropologist, that first made me question the "myth of the hidden disabled." I had myself for years experienced the difficulties of conveying my own views to various types of professionals, and I had seen how easily one could be labeled a "difficult mother." I was finishing a study on Norwegian families with disabled children, which was done with a child psychiatrist (Ingstad and

Sommerschild 1984), in which we had focused on the coping ability of such families. It was demonstrated clearly that life circumstances played a much more significant role than the *attitudes* of the parents in determining coping.

Thus my professional curiosity was raised. Could it really be that the situation was so much different in other cultures? Were traditional beliefs or "superstitions" (as they were called in fund-raising campaigns) about reasons for disabilities necessarily negative, and if so were they strong enough to overrule the love that most people feel for their offspring and other close kin? I doubted it, and I became determined to look deeper into the matter.

BOTSWANA

Methodology

Various coincidences brought me to Botswana, where I came to live with my family for two years (1984–1985) in one of the larger villages in the southern part of the country.[2] Botswana turned out to be a perfect place for studying the situation of disabled people in a developing country. Some years earlier it had been picked by WHO as one of the pilot countries for testing the model of community-based rehabilitation (CBR),[3] intended to be implemented later on a worldwide scale (for further discussion of CBR, see Ingstad 1991). Thus my study was designed to be both an in-depth study of the situation of disabled people in a non-Western (Tswana) culture, as well as a longitudinal study of the implementation of CBR in Botswana.

Because of the relatively long time I spent in the field, I was able to apply a multimethodological approach to the topic. Participant observation in the village as well as in households with disabled members and informal interviews with various categories of informants (disabled persons, relatives, folk healers, health personnel) formed the foundation of the study. On the basis of this I conducted semistructured interview sessions in 100 households with disabled members.[4] Each household was visited twice with one year in between visits. A study of time use was later done in a smaller sample of these households. Finally a KAP (knowledge, attitudes, practice) study was done in a representative sample of households without disabled members. This was done partly to get more systematic information on attitudes toward disabled persons in the general population, partly to evaluate this type of data against data gathered by means of other methods.

Hidden in "the Lands"

"You must understand that in this country people hide their disabled family members at the lands" was one of the first statements I heard when I visited various government offices trying to secure official permission to do my research. And this statement came from a very influential person involved in the implementation of CBR. Thus it might easily have been taken as a confirmation of all I had heard at home about disabled people in "developing" countries. But I was determined to find out how the situation was to be seen through the eyes of the disabled persons and their family members themselves.

"The lands" are the agricultural areas on which Batswana traditionally have relied for their cereals and vegetables. These are usually located some distance away from the village in which they spend the time between agricultural seasons and the "cattle post" where they keep their cattle (if any). Thus it is commonly said that the Batswana have three homes between which they move seasonally. This is a truth with some modifications. Modern development has brought schooling and (at least some) employment to the rural areas, thus making seasonal movements difficult for many household members. Prolonged periods of drought and opportunities for buying food also lessen the importance of agricultural and livestock production in the household economy and diet. Rural poverty is, however, a persistent problem, and most households try to keep up some agricultural activities, often by having unemployed members of the household move to "the lands" to take care of weeding, scare away birds from the crops, and mind small livestock.[5] Other household members would then come mainly for heavier tasks such as ploughing.[6] "Unproductive" family members quite often stay behind at "the lands" when the agricultural season is over, sometimes throughout the whole year. This is where they can get milk for their daily diet, and find wild roots, fruits, and berries even in times of severe drought. This is where they can bring small children and not have to worry that they will disturb the neighbors or run out into the traffic. Thus at "the lands," even out of season, we often find elderly women with a varying number of their grandchildren below school age and sometimes also a few youngsters as herd boys or helpers with housework.[7]

Disabled people may also be found at "the lands." Children in need of special care are often entrusted to the grandmother who has more time, experience, and perhaps more patience. Disabled youngsters or adults with milder impairments may have the role of helpers, and those with "strange behavior" have more freedom and cause less disturbance here than in the close neighborhood of a village.[8]

With all these varied categories of persons staying more or less permanently at "the lands," why is it then that only the disabled people are characterized as "hidden" there?

A Case of "Hiding"

During the course of my fieldwork I established a very good relationship with the two rehabilitation officers who were promoting CBR in the district. Also from them I frequently heard statements about disabled persons being hidden, abused, and neglected by their families. Eventually I asked them to take me to all the families in the district whom they thought exemplified such behavior. We interviewed them together and came up with a somewhat different picture, as can be illustrated by the case that follows.

In one village there was a compound with a mud hut without windows and a locked door from which screaming and howling were regularly heard. The hut was located next to a concrete house where the rest of the household seemed to be living. The rehabilitation officer said this family was "hiding" their adult mentally disturbed son by locking him up like this. The family, however, told a different story.

The man had been mentally retarded since birth, but peaceful as a child and in no way difficult to care for. When he was about eight, the family was advised by someone that they should send him to the mental hospital in Lobatse[9] so that he could get cured and become "normal." This was done.

The parents visited him regularly over several years but saw no improvement whatever. On the contrary, in the crowded ward at the mental hospital, he developed new symptoms, symptoms well known in similar institutions in more "developed" countries. He became restless and violent to the extent that his front teeth had to be pulled out so he could not bite people. On seeing this development, the parents started to request that he be discharged from the hospital and left in their care. By now, however, he had grown big and strong, and their request was repeatedly rejected on the grounds that they would not be able to control him.

The parents, however, did not give up. After several years of trying in vain, they finally turned to the local parliament member and asked for his help. This happened to coincide with the time (late 1970s) when it was decided to decentralize the psychiatric services and return as many as possible of the mental patients to their home communities. The young man was released to the family on the condition that they would build a special hut for him and keep him locked up so that he would not be able to harm others. They were told that they would be made personally responsible if anything happened.

The parents had complied, afraid that any breach of their promise would lead the authorities to return him to the mental hospital. However, they were quite aware of the sad life he was leading locked up in the hut like this, and they had taken him out occasionally to have meals with the family and walk around under guard in nearby surroundings. This, however, became increasingly difficult when the father died and there was only the mother and an adult sister in the household to control him. After a few episodes when he ran away and got violent, scaring the neighbors, he was more or less permanently confined to his hut.

Although she could probably have had him readmitted to the mental hospital and thus have relieved herself of the burden of care, the mother preferred to keep him at home. She had not asked the psychiatric services or special services for disabled for help, being afraid that this might lead to his removal.

When I visited him again one year later his condition was even worse. He was sitting naked in the hut, smearing himself with his stools and digging holes in the mud floor with his hands. All the furniture in the hut had been taken out so that he would not harm himself or others. We sat for a long time and talked to the family, advising them to let him out regularly to eat and be with others and to teach him simple tasks, but we had little hope when we left that they would manage to do so.

On my return to Botswana four years later (1989) I revisited the family unexpectedly, along with my former assistant. When we came to the compound, we saw the door to the hut open. Inside it was clean and tidy, with a made-up bed and a table and chair. When we looked toward the main house, we could hardly believe our eyes. There the man was, sitting, smiling with his toothless mouth, dressed in a clean white shirt and good trousers, and eating porridge from a bowl. He recognized us immediately and called out "lekgoa ya me " (my white person), followed by sentences much more coherent than he was able to speak before. His sister, who was alone with him at the time, explained that now his door was always open. He could sit in the yard alone when the family members were at work, and he walked around freely in the village, never attacking anyone. She even dared to sleep in the same room with him. He could stamp corn, sweep the floor,[10] and chop wood, and he even looked after the goats when they were at "the lands."

What had happened? On seeing the mother the next day, we were told that they had received no help or medication from the psychiatric services, no contact with the rehabilitation workers, and no help from folk healers. The only thing they had done, she said, was to follow the advice we had given them in 1985, with good help from the mother's new husband. No one who now saw the pride and joy in this mother's eyes when looking at her retarded son would doubt the love she had for him.

On revisiting the family in 1991 I found that their situation had become more difficult in that the mother's second husband had died in an accident, leaving them in economic uncertainty. The positive development of the disabled man had, however, continued, and he now preferred to spend most of the year at "the lands" with relatives, making himself useful in various ways. According to the mother, he was still asking for his lekgoa, wondering whether I would bring him some new trousers.

This story shows us that even what seemed like the most obvious case of a disabled person hidden away—a man locked up day and night in his hut— reveals a story of family love and concern when looked into more closely. Actually this poor village family without any special sources of influence had shown unusual strength in their long insistence on getting their son back when they saw that life at the institution was bad for him. The practical arrangements that outsiders interpreted as "hiding" and "abuse" were partly a result of this struggle, and partly necessary precautions that might have been relaxed had there been a better-developed (and better-functioning) system of support locally.

It also shows us how much can sometimes be done with very little (including some luck), and the danger of prejudging the situation of a family with a disabled member without full consideration of all the facts. Good judgment must be based on thorough knowledge of how family members see their own situation and an understanding of the possibilities and constraints under which their choices of action are made. Only then can we give advice that stands a chance of being realized and thus promote rehabilitation and integration of the disabled people in the community.

Among the eight cases that were shown to me by the rehabilitation workers as examples of hiding, neglect, or abuse, only two proved to be so to some extent when looked into more closely. And even in those two families we found that the situation of the disabled person was mainly a reflection of the general hardship that all household members were living under.

THE CONCEPT OF ATTITUDES

It is high time to question what we mean by attitudes toward disabled persons. This concept is most often used without any definition or clarification and seems to imply some sort of strange mixture between belief about the origin of disability, what people say that other people think or do, and what they think themselves. Only rarely are studies of actual behavior combined with the survey questions, and the social setting in which such behavior takes place is hardly ever examined. Thus attitude surveys come up with fairly similar conclusions in most countries: that disabled people are stigmatized and have poor chances in marriage, employment, and so on (Tekle-Haimanot et al. 1991).

Among the definitions for *attitude* in *Webster's Third New International Dictionary* we find:

> An organismic state of readiness to act that is often accompanied by considerable affect and that may be activated by an appropriate stimulus into significant or meaningful behavior. (1964, S.V. 4c)

From *The Social Science Encyclopedia* we learn that

> attitudes are predominantly a matter of affective evaluation. They represent the evaluations (positive or negative) that we associate with diverse entities, for example individuals, groups, objects, actions and institutions. (Kuper and Kuper 1985:51)

Finally, let us look at the definition used by the *International Encyclopedia of Social Sciences:*

An attitude is a relatively enduring organization of beliefs around an object or situation predisposing one to respond in some preferential manner. (Sills 1968:450)

In synthesizing these definitions we may say that *attitude* is seen as a concept comprising emotion, behavior/action, and beliefs. It is important to note the rather unclear distinction made between attitudes and beliefs in the last definition. This corresponds to usages most common in studies of attitudes toward disability, especially in third-world countries:

In African communities there are widespread beliefs that epilepsy is due to possession or bewitchment by evil spirits or the devil, and in some of the cultures the spirit is believed to be those of ancestors. There are also beliefs that the transmission of the disease is by physical contact, such as saliva. . . . Therefore attitudes toward epilepsy and the person with epilepsy in indigenous Africa are invariably unfavourable, because they reflect the mythical beliefs about the disease. (Tekle-Haimanot et al. 1991:203)

It is also worth noticing for our further discussion that none of the definitions suggests that attitudes may vary with the social situation in which they are acted out. There is no indication that they are socially as well as culturally constructed and *dynamic* in character.

The Relationship between Beliefs and Attitudes

In discussing the relationship between beliefs and attitudes it is useful to keep in mind the distinction made by Arthur Kleinman between *general beliefs* about sickness, which belong to the health ideology of the different health care sectors and exist independently of and prior to different episodes of sickness, and *explanatory models.* The latter are formed on belief systems but emerge in relation to specific illness episodes and therefore have to be analyzed in the context in which they occur (Kleinman 1980: 106). Explanatory models for the same case of illness or impairment may vary according to the *position* of the actors involved, thus influencing attitudes as "readiness to act" in different ways.

In all societies the beliefs about the causes of impairments may have consequences for action. Where biomedicine is the medical system that most strongly influences people's explanatory models, biomedical causation or diagnosis tends to influence the actions taken in relation to treatment and rehabilitation. The creation of alternative explanatory models and choices of alternative forms of treatment tend to take place only after biomedicine has failed to produce a cure or when the communication between patient and doctor has broken down (Ingstad and Sommerschild 1984). However, most people in Europe or North America would probably claim that their *attitudes* toward disabled people are not so much influenced by their knowledge or belief about the cause of the impairment. At least in Scandinavia, information through mass media, as well as the official policies promoted by the government, tends to play a much more important role for their "readiness to act."

In societies where the so-called personalistic medical systems (Foster 1976) play an important role, the connection between belief and attitudes may be more direct, but seldom as strong as the myth tends to indicate. If a particular type of impairment is believed ultimately to originate in the parents breaking an important taboo, this may lead to shame and reluctance to exhibit their misfortune in public. However, most such medical systems seem to have inbuilt a flexibility that makes it possible to construct alternative explanatory models that lessen or remove completely the stigma attached to an unfavorable "diagnosis." This is because most often it is the believed *origin* of the condition, and not the symptoms and their physical cause as such, which is seen as most important (Foster 1976).[11] Thus similar symptoms may have different origins, and the same origin of misfortune may cause very different symptoms.

On the other hand, possibilities for constructing explanatory models that place the blame for the misfortune on outside agents may create fewer feelings of guilt and shame in the parents than biomedical explanations that place much of the responsibility for a successful pregnancy on the mother.

My data from Botswana illustrate these issues. Here the only condition to which there is definitely attached a negative label is *mopakwane*, believed to originate in the parents breaking the prohibition against having sexual intercourse while the mother and newborn child are still in confinement (three months). Most of those given such a "diagnosis" would be called severely multihandicapped in biomedical terms, although some may be "only" severely malnourished or dehydrated.[12]

The stigma of mopakwane is primarily attached to the parents and not so much to the child; thus most parents of such children seem initially to have been both embarrassed and bothered by the comments of others. However, the majority eventually come to terms with the situation by revising their explanatory model and calling the condition something else. They now see the impairment as something that "just happened," which is a sort of residual category for conditions that cannot be correctly diagnosed and cured by divination and traditional remedies.

Another way to avoid the stigmatizing label is to claim that the child is *mpho ya modimo*, a gift from God. In line with the Tswana tradition of giving children a name that is meaningful for the life situation a child is born into, or for the parents' wishes or expectations, several of the children in my sample born with visible impairments had been given this name. The Tswana traditional god Modimo, and even the Christian counterpart that has taken over the same name, is mainly seen as a distant omnipotent power that demonstrates trust in people by giving them such special challenges.

Contrary to mopakwane, which places stigma on the parents, the blame of witchcraft tends to be placed outside the immediate family circle, on neighbors or more distant relatives. Thus in most cases witchcraft as a diagnosis causes neither guilt nor stigma for the disabled person or the parents. In rare cases, however, especially if the afflicted person is very influential or comes from a well-to-do family, she or he may be seen as the origin of the evil. The logic is that witchcraft worked on someone else may encounter magic protection that is stronger than the power of the sender and rebound upon its originator:

> Mary, a folk healer of some reputation, had been injured in a traffic accident and left with a considerable impairment. On return from the hospital she was very eager to spread the word around that this was not due to witchcraft, it was "just an accident." In private, however, she confided in me that it was witchcraft, all right, caused by a relative who was envious of her wealth and power.

We see from the example that Mary, being herself a person who might be suspected of administering witchcraft[13] (Ingstad 1989), found it more important to neutralize the incident than to place the blame where she felt it rightly belonged. It indicates that the connection between beliefs and attitudes is not simple and straightforward. It varies according to context and the position of the actors, and may be manipulated by all parties involved through the creation and re-creation of explanatory models.

Such a recognition must invariably lead to questioning the statement made by Redda Tekle-Haimanot and coauthors in the quotation in the previous section that attitudes toward (one type of) disability in Africa are "invariably unfavourable, because they reflect the mythical beliefs about the disease."

Biomedical explanations may be one way of neutralizing negative explanatory models rooted in the folk sector of health care. Thus one of the couples in my sample, who had been on the point of breaking up their marriage due to mutual accusations of "running around" after a mopakwane child was born, was greatly relieved when the nurse explained that the condition was due to brain damage caused by problems during delivery. The point was not to convince them that mopakwane did not exist, which they would probably not have believed anyway, but to give them an alternative neutral explanatory model which they could present to others. This gave them strength to meet the attitudes of other people whose explanatory models most often remained negatively influenced by the folk system of beliefs.

The Relationship between Social Position and Attitudes

We have seen that manipulation of explanatory models in order to minimize a possible stigma is one way that disabled persons and their near kin may try to influence the attitudes of people with whom they come into contact. To what extent the surroundings will accept such a redefinition of explanatory models varies.

Bernhard Helander (1990:41–44) has shown that disabled persons with similar impairments are treated differently within the same community if there are differences in the social position of the disabled persons and their families. Low status or bad reputation of the family may spread to the disabled person.

Similarly, of course, the presence of a disabled person in a family may influence the way the whole family is looked upon by others. This is what Erving Goffman (1963:30) calls "courtesy stigma." Nayinda Sentumbwe (this volume) uses spread in a different but related way—to show how one type of impairment is seen to affect and disable the whole person.

High or influential social position may, however, as in the case of Mary above, also have possible negative consequences in that the envy or enemies that such people may encounter in the community are reflected in the way they choose to explain the impairment and relate to the disabled person.

On the individual level, the existing relationship between the disabled person and the one expressing attitudes through words or behavior clearly makes a tremendous difference. Thus Batswana may agree in general that epilepsy is contagious through touch or saliva, but when it comes to their own child or close family member, they say: "I am not afraid, but treat him like anybody else and have not got epilepsy yet." Similarly there is agreement that to see a disabled person may be dangerous for a pregnant woman, especially if she gets frightened.[14] Disabled people, however, do not express any feelings of being restricted in their movement around the village for this reason, and the pregnant women rationalize their relationship to a disabled villager by saying that "I know him so I am not afraid of him." We thus see that attitudes, whether expressed in words or through behavior, are clearly relative to the position of both the person responding (or acting) and the disabled person.

The Relationship between Life Experiences, Emotions, and Attitudes

Previous life experiences are another important source of influence on people's attitudes and behavior toward disabled persons. In the study of families with disabled children in Norway we found that previous positive experiences in handling other types of crises became a source from which parents could draw when they got a disabled child. Even models from their natal home might help the parents to find a way of coping (Ingstad 1988; Ingstad and Sommerschild 1984). Roughly, we could identify two types of reactions to the experience of learning that their child was disabled: those who said that they got a terrible "shock," which it took them some time to overcome, and those who saw it as "just one of those things that happens in life."[15] On one hand, a "shock" often reflected high expectations for the child which now had to be revised; it also reflected a general expectancy in the Norwegian population that (most) children are born alive and healthy. "Just one of those things," on the other hand, often reflected a different view of life. Those parents had previously experienced that "life is not meant to be easy." Some of them came from the northern part of the country where the sea and rough climate for generations have been a challenge against which one survived or perished. Thus they did not expect a life free from worries, and did not feel that getting a disabled child made them that much different from other families.

Batswana families expressed a similar view. A life on the fringes of the Kalahari desert, where drought may wipe out the livestock and crops and where even common diseases like colds and diarrhea represent a threat to the life of children, invariably influences their reactions to disability. Thus when asked about her feelings about having a child with Down's syndrome, a mother who had lost three of her nine children said: "It is not him that I feel sorry about, but the ones that have died." For Batswana the potential tragedy of a disability is to a large extent measured according to the future role that the disabled person may be expected to play in a family. Thus a disability that does not prohibit the fulfillment of normal adult roles, or is compensated through rehabilitation or education, may even be seen as an asset: "I want my [physically disabled] daughter to be well educated. . . . [Unlike my other children] she is not likely to get married, and then she will work and support me when I am old."

We thus see that for both Norwegian and Batswana parents the reactions to a child's disability are influenced both by life experiences and by expectations of life in general and of the disabled person in particular. These reactions invariably influence—but do not alone determine—their relationship with the child.

A perspective on emotions not only as an individual concern but as culturally defined, socially enacted, and personally articulated (Lutz 1988:5) may also widen our understanding of the concept of attitudes. The emotional component of attitudes relates to the accepted way of expressing emotions in a particular society, as well as to the life experiences of people in that particular sociocultural setting, as discussed above. In Botswana, receiving a disabled newborn with little or no outward expression of grief and naming it Mpho—short for "a gift from God"—is in line with the culturally accepted way of handling emotions as well as an affirmation that the child is accepted as a positive challenge. Other people may laugh and make jokes about someone's impairment. Although that sometimes hurts the feelings of the disabled person, this also is in line with the acceptable way of meeting something unusual, and rarely is it interpreted or meant as an insult.

Disability as something out of the ordinary is likely to awaken emotions in people, whether they are directly involved through family ties or just observers. Disability is a visible proof of misfortune, but also in many cases it is a bill of exemption from some of the rules and obligations that hold for "normal" members of the society. The emotions disabilities call forth in others may be negative ones such as fear, contempt, or even envy when special benefits or privileges are awarded. Positively there may be pity, charity, and other forms of special treatment. Many disabled persons struggling for "normalization" have found the positive emotional reactions from others as difficult to encounter as the negative ones, and even harder to overcome.

Thus, people who are not in daily contact with a disabled person may also be expected to be influenced by whatever encounters they may have had. Actually, this is one of the main arguments behind the ideology of integration: that nondisabled children (and adults) should have positive experiences of persons with disabilities in school and thus acquire positive attitudes. This may not always work. A decade of integration of disabled children in mainstream Norwegian schools and child care facilities has surely been an eye-opener for many people, and many children now see disabled playmates as part of daily life. However, it has also led to resistance and even antagonism in cases where parents of normal children felt that the disabled child took too much of the teacher's attention or when disabled children were given priority in the struggle for scarce goods (for instance, places in nursery schools).

On the basis of what has been said so far I will argue that in asking about attitudes toward disabled people, it is highly relevant to know what sort of experiences with such people the informants have. A person with a disabled child or family member may be expected to answer differently from those who do not know such a person. Thus in the KAP study I made of disabled people in Botswana, I made it a point to include only people without disabled members in their household. The disabled people themselves and their family members were covered by more in-depth methods.

I have also argued that we must be very careful in identifying disposition or attitudes through expressions of emotions. We have to strive toward an understanding of the meaning people give to emotional expressions and how these are interpreted and acted upon by various categories of people in various cultural contexts.

The Relationship between Attitudes and Behavior

As we have already seen, the definition of attitude makes it clear that attitude is a *readiness* to act. Attitude is not necessarily the same as action nor does it determine action or behavior. Although this may seem obvious, the distinction is rarely made in literature on international rehabilitation (see quotation from SIDA/INFO above) or in studies of attitudes in non-Western societies.

One of the major weaknesses of KAP studies that are commonly used in this field is that they ask about attitudes and practices in a very general way and from there draw conclusions about behavior toward individual disabled persons. Since, as we have seen, there are many factors other than assumed dispositions to act that influence actual behavior, this may easily be misleading:

> One Tswana healer when telling about mopakwane exemplified the assumed hiding and shame of the parents by mentioning a neighboring household with a severely physically impaired son. I happened to know this family well and had seen for myself that the child, far from being "hidden," was well integrated in the neighboring school. The parents were very proud of his excellent marks and had high hopes for his future education. Their explanation of the impairment was witchcraft and not mopakwane.

In this case, whose attitudes should we take as a predictor of behavior toward the disabled child—that of the parents or that of the healer? The question obviously cannot be answered without reference to actual life situations and the actors involved. However, it demonstrates clearly the strong limitations of attitude and KAP surveys as indicators of the situation of disabled people in any society. By evaluating what people know, believe, and say that they (or others) do completely out of context, we risk creating stereotypes that have little to do with real-life situations. Thus KAP studies clearly have a methodological bias that needs to be taken seriously. They are neither reliable nor valid for measuring actual behavior (practice).

In order to understand how families cope with the care of a disabled child, how disabled people cope with their life situation, and how people relate to disabled friends and relatives, we must take living people as our starting point. To get a true picture we have to analyze actual life situations and identify the constraints and possibilities, beliefs and values that generate patterns of coping with disability (Ingstad 1991). We have to study how disabled people move about in social space and how they present themselves and are acted upon differently by various categories of relevant others.

CONCLUSION

A discussion of the concept of attitudes in relation to its various components and related topics leaves me, and probably also the reader, with a very uneasy feeling. Is this concept really useful as an analytical tool, and is it useful as a predictor for the life situation of disabled people in a particular community?

I shall answer the question with a very conditional yes. I will not dispute the fact that the concept of attitudes may serve certain analytical purposes, especially if we want to measure simple dimensions like parents' desire for schooling for a disabled child (e.g., "mainstream" or "specialized"). However, when it comes to more complex matters, I am doubtful. At least we must define the concept much more clearly than is usually done in writing about attitudes toward disabled people. I suggest that *attitude* be defined as "a statement about disposition to act toward a person, group, or object." By inserting the term *statement*, we remind ourselves about the nature of our data. Perhaps in this way we may avoid the danger of confusing statements with action, and the tendency to conclude that the life situation of disabled people in the community is the result of a single cause and effect. We also remind the reader/user that these statements are disconnected from any relational context.

By emphasizing attitudes, the international discourse on rehabilitation easily ends up in "victim blaming." Poor care for a disabled person is seen as a question of individual attitudes—most often that of the family or caregiving person—and changes become a question of attitude change. Attitudes of professionals or government are rarely questioned, and "the myth" becomes an excuse to justify paternalism and the righteousness of programs that are often created with little or no contact with the people they concern. In many—perhaps most—cases, however, the difficult circumstances of the disabled person are the result of the difficult life of the whole household or care unit. The problem may be poverty due to scarcity of resources, unemployment, or natural disasters such as drought—anything that makes the care unit extra vulnerable when one of its members becomes disabled. It may also be lack of support from outside, whether from neighbors or public services, as in the case of the young man "hidden" in the hut.

By focusing on attitudes in this way, two things are achieved. First, treatment of the individual disabled person and not the capacity of the care unit becomes the focus of attention. This is in line with the medicalization of rehabilitation and the inheritance from biomedicine in which restoring the functioning of bodily parts is one of the major concerns. The lack of ability of a care-giving person to follow up training instructions is thus interpreted as negative attitudes, and it is not seen in the total context of family resources and labor capacity. By limiting the perspective in this way, one loses the opportunity to make the care unit more viable and thus more able to take up the extra tasks that rehabilitation programs often introduce.

Second, "victim blaming" takes attention away from the fact that these are often political issues. It is a question of ability or willingness to develop appropriate rehabilitation and support services. It is also often a question of raising the standard of living for people in general, and thus also making households with disabled members more fit to cope. By changing social circumstances, we may change "attitudes" more easily and lastingly than by awareness campaigns. In this perspective a "myth of the hidden disabled" is useful not only for the charitable organizations collecting money but for governments in developing countries trying to avoid major investments in "unprofitable" sectors.

I am not suggesting that these consequences of the focus on attitudes are necessarily the result of conscious calculations. Rather, they are unintended consequences, but consequences that contribute to keeping an unfortunate myth very strong because it serves those who are in power.

What we see is a struggle for perspectives—or what Kleinman calls "clinical realities"—in which the strongest part is the winner and dictates the official truth:

> [But] the power to . . . legitimate a certain construction of reality as the *only* clinical reality, is not equally distributed. The professional sector is paramount because social power is in large part a function of institutionalisation, and the professional sector is heavily institutionalised whereas the popular sector is diffused. (Kleinman 1980:52)

Was the man in the hut protected from getting himself into trouble and thus from being sent back to a poor (and abusive) institution, or was he hidden and abused by his family? It all depends on the eyes that see and where one chooses to place one's loyalty. But the answer clearly has enormous impact on the way this family is approached by rehabilitation workers.

I am not suggesting that killing, neglect, or abuse of disabled people never happens, but I am rejecting the tendency to generalize abusive cases as images of *the way* of treating disabled people in developing countries while similar examples are seen as exceptions in the so-called developed part of the world. I am also rejecting attitude surveys and their consequences as a sufficient foundation for rehabilitation work anywhere. We should strive toward an approach in which the perspective of those concerned gets a prominent place in research as well as planning and implementation of programs concerning disabled people and their families. Only then can we hope to achieve a sustainable "rehabilitation for all by year 2000."[16]

NOTES

1. Norwegian organizations *by* disabled people had for two decades—in line with general trends of opinion in Scandinavia—been fighting fund-raising and private donations in any form, seeing such activity as an easy way out for the government. Interestingly enough, three of these organizations joined in a television campaign in 1981 to collect money for disabled people in developing countries. The question of whether fund-raising was the proper approach for other countries never seemed to bother them.

2. The fieldwork on which this article is based was made possible by grants from NORAD/Norwegian Ministry of Foreign Affairs and WHO. I am grateful to the University of Oslo for giving me two years sabbatical with half pay, which made it possi-

ble for me to go to Botswana for a two-year period. My husband was the district medical officer sent out on a contract by the Norwegian Development Cooperation. My children went to the village school.

3. This model is based on the mobilization of people in the local community, mainly family members, for the training of disabled people through the use of manuals with simple texts and drawings.

4. All types and severities of impairments were represented.

5. Small livestock is often not brought to the "cattle post."

6. Plowing has to be done by men since they are the only ones to handle cattle-drawn plows.

7. These are often children who for various reasons have failed to finish primary school, or have finished without being able to secure a job or further schooling. It also happens that children are taken out of school (or not enrolled) because they are needed at "the lands."

8. Village compounds are traditionally built adjoining one another, and seen from the air, they look like a cross-section of a beehive.

9. About two hours' travel by bus from where they lived.

10. This was the only case I ever encountered where the family was willing to teach a mentally retarded man "women's tasks."

11. In line with Foster (1976) I here see the personalistic medical systems as distinguished by their tendency to operate with several layers of causality. The first level, explaining the particular symptoms, are bodily processes as acknowledged by that particular medical tradition (dirty blood, moving womb, etc.). The second and higher level is the ultimate origin of the misfortune (witchcraft/sorcery, ancestor's anger, etc.).

12. This may be why the folk healers claim to be able to cure mopakwane if it is treated at an early stage.

13. Among the Tswana, folk healers are seen as people knowledgeable about prevention and cure of witchcraft, and also as the main source of witchcraft.

14. The fetus may be affected, giving the child the same type of disability.

15. *Livets tilskikkelse.*

16. The slogan for the UN Decade for Disabled Persons.

REFERENCES

Foster, George M.
    1976   Disease etiologies in non-Western medical systems. *American Anthropologist* 78(4):773–782.
Goffman, Erving
    1963   *Stigma: Notes on the Management of Spoiled Identity.* Englewood Cliffs, N.J.: Prentice-Hall.
Helander, Bernhard
    1984   *Rehabilitation for All: A Guide to the Management of Community-based Rehabilitation. 1. Policymaking and Planning.* WHO/RHB/84.1. Provisional version. Geneva: WHO.

1990   Mercy or rehabilitation? Culture and the prospects for disabled in Southern Somalia. In *Disability in a Cross-cultural Perspective,* ed. J. Bruun and B. Ingstad. Working paper no. 4. Oslo: Department of Social Anthropology, University of Oslo.

Ingstad, Benedicte
1988   Coping behaviour of disabled persons and their families: Cross-cultural perspectives from Norway and Botswana. *International Journal of Rehabilitation Research* 11(4):351–359.
1989   Healer, witch, prophet, or modern health worker? The changing role of Ngaka ya Setswana. In *Culture, Experience, and Pluralism: Essays on African Ideas of Illness and Healing,* ed. A. Jacobson-Widding and D. Westerlund. Uppsala: Almqvist and Wiksell International.
1991   The myth of the hidden disabled: A study of community-based rehabilitation in Botswana. Working paper. Oslo: Section for Medical Anthropology, University of Oslo.

Ingstad, Benedicte, and Hilchen Sommerschild
1984   *Familien med det Funksjonshemmede Barnet: Forløp, Reaksjoner, Mestring. Et Frambu-prosjekt* [The family with a disabled child: Process, reactions, coping. A Frambu project]. Oslo: Tanum-Norli.

Kleinman, Arthur
1980   *Patients and Healers in the Context of Culture: An Exploration of the Borderland between Anthropology, Medicine, and Psychiatry.* Berkeley, Los Angeles, London: University of California Press.

Kuper, Adam, and Jessica Kuper
1985   *The Social Science Encyclopedia.* London: Routledge and Kegan Paul.

Lutz, Catherine
1988   *Unnatural Emotions: Everyday Sentiments on a Micronesian Atoll and Their Challenge to Western Theory.* Chicago: University of Chicago Press.

Rosaldo, Renato
1989   *Culture and Truth: The Remaking of Social Analysis.* Boston: Beacon Press.

SIDA/INFO
1987   *Handikappade I U-länder* [The handicapped in developing countries]. Stockholm: SIDA.

Sills, David L.
1968   *International Encyclopedia of the Social Sciences.* New York: Macmillan Company and Free Press.

Tekle-Haimanot R., M. Abebe, L. Forsgren, A. Gebre-Marium, J. Heijbel, G. Holmgren, and J. Ekstedt
1991   Attitudes of rural people in Central Ethiopia toward epilepsy. *Social Science and Medicine* 32(2):203–209.

WHO
1981   *Disability Prevention and Rehabilitation: Report of the WHO Expert Committee on Disability Prevention and Rehabilitation.* WHO Technical Report Series, no. 668. Geneva: WHO.

Epilogue

FOURTEEN

Disability between Discourse and Experience

Susan Reynolds Whyte

A major aim of this book has been to examine the ways in which the cultural construction of personhood shapes the significance of sensory, mental, or motor impairments. In a variety of cultural settings, our contributors have posed the question, How does an incurable deficit affect an individual's possibilities and validity as a person? Since little research has been done on disability outside Europe and North America, this is a preliminary exploration; instead of drawing conclusions now, I raise some general issues and consider where we might go from here.

The anthropology of disability must place itself in relation to two radically different approaches to the question of impairment and personhood. On the one hand, there stands the sweeping cultural history of the French tradition, which characterizes the changing discourse on difference through historical epochs. Although the term *personhood* is not used explicitly, this work is ultimately concerned with how persons are construed in relation to biology, religion, ethics, and the institutional structure of society. On the other hand, there is a sharply contrasting approach that begins with individuals and tries to comprehend the experience of being an impaired person through first-hand accounts. One method has broad vision but risks stereotyping; the other has depth and nuance, but may lose sight of the changing social context in which individuals exist. Future research must draw from both of these approaches, and it must build on field research that contextualizes and differentiates the situations of persons with impairments.

Discourse analysis shares with other approaches in modern social science the assumption that phenomena are shaped by the ways people communicate about them; they are constituted through expressive practices. This is not to deny their material reality but rather to emphasize the processes through which that kind of reality is apprehended. Impairment or disability is culturally constructed through ways of talking and treating and writ-ing—through disability payments or begging as well as through professional treatises and the manipulation of stigma. A recent discussion of Michel Fou-cault's version of discourse analysis underlines his assertion that discourses are "practices that systematically form the objects of which they speak."

> For the final work discourse is meant to do, as social theory, is to suggest a con-cern not so much with meaning as with a kind of large-scale pragmatics . . . taking texts and talk and all sorts of other social practices as productive of ex-perience and constitutive of the realities in which we live and the truths with which we work. (Abu-Lughod and Lutz 1990:9–10)

It is the phrase "productive of experience" that I would like to prob-lematize. Discourses are ways of objectifying situations, issues, values, per-sons, and relationships. In the common use of the term, discourses "say" something; institutional practices imply something. At some level, a mes-sage is conveyed. How is the message understood? How does discursive prac-tice relate to the subjective experience of people with impairments? The relationship between a type of objectifying through discourse and the process of subjectifying—experiencing oneself and the situation in a given way—is the key issue here. Do people with impairments accept the con-structions of themselves that are offered? If they adopt the discourse, how do they transform it? Or do they resist it? In what contexts do they accept, ignore, contest, or rework a given discourse?

There is a growing body of literature about the subjective experience of disability in Western society, and some of it deals with the interface of ob-jectifying discourse and subjective reality. Much less has been written about this matter in other cultural settings. A recent book by Megan Vaughan (1991), analyzing shifts in biomedical discourses on the health of colonial Africans, points to precisely this problem in historical research. While it is possible to use textual material to examine the images of Africans inherent in campaigns against yaws, syphilis, and leprosy, it is difficult to know the ex-tent to which these images were appropriated by African people as part of their identity. What was it like to be labeled a leper and brought into the in-stitutional practices of colonial leprosy treatment?[1]

The methods of history and anthropology have different potentials here. Historians like Foucault or Vaughan or Stiker (to whom I shall turn in a mo-ment) work with texts about disability, disease, and health and to some ex-tent with records of the organization and practices of institutions, programs, and services. Ethnographers must listen and look and engage in dialogue in order to write of cultural discourses and practices concerning disability. Their material is experience—their own experience of other people's ex-pressions. This may be far less clear-cut than the programs of health plan-ners or the messages of historical texts. While rituals or answers to an interviewer's questions may seem to carry one coherent view of disability (a dominant view), daily life, ordinary conversations, and apparent strategies may be far more varied.

THE WESTERN CONSTRUCTION OF DISABILITY

The French scholar Henri-Jacques Stiker, in his history *Corps infirmes et sociétés* (1982), follows in the footsteps of Foucault in characterizing the cultural constructions of entire eras of European history. Stiker believes that societies reveal themselves in the way they deal with difference, and he sets himself the monumental task of portraying Western civilization through its discourse on bodily abnormality. He speaks of isotopes, levels, or registers in which difference may be expressed: biological, social, ethico-religious, medical. He traces the emergence of disability as a specific category of difference, and the responses that difference has invoked: charity, medical analysis, special education, and rehabilitation. His is a generalizing, sometimes provocative, vision, but it *is* a vision, in a field where few broad frameworks exist.[2] Here I can only sketch the outlines of a book that deserves to be known to anglophone researchers.

In the Middle Ages, impairments (infirmities, as Stiker calls them) were not specifically distinguished from other forms of misery or suffering. Infirmity and poverty were part of God's varied creation—the order of things. The response to difference was charity, spirituality, and morality. The giving of alms, individually or through the work of institutions (hospitals, monasteries, etc.) was an exercise of virtue, and suffering was a sign of divine presence. As Stiker characterizes the period, "deformity is neither indexed, nor excluded, nor organized, nor especially considered: it is there, and in the bundle of misery, it must be given mercy" (Stiker 1982:95).[3] In this system of charity, poverty and infirmity were seen as inevitable; the response was ethical rather than political or technical. But the ethical and spiritual integration of difference did not accomplish social integration. The infirm were marginal, cared for by their families or by charitable patrons, without any social function or identity as a distinct group.[4]

To these systems of charity, Stiker contrasts the developments of the sixteenth to nineteenth centuries. A medical, as opposed to a Christian, discourse on infirmity is established, and by the eighteenth century the concern is less to explain than to describe and make an inventory of impairments. The seventeenth century saw the beginning of the idea of confinement in hospitals. Whereas earlier, disabled people had been aggregated with the poor (not only as objects of charity in the Middle Ages, but under the Poor Laws of the sixteenth century in England), institutions specifically for disabled people were established. Significantly, the first of these was for soldiers and seamen who had suffered impairment in the line of duty; in Paris, the Hôtel des Invalides was founded in 1674 for invalid soldiers.[5] Nevertheless, confinement in institutions was never so general for people with sensory and motor impairments as it was for the mentally ill, whose era of confinement was described by Foucault (1973).

The idea of education or re-education of disabled people was a product of eighteenth-century Enlightenment. Stiker points to Denis Diderot's *Letter on the Blind* as part of a general European interest in the capacities of the impaired. In France, this was the era of the Abbé de l'Épée (1712–1789), who did pioneering work on sign language for deaf-mutes, and of Valentin Haüy (1745–1822), who established education for the blind (Louis Braille was a student at the institution he founded). The interest in the "Wild Boy of Aveyron," who had no language and was found living in the woods like an animal and brought to Paris in 1800, reflected this same concern with education as a way of developing the abilities of the impaired.

By the nineteenth century there were educational institutions for the deaf and the blind, and orthopedic institutions were established with techniques and machines for correcting the body. Families cared for those with motor and intellectual deficiencies, and only if they were unable to do so were people handed over to institutions for the poor, the old, and the infirm.[6]

World War I marked the beginning of rehabilitation as we know it, both in Europe and the United States. Stiker asserts that a broad paradigm shift occurred as Western societies dealt with the enormous numbers of mutilated men left behind by the war. As prostheses were developed, so also developed the more general notions of replacement, substitution, and compensation which in time were applied to all congenital and acquired impairments. As the catastrophe of war required reconstruction, so damaged people were to be rehabilitated, returned to a real or postulated preexisting norm of reference, and reassimilated in society. The process was not one of curing: "Curing is an expulsion and concerns health, reintegration is situated on the social level and replaces a deficit" (Stiker 1982:141).

Stiker sees in this period the beginning of the denial of difference that he finds characteristic of our time. Whereas earlier epochs situated the infirm as exceptional in some way, the modern intention (or pretension) is that they are ordinary and should be integrated into ordinary life and work. Infirmities do not raise metaphysical problems so much as technical ones, to be taken in hand and administered by social workers, vocational trainers, and medical and legal specialists. The assumption is that we master all the outcomes; every condition can be treated and adjusted, though not all can be cured.

ETHNO-TERATOLOGY: DISCOURSES ON ANOMALY

I began my review of the "genealogy" of contemporary European discursive practice with the charity discourse of the Middle Ages. Stiker goes further back, beginning his history with the Judaic scriptural texts and moving to the classical periods of ancient Greece and Rome. In his presentation, however, those early constructions of infirmity have no presence in today's social practices; Christianity constituted a break, and while the medieval theme of charity is still relevant, the older ones of evil, impurity, and humanity's relation to the gods are not. Some of these elements are evident in the ethnographic record, however. One mode of construing difference reported in the literature on non-Western societies is to fix upon anomaly and cast it in a cosmobiological discourse.[7]

Some kinds of infirmity are construed in terms of the biological integrity of the species and cast upon a cosmological plane of vast dimensions. As Mary Douglas puts it, anomaly may be used to consider deeper meanings of existence (1966:52–53). It is thought provoking and disquieting. Anomaly may be associated with evil as imperfection, as David Parkin (1985a:5–9) shows. Inspired by Paul Ricoeur (1967), he draws attention to the themes of rottenness or physical incompleteness or defilement as one way of understanding evil. This "archaic" system, which Ricoeur calls "cosmobiological" (and contrasts to the notion of sin committed by a guilty actor), was typical of the Hebrew world. Stiker (1982, chap. 2) points out that Leviticus identified impairments as legal impurities. Lepers, fools, and the blind, deaf, and lame were forbidden to present offerings. Biological wholeness was divine; its opposite was to be excluded from contact with the sacred.

In Western medicine, teratology (the term is derived from the Greek word for monster) is the study of congenital defects. The concern with deviations from biological integrity is an ancient one (Warkany 1971, 1977), and the conceptualization of anomaly cross-culturally is so varied that one is tempted to speak of ethno-teratology. Deliane Burck (1989:60ff.) summarizes some of the references in the literature on Southern Africa to "traditional" views of abnormalities considered so severe that they precluded an infant's being allowed to become a human. These included breech birth, cutting the upper teeth first, defecating while being born, and being delivered of a mother who had not menstruated between births.[8] Yet perhaps more commonly, differences of this sort are recognized as placing the individual in a special category: as less of a person, as unclean, as dangerous, but also sometimes as having or representing extraordinary powers. Twinship is one of the biological singularities that gives a special status in many cultures; in Africa twins might be killed or celebrated in various ritual transformations, but, according to the ethnographic record, they were seldom ordinary persons. This disposition to mark certain singularities of the individual's birth, development, and body or mind in a cosmological sense is very different from the present Western notions of disability. In Stiker's terms, it formulates the problem of difference by relating biological integrity to metaphysical or religious concerns of purity, order, defilement, and power.

Stiker's analysis of the discourse on difference in Western antiquity shows how myths elaborated on the meaning of deformity. In the story of Oedipus, exposed because of his misshapen foot, difference and identity (here in the form of incest) are the basic issues of the human condition. Other myths about mutilated and deformed gods made anomaly a sign that is "good to think with."[9] Stiker concludes that defects for which there was no place on the social level (malformed infants were offered to the gods through exposure in Sparta, Athens, and Rome) provoked philosophical and social reflection, and thus "on a magic, collective level" deformity had an eminent function (Stiker 1982:76).

An excellent contemporary example is provided by René Devisch from his work on cults of affliction in central Africa. Devisch describes the *mbwoolu* and the *khita* cults among the Yaka of southwestern Zaire as cults addressed to physically disabled people in a broad sense: those with gynecological problems, albinos, dwarfs, twins, infants whose "skull is too weak," children who fail to crawl or stand, and victims of polio, anemia, joint pains, accidents, severe and chronic fever, diarrhea, river blindness, and nightmares (Devisch 1990:111). In a detailed analysis of the symbolic process of initiation, Devisch shows how disability is represented and semantically transformed. The "origin of the anomaly" is unmasked and seized. The initiate addresses a set of eight or more statuettes in the mbwoolu shrine, which demonstrate the phylogenetic process: "the gradual coming into being of a man from a limbless body to one armoured with bony plates, from having only one leg, arm or breast to a fully fledged human body, from physical impairment or deformity to full ability, from a-sexuality to mature virile or female sexuality" (ibid.:123). The point is not that a cure is necessarily achieved but that the impaired person and the community are healed in a new understanding of the meaning of deficiency.

> As a result of the initiation, the disabled person no longer dwells in the twilight zones of social indefinition. Through the initiation and the permanent cult, the marginalising effects of the bodily defects and other disabilities are symbolically transferred to the figurines. These provide a liminal zone and a juncture with the society-at-large and its belief system. From now on, the physical flaws of the disabled person offer particular virtues for contact with the fundamental symbols of man's origin, phylogeny, and pre-ancestral space and time. *Mbwoolu* acts as a ritualization and rehabilitation of life's deficiencies into a culture-bearing process which may be cyclically renewed. (ibid.:125)

Devisch's point is that flaws become the vehicles for a powerful enactment of the human condition and its history, and those who bear the flaws attain a new persona. As occupants of a transitional space between society and the supernatural, they are regarded with respect, awe, and sometimes a touch of fear (Devisch, personal communication, 1992). In Stiker's analytical framework, this kind of discourse is diametrically opposed to the modern Western one on disability. Where rehabilitation emphasizes integration into a society of similar people through individual effort and social compensation, and the unspoken agreement to identify difference and pretend it does not exist, the Yaka cult dramatizes difference, giving it cosmological significance and creating persons with unusual powers.

DIFFERENCE AS MISFORTUNE: DISCOURSES ON CAUSE

Devisch attended the rituals that transformed flawed persons, but many ethnographic reports present the discourse on anomaly as "traditional practice" that is no longer followed. Killing twins is a thing of the past, though they may still be allowed to "wither away" as in Central Borneo (see chap. 2). In contrast, the discourse on cause is relevant and current. The scattered ethnographic reports about sensory, motor, and mental deficiencies often consist of accounts of the way people explain them. Cursing, sorcery, spirits, gods, transgression of order—these are the terms in which infirmity is presented. To judge from the ethnographic reports, and indeed from the contributions to this volume, there is far greater concern with etiology than there is with coping, stigma, adjustment, or social integration.[10] This is true not only for the African cases, where a strong tradition in ethnographic writing emphasizes explanations of misfortune, but also for the Punan Bah of Borneo (chap. 2) and the immigrant Turkish family in Sweden described in chapter 11. What does this expressed concern with cause mean in practice for people with impairments? Does it affect attitudes of others toward them or the way they are treated?

Looked at in the broad terms of juxtaposition, the discourse on cause has several striking characteristics. It casts impairment with other kinds of misfortune; the same range of causes may explain the collapse of granaries, failures in hunting, serious illness, and deafness. Just as the biocosmological discourse on anomaly conflates biomedically defined impairments with other singularities, so the concern with cause is not specific to the biomedical category of disability. Constructing difference as misfortune to be explained draws attention to relations with agents and to normative injunctions. Lameness may indicate the link to a spirit; madness may be the result of a sorcerer's malice; retardation may point to a parent's transgressions. The individual is conceived in a moral, relational world, where faults of the "mindful body" (Scheper-Hughes and Lock 1987) reflect faults in the social and spiritual order. Patrick Devlieger (chap. 5) argues that the concern with distorted relationships is fundamental for Songye and by implication for other African people. The concern with cause is an aspect of the definition of the person in terms of relations. Treatment must be addressed to the social and moral disorder, or, at the very least, it must recognize the relational nature of persons.

The attention to cause reflects more than an intellectual need to explain; it is often synonymous with a disposition toward treatment—a practice. This kind of discursive practice addresses causal forces by attempting to placate, counteract, or compensate them. As treatment it often seems unrealistic from a biomedical point of view. Although it can be argued that addressing distorted relationships is a form of healing, even when there is no remission of symptoms, afflicted people want to relieve the symptoms, not merely the causes of symptoms. They go on treating for one cause and another, until they give up and begin to speak of fate or the work of God, which no one can change. The way in which a therapeutic itinerary is tied to an interest in cause is explored by Bernhard Helander, writing on the Somali (chap. 4). There, many forms of disability are not sharply distinguished from illness;[11] thus therapy aimed at a presumed cause is the appropriate response. He suggests that when treatment is given up, so is any hope of making a change in the situation. Personhood is diminished as the individual becomes an object of mercy.

The assumptions about personhood and temporality implicit in the discourse on cause contrast sharply with those evident in the practice of rehabilitation. The latter involves the adjustment of the individual and integration into social activities; the person is responsible for coping and for trying to function as normally as possible. Others must provide technical assistance and try to compensate for and overlook differences. The question of who or what caused the condition in the first place is irrelevant, since nothing can be done about etiology. The temporality of disability for the individual and family is one of onset and recognition, followed by the process of adjustment, training, and individual development. The discourse on cause fastens upon a point in time, an event or disturbance occurring prior to the impairment. Attention is drawn back to that point and to the constellation of relationships in play at that time. Efforts are concentrated there, rather than on the formation of individual abilities and technical adjustment. The discourse on cause holds out the hope of transforming the symptoms; the discourse on rehabilitation promises adaptation to symptoms that cannot be changed.

Applying Stiker's notion of discourses on infirmity to contemporary non-Western cultures brings out a commonality between his type of culture history and much ethnography. Both focus on dominant discourses and thus tend to totalize one pattern in an era or society. In principle the historical approach is more cognizant of alternatives simply because of its emphasis on genealogy and transformation. Yet there is always a tendency, especially in describing more distant time periods, to point to *the* discursive practice.

LESSONS OF THE ELEPHANT MAN

Anomalies are good to think with, as Mary Douglas (1966) has taught us, so in imagining an anthropology of disability, let me turn briefly to the "human oddities" exhibited in museums, circuses, fairs, freak shops, and shows in nineteenth-century Europe and America. "Freaks," the term used at the time, included people billed as primitive and exotic, as well as those with physical and mental abnormalities: bearded ladies, "pinheads" (microcephalics), Siamese twins, "half men" (people who are missing limbs), dwarfs, and giants. Robert Bogdan (1988) describes what could be called a changing discourse in American culture history: the shift from seeing these people as entertaining and edifying curiosities to seeing them as pitiably sick, and finally to seeing them as disabled people being indecently exploited. Today freak shows seem anachronistic, and the pictures and pamphlets that formed an important part of the freak presentation are gathering dust in attics and special collections. But one "freak" has made the transition into our time with peculiar force: Joseph Merrick, the Elephant Man, "discovered" in a freak shop by a London doctor in 1884. Merrick suffered from a rare disease that progressively deformed his facial structure and body, inhibiting his movements and rendering him so grotesque that normal social intercourse was impossible. He was a man of mythical qualities, uniquely afflicted and singularly transformed physically and socially. In a book titled *Articulating the Elephant Man,* Peter Graham and Fritz Oehlsclaeger (1992) examine interpretations of his story: the reminiscences of Frederik Treves, the surgeon who lifted him out of the freak show and into both medicine and London society; the book about his humanity by anthropologist Ashley Montagu; the dramatic works, of which the best known is the prize-winning play by Bernard Pomerance; the film by David Lynch; the historical research; the children's books; the volume of poetry; and even the rock video by Michael Jackson. This study, like Bogdan's work on American freak shows, touches culture history and the social construction of bodily difference. Both describe a medicalization of abnormality: Bogdan (1988:66) points to the growing opinion that freaks belong in medical textbooks, not in side shows, and Graham and Oehlsclaeger (1992:45) describe with mild irony the way Treves *showed* his extraordinary specimen to the London Pathological Society, just as the police were closing down his freak show as an indecent spectacle. In Stiker's terms, these are shifts in discursive practice. But beyond illustrating the cultural process of medicalization, Joseph Merrick teaches us another fundamental lesson.

The articulation of the Elephant Man revealed different truths to different explorers: "Joseph Merrick has been transformed from a suffering individual to an exhibit, a shape-shifting curiosity whose different guises variously suit the needs of particular audiences, genres and interpreters" (Graham and Oehlsclaeger 1992:2). In one version (for theater audiences) he is subjected to the tyranny of the normal by a paternalistic doctor; in another (for child readers) he enjoys friendship and kindness from the staff of London Hospital. What never comes through, however, is Merrick as subject. The pamphlet that tells his life history (in the first person) for the freak show audience was probably written by his manager, and is a very simple account of his life for the consumption of customers. Even the doctor, Frederick Treves, who brings us closer to Merrick than anyone else, consistently refers to Merrick by the wrong name (he calls him John instead of Joseph) and dismisses his love for his mother, whom Treves misrepresents as having deserted him. Treves presents Merrick as a victim whose personhood was denied in being exhibited as a freak. In so doing, he denies Merrick's agency, for it was Merrick himself who sought out the opportunity of show life (ibid.: 46).

Graham and Oehlsclaeger keep coming back to a lesson about the representation of impaired persons: Merrick's own muteness in contrast to the abundant language of all those who showed him and made stories about him, putting words in his mouth. His disorder clouded the expressiveness of his face and the clarity of his speech; his class background and his social position first as a freak and then as an object of charity also limited the extent to which he could express his experience and thus come to terms with his misfortune. We know little of how Joseph Merrick articulated the Elephant Man; his own stories about his affliction are buried in the representations of others. It is just this issue of individual experience and expression that concerns many anthropologists today.

EXPERIENCE AND REPRESENTATIONS

Whether we approach difference in terms of discursive practice, as Stiker does, or whether difference becomes the stuff of myth, symbol, and story, as in the case of the Elephant Man, something essential is missing. What about the individuals and families living with and in spite of anomaly, misfortune, weakness, or disability? Discourse analysis does not leave much room for their subjectivity and agency.

> Such impersonal imaging of social life is unconvincing primarily because of its inaccuracy, its unsubtlety, its distance from the details of the ongoing work of social interaction: work by individuals in conjunction, creating themselves and their social relationships. (Indeed, if there were a political argument to be made, it would surely be that to miss reporting that individual work and substitute the dead hand of determinism—to replace, as would the Foucauldian, individual mentalities by conventional "governmentalities"—is a travesty.) (Rapport 1992:20)

The dangers of impersonal conceptualizations are particularly significant in the study of disability. Irving Zola (1982:199, 242) points to the tendency to separate and distance disability, to make it someone else's problem, and to render people with disabilities socially indistinct by stereotyping them. In a similar vein, Arthur Kleinman and Joan Kleinman (1991:276) argue that experience-distant analyses delegitimize and dehumanize their subjects. If there is a danger that disabled people are presented as Others, not like us, then there is a double danger in the study of people with impairments in other cultures. They are both foreign and disabled, and it is a difficult job to render them as subjects we can understand and identify with.

The effort to overcome distance and to bring experience near is well-established in medical sociology and in anthropological studies carried out in Europe and North America. In a 1990 collection of papers on qualitative methods in the study of chronic illness, the influence from phenomenology and the nearness of experience are strongly present. Peter Conrad, himself a pioneer in the study of the experience of disability, traces this approach back to the emergence of insiders' perspectives in symbolic interactionism (Conrad 1990:1260), as does Kathy Charmaz (1990), who uses grounded theory to analyze the ways people socially construct their chronic illness experiences. Within this tradition, the life stories of people with disabilities are told from their own perspective, if not in their own words. Accounts of the lives of mentally retarded people (Edgerton 1967; Langness and Levine 1966) for the first time presented them as subjects capable of having a coherent view of their lives and themselves. Extended dialogue with a woman lacking arms and legs revealed her vision of her basic normality (Frank 1984) and of her experience of embodiment (Frank 1986). Extensive interviews with chronic pain sufferers showed how they struggled to find a diagnosis and cure, dealing with questions about the physical, psychological, and social sources of their affliction (Good et al. 1992). In this book, Judith Monks and Ronald Frankenburg (chap. 6) analyze autobiographies written by people with multiple sclerosis to show how they conceptualize time in relation to their bodies and their selves. These published accounts disclose an unfolding through phases to a kind of narrative resolution of the opposition between self and infirm body. They differ from other accounts of individual experience in their more finished narrative form and in their reflexive and exemplary nature. Yet even dialogues or case stories constructed by the researcher share with them a sense of the immediacy of the individual's experience.

Traditionally, anthropologists have attempted to bring experience near by participant observation. The concept of participation is elastic, and fieldworkers do not always share the life conditions of "their people" in any sustained way. But there are at least three books about the experience of disability written by researchers who were participants in a very genuine sense.[12] Robert Murphy, Irving Zola, and Michael Dorris have all written insider accounts of experiences with impairment. All three are rich with information about the details of living with an impairment; the authors trace the development of their own subjective understanding of themselves, and all incorporate elements of their professional discourses in their accounts. But the balance between these elements is very different in the three books.

Zola undertook a short period of fieldwork in a village for disabled people in Holland. For a week, he put aside his cane and lived in a wheelchair, like the other villagers. This exaggeration of his disability brought him immediate acceptance and intense involvement with the "natives"; it also brought him to experience his own impairment and himself in a new way. His account, written in journal style, is both ethnographically informative and intimately revealing.

Murphy too presents his book as a product of field research: "And since it is the duty of all anthropologists to report on their travels, whether to Earth's antipodes or to equally remote recesses of human experience, this is my accounting" (Murphy 1987:ix). This is not just an experiential travelogue, however, as the sample reprinted in this volume (chap. 7) forcefully demonstrates. Murphy moves constantly from the immediacy of his own life, to assessments of American culture, to discussions of theoretical concepts and other research.

In contrast to Murphy and Zola, Michael Dorris (1989) never purported to write an ethnography, although his book, which won a literary prize, is also an account of participant observation by an anthropologist. He writes the story of life with his adopted son, who is diagnosed as having fetal alcohol syndrome. (Although this impairment is not located in Dorris's own body or mind, it is his affliction.) Dorris is not only a father and a gifted writer but also a Native American anthropologist, and his narrative switches to one of Indians, reservations, and alcohol, and his discovery of the professional discourse that provided a way of articulating his experience with his son. Murphy, and to a lesser extent Zola, analyze their personal experiences as a contribution to research. Dorris appropriates research findings and a social science perspective in order to give meaning and moral legitimacy to his experience of affliction.

These three books are exceptional in being written by afflicted participant observers. But most studies of the experience of disability are not written in the first person, and they must deal with the basic problem of anthropology—how to interpret other people who are different. In contrast to the celebration of otherness which emphasizes cultural difference, the concern with experience often points to the human universals that allow us to make a leap of empathy across differences of language, social situation, and embodiment.[13] The anthropologist's art lies in sensitivity to resonance, appreciating other people's experience on the basis of one's own (Wikan

1992). The phenomenological approach to suffering advocated by Kleinman and Kleinman (1991) defines experience as the felt flow of intersubjective social transactions in local moral worlds. In understanding the experience of others, we must be attentive to structures of relevance—"what is at stake" from their point of view (ibid.:277). The fact that some of the stakes are universally relevant as elements of the human condition is important in developing an approach to experience. Often it is the sense of experience shared at some level that makes an account powerful. Thus Robert Murphy writes of physical impairment "as an allegory to all life in society" (1987:ix) and of his "urge to penetrate the veneer of cultural differences and reach an understanding of the underlying unity of all human experience" (ibid.:87).

In practice, however, the experience of disability is still embedded in cultural assumptions and social relations, the "local moral worlds," of which even the most committed empathetic humanism must take account. Murphy accomplishes his universalizing purpose in part through an account of the values and attitudes of American culture. The cultural insights possible from the wheelchair perspective provide a unique assessment of American sociability and of American sociological theories about it. Here lies a central problem for studies of the experience of disability: how to retain the sense of resonance and common humanity, while attending to differences in world structure that shape (construct) the lives of other people.

This is a major theme in Vincent Crapanzano's *Tuhami* (1980), a remarkable book about his dialogue with a Moroccan man married to a she-demon. The man was apparently impotent and caught in a liminal situation of illness from which he seems unable to escape (ibid.:86–87). Crapanzano focuses on the process through which Tuhami reveals his world, and the book is usually read not as an account of the life of a disabled person but as a reflection on the nature of the ethnographic enterprise. It is also a narrative about the ambiguous construction of a life that is irremediably impaired. Crapanzano conveys a process of exploration, not only of the world of saints and demons, but of the uncertainty, contradiction, hope, and disappointment that make Tuhami human for his interlocutor and for us as readers.

In contrast, Peter Wilson's 1947 book about Oscar, a "madman" of the Caribbean island of Providencia, is more concerned with the "local moral world" in which individual experience of disability unfolds. Wilson describes how he came to know Oscar and how Oscar expressed himself about his life. But he also shows Oscar as a character in island society—thief, eavesdropper, and "man of words." Wilson lets Oscar illuminate Providencian values of respectability and reputation, and of privacy and autonomy as conditions for social relations. This too is an anthropology of experience, but one that is not focused on the subjectivity of one "disabled" individual. Wilson is present in the story (as Crapanzano was in Tuhami's), puzzling out Oscar, and so are other Islanders—fascinated, bemused, ambivalent, frightened by this crazy, powerful, intelligent, unpredictable man. The immediacy of Oscar is undeniable, not only because of his rich words, but because we see him, through Wilson, as a social person interacting with his neighbors. It is this capacity to grasp disability in an ongoing shared social context, from the viewpoints of different actors, and in relation to local values, that is unique to ethnographic fieldwork.

FIELDWORK, DISCOURSES, AND EXPERIENCES

An anthropology of disability must find inspiration in both discourse analysis and the study of individual experience, while maintaining the old appreciation of context and community that is rooted in ethnographic field-work.[14] Future work in the anthropology of disability needs the broad comparative perspective of cultural history like that of Stiker and Foucault. Their method helps us to contrast different cultural logics and to analyze our own basic assumptions. The analysis of changing institutional practice and the emergence of new social categories are particularly important in the study of disability in other cultures. The nature of professional discourses, the practices of various types of organizations, and the existence of national laws and policies are not always included as topics in ethnographic research. Yet it is through them, as well as through the analysis of symbols, rituals, and expressed values, that we can grasp the broad outlines of the themes of personhood and impairment.

The appreciation of narratives and case stories is equally important, as a way of acknowledging the legitimacy and irreducibility of individual experience. Such accounts remind us that subjectivity is far more complex, indeterminate, and idiosyncratic than discourse suggests. Here we see individuals appropriating or contesting the variety of discursive practice available to them. We see the process of interpretation and counterinterpretation, the movement of agents within webs of social relations, and the sense of self in relation to perceived cultural themes and values concerning personhood. Even though the individuality of the person and the self-reflection of the subject are not everywhere as extreme as in countries of the North, still impairments do occur in individual bodies or minds, and it is as subjects and agents that people deal with them.

Life stories are vastly enriched by fieldwork, where we must attend to the consistent cultural patterns that create shared worlds and the diversity of practice that complicates them. Without the context provided by fieldwork, people with disabilities are at risk of becoming their impairment in a new discourse of help and rehabilitation. They lose the cultural dimension of their personhood: Juma is blind, Sanjit is blind, Sally is blind. All that makes them multifaceted persons within a local world pales beside the overwhelming salience of a deficit.

The tendency to define people in terms of an infirmity follows from the delimitation of the research problem. Whether the researcher uses a local definition of a disability or a universal one, she or he cannot be sure that there will be many examples in the immediate community being observed. Thus research projects on "falling sickness," chronic pain, leprosy, or blindness are often done as interview studies, where the researcher locates those with the relevant problem and engages them in a discussion focused on the impairment. While this may be necessary in order to "collect" a number of cases, it has its limitations if not supplemented by some more extensive involvement with the family and community. As a social and cultural discipline, ethnography is committed to that piecing together of disparate information from various sources that aims to give a whole, or at least a broad, picture.

Contributions to this volume show how fieldwork can provide the material to sketch out concepts of personhood, causality, and value that constitute local moral worlds. Likewise, fieldwork affords familiarity with social forms and with specific situations in which social dynamics are at play. Ida Nicolaisen (chap. 2), for example, places impairment within a whole Punan Bah world of body images, spirits, subsistence activities, longhouse architecture, marriage practices, and the meaning of children. Nayinda Sentumbwe (chap. 8) gives us a framework of Ugandan gender relations, household structure, and marriage patterns within which the voices of the women he interviewed make sense.

Certainly, the job of characterizing general cultural and social themes in relation to health is more difficult in some settings; community studies of the type ethnographers have traditionally undertaken must be adapted to the more fragmented life worlds of the urban North. But even researchers working on individual experiences of disability in vast, complex, rapidly changing societies such as those of North America have underlined the necessity of considering broader social and cultural processes (Good et al. 1992:204–206).

The contributors to this volume have all framed impairment in terms of the social and cultural values that constitute persons. In doing so, they have touched, often implicitly, on three issues of discourse, experience, and social process that are important in what we have achieved so far and in where we might go from here.

Dominant and Divergent Patterns

It seems clear that discursive practice does not shape individual experience in a simple, mechanical way. The problem is to find a way of describing a dominant pattern while showing the extent to which people ignore or actively contest it. Let me take as an example the discourse on anomaly mentioned above. Reports that deformed or anomalous babies are disposed of in many non-Western societies must not be taken as "the culture of disability" in these settings. More often than not, people say that killing of faulty babies happened "in the olden days" (e.g., Burck 1989:61) or "traditionally." Such statements may say as much about modernity or Christian charity as they do about infanticide practices. David Parkin, writing of the Giriama of coastal Kenya, says that anomalous babies were seen as sources of evil and metaphysical danger, and that they were and often still are killed by community elders. But he goes on to say that parents do not accept this and that government chiefs, who cannot prevent the slaughter, advise parents to move to another area. "Indeed, the Giriama understand the conflict between parental love and the danger to the community that such children bring" (Parkin 1985b: 226). To say that the elders and not the parents represent Giriama culture would be an oversimplification. It would be better to speak of two views of disability, associated with different positions and types of authority. The dominant discursive practice, the discourse on anomaly, is resisted by parents, who express and presumably experience, another reality. As the old Punan Bah woman explained to Ida Nicolaisen, the father of the deformed spirit child took pity on him, and did not allow him to die.[15]

Anthropologists report that in some societies there is a continuing evaluation of the developmental integrity of the mindful body during the first years of life. Deviations may be understood to mean that the child is not a proper person, born to live. As always, such deviations are culturally relative; symptoms that biomedicine might define as curable may be grouped with permanent impairments as a single pattern. Nancy Scheper-Hughes's research in an urban community in northeast Brazil, one with a terribly high rate of infant mortality, identifies a category of "child sickness" or "doomed child syndrome" *(doença de criança)* that includes both conditions we might call disability (she gives the example of a child who never learned to talk or walk) and also weakness from infections and malnutrition. Such children are "marked by ugly or horrible symptoms that are seen as harbingers of permanent disability/deformity in the child" (Scheper-Hughes 1990:554). Scheper-Hughes argues that children perceived in this way are allowed to die through neglect, and that mothers are able to do this because they do not anthropomorphize infants immediately. They maintain distance from babies and do not attribute to them "such human characteristics as consciousness, will, intentionality, self-awareness and memory" (559).

Here again it is clear, both from Scheper-Hughes's own research (especially 1992) and from that of Marilyn Nations and L. A. Rebhun (1988), that this discursive practice is not the only practice. Children defined as suffering from "child sickness" are sometimes saved. Nations and Rebhun, whose fieldwork was more concerned with therapeutic situations, saw families struggling to keep their children alive against overwhelming odds in the form of poverty and a disastrously insufficient health care system. Often it was only after they had lost a child that they resigned themselves to the diagnosis of "doomed child syndrome."

Sensitive fieldwork reveals divergent patterns, while conveying overall themes. Aud Talle, writing of the Maasai (chap. 3), describes the intense equality with which all children are treated. Deformed or infirm children are given the same care as others—no less, but no more—with the result that many do not survive. But Talle also describes a seemingly different tendency among Maasai parents to educate their physically disabled children so that they might have an alternative to the strenuous occupation of nomadic pastoralism.

Professional Discourse and Lived Experience

A special variety of divergence is evident in the gap between how people are represented in an authoritative discourse and the character of their (often varied) experience. Professionals often have limited involvement with the people of whom they speak; they may come from outside the local society or from another social class. They are socialized into a professional world that is remote from the daily lives of ordinary people, and they communicate in terms appreciated best by their professional colleagues.

Researchers are experts authorized to pronounce on how "they" treat people with disabilities. In chapter 12, I take the example of epilepsy in East Africa to show how the process of analysis becomes one of misrepresentation. Much of the research I discuss there was published by medical specialists, but anthropologists also analyze, theorize, and generalize—indeed we must do so.

When anthropologists systematize, they too construct a discourse and must be sensitive to the way that portrayal relates to experiences. As Kleinman and Kleinman (1991) point out, anthropologists, like doctors, engage in a process of professional transformation when they cast a subject's experience in their own theoretical terms.

> Nor is it morally superior to anthropologize distress, rather than to medicalize it. What is lost in biomedical renditions—the complexity, uncertainty, and ordinariness of some man or woman's unified world of experience—is also missing when illness is reinterpreted as social role, social strategy, or social symbol . . . anything but human experience. (Kleinman and Kleinman 1991: 276)

This self-consciousness about what we are doing when we represent disability in other cultures is important methodologically in that it requires critical reflection on the way we learn about other cultures and the way we relate to the people whose worlds we are trying to convey. Our published representations form a discourse; they are also a form of practice that shapes reality.

Researchers are not the only people who put forward characterizations of how others deal with disability. Development planners, health professionals, social workers, rehabilitation experts, and aid agencies often formulate simplified pictures of how their target groups, patients, or clients think and behave. Often these are unflattering, thus justifying the need to intervene. Benedicte Ingstad (chap. 13) takes the example of the "myth of the hidden disabled"—the idea that people in a given culture isolate, hide, and neglect those with impairments, and shows how poorly this image corresponds to the real experiences of Botswana families with disabled members. There is a practical issue here in that "victim blaming" detracts attention from the efforts of the care unit and the need to strengthen it. There is also a political issue in that negative images encourage paternalism and excuse government inaction. Ingstad reminds us of the power of professional institutionalized discourse, and she shows how studies of "attitudes" toward disability by researchers fit with the discourse of development agencies and rehabilitation workers.

This brings us to a third major question raised in this collection: how we deal with change, development, and the complexity of cultures.

Multiple Discourses, Cultural Complexity, Historical Processes

It is easy enough to show that Stiker's modes of characterizing the discourse of an entire epoch can be used to portray contemporary cultures. But to restrict analysis to a classification of discursive practice is to miss the point. Stiker's method is "genealogical"; he is tracing patterns over time and showing how elements from one age linger on in the next. If we wanted to do that kind of analysis in ethnographic studies, we would have to identify different kinds of institutions and practices and show how they evolve over time. Historical studies of medical pluralism in non-Western contexts point the way. A task for future research is to follow the development of new discourses on disability in developing countries and to trace their interplay with older modes of dealing with impairment.

In Africa, for example, we would have to examine the way the discourse on weakness and charity has gradually gained ground with the spread of Islam and Christianity. Disabled people are treated as pitiable and as belonging to a category of vulnerable, resourceless persons deserving of mercy and help. The charitable demonstrate their goodness and the feeble their dependence. Near the mosques, on city streets, in missionary institutions, the discourse on charity is practiced. It does not replace that on the cause of misfortune; it supplements it. Rehabilitation programs form the most recent generation in this genealogy. They alone construct disability as a specific condition requiring technical and social adjustment of the individual and family. We can glimpse some of these historical processes in the studies from Africa in this book: the Somali beggars in Mogadishu, where the poor, the infirm, and the mad assume a common position of mendicancy (chap. 4); the rehabilitation home to which some Maasai families carry their phys-ically disabled children (chap. 3); the Ugandan institutions for the blind where the visually impaired meet potential spouses (chap. 8); and the treat-ment programs for epileptics (chap. 12). The most systematic examination of political processes and changing institutional forms is that provided by Ingstad (chap. 9) in her analysis of the transfer of rehabilitation discourses from North to South, and the current situation in Botswana.

Almost anywhere in today's world, the understanding of disability and personhood takes shape amid changing options; in some situations the complexity is extreme. Sachs's case study of an immigrant Turkish family in Stockholm (chap. 11) shows the contrast between Swedish biomedical and Turkish folk discourses that we would expect to find in a multicultural soci-ety. But she goes beyond this to describe the variation and uncertainty within the group of Turkish immigrant women familiar with the case. Liv-ing in Sweden while maintaining close links to their villages in Turkey, they confront radically different situations and must adjust their understandings of normality, responsibility, and the validity of "deviant" children.

Sachs organized her analysis around a single case and contrasted the per-spectives of Swedish health professionals and various Turkish actors. Frank Bruun (chap. 10) takes a more social-historical approach to the analysis of change and multiple discourses. He shows how closely representations of disability may be linked to a political agenda. Although he does not use the term *discourse,* his concern with institutions, media presentations, and power relations in the manipulation of meanings and emotions is certainly in line with the kind of culture history Stiker stands for. He suggests a ge-nealogy of the present situation with its three different coexisting images of disability. As an ethnographer, he is also able to fill in nuances and cite a case from a village where he lived, which he could illuminate from different points of view.

Between the discursive practice of governments and disability organiza-tions and the subjective experience of an individual living with impairment there is a wide space. This book shows how ethnographic fieldwork can fill in some of that space with analyses of meaning, value, and the significance of social position. We frame impairment as a cultural and social issue, rather than a medical or technical one. We ask general questions rather than per-forming detailed analyses on the functional implications of one or another deficit. We return frequently to the theme of personhood because it seems so central to the cultural understanding of disability. In this epilogue I have tried to take the discussion a step further by pointing to issues raised in this broad terrain between changing discourse and lived experience. An anthropology of disability will have to examine discourses, including its own, critically and with an eye to the disjuncture between authoritative discourse and the variety of experience. It will need tools for analyzing complex and changing situations where impairment and personhood are cast in different ways simultaneously and where processes of transformation are under way. We hope to have convinced our readers that it will also need the kind of comparative vision that this book offers.

NOTES

1. Don Bloch's novel *The Modern Common Wind* (1986) is an imaginative effort to describe leprosy and its treatment from an African point of view. Bloch shows people with leprosy living in a world in which leprosy treatment was one piece of a composite reality; the discursive practice of the treatment providers was transformed in the lived experience of the people receiving it. They did not appropriate the image of themselves and their disease offered by the white doctors in any direct way.

2. I would like to thank René Devisch for inviting me to Leuven to present a (primitive) version of this chapter, for stimulating my thinking about disability, and for introducing me to Stiker's book.

3. All quotations from Stiker are my own translations.

4. Stiker does speak of the specificity of deformed people in one respect, however. While the image of monsters at the unknown edges of the world evoked the terror of radical otherness, deformed people could show the reverse of society in a milder way. Dwarfs and hunchbacks, as jesters, could reflect on society in ways prohibited to normal people (Stiker 1982:85).

5. In England a hospital and fund were established, first for the navy and later for merchant seamen "who because of age, wounds, or other accidents became disabled from further sea duty and were unable to provide for themselves" (quoted in Straus 1965:7).

6. Robert Straus (1965) writes of nineteenth-century voluntary efforts to help the poor and disabled in the United States. In the effort to distinguish the deserving and the undeserving poor, impairment was a useful guideline, for impaired people were in need through no fault of their own (ibid.:10). Here, as in other programs directed at the poor, the emphasis was on work and training for work, in contrast to medieval notions of charity or Enlightenment ideas of uplifting through education.

7. I use the term *discourse* here, although it is not used in the literature I cite, to remind us that people are speaking and practicing (e.g., performing rituals) in modes that construct impairment in particular ways. The anthropologists who write about local worlds have also chosen a certain construction, a particular professional discourse.

8. Dorothy Mull and J. Dennis Mull (1987), examining infanticide among the Tarahumara of Mexico, found that most people had heard of cases of defective babies (including albinos and those with cleft palates) being killed at birth or allowed to die. Because the name-giving ceremony that confirms identity as a person can be delayed up to a year, human status can be deferred, making it easier to avoid seeing

the death of "damaged" infants as murder. However, it does not appear that this practice was positively enjoined as a way of implementing order in the world, as seems to have been the case in some other ethnographic reports.

9. In the ethnographic literature, mythical figures such as the North American trickster could change their bodies; gods and spirits of West Africa and the cults of Brazil can be misshapen or lame. In his monumental novel of Nigeria, Ben Okri uses this quality to powerful effect. The narrator, Azaro, is observing the weird mutant customers in Madame Koto's bar—albinos, midgets, beings "confused about the natural configuration of the human body"—and realizes that they are not human beings but spirits. "Their deformations were too staggering and they seemed unaffected by their blindness and their eyelessness, their hunched backs and toothless mouths. Their expressions and movements were at odds with their bodies. They seemed a confused assortment of different human parts" (Okri 1991:136).

10. The one does not necessarily exclude the other, as Marilyn Mardiros (1989) has shown. The Mexican-American parents in her study held both biomedical and social/moral explanations of the causes of their children's disability. But they also realized that the physical condition could not be fixed and that the main goal was rehabilitation—improving the daily well-being of the child and family.

11. Sentumbwe (chap. 10) also notes how Ugandans referred to his blindness as a sickness, implying the hope of a cure. In contrast, Europeans commonly distinguish between chronically diseased and handicapped people with opposite implications about prognosis and hope; handicapped people are (fortunately) stabilized at a given level of functioning, while the unfortunate diseased ones (e.g., those suffering from multiple sclerosis and muscular dystrophy) are not (Zola 1982:53).

12. Aside from these personal accounts, there are few examples of anthropologists who had disabilities themselves or in their families doing ethnographic studies. John Gwaltney, a blind student of Margaret Mead, was a pioneer in this respect, but his book (1970) makes little of his own blindness in comparison to the later self-reflective autobiographies. Nayinda Sentumbwe (this volume) allows his sight impairment but a modest place in his chapter; in a recent proposal for further research, he mentions the term "participant audition" only in a footnote. Others, like Paul Preston (1991) and Ingstad (Ingstad and Sommerschild 1984), used their family experience with disability as an entrance to and inspiration in their work, but not as data in their analysis.

13. The attempts to make such a leap of empathy across a vast time chasm are criticized by K. A. Dettwyler (1991), who reviews the archaeological evidence for compassionate treatment of impaired individuals in prehistoric times, concluding that neither compassion, cruelty, nor indifference leaves traces in the fossil record.

14. Some of what goes under the rubric of the anthropology of experience (Turner and Bruner 1986) attempts to combine the appreciation of discourse in the broad sense with an awareness of individual experience and expression. Edward Bruner distinguishes between experience, "how . . . reality presents itself to consciousness," and expressions, "how individual experience is framed and articulated" (1986a:6), but he is equally attentive to "the experience of anthropologically coming to know" (ibid.:10). In his own work on ethnography as narrative, he shows how Native American stories about themselves and ethnographer's stories about them share the same themes. Referring to Foucault, he asserts that anthropologist

and Indian are both influenced by the dominant discursive practice of their time (Bruner 1986b:149–150). I take his point, but I prefer to emphasize his own reservations: "... that the case is obviously stronger for American anthropologists and Native Americans, as they are members of the same larger society ... that many stories do not apply to culture change, that alternative stories exist simultaneously, that the sharing is not complete, that there are variations of the same basic plot, and that individuals manipulate stories" (ibid.:148).

15. From West Africa, Carolyn Sargent's (1982) study of Bariba obstetrics documents similar divergences from a dominant concern with biological aberration. Breech births, children born at eight months or with teeth, or children who slide on their stomachs at birth, as well as those with extreme birth defects, were considered witch children, and customarily they were killed at birth (Sargent 1982: 89–90). Sargent shows that Bariba cosmology concerning anomaly and danger was enacted, but she also makes it clear that options were kept open. By delivering alone, withholding information, or using the services of a local midwife bound to discretion, a woman might keep an aberrant child (ibid.:90–91, 111–113).

REFERENCES

Abu-Lughod, Lila, and Catherine A. Lutz
   1990   Introduction: Emotion, discourse, and the politics of everyday life.
             In *Language and the Politics of Emotion*, ed. Catherine A. Lutz and Lila
             Abu-Lughod. Cambridge: Cambridge University Press.
Bloch, Don
   1986   *The Modern Common Wind*. London: Paladin.
Bogdan, Robert
   1988   *Freak Show: Presenting Human Oddities for Amusement and Profit*. Chi-
             cago: University of Chicago Press.
Bruner, Edward M.
   1986a   Experience and its expressions. In *The Anthropology of Experience*, ed.
             Victor W. Turner and Edward M. Bruner. Urbana: University of Illi-
             nois Press.
   1986b   Ethnography as narrative. In *The Anthropology of Experience*, ed. Victor
             W. Turner and Edward M. Bruner. Urbana: University of Illinois
             Press.
Burck, Deliane Jannette
   1989   *Kuoma Rupandi (The Parts Are Dry): Ideas and Practices Concerning Dis-
             ability and Rehabilitation in a Shona Ward*. Research report no. 36. Lei-
             den: African Studies Centre.
Charmaz, Kathy
   1990   "Discovering" chronic illness: Using grounded theory. *Social Science
             and Medicine* 30(11):1161–1172.
Conrad, Peter
   1990   Qualitative research on chronic illness: A commentary on method
             and conceptual development. *Social Science and Medicine* 30(11):
             1257–1263.

Crapanzano, Vincent
    1980   *Tuhami: Portrait of a Moroccan.* Chicago: University of Chicago Press.
Dettwyler, K. A.
    1991   Can paleopathology provide evidence for "compassion"? *American Journal of Physical Anthropology* 84:375–384.
Devisch, René
    1990   The Mbwoolu cosmogony and healing cult among the Northern Yaka of Zaire. In *The Creative Communion: African Folk Models of Fertility and the Regeneration of Life,* ed. Anita Jacobson-Widding and Walter van Beek. Stockholm: Almqvist and Wiksell.
Dorris, Michael
    1989   *The Broken Cord.* New York: Harper and Row.
Douglas, Mary
    1966   *Purity and Danger: An Analysis of Concepts of Pollution and Taboo.* New York: Praeger Publishers.
Edgerton, Robert B.
    1967   *The Cloak of Competence: Stigma in the Lives of the Mentally Retarded.* Berkeley and Los Angeles: University of California Press.
Foucault, Michel
    1973   *Madness and Civilization: A History of Insanity in the Age of Reason.* New York: Vintage Books.
Frank, Gelya
    1984   Life history model of adaptation to disability: The case of a "congenital amputee." *Social Science and Medicine* 19 (6):639–645.
    1986   On embodiment: A case study of congenital limb deficiency in American culture. *Culture, Medicine and Psychiatry* 10:189–219.
Good, Mary-Jo DelVecchio, Paul E. Brodwin, Byron J. Good, and Arthur Kleinman
    1992   *Pain as Human Experience: An Anthropological Perspective.* Berkeley, Los Angeles, Oxford: University of California Press.
Graham, Peter W., and Fritz H. Oehlsclaeger
    1992   *Articulating the Elephant Man: Joseph Merrick and His Interpreters.* Baltimore: Johns Hopkins University Press.
Gwaltney, John L.
    1970   *The Thrice Shy: Cultural Accommodation to Blindness and Other Disasters in a Mexican Community.* New York: Columbia University Press.
Ingstad, Benedicte, and Hilchen Sommerschild
    1984   *Familien med det Funksjonshemmede Barnet: Forløp, Reaksjoner, Mestring. Et Frambu-prosjekt* [The family with a disabled child: Process, reactions, coping. A Frambu project]. Oslo: Tanum-Norli.
Kleinman, Arthur, and Joan Kleinman
    1991   Suffering and its professional transformation: Toward an ethnography of interpersonal experience. *Culture, Medicine and Psychiatry* 15 (3):275–301.
Langness, L. L., and Harold G. Levine
    1966   *Culture and Retardation: Life Histories of Mildly Mentally Retarded Persons in American Society.* Dordrecht: D. Reidel.

Mardiros, Marilyn
1989   Conceptions of childhood disability among Mexican-American parents. *Medical Anthropology* 12:55–68.
Mull, Dorothy S., and J. Dennis Mull
1987   Infanticide among the Tarahumara of the Mexican Sierra Madre. In *Child Survival: Anthropological Perspectives on the Treatment and Maltreatment of Children*, ed. Nancy Scheper-Hughes. Dordrecht: D. Reidel.
Murphy, Robert F.
1987   *The Body Silent.* New York: Henry Holt.
Nations, Marilyn, and L. A. Rebhun
1988   Angels with wet wings won't fly: Maternal sentiment in Brazil and the image of neglect. *Culture, Medicine and Society* 12(2):141–200.
Okri, Ben
1991   *The Famished Road.* London: Jonathan Cape.
Parkin, David
1985a   Introduction. In *The Anthropology of Evil*, ed. David Parkin. Oxford: Basil Blackwell Publisher.
1985b   Entitling evil: Muslims and non-Muslims in coastal Kenya. In *The Anthropology of Evil*, ed. David Parkin. Oxford: Basil Blackwell Publisher.
Preston, Paul
1991   Mother father deaf: The heritage of difference. Paper presented at the American Anthropological Association Annual Meeting, Chicago.
Rapport, Nigel
1992   Discourse and individuality: Bedouin talk in the Western Desert and the South Sinai. *Anthropology Today* 8(1):18–21.
Ricoeur, Paul
1967   *The Symbolism of Evil.* Translated by E. Buchanan. Boston: Beacon Press.
Sargent, Carolyn Fishel
1982   *The Cultural Context of Therapeutic Choice: Obstetrical Care Decisions among the Bariba of Benin.* Dordrecht: D. Reidel.
Scheper-Hughes, Nancy
1990   Mother love and child death in northeast Brazil. In *Cultural Psychology: Essays on Comparative Human Development*, ed. James W. Stigler, Richard A. Shweder, and Gilbert Herdt. Cambridge: Cambridge University Press.
1992   *Death without Weeping: The Violence of Everyday Life in Brazil.* Berkeley, Los Angeles, Oxford: University of California Press.
Scheper-Hughes, Nancy, and Margaret Lock
1987   The mindful body: A prolegomenon to future work in medical anthropology. *Medical Anthropology Quarterly*, n.s., 1:6–41.
Stiker, Henri-Jacques
1982   *Corps infirmes et sociétés.* Paris: Aubier Montaigne.

Straus, Robert
  1965   Social change and the rehabilitation concept. In *Sociology and Reha-
                bilitation,* ed. Marvin B. Sussman. Washington, D.C.: American Soci-
                ological Association.
Turner, Victor W., and Edward M. Bruner, eds.
  1986   *The Anthropology of Experience.* Urbana: University of Illinois Press.
Vaughan, Megan
  1991   *Curing Their Ills: Colonial Power and African Illness.* Oxford: Polity Press.
Warkany, Josef
  1971   *Congenital Malformations: Notes and Comments.* Chicago: Year Book
                Medical Publishers.
  1977   History of teratology. In *Handbook of Teratology,* vol. 1., ed. James G.
                Wilson and F. Clarke Fraser. New York: Plenum Press.
Wikan, Unni
  1992   Beyond the words: The power of resonance. *American Ethnologist*
                19:460–482.
Wilson, Peter J.
  1947   *Oscar: An Inquiry into the Nature of Sanity.* Reprint. New York: Vintage
                Books, 1975.
Zola, Irving
  1982   *Missing Pieces: A Chronicle of Living with a Disability.* Philadelphia: Tem-
                ple University Press.

CONTRIBUTORS

Frank J. Bruun. Ph.D. candidate at the University of Oslo, Section for Medical Anthropology. Fieldwork in Nicaragua and Botswana. Main research interests: disability and rehabilitation, the changing status of the elderly in developing countries, gender studies.

Patrick Devlieger. Ph.D. candidate in anthropology at the University of Illinois at Urbana-Champaign. Fieldwork in Zaire and Zimbabwe. Main research interests: cross-cultural research on disability, community research, the ethnography of transition of individuals with mental retardation.

Ronald Frankenberg. Professor emeritus of Sociology and Anthropology at Keele University. Professor Associate in Medical Anthropology at Brunel, the University of West London. Fieldwork in Wales, Zambia, and Italy. Main research interests: cultural performance of sickness, AIDS, disability.

Bernhard Helander. Associate Professor at the Department of Cultural Anthropology, Uppsala University. Fieldwork in Southern Somalia, Kenya, Tanzania, and Java. Main research interests: descent theory, medical anthropology, ethnography of speaking, anthropology of war.

Benedicte Ingstad. Professor of Medical Anthropology, Department of Community Medicine, University of Oslo. Fieldwork in Greenland, Norway, Botswana, and Gambia. Consultancies on rehabilitation in Zimbabwe, Tanzania, Ghana, Romania, and Nicaragua. Main research interests: disability in cross-cultural perspective, care for dependent people in the household, aging in developing countries, folk healers and folk medicine, sociocultural dimensions of AIDS, women in development.

Judith Monks. Research Fellow at the Centre for the Study of Health, Sickness, and Disablement, Brunel, the University of West London. Main research interests: sickness, disability, language, personhood, Latin America.

Robert Murphy. Professor of Anthropology at Columbia University until his death. Main fieldwork among the Mundurucu people of Brazil. Published work on myth and cosmology, social organization and gender, anthropological theory, and disability in America.

Ida Nicolaisen. Associate Professor at the Institute of Anthropology, University of Copenhagen. Fieldwork in Tchad, Niger, and Borneo. Main research interests: cultural identity and gender, ethnic identity, sociocultural transformation, cosmology, oral tradition, child development.

Lisbeth Sachs. Associate Professor of Social Anthropology, University of Stockholm. Researcher and supervisor at the Department of International Health Care Research (IHCAR) at the Karolinska Institute in Stockholm. Fieldwork in Turkey, Sweden, and Sri Lanka. Main research interests: comparative work on the medical problem of well-being, the creation of boundaries between health and unhealth in everyday health care, how new cultural syndromes are created, the processs of psychiatric diagnosis of somatization.

Nayinda Sentumbwe. Master's degree candidate from the University of Oslo. Fieldwork in Uganda. Main research interests: cross-cultural perspectives on disability, rehabilitation of the blind.

Aud Talle. Associate Professor of Social Anthropology, University of Stockholm. Research Associate at University of Bergen. Fieldwork in Tanzania, Somalia, and Kenya. Main research interests: the changing situation of pastoral nomad women as a result of development, female circumcision, sexuality, AIDS.

Susan Reynolds Whyte. Associate Professor at the Institute of Anthropology, University of Copenhagen. Fieldwork in Uganda, Kenya, and Tanzania. Main research interests: cosmology and personhood, gender, illness perceptions, medicines, the transformation of health care in developing countries.

INDEX

Designer:	U.C. Press Staff
Compositor:	BookMasters, Inc.
Text:	10/12 Baskerville
Display:	Baskerville
Printer:	Haddon Craftsmen, Inc.
Binder:	Haddon Craftsmen, Inc.